Monarch butterfly

A Round Stone Press Book

Published by The Book Division
National Geographic Society
Washington, DC

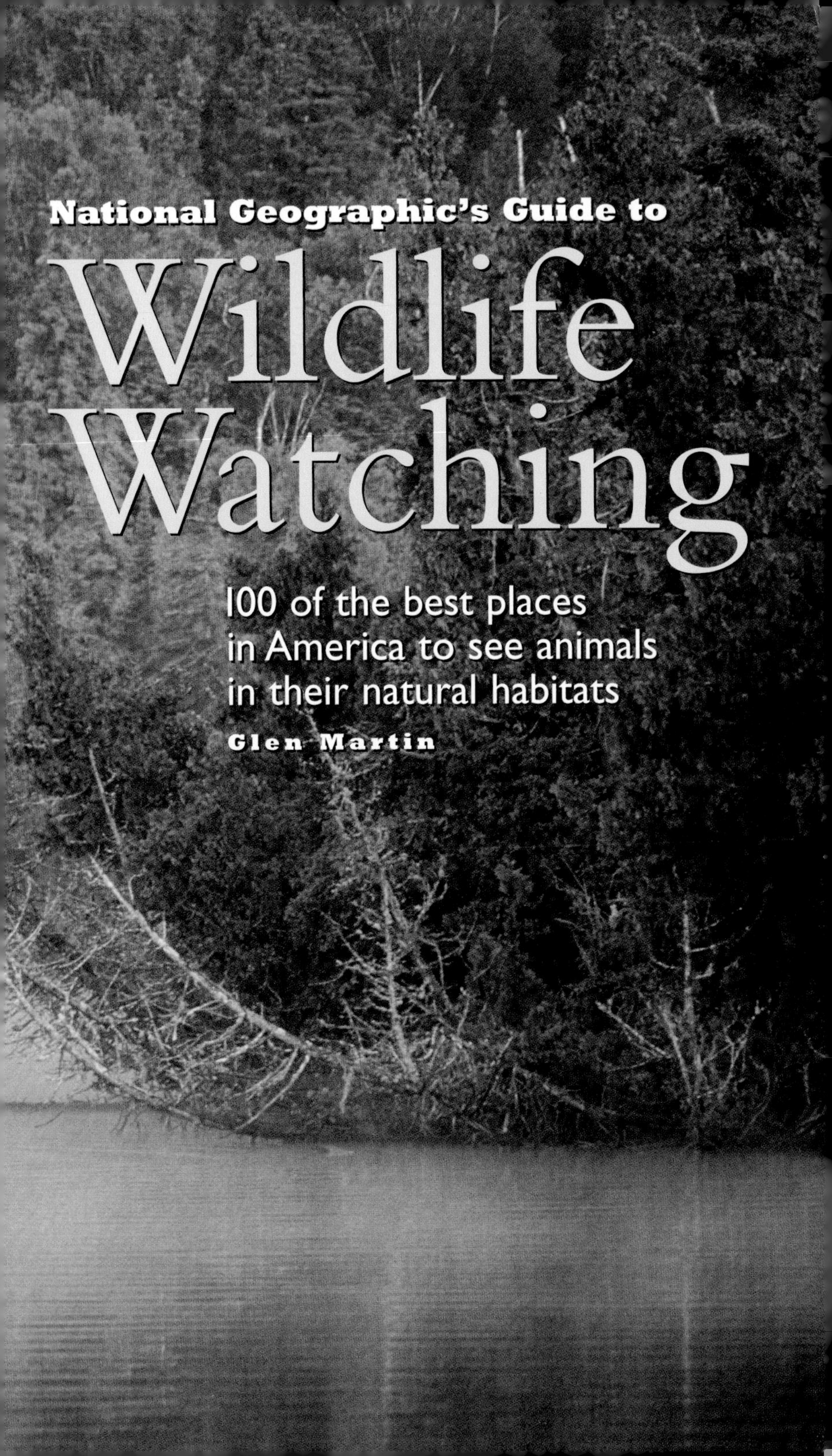

National Geographic's Guide to

Wildlife Watching

100 of the best places
in America to see animals
in their natural habitats

Glen Martin

Produced by Round Stone Press, Inc.

Directors: Marsha Melnick, Susan E. Meyer, Paul Fargis

Senior Editor: Nick Viorst

Project Manager: Kathryn Clark

Designer: Wendy Palitz

Maps: Natasha Perkel

Photo Editor: Marilyn Gibbons

Production Design: Smythtype

Printed in U.S.A.

Library of Congress Cataloging-in-Publication Data

Martin, Glen, 1949-
    National geographic's guide to wildlife watching: 100 of
the best places in America to see animals in their natural
habitats / Glen Martin.
        p.   cm.
    "A Round Stone Press book."
    Includes index.
    ISBN 0-7922-7130-0 (reg.)
    1. Wildlife viewing sites—United States—Guidebooks.
2. Wildlife watching—United States—Guidebooks.
I. National Geographic Society. Book Division. II. Title.
QL155.M37 1998
591.973—dc21   97-46750
                                                     CIP

Cover: Bull caribou, Alaska

Previous pages: Moose, Isle Royale National
Park, Michigan

Following page: Raccoons

CONTENTS

◼ Western States

■ Central States

Contents

Eastern States

100 SITES FOR WATCHING WILDLIFE

To find the name of the site that corresponds to each numbered box, see the Table of Contents (pp. 5-9).

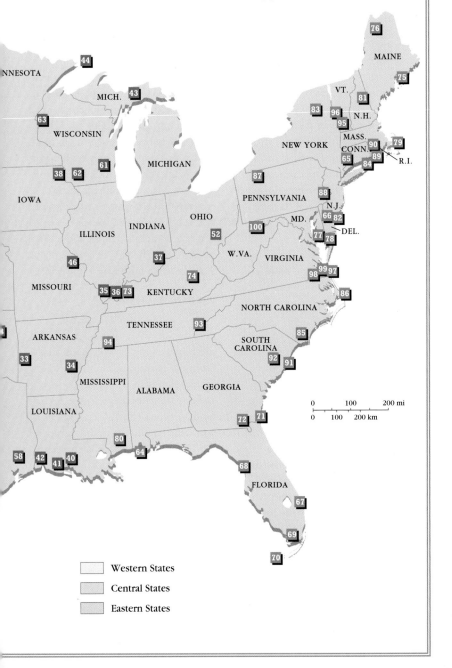

WHERE THE WILD THINGS ARE

It has been almost a hundred years since Theodore Roosevelt used the bully pulpit of the Presidency to make the word "conservation" part of the American vocabulary. A man truly infatuated with the wild, Roosevelt was appalled by the mindless slaughter of the continent's big game and by the wholesale destruction of forest, swamp, and plain in the quest for minerals, timber, and plowable land. As President, Roosevelt gave the country some of its most significant national parks, and he helped the average citizen understand the inherent value of the American wilderness. He left a great natural legacy that has been enhanced by men and women of succeeding generations who have shared his vision.

So how would T.R. view today's wild America? Candidly, he would be saddened. The forestry methods of his era were in some ways far more progressive than those in use today. Roosevelt and his compeer, Gifford Pinchot, the first director of the U.S. Forest Service, favored selective cutting for timber harvest—not the clear-cutting that has ravaged vast portions of the West and southeast Alaska. He would be stunned by the loss of 90 percent of our wetlands, by the destruction of fisheries by dams and pollution, by the paving of wildland for strip malls and parking lots.

But the indomitable Roosevelt would also find much reason for hope. Millions of acres in the United States are now protected by the government or private conservancy groups. Many species that were on the brink of extinction in Roosevelt's day have been resuscitated—bison, mountain lion, elk, and great egret among them.

Roosevelt would also be impressed by the place that environmentalism holds in our culture. In his day he was, almost literally, a voice crying in the wilderness, supported only by Pinchot, John Muir, and a few other prescient lovers of untamed country. Today conservation is championed by private citizens, government agencies, even large corporations. The walk doesn't always match the talk, of course, but at least everyone understands the stakes.

Wildlife Habitats

Largely as a result of Roosevelt's intervention, 20th-century America still boasts incredible wildlife diversity. From the swamplands of the Deep South—home to anhingas, alligators, and roseate spoonbills—to the Arctic tundra—where musk-oxen and caribou forage under the midnight sun—the United States offers magnificent wildlife-watching opportunities.

Hanker to see rare tropical birds in their native rain forests? Try Waikamoi Preserve on the Hawaiian island of Maui. Want to observe in-the-field sea turtle protection efforts? Check out Blowing Rocks Preserve in Florida. Or raft the Selway River in Idaho, to spy black bear, mule deer, and elk in one of the world's most remote and pristine gorges. Watch hundreds of bald eagles fishing for salmon on Alaska's Chilkat River, or look for nesting wood warblers in the lush canopy of Hiawatha National Forest in upstate Michigan. For all the deleterious impact civilization has had on its wildlands, America is still a paradise for wildlife and wildlife lovers.

This book focuses on 100 of the country's most remarkable wild places. There was no attempt to highlight the "best"—such a qualifier is ultimately subjective in any event. Rather, we featured preserves, refuges, and protected wildlands that meet certain criteria. First, we wanted to include at least one site from every state. We also wanted refuges that supported species and habitats that were either unique or were particularly representative of the surrounding biome, and sites that were managed by organizations with a mission to protect those species and habitats—the Nature Conservancy, the National Audubon Society, state and federal park services, among others. We tried to reflect the diversity of the United States in our choices, offering sites from desert to wetland, from mountain fastness to lonely seacoast, from lush tropical hammock to Arctic steppe and tundra. And finally, we wanted to give readers choices in terms of access and cost.

Arctic National Wildlife Refuge is one of the wildest places left on the globe. North America's rarest large mammals live here unmolested, as they have since the waning of the last ice age. The vistas are empty from horizon to horizon. There is no place like it on earth. But it takes money, time, and effort to visit this remarkable refuge, and it is no place for the novice to wander alone. On the other hand, many of the preserves in this book are literally walks in the park, suited for casual day trips, with no particular outdoor expertise required to enjoy them. Take the John Heinz National Wildlife Refuge at Tinicum, Pennsylvania, for example. This lovely slice of wetland is tucked into the flank of Philadelphia's busy international airport, providing peace and relaxation for thousands of birds and thousands of urban birders.

Some sites feature auto tour routes, ideal for the elderly or disabled (or merely fatigued) visitor. Others are best explored by canoe, powerboat, horseback, or mountain bike. In short, there is something here for everyone.

Habitat Preservation

In the strictest sense, this is a guide to wildlife habitats rather than wildlife. Wild animals do not live in a vacuum. Self-sustaining populations require high-quality habitats that meet their specific needs for food, reproduction, and simple elbowroom. The crisis that afflicts America's wildlife isn't the result of a lack of open space—the majority of the country remains unpaved. The major problems are fragmentation and degradation of the land. A single road or pipeline punched through a favored migration route can decimate a caribou herd. Draining one-quarter of a blackwater swamp can cut wildlife populations by one-half. You can't remove one-quarter of the components of a computer and expect it to work. Wild systems must remain intact to support optimum populations of wildlife.

Can the damage that has already been done be repaired? Fortunately, the answer is sometimes yes. Wildlife conservation is entering a new and exciting era, shifting from a period of simple preservation to active and aggressive restoration. Many of the sites featured in this book represent the vanguard of this movement. At the Carrizo Plain Natural Area in California, for example, prescription burning, fence removal, tree planting, and reintroduction of tule elk and pronghorn are all being employed to revive the historic arid plateau ecology that characterized the region before the advent of white settlers. In other parts of the country, corridors are being established through conservation easements to link up core preserves, greatly enhancing the mobility—and hence, survivability—of migratory wildlife.

While we feature many places that have abundant populations of "charismatic megafauna"—big, attractive animals such as deer, elk, moose, and bear—we don't want to forget the little animals that are so easily overlooked. Reptiles, amphibians, and migrant songbirds are as wild as the grizzly bear rooting in a meadow for camas bulbs. All contribute to the web of life that supports the wilderness. A treefrog, in fact, is a more significant wildlife sighting than a white-tailed deer, given that amphibians are in precipitous decline and whitetails are exceedingly common. When visiting Great Smoky Mountains National Park, keep in mind that herpetologists refer to it as the salamander capital of North America. More than 20 species of the little lizardlike amphibians live here. To some that distinction may seem dubious, even laughable. But salamanders are prime indicators of environmental quality in general and water purity in particular. Their abundance points to a healthy wildland system.

Watching Wildlife

As veteran wildlife observers know, there are no guarantees. Neophytes to wildlife-watching are sometimes disappointed when they head to a refuge and see few, if any, wild creatures. Wild animals, it must be remembered, are just that—wild. They fear human beings, whom they rightfully consider fearsome predators. When people show up, wild animals typically depart.

Natural coloration or camouflage, which protects many animals from those that hunt them, is another difficulty for human viewers. It is usually an animal's motion that will catch the eye of an observer. Finally, many wild species, mammals in particular, are nocturnal. If you go to a preserve in the middle of the day, the animals you might hope to see will be peacefully snoozing in some burrow or thicket. It's generally a good idea to visit as close to dawn or dusk as possible.

To observe wild animals, then, you must more or less think as they do. Stealth is the prime directive. Walk quietly: Even the scraping of brush against clothing can spook wary animals. Good binoculars are essential. Carry them at all times, and use them often to scan the landscape. Stop often and sit quietly for long periods of time in areas that afford good overviews of the countryside. Sit near places where animals are known to congregate, such as mineral licks or trails leading to water. Sitting, in fact, is probably the single best way to observe wildlife. By remaining motionless, you become part of the landscape. Birds emerge from the foliage, turtles crawl up on logs to sun, deer and moose browse in plain view unconcernedly, and coyotes and foxes wander past in their unceasing quest for rodents.

When moving up on animals for a closer look, always approach them from a downwind position. Mammals especially rely on their noses far more than their eyes. A strong odor of aftershave or perfume wafting on the breeze will send them fleeing.

Remember that every species has its season. In the continental United States, ducks and geese congregate in their greatest numbers in the autumn and winter. Warblers are best observed in the spring, when they are displaying their distinctive breeding plumage and are conspicuously involved in mating and nest building. Deer and elk are at their boldest in the fall, the season of the rut. At the National Elk Refuge in Wyoming, elk gather in the winter. In short, take a little time to learn about the species you want to see before you seek them out.

Be Prepared

The climate and the weather are the most critical considerations in any outdoor foray, since both hypothermia and hyperthermia can occur quickly. In cold weather, dress in warm layers, adding or shedding clothing as necessary. Avoid getting wet. Carry snacks, including warm liquids, whenever possible. In hot weather, wear light, loose clothing. On torrid days your most important article of apparel is

your hat—make sure it's large enough to protect both your head and neck from the sun. Carry sunscreen and apply it liberally and often, and bring along plenty of water.

Regardless of the weather, baby your feet. The wildlife enthusiast has at least one thing in common with the infantry soldier—both rely on their feet. Boots should be thoroughly broken in and comfortable, and they should have rubber soles. Wear clean socks, preferably wool.

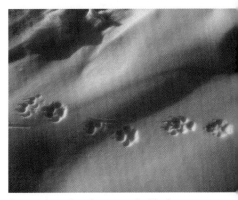

A coyote's tracks—four toes, all with claws—are easily seen in the snow.

Wildlife observation is enhanced by taking photographs, and this can be expensive. Exceptional shots require exceptional cameras and appropriate lenses. A "long glass," or telephoto lens, is a prerequisite for serious wildlife photography. Professional "shooters" routinely use lenses of 1,000mm or more. Amateurs can get by with lenses in the 400mm to 600mm range. Some folks even succeed with disposable cameras and a lot of luck.

Watching wild animals doesn't involve hazards on the level of white-water kayaking or rock climbing, but there are some minor dangers. On rugged terrain, spraining an ankle, or even breaking a leg, is rather easy to do. Watch your step. The same advice applies to travel in snake country. It's easy to avoid being bitten by snakes: Simply don't put your hands or feet on them. In venomous snake habitat, travel slowly and watch where you're stepping and where you're placing your hands.

Never try to touch or feed wild animals. Even harmless-seeming species, like squirrels or chipmunks, can transmit diseases. Some large species present particular problems. Grizzly bear attacks are not common, but they do occur. In griz country, the operative phrase is "never surprise the bears." Talk loudly, sing, or rattle pebbles in a can when moving through heavily vegetated areas. Above all, do not approach or get between a sow and her cubs. It is not a bad idea to carry "bear spray"—supersize cans of industrial-strength pepper spray.

In Alaska moose are known for their testiness and aggression against human beings; give them plenty of leeway. Recently a number of attacks by mountain lions have been recorded in California and Colorado. While hikers in the wild are much more likely to be killed by lightning than by a mountain lion or other wild animal, it's still a good idea to be cautious. In particular, don't let children wander—they are in the most danger from mountain lion predation. In the unlikely event that you are confronted by a mountain lion, yell, stand on tiptoe with arms spread to look larger, and throw rocks. Don't run. It's also important to keep an eye on children when traveling in wild areas of Florida

and other locations in the Deep South where alligators occur.

One final thing: When all is said and done, wildlife observation also requires a good deal of luck. The wild is not a theme park, and there are no guarantees. Despite the best-laid plans, despite the expenditure of time and money (and, on occasion, plenty of it), despite the employment of the finest binoculars and cameras, despite painstaking stalking, paddling, or crawling on your belly through briars and mud, sometimes it all comes to naught. Sometimes you end up with nothing for your troubles but sunburn, chigger bites, and burrs in your socks. But cheer up—remember the old query that fishing guides dredge up whenever their clients are "skunked": Ain't it great just to be out here?

Using This Book

Readers of *National Geographic's Guide to Wildlife Watching* may be interested in learning about the sites in a particular region of the United States— either to find out what's close enough for a short excursion from home or as a resource in planning a trip to a different area of the country. With this in mind, we have divided the country into three regions—The Western, Central, and Eastern States. The states within each region are organized alphabetically. The featured wildlife areas, or sites, are listed alphabetically within their state and are numbered from 1 through 100. An overall map of the United States (see pp. 10-11) shows each region and displays the location of all 100 sites. The names of the sites are found in the Table of Contents.

So if, for example, you're thinking about a trip along the Pacific Coast, turn to the Western States section where you'll find California, Oregon, and Washington, with a total of nine sites. Or, if you live in Baltimore, turn to the Eastern States section to find, in Maryland and Delaware alone, three sites to visit.

Each site is accompanied by a locator map and directions for getting there. In most cases, directions are for road travel from the nearest large city. This information will be useful for planning your visit; but always use a good road map. Sometimes a site can only be reached by plane or boat, and in those cases, we've included the phone numbers for service providers.

Other practical information includes each site's hours of operation, best months to visit, fees, and handicapped accessibility. We've provided details for camping and for any on-site accommodations (although inclu-

sion of a campground or hotel does not mean that it is endorsed by the National Geographic Society). Many sites, particularly parks, maintain lists of accommodations in their area that they will send you on request. Keep in mind that many sites close on national holidays. And since information can change without notice, it's a good idea to call ahead.

The final section of the book, About the Animals, serves as a field guide to 100 of the animals found at the sites. It would have been impossible to provide this information on all of the nearly 1,000 different species mentioned in the book, so we've selected those that are widespread (like the white-tailed deer), uniquely American (like the manatee), or very rare (like the black-footed ferret). Each is cross-referenced to the featured sites at which that animal may be found. Readers who wish to find sites featuring a particular bird or beast might start their search here.

MAP KEY AND ABBREVIATIONS

MAP KEY		ABBREVIATIONS	
(80)	Interstate Highway	C.M.A.	*Cooperative Management Area*
		HWY.	*Highway*
(80)	U.S. Federal Highway	I.	*Island*
		L.	*Lake*
(80)	State Road	Nat. For.	*National Forest*
		N.W.R.	*National Wildlife Refuge*
(106)	County, Local, or Other Road	N.P.	*National Park*
		N.F.	*National Forest*
■ / ■	Featured Wildlife Site	N.R.A.	*National Recreation Area*
		PKWY.	*Parkway*
■	Other Forest, Park, Wilderness Area	RD.	*Road*
		R.	*River*
■	Built-up Area	S.P.	*State Park*
		TPK.	*Turnpike*
⊛	State Capital	W.A.	*Wildlife Area*
		W.M.A.	*Wildlife Management Area*

A Dall's sheep among Alaska's high peaks

Alaska Chilkat Bald Eagle Preserve

In autumn, this spot of warm water on the Chilkat River attracts thousands of bald eagles looking for a meal of salmon.

SITE 1 Something truly miraculous happens each year on southeastern Alaska's Chilkat River. From spring through early fall, glacier and snowmelt surge into a vast alluvial fan of sand and rubble at the confluence of the Chilkat, Tsirku, and Kleheni Rivers. The water flows into this basin faster than it can flow out, creating a huge underground reservoir. By late autumn the water is 10 to 20 degrees warmer than the water of the adjacent rivers. This relatively warm water slowly seeps back into the Chilkat throughout the winter, creating a 5-mile oasis of open water in a wilderness of ice and snow.

All five species of Pacific salmon—chinook, coho, chum, sockeye, and pink—spawn here. By the middle of November the river is choked with chum "downstreamers," spawned-out, beat-up salmon that are more dead than alive. Their food value to humans at this point is negligible. To fish-loving bald eagles, however, they are manna. The moribund chums, combined with the open water that allows easy access to the fish, have conjoined to make the Chilkat the bald eagle capital of the world.

During the height of the fall congregation from November through mid-December, more than 4,000 eagles have been counted within this 48,000-acre preserve. Between 200 and 400 eagles live at the refuge year-round, and approximately 80 nests have been identified. In early April visitors can see the spectacular aerial courtship and mating flights of the resident eagles when the birds dive in unison and interlock talons.

There are other significant wild

At Chilkat, you can see bald eagles from roadside turnouts along the river.

species that inhabit this mountainous, heavily forested area: brown bear, black bear, lynx, gray wolf, mountain goat, moose, mink, marten, and snowy owl. A threatened seabird, the marbled murrelet, is found here as well. The lucky visitor may well see some of these animals. But the real reason to visit Chilkat is the eagle congregation. There are other sites where eagles gather, of course, but none approach the Chilkat in the number of birds and the grandeur of the habitat.

Access is mostly restricted to car viewing along the Haines Highway. (Because foot traffic can disturb the birds, only limited hiking on developed trails between the highway and the river is allowed.) Eagles can be seen all along the course of the Chilkat during the height of the congregation, but the river flats between Mileposts 18 and 21 on the Haines Highway are the most productive places for viewing. The Haines Highway is a narrow and serpentine road. Watch for oncoming traffic, never pass on curves, and always use the designated turnouts.

Though the eagles feed aggressively throughout the salmon season, they are extremely susceptible to disturbance. They need to eat as much and as often as possible to develop enough body fat to sustain them through the long and bleak winter, and any agitation can throw them off their feed. By the same token, all fish and fish carcasses should be left undisturbed. The salmon production of the Chilkat can seem positively profligate—and certainly odoriferous. But 3,000 eagles consume a lot of ripe salmon over the course of a season, and every fish that is mindlessly kicked into the brush or

submerged in the river is one less fish for the eagles.

The eagles are vital to the local Tlingit Indians. The eagle is a significant totemic creature to this tribe, and the members are dedicated to the protection of the magnificent birds. The tourist dollars brought in by the fall congregation help stabilize the local economy and assure a place for both eagles and native peoples in southeastern Alaska.

Arctic National Wildlife Refuge

This vast Arctic wilderness is one of the last and best places in America to witness a spectacular caribou migration.

SITE 2 This is it. The Arctic National Wildlife Refuge is incomparable, one of the best places in North America for viewing wild animals in their natural setting. And what a setting it is: A yawning expanse of tundra, coastal plain, forests, rivers, and wetlands, its diversity of habitats gives rise to a wonderful diversity of animal life. The snow-capped Brooks mountain range runs from east to west, dividing the refuge into north- and south-draining slopes. At 19.5 million acres, this refuge in the northeasternmost corner of Alaska is bigger than all the national wildlife refuges in the lower 48 states combined.

This is wilderness in the most complete sense of the word. Even getting here is an adventure, requiring moderate difficulty and considerable expense. There's only one practical way in and out—bush plane. Pilots drop off recreationalists and guides at crude upland landing strips. Once in the interior, visitors typically backpack for one or two weeks or raft down any of eight major rivers on the north slope (or six on the south slope). For first-timers a guided river trip may be the best option because a great deal of country is covered in a relatively short time, enhancing the wildlife-viewing opportunities. Plus, river running usually leaves plenty of time for day hiking and angling.

Arctic NWR is best known for its spectacular caribou migrations. A caribou migration is a heart-stopping experience: Picture untold thousands of antlered beasts loping beneath the midnight sun, the tundra stretching endlessly to the horizon, the air resounding with the pounding of hoofs. This majestic tableau has unfolded in the same way for tens of thousands of years, and this is one of the last places on earth where it still occurs.

The southern portion of the refuge and northwestern Canada is the heartland for the Porcupine herd (named for the Porcupine River), which numbers about 150,000 caribou. Each year this herd makes a 700-mile round-trip migration to and from their calving grounds on the coastal plain along the Beaufort Sea. In April they head north from the winter range. By late May they have reached the calving areas and the pregnant cows begin to give birth. In late June and early July, the animals concentrate in herds numbering in the tens of thousands and move along the coast and onto the north slopes of the mountains, seeking relief from the Arctic's fearsome mosquitoes. By mid-July the herds head south and east to their wintering grounds.

Much is unpredictable within this broad dynamic. The Arctic coastal plain is huge, and no one can say precisely where the animals will calve; similarly, it is difficult to determine exactly where they will winter. The best hope is to be on the Beaufort Sea coast or on the north slopes of the Brooks Range in late June and early July, or in August to float the

Caribou gather in herds numbering in the tens of thousands at the Arctic NWR.

rivers that transect the southward migration routes.

The musk-ox, a rare and wild ox of the far north, also lives at the Arctic NWR. Eliminated from Alaska's coastal plain in the late 19th century, 64 of these shaggy bovines were reintroduced here in 1969 and 1970. The population has since grown and is now stable at about 300 animals. These huge animals form small herds, which can be observed along the rivers of the coastal plain.

All three species of North American bears are found here. Polar bears inhabit the Beaufort Sea coast, where they prey on bearded seals and ringed seals. Grizzly bears, a subspecies of brown bears, inhabit the inland, mountainous regions. Black bears are relatively common in the southern portion of the refuge. As always, when in bear country follow the standard precautions: Stay off game trails, avoid dense coverts, don't cook near sleeping sites, never get between a sow and her cubs, and make plenty of noise going through thickets.

A number of gray wolf packs hunt the refuge; they are found primarily in the mountainous areas, along rivers. Dall's sheep are also numerous

THE FACTS

Noteworthy Animals: Caribou, musk-ox, polar bear, grizzly bear, black bear, gray wolf, Dall's sheep, moose, wolverine, lynx, arctic fox, arctic hare, snowy owl.

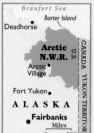

Getting There: Arctic National Wildlife Refuge is accessible by chartered bush plane. Alaska Airlines (800-426-0333) and charter services fly to Fort Yukon (160 miles northeast of Fairbanks), Arctic Village (100 miles northwest of Fort Yukon), Barter Island (450 miles northeast of Fairbanks), and Deadhorse (450 miles northeast of Fairbanks).

Open: Daily, 24 hours, year-round.

Best Times to Visit: June through August.

Visitor Information: U.S. Fish and Wildlife Service, Fairbanks office (907-456-0250), open Monday through Friday, 9 a.m.-5 p.m., year-round. No on-site visitor center.

Outfitters and/or Guide Services: For licensed guides, air-taxi operators, and outfitters, call the U.S. Fish and Wildlife Service (907-456-0250). The average cost of a bush plane is $125 per hour. For organized trips, call Sierra Club Outings (415-977-5630).

Entrance Fees: None.

Disabled Access: None.

Camping: Primitive camping; no permit or fees required.

throughout the mountains. These pure white sheep often require some tough hiking to observe, so be prepared for rugged terrain, long hours, and inclement weather. Other mammals that might be seen include moose, wolverine, arctic fox, marten, and arctic hare.

Approximately 165 migratory bird species have been recorded at the Arctic NWR, and it is a critical stopover for migrating waterfowl, most notably snow goose, Canada goose, tundra swan, oldsquaw, king eider, northern pintail, and brant.

This is, naturally, a stronghold for birds emblematic of the Arctic: Steller's eider, gyrfalcon, snowy owl, arctic loon, arctic tern, and Sabine's gull. The refuge also supports a healthy population of peregrine falcons and the northernmost breeding population of golden eagles on the continent. Birds are readily observed throughout the refuge, a happy circumstance due to the unparalleled quality of the habitat and the fact that the tourist season occurs at the same time as the nesting season.

There are two ways to see the refuge: with an outfitter or on your own. Outfitters are familiar with the territory, know about recent wildlife sightings, and handle all the arrangements for transportation and camping. Some environmental organizations, most notably the Sierra Club, also sponsor organized trips. Unless you have considerable experience in the wild, don't go it alone—arrange for a competent guide.

The refuge is open for access year-round, but Arctic winters are fierce, to put it mildly. Most visits occur during the summer, peaking in July. Relatively moderate weather, of course, is the primary attraction for a high-summer visit, but there's another equally compelling reason: The sun literally never sets, adding many more hours to the wildlife-viewing day. Also, many Arctic animals that are by habit nocturnal, such as the lynx, must prowl for their sustenance during the summer light, which further increases the chance of a sighting.

Kenai National Wildlife Refuge

This remote, yet accessible, Alaskan wilderness offers visions of caribou, moose, Dall's sheep, and stunning scenery, too.

SITE 3 While Alaska is renowned for its spectacular wildlife-watching sites, getting to them can be difficult. There are few roads in our largest state, so bush plane is the requisite mode of transport for most of Alaska's wildlife refuges, national parks, and national monuments. Kenai National Wildlife Refuge is one notable exception. Located about 150 miles south of Anchorage, it can be reached by all-weather Alas. 1. Even the drive to the refuge is spectacular, offering excellent chances for seeing wildlife as well as stunning scenery.

Kenai is suitable for a day trip from Anchorage, though it warrants more than that. At 1.9 million acres, it is roughly the size of West Virginia and is characterized by steep terrain and mixed forests of black spruce, white spruce, aspen, birch, cottonwood, and willow. Most of Alaska's large mammals—brown bear, black bear, moose, caribou, Dall's sheep, gray wolf, lynx, and wolverine—are found here, as are many smaller species, including marten, river otter, ermine, beaver, and snowshoe hare. Pick up a map and advice from refuge staff at the Visitor Center. Camp or stay at a motel in nearby Soldotna or Homer and drive Alas. 1 and Alas. 9, which traverse much of the refuge.

Getting deep into the interior is

Brown bears, best viewed at a safe distance, are a familiar sight in Kenai's dense brush.

moderately difficult due to the lack of an extensive backcountry trail network (bush planes are still the rule), but there are a few easily accessible trails. Try the Kenai River Trail (about 40 miles east of Soldotna) for brown bears and black bears, the Seven Lakes Trail (about 30 miles east of Soldotna) for both moose and bears, or the extremely rugged and steep Skyline Trail (about 35 miles east of Soldotna)

for the chance of seeing a wide variety of different species. The 20-mile Funny River Trail is the best option for a multiday backpacking trip and it offers some good angling as well as potential wildlife sightings.

Canoeing here is an incomparable wilderness experience, and is relatively easy to arrange and execute. Canoeists have the option of two excellent routes. The Swanson River route

The solitary marten spends much of its time in trees.

traverses 40 lakes and 46 miles of stream for a total of 80 miles; the Swan Lake route covers 30 lakes and 33 miles of stream. The put-ins for both are in the northern half of the refuge.

Relatively effortless wildlife viewing is provided by the Russian River Ferry, which crosses the Russian River at Cooper's Landing about 45 miles east of Soldotna on Alas. 1; passengers should scan nearby Round Mountain with binoculars for Dall's sheep.

Waterfowl are incredibly abundant, especially during the spring nesting season. In addition to an important nesting population of trumpeter swans, the refuge supports large numbers of visiting Canada geese. Other species include greater scaup, harlequin duck, black scoter, and Barrow's goldeneye.

From late spring through summer, migrating and nesting shorebirds are common, most notably semipalmated plover, greater yellowlegs, spotted and least sandpipers, common snipe, and red-necked phalarope.

Most notable among Kenai's birds of prey is the bald eagle, which is well distributed throughout the refuge. Also look for boreal owls. Other birds here include a great array of migratory warblers, sparrows, and thrushes, as well as the uncommon northern shrike and birds that are associated with the far north, such as the Bohemian waxwing, snow bunting, and gray-crowned rosy finch.

The Kenai River supports 28 species of fish and boasts the world's record for chinook salmon (97 pounds). Not surprisingly, fishing is popular with both residents and visitors, particularly for the five resident species of salmon. The salmon season—midsummer

THE FACTS

Noteworthy Animals: Brown bear, black bear, moose, caribou, Dall's sheep, gray wolf, lynx, wolverine, marten, trumpeter swan, bald eagle, chinook salmon.

Getting There: From Anchorage, Alaska Airlines (800-426-0333) runs commuter flights to Kenai and Seward; rental cars are available in both cities. Driving from Anchorage, take Alas. 1 south for 110 miles. For the Visitor Center, drive into Soldotna, across the Kenai River bridge, turn left onto Funny River Road, then right onto Ski Hill Road, and watch for signs. The center is about 2 miles from Soldotna.

Open: Daily, 24 hours, year-round. Russian River Ferry (no phone) operates only in summer.

Best Times to Visit: April through September.

Visitor Information: Kenai National Wildlife Refuge Visitor Center (907-262-7021) open Monday through Friday 8 a.m.-4:30 p.m.; 10 a.m.-5 p.m. weekends; year-round.

Entrance Fees: None.

Disabled Access: The Visitor Center is wheelchair accessible, and a fishing area near the Russian River Ferry is reserved for disabled anglers.

Camping: Primitive camping allowed throughout the refuge; no permit or fees required. Two developed campgrounds; fees; no reservations.

through fall—is also the best time to see brown bears, which gorge on the migrating fish.

One final caution: Brown bears generally shy away from humans, but they should not be approached under any circumstances, especially when feeding or when cubs are in the area. When hiking densely vegetated trails, make plenty of noise; brown bears hate surprises.

Aravaipa Canyon Wilderness and Preserve

A lush oasis in the desert provides succor for rare indigenous animals such as bighorn sheep, ringtails, and collared peccaries.

SITE 4 About 50 miles northeast of Tucson lies one of the Southwest's great natural treasures: Aravaipa Canyon. Over the eons the waters of Aravaipa Creek have carved a majestic barranca, or gorge, out of the desert floor. Its central 10 miles comprise a glorious 42,000-acre wilderness, preserved through a conjunction of holdings administered by the U.S. Bureau of Land Management (BLM) and the Nature Conservancy of Arizona.

The bighorn sheep is the star species of Aravaipa. Decimated throughout most of its range by hunting and the expansion of domestic livestock areas, this magnificent wild ovine is holding its own in the Aravaipa. The population numbers between 40 and 70 individuals, depending on the year.

Other large mammals found here are mule deer, black bear, bobcat, mountain lion, coyote, collared peccary, coati, and ringtail. As every naturalist knows, wild animals, especially predators, may be difficult to spot, even in areas where they are relatively plentiful. Perennially flowing Aravaipa Creek is an aid in this regard, since it's the main water source for a huge portion of the surrounding area. A simple creekside stroll is ample proof of this fact: Tracks are everywhere. Hiking at dawn and dusk along the creek is probably the best way to glimpse the canyon's more reclusive species. Walk slowly and quietly,

refrain from talking, and take time to stop and scan the surrounding terrain.

Though certainly not as dramatic in appearance as bighorn sheep, Aravaipa's aquatic residents are at least as important from the perspective of biodiversity. Seven native fish species inhabit the creek. Two—the loach minnow and spikedace—are on the federal list of threatened species.

Aravaipa Canyon is at the edge of the northernmost range for several

tropical birds, and its combination of water, lush riparian zones, and pristine desert habitat make it a bird's (and birder's) paradise. More than 200 species are either permanent or migratory residents of Aravaipa, including locally rare raptors such as the peregrine falcon and golden eagle. Hawk species include zone-tailed, Harris', and Swainson's hawks.

Songbirds found only in the extreme Southwest haunt the canyon. Yellow-billed cuckoos are relatively common. Look for Abert's towhee; beardless-tyrannulet; Virginia's, Lucy's,

Grace's, red-faced, and olive warblers; vermilion and dusky-capped flycatchers; Bell's, gray, and Hutton's vireos; hepatic tanager; pyrrhuloxia; greater pewee; tropical kingbird; and yellow-eyed junco. Lucky visitors may spot an elegant trogon. These emerald green-and-crimson birds are related to the quetzal of Central and South America. Although most live in Mexico and points south, some breed in the mountains of southeastern Arizona. Gambel's, scaled, and Montezuma quail, three species endemic to the Southwest, are also found here.

Harris' hawks nest in the mesquite brushlands and cactus deserts of the American Southwest.

Aravaipa also boasts a great diversity of reptiles. Eight different rattlers are found here: massasauga, western diamondback, black-tailed, Mojave, tiger, Arizona black, banded rock, and the endangered twin-spotted. The venom of the Mojave rattlesnake is unique in that it contains a potent neurotoxin along with the hemotoxin typical of North American pit-viper venoms. Its bite can be extremely serious. Other resident snakes include Arizona coral, gopher snake, bullsnake, and common kingsnake.

Look for gila monsters, the venomous and beautiful lizards long associated with the Southwest, in the early morning along roadways and in rocky areas. Desert tortoises and western box turtles are also found here. Resident amphibians include the Colorado River toad, Great Plains toad, and leopard frog.

Because of the wilderness designation of the federal holdings, it is necessary to obtain a permit from the BLM before hiking.

Lands owned by the Nature Conservancy are administered rigorously as a refuge, and hiking is by permission only. To maximize the Aravaipa experience, take one of the day hikes, backpacking trips, or horseback trips that are regularly scheduled by the Conservancy.

There is a road through the Conservancy lands, allowing casual visitors to view a good portion of the private refuge from their cars. In some ways this is one of the best means for viewing the local wildlife. Animals that are spooked by human beings on foot are often blasé about vehicles.

Cabeza Prieta National Wildlife Refuge

Early morning is the best time to look for gila monsters and desert tortoises in this vast and scorching Arizona desertscape.

SITE 5 At 860,010 acres, Cabeza Prieta is the largest national wildlife refuge in the lower 48 states. The enormity of the terrain (it takes at least 16 straight hours to drive across the refuge on its rutted four-wheel-drive tracks), the lack of water, and the distance from anything even remotely resembling civilization all demand that visitors approach this refuge with respect and a knowledge of their own limitations. There is nothing here except the eternal Sonoran Desert and the wildlife that inhabits it.

To see wildlife in this sere setting, however, one must be willing to be up and moving when the animals are doing the same: at dawn and sunset. Many desert species are nocturnal and at least partially subterranean, and Cabeza Prieta's wildlife is no exception. Get up well before the sun, hole up after the early morning, and resume observations at dusk. Slow nighttime driving along stretches of level, safely graded road can also be rewarding.

The desert is conservative in every sense; it does not teem with wildlife. Be prepared for patient, long-term observation. Before you set out, stop at the headquarters in Ajo and ask about locations of recent sightings.

Probably the most significant

The rare desert tortoise has an average lifespan of fifteen years.

When a gila monster is well fed, its tail swells with fat. The tail shrinks as fat is depleted.

celebrity species at Cabeza Prieta is the bighorn sheep. Efforts to reintroduce this endangered ungulate have met with some success here. They are found in mountainous areas of the preserve, particularly near seasonal or permanent sources of water. Pronghorn and mule deer are likely to be found in the same general areas. Smaller mammals here include kit fox, coyote, bobcat, badger, black-tailed jackrabbit, and white-throated woodrat.

The refuge is one of the best places in North America to observe reptiles, particularly lizards. It is at the heart of the gila monster range. These large lizards, spectacularly colored with bands of black and orange or black and pink scales, are poisonous, but they are also sluggish and will bite

only if molested. Also look for desert iguanas, chuckwallas, and zebra-tailed lizards. For a few hours after sunrise, lizards perch on rock outcroppings to warm up; later in the day they retreat to crevices or burrows.

The refuge is likewise a stronghold for various snakes, including six species of rattlesnakes. The sidewinder is the most common rattlesnake and is easily recognized by its sideways method of locomotion and the "horns" just over its eyes. Snakes are often seen in the evening, warming themselves on roadways and large rocks, which radiate thermal energy long after the sun sets.

Unlike turtles, all tortoises are strictly terrestrial. The desert tortoise, a threatened species, is found in Cabeza. This species is truly nocturnal and the best chance of seeing one of these rare reptiles is in the early morning as it heads back to its burrow.

Cabeza Prieta doesn't support great swarms of birds, but a number of species seldom noted in more northern latitudes thrive here. Flycatchers find the refuge especially hospitable. Individual species include vermilion and brown-crested flycatchers, and Cassin's and western kingbirds. The refuge is also one of the best places in North America to see thrashers, those long-tailed, curve-billed birds associated with western scrublands. Individual species that have been documented here include sage, Bendire's, curve-billed, crissal, and Le Conte's thrashers.

The greater roadrunner, the crested ground-walker emblematic of the Southwest, is also quite common. Watch for roadrunners in the scrub, running down snakes, lizards, and fledgling birds.

Raptors, most notably red-tailed hawks, soar on the thermals. Also look for the beautifully plumaged Harris' hawk, American kestrel, ferruginous hawk, and gray hawk. The ferruginous pygmy-owl is virtually endemic to the refuge; elf, burrowing, and great horned owls are also here.

In order to allow maximum viewing time in the morning and at twilight, try to camp at Cabeza Prieta for two days or longer. Primitive camping is allowed throughout the refuge, but remember that the desert is a delicate place, easy to wound and slow to heal. No wood fires are allowed, and human wastes should be retained in a chemical toilet and packed out.

While accommodating the desert's

THE FACTS

Noteworthy Animals: Bighorn sheep, kit fox, gila monster, desert tortoise, zebra-tailed lizard, chuckwalla, sidewinder, greater roadrunner, brown-crested flycatcher, sage thrasher, ferruginous pygmy-owl, burrowing owl, Harris' hawk.

Getting There: From Phoenix, take I-10 about 30 miles west to Buckeye, turn south on Ariz. 85, and drive about 70 miles to the refuge's headquarters on the north end of the town of Ajo. From Tucson, drive west about 130 miles on Ariz. 86 to Ajo. From Yuma, take I-8 east 90 miles to Gila Bend, then drive south on Ariz. 85 about 40 miles to Ajo.
Open: Daily, 24 hours, year-round. Stop at headquarters to obtain entrance permit and to check on road closures due to weather.
Best Times to Visit: October through June.
Visitor Information: Cabeza Prieta National Wildlife Refuge headquarters (520-387-6483) open Monday through Friday, 7:30 a.m.-4:30 p.m., year-round.
Entrance Fees: None.
Disabled Access: None.
Camping: Primitive camping; permit required; no fees.

fragility, never forget its essential unforgiving nature. Refuge staff are happy to dispense plenty of solid advice, but their mandate is not search-and-rescue. Out here, you're on your own. Pack at least one gallon of water per person per day—preferably more. Make sure your vehicle is in good shape, and carry spare fan belts and radiator hoses. In short, to commit to exploring Cabeza Prieta is to commit to a safari. Luckily, the rewards are as monumental as the challenge.

Muleshoe Ranch Cooperative Management Area

This popular desert refuge attracts hummingbirds, mule deer, and coatis to its well-watered arroyos throughout the year.

SITE 6 The watersheds of seven permanent streams flow through this spectacular 48,120-acre high desert refuge in southeastern Arizona, creating some of the lushest wildlife habitat in the Southwest. Early ranchers coveted this land because of the permanent surface water, an extremely scarce resource in the Southwest. The ruins of early homesteads are still scattered throughout the region. But the streams that once fed and watered thousands of cattle now succor wildlife. About 80 percent of the region's wild species depend on riparian zones during some time in their lives; small wonder, then, that Muleshoe Ranch burgeons with wildlife.

Jointly managed by the Nature Conservancy, the U.S. Forest Service, and the U.S. Bureau of Land Management, the Cooperative Management Area (CMA) has admittedly tough

The western diamondback rattlesnake can grow to a length of nearly seven feet.

access. The sole route in and out is the 27-mile unpaved Jackson Cabin Road 27. A two-wheel-drive vehicle will make it unless heavy rains have occurred, but a sturdy four-wheel-drive vehicle is a must for accessing the backcountry. Many locals prefer to enter the CMA by horseback or on foot. Two established trails, the High Lonesome and the Scenic Vista, begin at different points along the road. Take your time when hiking and stop often to scan the surrounding terrain: Animals of the high desert are notoriously tough to spot.

Desert wildlife follow a rigorous seasonal clock; what visitors see at Muleshoe depends on when they're there. Generally speaking, the best wildlife viewing is always near water—that is, in and around the arroyos—at dawn and dusk.

January and February are the best months to see coatis, or coatimundis. These playful and intelligent predators live in large troops that roam through the canyons. The purpose of these bands appears to be mutual forgaging and sheer sociability. Coatis, which are related to raccoons, have long delicate snouts and semiprehensile tails. Mule deer, the large deer native to the West, are often spotted browsing on scrub.

Muleshoe supports a stunning diversity of woodpeckers, which are particularly abundant in the winter months. Individual species include

The social and vocal coati is a pointy-nosed relative of the raccoon.

Lewis', acorn, gila, ladder-backed, hairy, Strickland's, and three-toed woodpeckers; Williamson's and red-naped sapsuckers; and northern flicker. Winter is also a good time to look for endemic songbirds such as the green-tailed towhee and the yellow-eyed junco.

March and April mark the end of hibernation and the beginning of the nesting season. Rock squirrels, spiny lizards, and leopard frogs emerge from their winter dens, while rare raptors such as zone-tailed hawks, common black-hawks, and gray hawks nest in the canyonlands. Any large, bulky nests in tall trees or on cliffs are likely to be theirs.

Muleshoe also harbors a great many songbirds that are either rare or absent in other regions of the U.S., and they are at peak populations in May and June. Be on the lookout for vermilion, gray, brown-crested, and dusky-capped flycatchers; Lucy's, yellow-rumped, and Grace's warblers; hepatic tanagers; crissal, curve-billed, and Bendire's thrashers; and canyon and cactus wrens.

Peregrine and prairie falcons, Cooper's hawks, and golden eagles scour the canyons and highlands in

the early summer months. The owls—elf, western screech, flammulated, ferruginous pygmy-, and great horned—are raising their young at this time and may be seen at dusk flying to their nests with captured prey.

The summer rains usually begin in July and last throughout September. Now, when growth is relatively lush, foraging by all species is top priority. Collared peccaries, wild pigs native to the desert, haunt mesquite bosques, feeding actively. Reptiles—including desert tortoise, Arizona coral snake, Arizona black and western diamondback rattlesnakes, and Sonora whipsnake—are at the height of their activity. Coveys of Montezuma and Gambel's quail gather together, and bighorn sheep, bobcat, mountain lion, and coyote traverse the wilderness areas, seeking food.

Around the ranch headquarters, high summer is the best time to monitor the hummingbird feeders. Among the individual species that frequent the feeders are broad-billed, violet-crowned, black-chinned, Costa's, and broad-tailed hummingbirds.

In the late fall, mule deer enter the rut; they are particularly easy to observe at this time since their natural wariness diminishes. November and December are, relatively speaking, downtimes for the CMA. Still, for the wildlife enthusiast, there is much to see: Winter birds such as the sharp-shinned hawk, white-crowned sparrow, and northern flicker are arriving, and the coatis have begun to form their large troops.

Spring and fall, when the temperature extremes of the desert are muted, are the most comfortable seasons for a visit. But in any season, Muleshoe is best appreciated over several days. Backcountry camping is allowed on public lands. From September through May, the Nature Conservancy offers accommodations in comfortable casitas near ranch headquarters.

Año Nuevo State Reserve

Northern elephant seals, sea lions, and sea otters dominate the waters and beaches of this northern California refuge.

SITE 7

Four species of pinnipeds frequent Año Nuevo State Reserve, a 4,000-acre tract of sandy beach, open ocean, and rocky islets north of Monterey. Northern elephant seals, California sea lions, northern sea lions, and harbor seals all breed here in large rookeries. Two other species, the Guadalupe fur seal and the northern fur seal, are occasional visitors.

Bull northern sea lions can tip the scales at a ton or more. But they're lightweights compared to the northern elephant seal, one of the world's largest seals and the chief attraction at the refuge. Bull elephant seals can reach 20 feet in length and may weigh four tons; at times even the cows weigh more than a ton.

An elephant seal rookery during the breeding and pupping seasons is a spectacle of fantastic proportions. Thousands of these massive creatures crowd the shore. The tableau is dominated by huge "beachmasters," dominant bulls zealously guarding their harems and turf. Fights between the beachmasters are common, consisting of sumo-wrestlerlike charges, biting, and sonorous bellows issued from their huge proboscises.

The rookeries also function as a well-stocked larder for great white sharks, the primary predator of all California pinnipeds. Old scars and wounds from shark attacks are usually observable on a number of seals or sea lions.

While Año Nuevo's pinnipeds are the primary draw, there are other animals in residence. Sea otters—certainly among the most charismatic and endearing of mammals—disport in the

In early December bull elephant seals arrive at Año Nuevo to claim space for their harems.

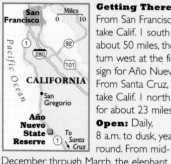
refuge's waters, diving for abalone and sea urchins and obligingly devouring them while floating on their backs within camera range of visitors.

This is also a wonderful place for birding. More than 320 species of birds use the reserve, including such local rarities as marbled murrelet, rhinoceros auklet, snowy plover, black swift, and bank swallow. Brown pelicans are often seen skimming over the waves in search of fish or preening on offshore rocks.

Shorebirds are particularly abundant in winter and spring. Black-bellied plover, black oystercatcher, willet, short-billed and long-billed dowitchers, wandering tattler, whimbrel, long-billed curlew, marbled godwit, ruddy and black turnstones, surfbird, sanderling, and dunlin all might be seen probing in the sand behind retreating waves as they search for crustaceans.

Raptors are common, especially during their late fall and winter migration. Species include red-tailed, red-shouldered, sharp-shinned, and Cooper's hawks; merlin; osprey; great horned owl and western screech-owl. The northern pygmy-owl, a tiny woodland owl about the size of a starling, also frequents the reserve.

Not surprisingly, the extravagant wildlife attract extravagant numbers of visitors. Most come during the pinniped breeding and pupping season, which runs from around mid-December through March. During this time the only access to the beaches dominated by elephant seals is through a three-hour guided walking tour. About 45,000 people gain entrance to the reserve through these walks each year.

During the rest of the year individual exploration is allowed, but access to sensitive areas is still tightly controlled by patrolling rangers. Obey all signs and rules at the reserve—high usage translates as exceptional pressure on wildlife, particularly the marine mammals. Given its popularity and the sensitivity of resident wildlife, Año Nuevo would be lost without constant vigilance.

Carrizo Plain Natural Area

Endangered species, including the San Joaquin kit fox, are being lured back by restoration efforts at this central California preserve.

SITE 8 This preserve—250,000 acres of arid plains in central California—is a joint venture between private conservancy groups and government agencies, including the Nature Conservancy, the U.S. Fish and Wildlife Service, the U.S. Bureau of Land Management, and the California Department of Fish and Game. This preserve is one of the best places in the world to witness habitat restoration on a landscape scale. The goal is to turn back the clock at Carrizo, to restore portions of the ecosystem to what it was thousands of years ago, when grizzly bears roamed the region and Native Americans hunted such tasty megafauna as tule elk and pronghorn.

The grizzlies won't be returning, but the goal of restoring the plain closer to its original condition seems increasingly attainable. Efforts to reestablish the native bunchgrass ecology have yielded heartening results. The natural area is home to a number of endangered species, including the San Joaquin kit fox, Nelson's antelope squirrel, giant kangaroo rat, and blunt-nosed leopard lizard. All have flourished since the project was launched a decade ago. Pronghorn and tule elk have been reintroduced and are propagating impressively, each species numbering several hundred animals. The preserve is adjacent to a designated release site for the California condor, a species now bred wholly in captivity. Someday condors may again forage on the Carrizo.

But endangered species aren't the only animals that have benefited from the preserve's creation. Raptors of all kinds are abundant: Black-shouldered kites; red-tailed, rough-legged, and ferruginous hawks; prairie falcons; merlins; American kestrels; and even golden eagles are seen with regularity. Great horned owls and common barnowls haunt the preserve's cottonwood

Conservation efforts have brought the pronghorn back from the edge of extinction.

39

THE FACTS

Noteworthy Animals: Pronghorn, San Joaquin kit fox, Nelson's antelope squirrel, giant kangaroo rat, tule elk, coyote, bobcat, golden eagle, ferruginous hawk, rough-legged hawk, sandhill crane.

Getting There: From Los Angeles, take I-5 north about 100 miles to Calif. 58 (near Bakersfield). Follow Calif. 58 west for 40 miles to Soda Lake Road, which is clearly marked. Drive 7 miles to the Goodwin Education Center.

Open: Daily, dawn to dusk, year-round.

Best Times to Visit: December through May.

Visitor Information: Goodwin Education Center (805-475-2131) open Thursday through Sunday, 9 a.m.-5 p.m., December through May. At other times, call the U.S. Bureau of Land Management, Bakersfield office (805-391-6000).

Entrance Fees: None.

Disabled Access: Some of the rest rooms, picnic areas, and trails are wheelchair accessible.

Camping: Primitive camping; no permit, fees, or reservations required.

groves and rock outcroppings, as attested by the numerous droppings and pellets (masses of hair and bone that the birds regurgitate after ingesting prey). Watch for these powerful owls at twilight, when they emerge for their nightly hunts. Burrowing owls perch on fence posts or ground squirrel mounds throughout the area.

Visitors will also want to keep an eye out for bobcats, coyotes, and mountain lions. These predators are quite wary, and their encounters with humans are rare.

A central feature of the preserve is Soda Lake, a 5-mile-long ephemeral body of brine that fills up with the winter rains and disappears by summer. The lake, or more particularly its population of fairy shrimp and brine shrimp, attracts hundreds of overwintering sandhill cranes. Two types of long-legged wading birds, black-necked stilts and American avocets, avidly feed in the lake's shallows.

Spring may be the best time to visit Carrizo. Not only are the wildflower displays stunning—entire square miles of California poppies, cream cups, owl's clover, and other species, following each other through the season in a stately, variegated procession—but the temperatures are balmy and enjoyable. By midsummer, the preserve has become an oven, with little shade and daytime temperatures exceeding 100°F. That's not to say summer isn't a good time to visit; just try to time your explorations for early morning or sunset. Many of the most interesting species are crepuscular or nocturnal in habit, and the temperatures are tolerable during those times. Plan to spend some evenings at Carrizo for nocturnal wildlife viewing. The complete absence of light pollution at the preserve also makes it a wonderful place for stargazing and observing meteor showers.

It's possible to hike in Carrizo, but the preserve is so expansive that viewing it from a car (not necessarily four-wheel drive) or mountain bike is probably more practical. Cars and bikes are prohibited from traveling off-road, but a network of roads provides good access to most of the area. Oddly enough, animals are less spooked by motor vehicles and bikes than by people on foot.

Gray Lodge Wildlife Area

Thousands of snow geese seeking food and shelter swoop down upon this California refuge during their fall migration.

SITE 9 North American waterfowl experienced a discouraging decline in the 20th century. The destruction of breeding grounds and overwintering habitat that resulted from agricultural and urban development sent duck and goose populations plummeting, from 500 million in the late 19th century to 23 million in 1990. But recent domestic conservation programs and international accords between the United States, Canada, and Mexico have turned things around dramatically. In 1997 migratory waterfowl populations stood at 100 million birds, the highest level in 20 years. Wild ducks and geese are on the rebound. And while they may never again darken the sky from horizon to horizon, their fortunes are good and getting better.

Of the continent's four major flyways—the continental routes waterfowl use to migrate between their nesting areas and wintering grounds—the Pacific flyway offers some of the most dramatic migratory spectacles. Each fall about 25 million ducks and geese wing their way south along this West Coast aerial route; at least 10 million of them end up in northern California's Sacramento Valley, where a vast complex of wildlife refuges and sprawling rice farms provide an abundance of food and shelter.

Virtually all the refuges afford excellent birding opportunities, but one is exceptional. The Gray Lodge Wildlife Area, which is managed by the California Department of Fish and Game, is an 8,400-acre amalgam of marshes, ponds, and mature forests that hosts between 500,000 and 1,000,000 waterfowl each winter. The sight of tens of thousands of greater white-fronted and snow geese spiraling down to the refuge after an early morning feeding on nearby rice fields is not soon forgotten.

Among the migratory fowl that winter at Gray Lodge are green-winged teal and cinnamon teal, two closely related species of small, brightly colored, fast-flying ducks. Northern shoveler, wood duck, gadwall, common goldeneye, ring-necked and ruddy ducks, and bufflehead throng at the refuge. Snow geese, greater white-fronted geese, and Canada geese are winter residents as well. In the spring, American wigeon, mallards, and northern pintail are seen participating in elaborate mating rituals, such as "courting flights": aerial steeplechases in which the drakes chivy the hens across the sky, hoping to coerce them into mating.

Shorebirds—specifically American avocets, black-necked stilts, long-billed dowitchers, and long-billed curlews—are common in the winter and spring.

Wading birds abound. An egret and heron rookery occupies one corner of the refuge, and up to 50 pairs of great blue herons and great egrets brood there, competing raucously for nesting space. Other water-associated birds that favor Gray Lodge are sandhill

cranes, snowy egrets, green-backed-herons, black-crowned night-herons, and white-faced ibis.

Northern harriers, American kestrels, merlins, red-tailed hawks, and rough-legged hawks haunt the refuge's open areas. Red-shouldered, Cooper's, and sharp-shinned hawks nest in the trees. Bald and golden eagles are relatively common sights. Great horned owls can be found whiling away the day in the thickets, and the lucky visitor may stumble on the increasingly rare burrowing owl, a species in decline due to habitat loss.

Songbirds are common in the wooded areas. Look for black phoebes, rufous-sided towhees, northern orioles, and western tanagers in the woods. Western bluebirds, western kingbirds, and meadowlarks are likely sightings in more open areas.

Mammals are not the primary reason for visiting Gray Lodge, although coyotes, gray foxes, river otters, beavers, muskrats, raccoons, and opossums are all in permanent residence. A large herd of black-tailed deer migrates between the refuge and nearby Sutter Buttes. The deer are of particular interest because they harbor a persistent albino strain in their genetic matrix. Sightings of pure white deer are regularly reported.

The entire refuge is open for hiking from February through September. Although hunting is allowed from mid-October through January, a 2,500-acre zone remains open for wildlife-watching. This zone includes a 3-mile auto tour loop, an observation

Nearly extinct at the turn of the century, the great egret has reclaimed its original range.

THE FACTS

Noteworthy Animals: Northern pintail, green-winged teal, American wigeon, long-billed dowitcher, great egret, black-necked stilt, greater white-fronted goose, snow goose, red-tailed hawk, northern harrier, merlin.

Getting There: From Sacramento, take Calif. 99 north as it splits off toward Chico. Follow Calif. 99 through Yuba City. The turn-off to Gray Lodge is about 10 miles north of Yuba City

at Live Oak, or alternately another 5 miles north at Gridley. From Live Oak, turn left at the light for 10 miles to Almond Orchard Road (later called Pennington Road). Turn north and drive 2 miles to the refuge entrance on the left. From Gridley, drive into town, turn left on Sycamore Street, and follow it about 6 miles onto Pennington Road. For both routes, follow the gray signs to the refuge office, hunter/birder registration check station, and parking lot.

Open: Daily, dawn to dusk, year-round.

Best Times to Visit: Year-round.

Visitor Information: Gray Lodge Wildlife Area (916-846-5176) naturalist's office open Monday through Friday, 8 a.m.-4:30 p.m., year-round.

Entrance Fees: $2.50 per person; usually self-registration at parking lot. Free entry with a current hunting or fishing license or membership in California Wildlife Campaign.

Disabled Access: North of parking lot 14, there is a wheelchair-accessible 0.3-mile trail to a viewing platform. Roadway turnouts serve as excellent viewing sites.

Camping: None on-site.

---

platform, and 2 miles of hiking trails. One of the special attractions at Gray Lodge is a photography blind, available by reservation only. Photographers who spend a day here are virtually guaranteed some of the most dramatic wildlife images of their careers.

Gulf of the Farallones
National Marine Sanctuary

This refuge in the midst of the open ocean is one of the best places in the world to observe gray whales on their annual migration.

SITE 10 A few miles from San Francisco lies one of the wildest animal sanctuaries in the Western Hemisphere, a place where great mammals feed, millions of birds disport, and the hand of humanity still weighs lightly. Not surprisingly, this preserve is in the midst of the open sea.

The 1,255 nautical miles of the Gulf of the Farallones National Marine Sanctuary (GFNMS) owe their abundance of wildlife to the conjunction of a few factors. First is the upwelling—strong, cold offshore currents that pump nutrients from the depths of the ocean to warmer nearshore waters, fueling constant plankton blooms that form the cornerstone of a vast food web. This "food pump" supports everything from enormous shoals of tiny shrimplike krill to the huge gray whales that eat them.

Then there are the Farallon Islands and Cordell Bank, the former a series of islets just 25 miles west of San Francisco, the latter a submerged reef that adjoins the islands. The islands support rookeries for northern elephant seals, California and northern sea lions, and numerous species of nesting marine birds. Cordell Bank provides food and shelter for a great variety and quantity of fish, which in turn attract seabirds and marine mammals in mind-boggling numbers.

The gulf is one of the best places

in the world to observe the annual migration of gray whales. About 23,000 of these massive creatures migrate each fall from Alaska to their breeding territories in the lagoons of

Baja, Mexico; they return along the same route in spring and spend the summer feeding in Arctic waters. The sight of a 30-ton whale breaching the waters or "spyhopping" (lifting their heads above the water for a prolonged look around) is unforgettable.

Whale-watching boat tours are the most practical way to visit this watery sanctuary. (The islands themselves are off-limits to visitors.) Blue, humpback, and gray whales are common sightings; sperm whales and beaked whales are sometimes seen. Cetaceans such as Dall's porpoises and Risso's dolphins often follow the boats. Recently, small numbers of northern fur seals have begun visiting the island.

You can hear the sharp barking of male California sea lions throughout the Farallon Islands.

THE FACTS

Noteworthy Animals: Blue whale, gray whale, humpback whale, orca, Dall's porpoise, northern sea lion, California sea lion, common murre, pigeon guillemot, rhinoceros auklet, tufted puffin.

Getting There: Numerous whale-watching charters operate in the Bay Area—leaving from San Francisco's Fisherman's Wharf, Sausalito, Emeryville, Half Moon Bay, and elsewhere—with trips daily in the summer and on weekends from November through April. Check local directories or the San Francisco Information Center (415-391-2000). Trips generally cost $35-$60 per person and most boats will not take passengers under 12 years of age.

Open: Daily, 24 hours, year-round.

Best Times to Visit: March through May; September through November.

Visitor Information: Gulf of the Farallones National Marine Sanctuary Headquarters at Crissy Field Coast Guard Station, The Presidio, San Francisco (415-561-6622). Visitor Center (415-561-6625) open Monday through Friday, 9 a.m.-4:30 p.m.; weekends, 10 a.m.-3:30 p.m., year-round.

Charters or Guide Services: The Oceanic Society Expeditions (415-474-3385) runs whale-watching trips in summer and winter.

Entrance Fees: None.

Disabled Access: Varies from boat to boat.

Camping: None on-site.

Bird displays can be stunning—common murres, shearwaters, pigeon guillemots, gulls, fulmars, petrels, and cormorants by the thousands, skimming the waves and actively feeding on the water. The refuge marks the southernmost range for tufted puffins, squat, stubby-winged birds with huge parrot-like beaks. Other species likely to be seen include black-footed albatross, Cassin's auklet, and rhinoceros auklet. The two auklet species are recovering after years of decline. Rhinoceros auklets established nests on the Farallon Islands in 1997, after a 100-year absence.

But it's not just the abundance of species that makes the Farallones such a spectacular place to visit—it's also the interaction between species. The sight and sound of thousands of seabirds ravaging a square-mile school of anchovies defies description. The waters adjacent to the Farallon Islands are also one of the favored haunts in North America for great white sharks, and it is not terribly uncommon for visitors to witness these stately and awesome predators attacking seals and sea lions near the rookeries. Rarely, orcas will be seen assailing gray whales—not a sight for the faint of heart or weak of stomach, perhaps, but certainly a wildlife spectacle of mythic dimension.

Though the Gulf of the Farallones National Marine Sanctuary is literally just off the coast from San Francisco, a visit typically requires an entire day. The boats cover a lot of nautical miles during their tours of this gigantic expanse of water. Seas can be rough, so those prone to motion sickness should take appropriate precautions. Wear deck shoes or short rubber boots, and pack layers of warm and waterproof clothing—the weather can be changeable. A hat, sunscreen, and binoculars are the only equipment necessary for this wilderness trek.

Point Reyes National Seashore

Both land and sea creatures—tule elk and California sea lions foremost among them—are found at this refuge near San Francisco.

SITE 11 Just 20 miles north of the Golden Gate Bridge lies a stunning landscape of primeval forest, craggy bluffs, and pristine beach, a wilderness burgeoning with wild animals great and small. There are many wonders associated with Point Reyes, but perhaps the greatest is its very existence: The fact that an 86,000-acre wildland can thrive at the margins of one of the country's densest population centers is something of a miracle.

A good way to begin a visit is with a stop at the Bear Valley Visitor Center, just off Calif. 1 at Olema, to pick up road and trail maps, check out the excellent interpretive program, and ask rangers for advice. From there most first-time visitors head north to observe the tule elk herd.

The smallest subspecies of North America's wapiti or elk, tule elk are sizable beasts, with bulls topping the scales at 800 pounds. About 300 elk roam a 2,600-acre paddock at the northern tip of the peninsula, which is cordoned off from the rest of the preserve by stout fencing. Most of the property adjacent to Point Reyes is ranchland, and the robust ungulates would raise havoc with domestic livestock and crops if allowed to range freely. You have to hike to see the elk;

The antlers of a male tule elk often measure as much as four feet across.

only foot traffic is allowed in their sanctuary. They're liable to be spotted anywhere—grazing on the grassy knolls, resting in the brushy draws, even ambling along the beach.

The elk are of particular interest during the late summer and early fall, when the rut is in high gear. The haunting, high-pitched bugling of the lust-crazed bulls penetrates the foggy air as they challenge one another over mating rights to the cows. Antler-clattering engagements between rival bulls are common at this time. Visitors should be aware that bull elk lose much of their natural timidity during the rut, and challenges to human beings have been known to occur.

Native black-tailed deer range throughout the preserve, as do several hundred fallow and axis deer, exotic species naturalized from the Mediterranean and India, respectively. Many visitors who see snow white fallow deer (they display a variety of colors, from white to black) mistake them for albino native deer. Locally common mammals include bobcat, coyote, gray fox, long-tailed weasel, badger, striped and western spotted skunks, black-tailed jackrabbit, and mountain beaver (the Point Reyes subspecies is endangered). They all live and range freely throughout Point Reyes, and any of the park's trails is likely to yield sightings.

The forests of Bishop pine and Douglas-fir are excellent birding grounds. During the late fall and early winter, tens of thousands of raptors funnel through here on their way south. Look for red-tailed and red-shouldered hawks, peregrine falcon, white-tailed kite, northern harrier,

sharp-shinned and rough-legged hawks, American kestrel, and merlin. Owls—great horned, western screech-, common barn-, long-eared and short-eared, northern saw-whet, and the endangered northern spotted—are year-round residents.

Woodland songbirds are numerous, especially during the spring and fall migrations. The interfaces between the coniferous forest and the coastal scrub (usually a few hundred yards from the beach) are particularly good places to birdwatch. The brilliant gold-and-scarlet western tanager is commonly reported. So is the varied thrush, which is identified by its orange wing bars and a black breast band. Western wood-pewee, western flycatcher, black phoebe, and western bluebird are seen as well.

Point Reyes is a good site for western warblers. Orange-crowned, yellow, yellow-rumped, black-throated gray, hermit, and Wilson's warblers might be spied as they rustle through the foliage.

But the land is only half the story of Point Reyes. The other half is the sea. On the western border of the refuge is the wild Pacific, ceaselessly pounding the miles-long beach. To the south is Drakes Estero and to the east is Tomales Bay, which together constitute some of the richest estuarine habitat on the West Coast.

An abundance of pinnipeds frequent these waters, most notably California sea lions, northern elephant seals, and harbor seals. The primary predators of these large marine mammals, great white sharks, are also common. Indeed, the mouth of Tomales Bay is one of the world's primary nurseries for great whites.

Point Reyes is also known for its fine whale-watching opportunities. Between late December and mid-March, the Point Reyes Lighthouse offers a good perch from which to look for migrating gray whales.

Virtually all aquatic birds native to the West Coast are found here. Some notable species include the endangered brown pelican, black brant, red-throated and common loons, double-crested cormorant, western grebe, great and snowy egrets, Forster's tern, common murre, great blue heron, and black-crowned night-heron.

Ducks are common during the winter migrations. Look for them in Tomales Bay, on the east side of the refuge. Visitors are likely to spot common, white-winged, and surf scoters, American wigeon, northern shoveler, northern pintail, mallard, gadwall, ruddy duck, canvasback, redhead, greater scaup, and common goldeneye.

Shorebirds teem on both the beaches and the estuaries. Among the species busily probing the sand and silt for tasty invertebrates are apt to be black-bellied and snowy plover, killdeer, black oystercatcher, willet, whimbrel, spotted and western sandpipers, sanderling, long-billed curlew, marbled godwit, ruddy and black turnstones, black-necked stilt, American avocet, dunlin, and short-billed dowitcher.

While Point Reyes is an ideal day trip from San Francisco, it's also expansive enough to warrant a weekend backpacking foray with an overnight stay at one of the four primitive campgrounds maintained by the National Park Service. Visitors can also hike,

THE FACTS

Noteworthy Animals: Tule elk, black-tailed deer, axis deer, fallow deer, mountain beaver, gray whale, California sea lion, harbor seal, northern elephant seal, brown pelican, common scoter, American avocet.

Getting There: From San Francisco, take US 101 north for about 15 miles to the Sir Francis Drake Highway exit (just before San Rafael). Turn west and drive about 20 miles to Olema. Turn right on Calif. 1, then make an immediate left on Bear Valley Road. From there it is 0.5 mile to the Bear Valley Visitor Center.

Open: Daily, dawn to dusk, year-round.

Best Times to Visit: Year-round.

Visitor Information: Bear Valley Visitor Center (415-663-1092), open Monday through Friday, 9 a.m.-5 p.m.; weekends, 8 a.m.-5 p.m.; year-round. Two other Visitor Centers—one at the lighthouse, the other at Drakes Beach—have more limited, irregular hours.

Entrance Fees: None.

Disabled Access: The Bear Valley Visitor Center and the adjacent Earthquake Trail are completely accessible. The Abbot's Lagoon Trail is wheelchair accessible for about the first mile of its length—up to an overlook with a magnificent view of the lagoon and its resident birdlife. The tule elk preserve headquarters is also wheelchair accessible.

Camping: Primitive camping, permit required; fees; reservations essential, accepted up to two months in advance. Call 415-663-8954 Monday through Friday, 9 a.m.-2 p.m.

bike, or ride horses along well-maintained trails. Other options include a stroll on the beach, surf-fishing, or even a walk along the San Andreas Fault on the Earthquake Trail.

Aiken Canyon

Wild turkeys, greater roadrunners, golden eagles, and Mexican spotted owls all thrive in this woody canyon preserve.

SITE 12 One of the West's richest wildlife habitats—the gambel oak and mountain mahogany scrublands endemic to the southern portion of the Rocky Mountain foothills—is also one of its most threatened. These trees often grow alongside juniper, pinyon pine, and needlegrass; taken together, they make an extremely well-stocked larder for wildlife. Pinyon pine nuts and gambel oak acorns, in particular, are bursting with protein, carbohydrates, and fat, providing a nutritional bonanza for a great variety of wildlife species. Some animals directly consume the nuts; others prey on the acorn eaters.

Unfortunately, Colorado's foothill country is as attractive to humans as it is to wildlife. Development swallows up more and more of these productive woodlands with each passing year. But Aiken Canyon, a 1,600-acre preserve that is administered by the Nature Conservancy, might help change this unfortunate trend. The refuge contains some of the best gambel oak habitat in the state, and preserve managers are working with private landowners in an effort to make the canyon the cornerstone of a general habitat preservation plan for the entire region. And, because the preserve is bounded on the east by the 237,000-acre Fort Carson and on the west by the 1,700-acre Beaver Creek Wilderness Study Area, the area closed to development is greatly extended.

Drawn by the abundant food, more than a hundred different bird species have been documented at the canyon. Woodpeckers are abundant, including such species as hairy and downy woodpeckers and the boldly marked

northern flicker. Red-breasted, white-breasted, and pygmy nuthatches can be seen nimbly creeping straight up and down the tree trunks.

A robust population of wild turkeys inhabits the canyon. In the spring the aggressive gobbling of the toms is heard as the males lay claim to hens and territory. In the fall the turkeys are likely to be positioned beneath the oaks, scratching in the leaf litter to locate acorns. The canyon marks the far northern edge of the greater roadrunner's range. These bushy-crested ground birds can be recognized by the way they race along, then stop abruptly, look about, and rapidly pump their tails.

The rare and threatened Mexican spotted owl thrives only in deep forest.

prey heavily on the preserve's population of ground squirrels and rabbits. Other birds of prey that have been sighted in the canyon include prairie and peregrine falcons, and Cooper's and red-tailed hawks. Watch for them perched motionless in the oaks or on fence posts, or soaring effortlessly on afternoon thermals. Owl species known to reside here include the great horned owl, western screech-owl, and the petite northern pygmy-owl. The rare Mexican spotted owl has also been documented in deep timber areas of the preserve. This species is designated as threatened under the federal Endangered Species Act, and there are only about 40 of these big owls in all of Colorado.

Many large mammal species emblematic of the West—including black bear, mountain lion, and Rocky Mountain elk—are known to inhabit the refuge, but the chances of a sighting are relatively slim. Their tracks and scat may be all that a visitor finds. Sightings of mule deer and smaller creatures, such as the Colorado chipmunk, rock squirrel, Abert's squirrel, black-tailed jackrabbit, and desert cottontail, may have to suffice.

The preserve is an easy drive from Denver and an ideal day trip. There are several miles of developed trails, providing good access for walkers and hikers. No vehicles of any kind, including bikes, are allowed on-site. Go it alone or sign up for one of the regularly scheduled tours, which give an excellent grounding in the gambel oak biome and its resident creatures. Conservancy staff members are usually on hand to answer questions and suggest hiking routes.

Songbirds include the blue-gray gnatcatcher, western bluebird, scrub jay, Virginia's warbler, rufous-sided towhee, and black-headed grosbeak. Pinyon jay and plain titmouse are here, too; like the greater roadrunner, they are at the far northern reaches of their range.

Star among the resident raptors is the golden eagle, which favors these dry, woody uplands. Golden eagles are far better hunters than bald eagles, and

Arapaho National Wildlife Refuge

High in the Rocky Mountains of Colorado roam charismatic megafauna, including elk, moose, mule deer, and pronghorn.

SITE 13

North-central Colorado, with an average elevation of 8,000 feet, is home to the highest national wildlife refuge in the lower 48 states. Up here temperatures can plunge at any time after the summer solstice, so savvy visitors pack thermal underwear for a visit to Arapaho regardless of the season.

Administered by the U.S. Fish and Wildlife Service, this 23,267-acre holding is an excellent place to observe the big game species typical of the Rocky Mountains. Almost half the acreage, located along several miles of the Illinois River, consists of irrigated meadows and riparian willow thickets, with the rest being primarily sagebrush-grassland uplands. Such a wealth of forage is a powerful draw for elk, moose, mule deer, and pronghorn. With any luck, on any trip between spring and early fall, visitors should see individuals from all four species.

Summer is a particularly good time to see pronghorn, when several hundred of the handsome animals graze in the irrigated meadows. Moose are out foraging with their calves at this time, too. In late fall and winter, herds of Rocky Mountain elk and mule deer congregate on various parts of the refuge.

Among the small mammals that might be encountered by visitors is the badger, a scrappy, short-legged, striped-back predator that once ranged widely in the West. Other commonly seen mammal species include coyote, beaver, mink, long-tailed weasel, striped skunk, white-tailed prairie dog, white-tailed jackrabbit, and Nuttall's cottontail.

Arapaho, especially in the area known as North Park, is one of the best brood areas for waterfowl in the Rocky Mountains. During the spring expect to see nesting pairs of ruddy duck, gadwall, lesser scaup, mallard,

Sage grouse, declining in range and numbers, depend on sagebrush for shelter and food.

northern pintail, teal (blue-winged, green-winged, and cinnamon), northern shoveler, American wigeon, and redhead. Each year as many as 7,500 ducklings are hatched and raised to maturity here.

Migrating shorebirds are also likely

Mule deer forage in the mountains in summer and return to lower elevations in winter.

spring sightings. Look for killdeer, mountain plover, spotted sandpiper, common snipe, and Wilson's phalarope.

Western songbirds also thrive at Arapaho and are particularly evident in the summer. The western kingbird, a big, bold, lemon-breasted flycatcher, might be seen perched upon fence wires. Horned larks, which are immediately recognizable by the two feather "horns" over the eyes, are common in the grasslands. Other species that have been documented here include sage thrasher, warbling vireo, yellow warbler, common yellowthroat, green-tailed towhee, MacGillivray's warbler, Wilson's warbler, bobolink, and red-winged blackbird.

Sage grouse are also found throughout Arapaho. Each spring the males stamp out an intricate dance on their ancestral dancing grounds, or leks, stimulating the hens' interest in mating. The leks are located just beyond the refuge's borders, but refuge staffers can direct visitors to them.

Open country and abundant small prey make Arapaho a wonderful site

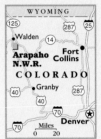
for raptors. Prairie falcons in particular are found in abundance. Swainson's hawks are also common, and golden eagles live here year-round. Also look for northern harriers, rough-legged hawks, ferruginous hawks, red-tailed hawks, American kestrels, merlins, burrowing owls, and even the occasional bald eagle.

The wide expanses of irrigated meadowlands have caused the local populations of chorus frogs to boom, and their twilight antiphonies, heard from late spring through midsummer, are extremely enjoyable.

Arapaho makes a good one-day side trip for anyone visiting nearby Rocky Mountain National Park. Biking and driving are the most practical ways to explore. An auto tour route (which is also admirably suited for bicycles) winds through the entire preserve, providing vistas of all the major habitats. Signs along the way provide information on the significance of each area and the type of wildlife to look for at that spot.

Phantom Canyon Preserve

As hawks and eagles soar high above this pristine river gorge, pronghorn and mule deer graze below.

SITE 14 The North Fork Cache La Poudre River (so named by early fur trappers, who stashed their black powder here) is one of Colorado's few major river canyons that remains inaccessible by road. There has never been a route along this steep gorge; two pioneer trails, the Cherokee Trail and the Overland Trail, passed nearby but didn't penetrate the canyon. Explorer John Charles Frémont eloquently expressed the beauty of the North Fork Cache La Poudre gorge in 1843. His words still ring true:

It was a mountain valley of the narrowest kind—almost a chasm; and the scenery very wild and beautiful. Towering mountains rose about; their sides sometimes dark

Typically, yellow-bellied marmots grow to ten pounds in weight and fifteen inches in height.

with forests of pine, and sometimes with lofty precipices, washed by the river. Below, the green river bottom was a wilderness of flowers, their tall spikes sometimes rising above our heads as we rode among them.

This 1,700-acre preserve incorporates a good portion of the canyon proper and a sizable chunk of the surrounding rim. The habitats are varied. Much of the rimland is a mixture of short-grass prairie and ponderosa pine savanna. The south slopes of the canyon are characterized by thick growths of antelope bitterbrush, mountain mahogany, and flowering perennials, while the north slopes are lushly forested in Douglas-fir, ponderosa pine, and Rocky Mountain juniper. The bottom of the canyon and its various side gorges support riparian forests of narrowleaf cottonwood, river birch, alder, chokecherry, wild plum, and willow.

Wildlife is both diverse and abundant in this rich landscape, with large mammals particularly well represented. Black bear and mountain lions haunt the woodlands; Rocky Mountain bighorn sheep are often seen near the mouth of the canyon; pronghorn are common on the rimland prairie; Rocky Mountain elk, mule deer, and white-tailed deer are all likely to be sighted throughout the canyons. Smaller mammals that may be spotted fleetingly include bobcat, coyote, badger, porcupine, and yellow-bellied marmot. Two rare mammals—Ord's kangaroo rat and Townsend's big-eared bat—have also been recorded here.

Above all, Phantom Canyon is premier raptor country. Eagles, hawks, and owls are all drawn by the abundance of small prey and the superb nesting habitat. At least three separate golden eagle territories occur in the canyon. Other species that brood in or around the preserve include prairie falcon, northern harrier, American kestrel, and red-tailed hawk. During the fall migration, ospreys, Swainson's hawks, Cooper's hawks, and sharp-shinned hawks are also seen. Bald eagles winter along the North Fork Cache La Poudre—particularly near Halligan Reservoir, which is upstream from the preserve.

The canyon also has some of the best songbird habitat in the region. Species include western tanager, lazuli bunting, mountain bluebird, Virginia's warbler, yellow-rumped warbler, yellow warbler, Wilson's warbler, lark bunting, evening grosbeak, solitary vireo, canyon wren, and rock wren. In winter Townsend's solitaires are found in the juniper thickets, each individual fiercely defending its well-defined territory; juniper berries are the primary winter sustenance for these slender, gray-and-white birds.

Among locals the canyon is best known for its stellar trout fishery. Huge brown trout and hybridized rainbow-cutthroat trout swim in the deep pools of the river. Angling is permitted on a lottery system, but the policy is strictly catch-and-release and

restricted to artificial lures with barbless hooks. (As of 1997, fishing had been temporarily suspended because uncharacteristically large water releases from the Halligan Reservoir had deposited large amounts of sediment into the riverbed. The fishery will remain in recovery until the river removes the silt, which may take several years.)

Rocky Mountain bighorn sheep maintain a secure foothold at Phantom Canyon.

Back on the ground, keep an eye out for prairie rattlesnakes. They are just about everywhere. Exercise reasonable caution when hiking and do not interfere with any snakes that you encounter. These beautiful reptiles are essential to the ecological health of the preserve.

The Nature Conservancy hosts a great variety of programs at Phantom Canyon, including pleasure hikes and trips that focus on different scientific disciplines: bird taxonomy, geology, aquatic invertebrates, riverine habitats, and general natural history. Some field trips entail fees; others do not. Call for information, and book reservations early—slots fill up fast. There is also a summer internship program at the canyon for people interested in participating in stewardship or restoration work.

Hanauma Bay Nature Preserve

This popular spot on the Hawaiian island of Oahu offers snorklers close-up views of colorful tropical fish and live coral.

SITE 15 Two things up front: First, this is the best place in the Hawaiian Islands for the casual visitor to see huge numbers of tropical fish. Second, this is probably the most heavily visited dive spot in the world. The entire Great Barrier Reef in Australia—all 1,000 linear miles of it—gets about three million visitors a year, while tiny 100-acre Hanauma Bay on Oahu hosts two million visitors a year.

That's a lot of people. And there are a lot of fish. The number of fish in and around the bay is abnormally high. This is partially due to the fact that the area is a protected environment, but fish populations are also inflated as a result of years of snorkelers hand-feeding them everything from frozen peas and bread to trout chow.

Anyone who dons a mask and snorkel and jumps into the bay, then, is not going to see a strictly natural habitat. The number of fish is much higher than one would see in an unmanipulated environment, and the species mix is completely different. The feeding has encouraged a boom in aggressive species such as rudderfish: large, silvery fish that tend to scare off more timorous and delicate reef species. Indeed, rudderfish sometimes become so forward that they nip unwary divers.

But while Hanauma Bay may not be pristine, it constitutes an important marine resource and offers a terrific snorkeling experience. Marine life positively teems here, most particularly reef fish with names as colorful as their bodies: unicorn fish, hogfish, ornate butterflyfish, teardrop butterflyfish, multiband butterflyfish, onespot butterflyfish, raccoon butterflyfish, file fish, moorish idol, trumpet fish, blue trevalle, stingray, half beak, forceps fish, mullet, and false mullet. Also look for yellow tang and sailfin tang, flattish, boldly marked fish with long snouts. Coronet fish, which have long, snakelike bodies and exceptionally long mouths, lurk on the sandy sea bottom. Moray eels, voracious though generally cautious predators, haunt crevices and caves. Green sea turtles visit the bay, though they generally avoid areas of high snorkeler density.

Even the wariest reef dwellers—parrotfishes, most notably—have been lulled by the feeding at Hanauma Bay. Look for bulletheaded parrotfish and spectacled parrotfish, both blue-green in color with large scales. Cleaner wrasses, which are small and brilliantly hued, earn their livelihood by removing parasites and debris from the bodies and mouths of larger fish. They usually set up "cleaning stations" near areas of considerable fish traffic. When a large fish spots a cleaner wrasse, it approaches, stops, and adopts a nonaggressive posture, signaling the wrasse that it can safely commence its work.

Invertebrate life is also relatively abundant, especially in the outer bay. Octopuses are numerous. There are several species of beautiful flatworms

The butterflyfish's small flattened body allows for easy movement through coral reefs.

and fanworms with feathery gills. Cleaner shrimp and banded coral shrimp, sea urchins (rock-boring, spiny, and slate pencil), rock crabs and ghost crabs, sea stars and sea cucumbers are present, too. Nudibranchs are bright-colored sea slugs that creep among the colonies of live coral. Take particular care not to step on, break off, or even touch any coral, dead or alive. Under considerable stress here, these corals are the essential building blocks of tropical reefs.

The managers of Hanauma Bay Nature Preserve are attempting to restore the bay's ecosystem by restricting the number of visitors and moving toward a no-feeding policy. Presently, visitors are asked to voluntarily refrain from feeding the fish.

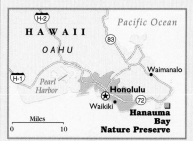
Several rules are strictly enforced: Namely, no smoking and no littering. Cigarette butts, which are toxic, ultimately wash into the bay. Plastic bags have been linked with sea turtle mortality—they resemble jellyfish, the turtles' favorite food.

The preserve offers a number of services, including snorkel rental, a snack bar, showers, and lifeguards. Note that the bay posts the highest drowning figures of any Oahu beach, not because the water is treacherous (although it sometimes can be) but because the heavy usage increases the likelihood of mishap. Snorkelers should be honest about their swimming ability and should not venture into the outer bay unless they are experienced swimmers.

Waikamoi Preserve

Beautiful native birds, such as the Maui parrotbill and the crested honeycreeper, can be spotted in this mountain forest.

SITE 16

To the casual visitor the Hawaiian Islands seem incredibly lush. Vegetation is riotous, forming a thick canopy over steep, fluted ridges and valleys. Most of this forest, at least at lower elevations, is naturalized, composed of nonnative trees, shrubs, and flowers that have overtaken indigenous species. As the native plants have disappeared, so have Hawaii's singularly beautiful endemic birds, supplanted by more robust exotic species that thrive in the altered habitats. But there are still a number of places where the old Hawaii, the Hawaii primeval, can be witnessed in all its splendor. One of the best is Waikamoi Preserve on the island of Maui.

Waikamoi, on the north slope, adjacent to Haleakala National Park, comprises 5,230 acres of rugged rain forest, shrubland, grassland, and old lava flows. Hundreds of native Hawaiian plant species are found here, along with their associated insect pollinators, symbiotes, and dependents. And living among the plants and the insects are Hawaii's rarest natural treasures: her forest birds.

This is the world's last stronghold of the rare Maui parrotbill. A shy,

The brilliantly colored iiwi sips nectar from an akala, or Hawaiian raspberry.

stub-tailed bird with greenish plumage, it has an exceedingly large, hooked parrotlike bill. The sighting of a Maui parrotbill constitutes a red-letter day for any birder, beginner or veteran. Another rare endemic bird is the crested honeycreeper (or ako-hekohhe), a gorgeous bird identified by its orange nape and bushy white forehead crest.

Many more native forest birds can be seen in the preserve. The apapane is a crimson nectar-imbiber with a curved bill; look for it in flowering trees. The amakihi is a small greenish bird with a dark curved bill that for-ages among shrubs and foliage. The iiwi is a vermilion nectar-sucker with black wings, a black tail, and a curved bill. The Maui creeper (alauahoio) is a greenish bird similar in appearance to some North American wood warblers.

Other native birds that are found at Waikamoi include the pueo, Hawaii's only native owl. It is sometimes spot-ted gliding above the treetops as it searches for prey. The nene, Hawaii's renowned flightless goose, is also a Waikamoi resident, but it lives in re-mote areas of the preserve not general-ly accessed by the public. Because it can't fly, the nene is extremely vulner-able to rats and mongooses, the bane of ground-nesting birds everywhere.

Waikamoi is remote and extremely rugged. The Nature Conservancy of Hawaii, the administering agency, restricts access both to ensure visitor safety and to protect the preserve's delicate habitats and the rare species that dwell in them. The only access is by means of guided hikes, for which reservations are usually neces-sary. This is rugged hiking; wear

good boots and bring a hat, sunglass-es, and sunscreen. Supplies are not available on-site, so come prepared. On the third Saturday of each month, volunteers work in the preserve, eliminating invasive nonnative weeds. All interested parties are welcome.

Flat Ranch

These grassy wetlands provide critical habitat for a variety of species, such as coyotes, cutthroat trout, and sandhill cranes.

SITE 17 Of all the major habitat types in the mountainous West, undisturbed wetlands are the rarest. Most have been drained for pasturage or had their water sources diverted for irrigation. But Flat Ranch, a 1,450-acre holding of expansive marshes and grassy wetlands on the Henry's Fork Snake River, is a lovely exception. Charged by springs flowing from the Yellowstone Plateau, this critical parcel owned and operated by the Nature Conservancy of Idaho both extends the Yellowstone-Grand Teton biome and provides critical habitat for waterfowl and wading birds.

Given its proximity to Yellowstone National Park (a mere 7 miles as the crow flies), it's not surprising that Flat Ranch supports many of the same species that have made that park famous. Grizzly bears have occasionally been sighted in the area, and black bears are quite common. Coyotes stalk mice and voles in the water meadows. Moose, great lovers of aquatic vegetation, have claimed the refuge as a favorite regional larder, and visitors often see them browsing in the marshes. The ranch is also on the historic migration route for the area's Rocky Mountain elk and pronghorn herds. The elk calve here in the spring, and large numbers of pronghorn spend their summers on the preserve, gorging on the rich wetland grasses and sedges. Other animals here include water-loving species such as beaver, muskrat, and river otter.

The marshy flats are a haven for waterbirds. At least a hundred pairs of sandhill cranes nest at Flat Ranch

Coyotes can leap more than a foot in the air and run at speeds of up to 40 mph.

each year. So do hundreds of long-billed curlews, a large, curved-bill shorebird that is increasingly rare over most of its range. Other nesting waterbird species include Canada goose, northern pintail, teal (green-winged, blue-winged, and cinnamon), northern shoveler, gadwall, harlequin duck, mallard, killdeer, mountain plover, willet, and spotted sandpiper.

Among the numerous songbird species are yellow, yellow-rumped, orange-crowned, and MacGillivray's warblers; solitary, warbling, and red-eyed vireos; and yellow-breasted chat. Raptors include peregrine falcons, ospreys, northern harriers, and most notably, bald eagles, which gather in the spring to prey on spawning native cutthroat trout.

The cutthroat, in fact, deserves special mention. This large, dramatically colored native trout is threatened across much of its range. Henry's Lake and upper Henry's Fork and its tributaries are one of the cutthroat's last strongholds, and hundreds of big, gravid females congregate on the refuge's redds to lay their eggs, which are then fertilized by milt released from ardent males. The spectacle of these hefty, gaudy trout rolling over their spawning beds is extraordinary. The cutthroat indicate that Flat Ranch is still a functioning ecosystem, one that can count all of its constituent parts in good working order.

The vigor of this riverine meadow and wetland system is all the more remarkable because the Conservancy still runs it as a working cattle ranch. The object is to demonstrate to ranchers and visitors alike that conservation and agriculture can profitably coexist.

Although Flat Ranch is only about 20 miles from the West Entrance to Yellowstone National Park (see p. 106), it is worlds away from the summer crowds. The best way to see Flat Ranch is by canoe, floating the 4 miles of river along the preserve lands. The most popular put-in is about a mile north of the preserve where US 20 crosses the Henry's Lake outlet. The Conservancy owns a few canoes, which it lends out. Call ahead to see if one is available. Fishing is allowed in season, though a catch-and-release philosophy is strongly encouraged.

Selway-Bitterroot Wilderness

River runners who navigate the wild Selway combine a thrilling white-water ride with glimpses of black bears, mule deer, and moose.

SITE 18 A vast corridor of wilderness extends from the Canadian border through the Idaho Panhandle and eastern Montana, tracing the Bitterroot mountain range for 400 miles to the high desert of southern Idaho. At its heart is the Selway River, running free and clear through some of the wildest country left in the continental states.

The 60-mile run down the Selway is the experience of a lifetime, combining exciting white water with unparalleled wildlife-viewing opportunities. The trip is challenging, especially early in the season, when the river is high and the white water is thunderous. Commercial outfitters are usually fully booked several months to a year in advance. Private permits are issued by the river's administering agency, the U.S. Forest Service, but they're difficult to obtain because each year about 10,000 applications are received for 100 slots. Besides, unless you're an advanced white-water rafter or kayaker with considerable experience, the Selway is too much of a challenge to tackle alone.

Outfitters typically handle all the logistics, from rowing the rafts to cooking dinner; guides are also generally knowledgeable about the geology, flora, and fauna of the river and provide running commentary between the rapids. The character of the river changes radically with water level. During the spring runoff, the Selway runs high and the white water can be intense. By late summer, the flow has slackened so that the typical run is a contemplative float punctuated by sharp rapids.

Large mammals teem throughout the Selway system. Sightings may be numerous or relatively scant, depending on the season, weather, and simple luck. Keep a close watch on the riverbank, particularly at the confluences of side creeks, where you may see

mountain lions, lynx, bobcats, or wolverines. Black bears live all along the river, and can be seen at any point—even in camp, if wild food has been scarce in the past year.

The Selway drainage supports the largest population of Rocky Mountain elk in Idaho; look for these massive members of the deer family in spring and early summer, especially in the river's upper reaches. Rocky Mountain bighorn sheep and mule deer also forage at high elevations during those seasons, and mountain goats are ob-servable along the canyon walls. Moose, sometimes with calves in tow, are seen along the calmer stretches of the lower river, rooting for aquatic vegetation and sedges. Fishers and marten inhabit the big timber along the river course, partic-ularly in the lower portions. River otters are particularly in evidence in late summer, when water levels are relatively low.

The Selway has been designated as a federal release site for gray wolves. A colony has been established, and

Moose calves, born in the spring, are completely weaned by the time they are six months old.

for their large size, striking gray plumage, and red eyes—nest along the entire length of the river. Other resident raptors that are commonly seen soaring overhead includes golden eagles, sharp-shinned and red-tailed hawks, and American kestrels. Swainson's, ferruginous, and rough-legged hawks are sometimes seen along the upper stretches of the river.

Far as it is from migratory waterfowl routes, the Selway doesn't see much in the way of ducks or geese. A notable exception is the harlequin duck, a dramatically marked bird that spends spring and summer on high mountain streams and winter along the rugged coastal headlands. This beautiful little duck is often observed gliding down the river or dabbling in the eddies for invertebrates.

American dippers—gray, exceptionally alert, robin-size birds—are abundant along the riverbed, and can often be seen diving into the riffles, where they walk along the bottom searching for aquatic nymphs.

Reptiles and amphibians are scarce, but one notable resident is the tailed frog, a primitive species that can only live in cold water of exceptional purity. Its abundance in the Selway is reliable testimony of the river's unusually high water quality.

Guided trips are arranged with plenty of time for side hikes, swimming, and fishing. No Selway trip would be complete without engaging in the river's gold-medal cutthroat trout fishing. Big fish are the rule here, many exceeding 18 inches. Use artificial lures and barbless hooks only, please—the angling is strictly catch-and-release.

appears to be rapidly expanding both in numbers and range. Because it encompasses the biggest chunk of untouched wilderness in the lower contiguous states, the Selway-Bitterroot Wilderness is also under consideration as a release site for grizzly bears.

The Selway is home to one of the greatest concentrations of northern goshawks on the continent. These fierce woodland accipiters—notable

Glacier National Park

More than 200 grizzly bears roam in the wide open spaces of this protected land in Montana, high atop the Continental Divide.

SITE 19 Glacier National Park is the living embodiment of the wild, and largely vanished, mountainous West. All the big mammals associated with the northern Rocky Mountain biome call this one-million-acre park home: grizzly, black bear, mountain lion, lynx, gray wolf, bighorn sheep, mountain goat, Rocky Mountain elk, moose, mule deer, and white-tailed deer. Three rare large mustelids—wolverine, marten, and fisher—also inhabit the park. Other residents include bobcat, coyote, badger, mink, long-tailed weasel, river otter, and snowshoe hare.

The park, which straddles the Continental Divide, takes its name and its shape from the huge glaciers that sculptured the landscape during the ice age. As they moved slowly southward, the glaciers scoured the earth beneath them, leaving behind high peaks and deep valleys, pristine lakes and thundering waterfalls, and dozens of small glaciers. The park is crossed by the scenic Going-to-the-Sun Road and more than 700 miles of developed trails.

Grizzly bears are the undisputed lords of this mountainous realm. For its size, Glacier has the greatest concentration of these huge humpbacked bears in the lower 48 states; more than 200 range the park and surrounding environs. Grizzlies range lower elevations in the spring and autumn and higher elevations in the summer. After emerging from their winter dens in the spring, they head for the lowlands to feed on succulent greens and winter-kill ungulate carcasses. In summer the bears repair to the high scree slopes to hunt ground squirrels and marmots and lap up colonies of ants and army cutworm moths. Fall brings them low again to gorge on berries and tubers. The more opportunistic bears may attempt to forage for garbage or human victuals in campsites and along roadsides at any time of the year.

Black bears inhabit the same range and follow more or less the same seasonal clock as grizzlies. Remember, however, that close contact with bears of both types is to be

Grizzly bears are omnivorous, eating everything from grass to insects to candy bars.

assiduously avoided; maintain a respectful distance and take particular pains to give females with cubs plenty of leeway. Ask for orientation materials at the Visitor Centers and follow the guidelines. Exercise caution always.

In the late spring and summer, mountain goats frequent Walton Goat Lick, a highly mineralized natural seep off US 2. The goats, which are often visible at middle to high elevations throughout the park, come down from the heights to avail themselves of the mineral salts and may be observed from a designated viewing area near the road. Bighorn sheep are occasionally seen along the Highline Trail and at Many Glacier Valley.

White-tailed deer occur throughout the park, while the larger mule deer prefer the western side. Moose favor the park's various lakes and marshlands, while elk range far and wide.

Predators are not at all uncommon,

Bighorn sheep, highly social animals, live in herds made up of rams, ewes, and lambs.

but they are reclusive. Each year visitors and staffers see mountain lions, wolverines, wolves, marten, and fishers, but it's strictly by luck.

Glacier supports at least nine nesting pairs of bald eagles. It's also a stronghold of the northern goshawk, the most aggressive of our woodland raptors. Other birds of prey that hunt here include the golden eagle, osprey, peregrine falcon, northern harrier, red-tailed hawk, Swainson's hawk, American kestrel, great gray owl, great horned owl, long-eared owl, short-eared owl, boreal owl, and northern saw-whet owl. Gyrfalcons—the largest of the continent's falcons—visit regularly in the winter, as do snowy owls and, rarely, northern hawk-owls.

Common loons are omnipresent in

THE FACTS

Noteworthy Animals: Grizzly bear, black bear, gray wolf, lynx, bobcat, wolverine, fisher, marten, badger, bighorn sheep, Rocky Mountain elk, mountain goat, moose, mule deer, golden eagle.

Getting There: From Kalispell, take US 2 northeast about 35 miles to the West Entrance of the park. Winter access may be difficult; call for road conditions.
Open: Daily, 24 hours, year-round. Going-to-the-Sun Road open mid-June through mid-October.
Best Times to Visit: June through October.
Visitor Information: Glacier National Park Headquarters (406-888-7800) at West Glacier just past the Middle Fork Flathead River. There are four Visitor Centers: Apgar (West Entrance), Logan Pass and Many Glacier Ranger Station (both in the center of the park), and St. Mary (eastern section, on US 89). Each is open daily, May through October; Apgar remains open on weekends year-round.
Entrance Fees: $10 per vehicle, valid for seven days.
Disabled Access: All Visitor Centers are fully accessible. US 2 and US 89 afford roadside viewing. Trail of the Cedars has flat boarded sections for wheelchair accessibility.
Camping: Thirteen developed campgrounds in Glacier National Park; fees; reservations accepted, but not mandatory. Permit required for backcountry camping.
Accommodations: For reservations and information on lodges, hotels, and motels within the park, call 602-207-6000. For chalet rentals, call park headquarters.

aquatic birds that are commonly spotted by observant visitors include eared grebe, American bittern, Barrow's goldeneye, harlequin duck, blue-winged teal, gadwall, redhead, and common merganser.

Groundbirds are doing very well in Glacier. Spruce grouse, blue grouse, ruffed grouse, and white-tailed ptarmigan are all residents.

Woodpeckers thrive in the thick coniferous forests; individual species of note include northern flicker; pileated, Lewis', downy, hairy, three-toed, and black-backed woodpeckers, as well as yellow-bellied and Williamson's sapsuckers.

Look (and listen) for passerine songbirds such as the western tanager, mountain bluebird, and western bluebird. Red crossbills and white-winged crossbills are first located by their loud twittering. These pink-plumaged birds feed openly and quite fearlessly; at close range their distinctive crossed bill tips are visible.

Visitors can spend days, or even weeks, profitably exploring Glacier National Park. Options range from superb and nearly effortless roadside wildlife viewing to some of the finest and most challenging wilderness backpacking in all of North America. Trails span a wide range of difficulty levels, from an easy stroll to extended backcountry travel. The rock climbing, canoeing, fishing, and cross-country skiing are all first-rate.

During the summer National Park Service rangers conduct natural history hikes and campfire programs. Participation in these events can greatly enhance appreciation of the park's diversity and its denizens.

the park's lakes and ponds during the spring and summer, their wild and mournful cries enriching many an evening around the campfire. Other

Pine Butte Swamp Preserve

In addition to guided hikes and horseback rides, visitors to this Montana ranch can study mammal tracking or paleontology.

SITE 20 The eastern front—or eastern slope—of the Rocky Mountains is a region of profound contrasts. This is where the flat expanse of the Great Plains ends, abruptly butting up against the awesome massif of the Rocky Mountains. It's a place of abundant ecotones, ecological niches created by abrupt changes in elevation, geology, and vegetation in a relatively constricted area.

Pine Butte Swamp Preserve, an 18,000-acre Nature Conservancy holding of prairie, wetland, coniferous forest, and aspen groves, provides an exceptional look at the front in all its biodiverse splendor. Because of the fragility of the area, however, general public access is restricted to the Bud Guthrie Memorial Trail, a half-mile track that traverses an area of prairie overlooking the wetlands. There is one guided hike on the preserve each week that is open to a limited number of the general public. The Nature Conservancy also hosts guided visits; even then, access is limited and strictly regulated. Human-free space is critical to the survival of this unique habitat and its resident creatures.

A tremendous number of wild species converge here—the grizzly bear foremost among them. This is the last place in the United States where grizzlies utilize a prairie habitat. The bears roam from spring through fall, but they are particularly abundant in the spring, immediately after they emerge from hibernation. Famished after their long winter fast, they gorge on succulent grasses, perennials, and tubers. Candidly, don't expect to find swarms of bears cavorting on the prairie. For one thing, the typical sow grizzly commands about 100 square miles of foraging terrain. Also, these are not "park bears," comfortable with the presence of human beings. They are truly wild, wary animals and are more nocturnal than most other grizzlies. There are usually only about 10 grizzly sightings a year, and these are typically from a distance of 1 to 2 miles; it is more common to find the bears' scat, tracks, and excavations from their quests for subterranean food.

Other large mammals that inhabit the preserve include black bear, mountain lion, elk, and mule deer. Lynx have been recorded here, and it's likely that gray wolves are naturally recolonizing the area from the north; but again, sightings of these wary canids are highly unusual. Among the smaller mammals that may be encountered are bobcat, badger, coyote, red fox, mink, beaver, porcupine, white-tailed jackrabbit, and Richardson's ground squirrel.

Pine Butte also supports a great array of birds, which are the refuge inhabitants most likely to be seen by visitors. Spring and fall migrations bring waterfowl, including the white pelican, green-winged teal, northern pintail, northern shoveler, gadwall, and redhead. Wading birds, such as American bittern and great blue

A coyote mates in the late winter and will sometimes stay with the same partner for life.

heron, are commonly seen hunting fish, frogs, and snakes. Nesting waterfowl species include Canada goose, mallard, common merganser, blue-winged teal, and cinnamon teal. Among the nesting shorebirds are spotted sandpiper, long-billed curlew, and common snipe.

There are breeding populations of golden eagles, the West's peerless hunter of small mammals. The lucky visitor may see one of these magnificent birds diving on a jackrabbit or ground squirrel. Northern goshawks nest in the deep forests, while prairie falcons, northern harriers, American kestrels, and merlins prefer forest margins and meadows. Northern pygmy-owls and long-eared owls congregate in pine copses. Other resident species include short-eared, western screech-, great horned, and northern saw-whet owls. Look for them near dawn and dusk, gliding on silent pinions as they scan the ground for prey.

Gorgeous western tanagers and northern orioles make their nests here in the spring. This is wonderful territory for western wood warblers, shy birds that favor the deep woods and forest margins; breeding species include yellow, yellow-rumped, and common yellowthroat. Sparrows, fly-catchers, swallows, and wrens are also here in force.

As participants in various Nature Conservancy programs, visitors can study a wide range of subjects—everything from mammal tracking to paleontology. (The preserve encompasses Egg Mountain, a renowned archaeological dig that several years ago yielded fossils of a dinosaur egg clutch.) Guests stay on-site at the

THE FACTS

Noteworthy Animals: Grizzly bear, coyote, mountain lion, bobcat, lynx, badger, Rocky Mountain elk, beaver, golden eagle, northern goshawk, prairie falcon, northern pygmy-owl.

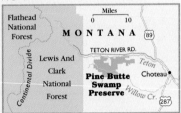

Getting There: From Choteau, take US 89 north for 5 miles. At Teton River Road, turn left and proceed west for 17 miles to the preserve office.

Open: Bud Guthrie Memorial Trail open daily, dawn to dusk, year-round. Hiking access limited; call in advance for permission.

Best Times to Visit: June through October.

Visitor Information: The Nature Conservancy of Montana, Site Manager's Office (406-466-5526), open Monday through Friday, 9 a.m.-5 p.m., year-round.

Entrance Fees: None.

Disabled Access: Accessible facilities are planned for the guest ranch, but not yet in place.

Camping: None on-site. Numerous campgrounds are located nearby in Lewis and Clark National Forest (406-791-7700).

Accommodations: Weekly rates at the guest ranch range from $775 to $1,050 per person (depending on the season) and include all meals, naturalist programs, and horseback riding. Group rates are available. For information, call 406-466-2158.

Pine Butte Guest Ranch. Resident naturalists lead hikes and horseback rides on and off the preserve.

Pine Butte abuts the Bob Marshall Wilderness, which affords wonderful backpacking and superlative trout fishing. Glacier National Park (see p. 69) is just 60 miles northwest.

Ruby Mountains Wilderness and Ruby Lake National Wildlife Refuge

Two vastly different sites—one a mountain fastness, the other a marshy wetland—support scores of mammals and birds.

SITE 21 Nevada is popularly considered a land of flat and relentless sand, sagebrush, and salt pans. To a large extent this is true. But there is another Nevada—the Nevada of mountains and wetlands. The mountains rise from the plain like schooners on the open ocean. More accurately they are arks, supporting animals typically found in the Rockies or the Cascades. The wetlands are desert oases, sustaining many species that could not survive in the sun-blasted, waterless expanses that surround them.

There is no better place observe these unique environments than the Ruby Mountains. Here a remote mountain wilderness and one of the West's premier high-desert wetlands lie within a few miles of each other, affording visitors the opportunity to see the best wild Nevada has to offer.

There is no easy way into Ruby Mountains Wilderness, which realistically is accessible only from early summer through mid-autumn. This is, essentially, a pure backcountry experience: You go by foot or horseback, following the 40-mile Ruby Crest National Recreation Trail across the ridges. The sweat equity, however, more than pays off. This 90,000-acre wilderness ranges between 6,000 and 11,300 feet in elevation, and is characterized by mixed coniferous forests. In two places there are copses of spruce and white fir, arboreal remnants from the last ice age.

Some of the West's most familiar large mammals are scarce or totally absent here. There are no black bears, for example. Elk, disliked by local farmers because they consume alfalfa with untoward enthusiasm, are few. Mountain lions, like most large predators, are likewise scarce. But the area has the largest population of mule deer in the state. Rocky Mountain bighorn sheep and mountain goats gambol among the crags at the highest elevations. Bobcats and coyotes are the largest commonly observed predators. Badger, long-tailed weasel, ermine, and striped skunk are also found here. Herbivorous mammals include white-tailed jackrabbit, yellow-bellied marmot, and pika. Also known as "rock rabbits," pikas live in scree slopes, harvesting dry grasses for consumption during the winter.

Nevada's cordilleras are potent attractions for birds because they promise water, food, and shade in an otherwise hostile desert environment. Ruby Mountains Wilderness is thus one of the best places in the state for nesting and migrating birds of prey.

Golden eagles reign supreme among the local raptors and are often seen riding the thermals or perched on conifer snags, looking for jackrabbits and ground squirrels. Also be alert for northern goshawks; red-tailed, sharp-shinned, Cooper's, Swainson's, ferruginous, and rough-legged hawks; and

American kestrels. Lucky visitors may also see an occasional prairie falcon, a beautiful relative of the better known peregrine falcon.

The Ruby Mountains support a number of gallinaceous birds, including chukar and sage grouse. The most significant species from a birder's viewpoint, however, is the Himalayan snowcock—an introduced species from Asia. The only places on earth to see this rare bird are the Himalayas, the Wallowa Mountains of Oregon, and the Ruby Mountains. Birders from across North America undertake pilgrimages to the highest realms of the Ruby Mountains simply to add this big, beautifully marked, partridge to their life lists.

Just southeast of Ruby Mountains Wilderness sprawls the 37,600-acre Ruby Lake National Wildlife Refuge, which offers a wholly different experience—both in terms of wildlife and access. Unlike Ruby Mountains Wilderness, the refuge requires no strenuous effort to explore it. Central to the refuge is a 17,000-acre spring-fed marsh bordered by meadows, grasslands, and shrub-steppe uplands. The marsh is transected by levees and roads, making it easy for visitors to view marsh wildlife. An excellent auto tour route with several overlooks has also been established.

Known to support at least 200 species of birds, Ruby Lake is the most significant nesting area in the lower

Only about seven inches long, a typical pica weighs less than five ounces.

77

THE FACTS

Noteworthy Animals: Mule deer, Rocky Mountain bighorn sheep, mountain goat, pronghorn, pika, golden eagle, Himalayan snowcock, canvasback, sage grouse, trumpeter swan, tundra swan.

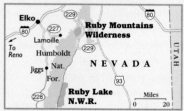

Getting There: Ruby Mountains Wilderness: From Elko, take Nev. 228 south 5 miles to Nev. 227. Follow Nev. 227 east 15 miles; the wilderness entrance turnoff is 0.5 mile before Lamoille. Ruby Lake National Wildlife Refuge: From Elko, take I-80 east about 20 miles to Nev. 229 (unpaved). Follow Nev. 229 south about 75 miles to refuge headquarters.

Open: Ruby Mountains: daily, 24 hours, year-round. Access impractical once the snow falls. Ruby Lake: daily, dawn to dusk, year-round.

Best Times to Visit: April through October.

Visitor Information: Ruby Mountains Wilderness: U.S. Forest Service, Elko office (702-738-2151 or 800-715-9379), open Monday through Friday, 7:30 a.m.-4:30 p.m., year-round. There is no visitor center, but the office provides maps and information. Ruby Lake National Wildlife Refuge Headquarters and Visitor Center (702-779-2237) open Monday through Friday, 7 a.m.-4:30 p.m., year-round. Information kiosks throughout the site.

Entrance Fees: None.

Disabled Access: Ruby Mountains Wilderness: None. Ruby Lake NWR: Visitor Center, one fishing area, and auto tour route fully accessible.

Camping: Ruby Mountains Wilderness: Primitive camping allowed; no permit or fees required. Ruby Lake NWR: None on-site, but developed campsites available at the adjacent Ruby Marsh Campground. For information call Ruby Mountains Ranger District, Humboldt National Forest (702-752-3357).

48 states for canvasback, a large diving duck that has experienced significant decline across the continent. About 3,500 "cans" and 2,500 redheads (a related species) are produced at the refuge each year. From May through July, the ducklings gain weight on a rich diet of invertebrates and become fully fledged adults.

At the peak of the fall migration in late September and October, the marsh supports about 60,000 ducks and geese. Along with canvasback and redhead, look for Canada goose, gadwall, mallard, northern pintail, cinnamon teal, green-winged teal, bufflehead, and northern shoveler. Both trumpeter and tundra swans winter here in moderate numbers; look for them in areas where active springs have kept the ice at bay.

Nesting colonies of shorebirds and wading birds are also highly visible along the mudflats. Individual species include white-faced ibis, great blue heron, black-crowned night-heron, great egret, snowy egret, and American avocet.

Migrating songbirds flit throughout the refuge. Flycatchers, warblers, and thrashers are particularly abundant; look for western flycatcher, orange-crowned warbler, and sage thrasher, among many others.

From spring through fall, the refuge is a good place to see pronghorn. Also, it's located on a major winter migration route for mule deer. The deer start moving out of the mountains with the first heavy snows in the high country, usually by late November. By December, it's not unusual to see herds of several hundred animals browsing near Refuge Headquarters.

Stillwater National Wildlife Refuge

Enormous congregations of white pelicans flock to this newly
established sanctuary of marshes and lakes in Nevada.

SITE 22 The Great Basin—a vast western sink that includes virtually all of Nevada and portions of Oregon, Idaho, and Utah—is for the most part a trackless inland sea of sagebrush and alkali flats. There is certainly a monochromatic grandeur to this mammoth depression. The beauty is in the vastness and sameness of the landscape, in the seeming immutability of the gray-green horizons. But there are also oases here—alkaline marshes and lakes that teem with birds and other wildlife. One prime example is the Stillwater National Wildlife Refuge.

Stillwater is one of the newest holdings in the federal refuge system. Established in 1990, it consists of a 77,500-acre core tract held directly by the U.S. Fish and Wildlife Service, plus a buffer area of 162,000 acres owned by the U.S. Bureau of Land Management but managed by the USFWS. The huge size of this refuge is significant in itself, but the superb quality of the habitat is as important as the quantity of acreage. During the last few years, refuge managers have secured guaranteed rights to 10,000 acre feet (a measurement equal to 1 acre in surface area and 1 foot in depth) of water annually, as well as significant funding for additional acquisitions. The wetlands created by the judicious application of this water has made the desert bloom—not in cotton, corn, or soybeans but in wildlife. About 20,000 acres are now in marshland, and this figure will rise as more water becomes available.

About 12,000 white pelicans—one of the largest congregations in the United States—forage in the Stillwater area during the spring and summer breeding season. These freshwater pelicans nest at 750-acre Anaho Island on Pyramid Lake, located about 50 miles northwest of the town of Fallon. They fly regularly to the refuge to fish for the carp and tui chub that thrive in the shallow alkaline marsh waters. Radiotelemetry research conducted on these birds indicates that members of the species are far more wide-ranging than once thought. One bird was tracked to the Great Salt Lake—about 450 miles to the east—just 12 hours after being located at Stillwater.

This refuge is one of the most significant sites in the Great Basin for migratory waterfowl and shorebirds and one of the best places in the West for viewing tundra swans. In the fall and winter, as many as 5,000 of these stately snow white birds may be found here. The sight of several hundred swans winging their way across the marshes at dawn, their breast feathers stained pink by the rising sun, is the stuff of indelible memories.

Canvasback ducks—huge ducks with rust-colored heads—stage here in phenomenal concentrations that sometimes number 25,000 birds. This is also one of the most important breeding areas in the United States for redheads, a duck that is similar to the

The American avocet picks up crustaceans by swishing its bill through the water.

canvasback and, like the canvasback, is experiencing troubling declines.

In total, as many as 250,000 waterfowl may be found here during the height of the fall migration—usually late October to late November. In addition to swans, canvasbacks, and redheads, other species that pass through Stillwater include Canada goose, green-winged teal, cinnamon teal, mallard, northern pintail, northern shoveler, gadwall, lesser scaup, common goldeneye, bufflehead,

common merganser, and ruddy duck.

Shorebirds also gather in stunning numbers—up to 200,000 strong during the peak of migration. Scan the refuge's mudflats for the diminutive snowy plover and the gangly black-necked stilt. Other species to look for are killdeer, American avocet, western sandpiper, long-billed dowitcher, common snipe, and Wilson's phalarope. The white-faced ibis, an elegant and long-billed wading bird rare in the Western states, is also found here.

THE FACTS

Noteworthy Animals: White pelican, tundra swan, canvasback, redhead, white-faced ibis, bald eagle, American avocet.

Getting There: From Reno, take I-80 east about 30 miles to US 50. Follow US 50A for 30 miles to the town of Fallon; proceed another 5 miles on US 50, then take the turnoff marked by the National Wildlife Refuge sign. The refuge begins about 15 miles past the first sign. In winter and spring, call ahead to check on the road conditions.
Open: Daily, dawn to dusk, year-round.
Best Times to Visit: April through June; October and November.
Visitor Information: Stillwater National Wildlife Refuge, Fallon office (702-423-5128), open Monday through Friday, 7 a.m.-5 p.m., year-round. No visitor center on-site.
Entrance Fees: None.
Disabled Access: Facilities are planned but not yet developed.
Camping: None on-site.

Bald eagles winter at the refuge, and golden eagles are year-round residents. Northern harriers, recognizable by their white rumps, fly just a few feet above the wetlands. Peregrine falcons and ferruginous hawks are here, as are Swainson's, red-tailed, and rough-legged hawks; prairie falcons; merlins; and American kestrels. Look for them perched on fence posts, power poles, and trees, especially during the fall migration.

Mammals are relatively scarce, as they are throughout the Great Basin. However, the marsh does support a sizable herd of mule deer. Muskrat is the most common species; lesser numbers of beaver, mink, coyote, kit fox, black-tailed jackrabbit, and striped skunk also make their homes at the refuge. The scant cover means that chances of mammal sightings are good.

Because the refuge is so recently established, it is not fully developed. There are no wildlife blinds, no maintained hiking trails, no interpretive center. But there are more than 200,000 acres of pristine marsh and uplands with good road access, making this a birder's paradise in every season.

Gila Riparian Preserve

The endangered willow flycatcher is just one of the rare birds likely to spotted along the banks of the Gila River.

SITE 23 The Gila is the Southwest's last major free-flowing river. All the rest have been dammed, diverted, or even extirpated —sucked dry by thirsty cities and farms. But on the Gila a sizable portion of desert riparian corridor has been preserved: 7,308 acres, to be precise. In terms of wildlife species, this is the most diverse deciduous woodland habitat in New Mexico.

The Gila is a transition zone for northern and southern continental wildlife, which means that species from the northern Rocky Mountains and Mexico commingle here. Wildlife

The gila woodpecker builds its nest in holes in giant saguaro cactus or mesquite trees.

sightings—of birds particularly—are therefore unpredictable and often delightfully serendipitous. About one-third of all of North America's bird species have been sighted in the preserve. It is particularly rich territory for flycatchers. These birds are named for their distinctive method of catching prey in which they suddenly flit down from a branch and snag an insect on the wing. In addition to the willow flycatcher, whose numbers are declining in the Southwest, there are vermilion, ash-throated, and brown-crested flycatchers. The gila woodpecker, which is found only in New Mexico, and Arizona, also lives here.

As rich as the preserve is for birds, it's only going to get better. Cottonwood and sycamore forest and marsh restoration projects are ongoing—not just at the refuge, which is cooperatively managed by the state of New Mexico, federal agencies, and the Nature Conservancy, but along 40 additional miles of adjacent public and private lands as well. Many private landowners along the Gila's corridor are enthusiastically participating in riparian zone rehabilitation.

As the wetlands and cover have increased, so have populations of towhees and vireos. Expect to see Abert's, brown, and green-tailed towhees; and Bell's, solitary, and warbling vireos. Warblers are also increasing with the woodlands, most notably Lucy's warbler and yellow-throated warbler.

This is wonderful country for raptors. Breeding pairs of bald eagles have recently begun nesting in the cottonwoods along the Gila. Rare zone-tailed and black hawks frequent the canyons, as do peregrine falcons. Other hawks here include American kestrels and red-tailed and ferruginous hawks. Sightings of great horned owls, burrowing owls, and ferruginous pygmy-owls are relatively common.

Rocky Mountain bighorn sheep have enjoyed a successful reintroduction into the area. Mule deer, coyote, and coati frequent wooded areas. Sometimes beavers are spotted swimming in the river at dusk. Mountain lion, black bear, collared peccary, and swift fox are present, but because they are secretive, sightings depend largely on luck. Their tracks, however, are often evident along the riverbanks. In 1995 in the nearby Animas Mountains (about 50 miles south of the preserve), a jaguar was treed by a photographer using hounds. It's unlikely that jaguars are breeding in the region—the animal was a young male, undoubtedly roaming far from its native range. Still, the incident thrilled local naturalists.

Reptiles abound—most notably gila monsters, softshell turtles, and mud turtles. Kingsnakes, bullsnakes, black-tailed rattlesnakes, western diamondback rattlesnakes, and western box turtles are also resident species. Give the rattlesnakes a wide berth, but don't be unduly concerned; if you don't bother them, they won't bother you.

The river itself harbors species of note, most particularly the spikedace and loach minnow, both endangered.

Though beleaguered by nonnative species, these small, quick-swimming species may benefit, according to naturalists, from plans to reintroduce river otters. Otters prefer large, slow-moving fish such as carp and suckers and typically leave smaller fish alone.

Late spring and early summer are wonderful times to visit the preserve. This is a relatively large area, impossible to explore thoroughly in one day, so plan to spend two days or more, using a campsite or motel room as a base. An extensive trail system allows good access throughout the preserve, though the going is sometimes rugged.

Malheur National Wildlife Refuge

This wetland offers food and shelter to scores of swans, geese, cranes, and ducks winging their way along the Pacific flyway.

SITE 24 Most people would describe Oregon as an uncommonly lush state, blessed with old-growth temperate forests and omnipresent gentle rain. That's true, on the western slope of the Cascade Range. But about two-thirds of the state is high desert or arid woodlands. Water is scarce east of the Cascades—and when it occurs, wildlife accretes to it like rust to cast iron.

Malheur National Wildlife Refuge, which is administered by the U.S.

Fish and Wildlife Service, is a prime case in point. At nearly 186,000 acres, it is dominated by two huge bodies of water, Malheur Lake and Harney Lake. At least they're lakes on the maps—in reality they're vast wetlands, subject to great flux in water levels. Sometimes the lakes are full to the brim; sometimes they're a maze of marshes, channels, and sedge lands.

The refuge is located precisely in the middle of the Pacific flyway, which supports the most waterfowl

Mallards are just one of the many species of migratory ducks that throng at Malheur in the fall.

of the four continental flyways—the primary routes used by migratory waterfowl flying between their breeding and wintering grounds. Ducks and geese have to fly more than 1,000 miles from their nesting grounds in Canada to reach Malheur, the first significant wetland on the route. When they arrive, they do so by the hundreds of thousands, eager to feed, socialize, and rest.

Numerous rare waterbird species stage at Malheur. Several thousand greater and lesser sandhill cranes stop off here during the spring migration to load up on invertebrates before heading north to their brooding grounds. In the autumn the refuge hosts more than 10,000 tundra swans. Additionally, 50,000 or more geese—greater white-fronted, snow, Ross', and several races of Canada geese—descend in huge flocks over meadows and grainfields.

The fall populations of migratory ducks can easily exceed a million individuals of many different species. There are big, green-headed mallards and dainty green-winged, blue-winged, and cinnamon teal. Some, such as northern shovelers, with obvious spatulate bills, and buffleheads, small diving ducks with huge, dramatic crests, are immediately identifiable. They are joined by large numbers of canvasbacks, redheads, lesser scaup, and common goldeneyes.

In the spring wading birds and shorebirds stop over regularly. Great blue and green-backed herons, American bitterns, and great and snowy egrets hunt for fish and frogs in the shallows. Virginia rail and soras haunt the tall bulrushes. Black-necked stilts, American avocets, willet, spotted sandpipers, long-billed curlews, Wilson's phalaropes, and common snipes congregate on mudflats and shallow marshes, probing the mud furiously for worms, larvae, and other succulent invertebrates.

In the fall Swainson's hawks roost in the trees in astounding numbers, some aggregates reaching 200 or more birds. Ospreys, golden eagles, and overwintering bald eagles are common sights at Malheur. Other birds of prey here include red-tailed, red-shouldered, ferruginous, and rough-legged hawks; American kestrel; merlin; and great horned, barred, burrowing, northern saw-whet, short-eared, and western screech-owls.

Among birders Malheur has a reputation as a hot spot for anomalous species, particularly songbirds. During the last weekends in May and the first weekends of June—the peak of the passerine songbird spring migration—serious birders come from as far away as Seattle and San Francisco, hoping to add one unusual bird or another to their life lists. They seldom go away disappointed.

In recent years exclusively eastern species of warblers, including palm, prothonotary, golden-winged, Canada, and cerulean warblers, have shown up. In 1995 a streak-backed oriole—a bird that dwells primarily in Central and South America—was identified and confirmed. Other confirmed

THE FACTS

Noteworthy Animals: Sandhill crane, tundra swan, Canada goose, mallard, cinnamon teal, American bittern, willow flycatcher, golden eagle, Swainson's hawk, pronghorn, mule deer, river otter, beaver.

Getting There: From Bend, take US 20 east 130 miles to Burns and pick up Oreg. 205 south for 25 miles. Take Princeton/Narrows Road, which cuts in from the left, and follow the signs 6 miles to Refuge Headquarters.

Open: Daily, dawn to dusk, year-round.

Best Times To Visit: April through October.

Visitor Information: Malheur National Wildlife Refuge Headquarters and Visitor Center (541-493-2612) open Monday through Thursday, 7 a.m.-4:30 p.m.; Friday until 3:30 p.m.; some weekends, March through October.

Entrance Fees: None.

Disabled Access: The Visitor Center and one recreational fishing area are wheelchair accessible.

Camping: None on-site. Paige Springs Campground, maintained by the U.S. Bureau of Land Management (541-573-4400), is a few miles south of the refuge, near Frenchglen; fees; no reservations.

vagrant species include the scissor-tailed flycatcher, emperor goose, red phalarope, and blue jay.

Songbirds typically congregate at one of three sites at Malheur: Refuge Headquarters and the two tiny crossroads burgs of Frenchglen and Fields. These sites contain the majority of the refuge's riparian woodland habitat, where warblers and their allies concentrate. Species and numbers at each site change radically from day to day during the height of the spring migration. Most songbirds migrate at

night and spend no more than a complete diurnal cycle at each rest stop, so serious birders should plan to spend several days at Malheur during the spring to bolster their chances of a rare sighting.

Flycatchers, including willow, dusky, and ash-throated, Say's phoebe, and western kingbird, are abundant. Horned larks are found in the dry upland areas surrounding the marshlands. Marsh wrens—bold and inquisitive, particularly if you sit quietly—abound in the tall grasses. On closer inspection, telltale flashes of yellow in the trees or shrubs will reveal a western tanager or northern oriole.

Also look for black-capped chickadee (especially in winter); bushtit; western bluebird; hermit thrush; American pipit; solitary vireo; and common yellowthroat, orange-crowned, yellow, black-throated gray, Wilson's, and MacGillivray's warblers.

Although birds are the main attraction, about 60 different species of mammals reside at or pass through the refuge. Beavers, badgers, river otters, mink, and muskrats are seen along marshlands at dusk or dawn. Pronghorn, mule deer, and on rare occasions Rocky Mountain elk are spied browsing the interfaces of marshes and uplands.

A 42-mile auto tour route begins at Refuge Headquarters or Frenchglen and provides excellent access to the best birding spots. Malheur is just 35 miles south of the Ochoco and Malheur National Forests, public lands that are remote and lightly used. These national forests provide wonderful backpacking, mountain-biking, and day-hiking opportunities.

Rogue River

A rafting trip down this Oregon river offers an exhilarating ride as well as sightings of black bears and black-tailed deer.

SITE 25 Thanks to the federal Wild and Scenic Rivers Act, 64 miles of the lower Rogue River have been protected. The river has three classifications (wild, scenic, and recreational) based on accessibility and development. The wild section, which runs 33 miles from Grave Creek to Watson Creek, has remained pristine, free of the development that has blighted so many of the rivers of the Pacific Northwest. This portion of the Rogue is accessible either by watercraft (raft, kayak, or drift boat; jet tour boats have access from Gold Beach to Blossom Bar, which is 10 miles into the wild section) or by foot. The Rogue River Trail skirts the river's north bank from Grave Creek to Slide Creek (a distance of 50 miles with 17 miles of scenic and recreational designated river).

Both access options have their strong points. The trail offers a superb wilderness backpacking experience on 40 miles of well-maintained tread. The gradient is moderate, and the hiking is relatively easy. Allow four to five days for the average hike, and be aware that landslides and high water may complicate passage after heavy rains.

Many people choose to float the river. The most convenient option is to arrange a trip through a professional rafting company. Most companies book three- to five-day trips. Guides handle all fees, permits, camp duties, and itineraries. They will also arrange side hikes if clients express interest.

As it plunges through old-growth forests of Douglas-fir, incense cedar, black oak, and madrone, the Rogue encompasses some of the richest wildlife habitat in the Pacific Northwest. Traveling by watercraft allows wildlife buffs to approach animals closely without being seen. All living things must ultimately come to water, so the long pools and lovely riffles of the Rogue offer prime viewing opportunities on every trip.

An ideal time to visit is from midsummer through early fall, when the weather is warm and the river hosts chinook salmon. The spawning runs can be impressive, and the "downstreamers"—spawned-out, moribund salmon—attract black bears. Bears also forage along the river in summer and fall for the plentiful blackberries, acorns, and tubers. It is a rare summertime Rogue trip that does not include a bear sighting or two.

Along the river's edge, families of river otters frolic, black-tailed deer browse, and great blue herons, great egrets, and green-backed herons fish stolidly. Common mergansers frequent the river's calmer stretches. On side hikes into the surrounding woodlands, the exceptionally lucky observer might catch a fleeting glimpse of a marten or fisher. Beavers live all along the Rogue but are rarely seen because of their nocturnal habits.

Birds of prey, including ospreys, bald eagles, and red-shouldered and red-tailed hawks, soar high above the

THE FACTS

Noteworthy Animals: Black bear, marten, fisher, black-tailed deer, river otter, bald eagle, great blue heron, osprey, pileated woodpecker, red-tailed hawk, northern spotted owl.

Getting There: From Grants Pass, take I-5 north for 5 miles and turn west onto Merlin/Agness Road. Proceed west for about 8 miles to the Smullin Visitor Center at Rand.

Open: Daily, dawn to dusk, year-round.

Best Times to Visit: May through October.

Visitor Information: U.S. Bureau of Land Management, Medford office (541-770-2200). For further information and boating permits, contact the Smullin Visitor Center (541-479-3735), open daily, 7 a.m.-4 p.m., May through mid-October. At other times permits are self-issued.

Entrance Fees: None for hiking. Float permits are $20 per person. In the summer, heavy usage necessitates a permit lottery ($4 application fee). Applications accepted from December to February.

Outfitters and/or Guide Services: Call the Grants Pass Chamber of Commerce (541-476-7717) for a list of outfitters. Raft trips cost $100-$200 a day for a three- to five-day trip.

Disabled Access: There is a wheelchair trail on the south side of Ranie Falls.

Camping: Call the Smullin Visitor Center for details.

canyon. Northern goshawks might be spotted as they perch in the conifers. At dusk, great horned owls glide on silent pinions, hunting for mice and voles in riverside meadows. The endangered northern spotted owl makes its home along the river, as does the great horned owl, common barn-owl, northern pygmy-owl, long-eared owl, and northern saw-whet owl.

Pileated woodpeckers are as often heard as seen, their eerie cries resounding through the trees. Look for other woodland birds such as the western tanager; black-headed grosbeak; brown and rufous-sided towhees; varied, hermit, and Swainson's thrushes; yellow and yellow-rumped warblers; and common yellowthroat. Frequently seen reptiles include gopher snakes, kingsnakes, Pacific rattlesnakes, garter snakes, and Pacific pond turtles.

A black bear climbs trees to protect himself and to feed on nuts and berries.

The white water is extremely exhilarating, though not truly fierce. Thirty-five miles of Class II rapids—punctuated by one Class III, two Class IV, and one Class VI rapid—and a number of good trails make for a multifaceted outdoor adventure, as well as a wildlife-viewing expedition. Check out Zane Grey's cabin, located just downstream from Battle Bar. (The Rogue was the author's favorite stream for steelhead and salmon fishing.) Whiskey Creek Cabin, a miner's homestead, is on the National Register of Historic Places. Rogue River Ranch, near Mule Creek, has a museum devoted to the history and culture of local indigenous people.

The wild and scenic section of the Illinois River (Kalmiopsis Wilderness Area) is nearby, and even more dramatic—both in terms of wildlife and white water—than the Rogue. It also constitutes a much more demanding trip. Its river-running season is short (spring only), and some of the rapids are ferocious and suitable for experienced river runners only.

Bear River Migratory Bird Refuge

This spot where the Bear River joins the Great Salt Lake is one of
the West's most significant wintering grounds for waterfowl.

SITE 26 Contrary to popular belief, the Great Salt Lake is not a biological desert. It teems with tiny brine shrimp and insects, attracting aquatic birds from throughout the mountainous West and the Great Basin. Still, the intensely salty water is hardly conducive to great biological diversity. That changes at the delta of the Bear River, which flows into the lake near Brigham City.

The white pelican inhabits fresh inland waters, such as the rich delta of the Bear River.

Here the conditions of a marine estuary are mimicked: Fresh water flows into saltwater, creating a wide spectrum of salinity and the whole array of typical wetland habitats, from mudflats to deep marsh. A tremendous variety of microorganisms, plants, and invertebrates find agreeable niches in this brackish world; together they comprise a larder that wildlife find irresistible.

Indeed, the 72,000-acre Bear River Migratory Bird Refuge is probably the most biologically significant wetland complex in the mountainous West. Managed by the U.S. Fish and Wildlife Service, it is much like the Okavango River Delta in Botswana, another choice wetland formed by a river pouring into an alkali sink. That is, a magnet that attracts wildlife from a vast and generally inhospitable region. Waterfowl, in particular, congregate at Bear River in astounding numbers. During the height of the fall and winter migration, more than 600,000 of them may be found at the refuge.

This is the West's most significant wintering ground for tundra swans. In some years, 30,000 of these stately birds arrive. Smaller numbers of rare trumpeter swans also winter at the refuge. Because the two species are so similar in appearance and sociability, it's often difficult for less-than-expert birders to tell them apart, especially at a distance. However, the tundra swan has a small yellow spot on its bill; the trumpeter's bill is all black.

As many as 10,000 Canada geese also spend the winter at the refuge. In spring the geese nest throughout the wetland areas in impressive numbers, as do ducks. Pintails can be recognized by the drake's long, pointed tail. Other nesting ducks include mallards, green-winged and cinnamon teal, northern shovelers, gadwalls, American wigeon, canvasbacks, redheads, lesser scaup, and common mergansers.

Spring also signals the arrival of thousands of shorebirds on the invertebrate-rich mudflats. One of the most commonly sighted shorebirds is Wilson's phalarope, identified by its chestnut throat and black eye stripe. They may be joined by the long-billed curlew, black-necked stilt, American avocet, greater and lesser yellowlegs, willet, spotted and least sandpiper, common snipe, and killdeer.

Several thousand white pelicans—declining over most of their range because of habitat destruction and pesticides—come to feed at the refuge. These huge snow-white birds are more gregarious than their cousin, the exclusively marine brown pelican, and typically favor the large inland lakes of the West.

The most noteworthy birds of prey are bald eagles and peregrine falcons. Eagles are especially numerous during the winter migration, when they can prey on ducks that have been crippled by hunters or snag carp in the ice-free portions of the marshes. Also look for northern harriers, large white-rumped hawks that cruise quite close to the ground, hoping to flush small rodents or crippled ducks.

Other raptors include golden eagle, prairie falcon, osprey, Swainson's hawk, ferruginous hawk, red-tailed hawk, merlin, great horned owl, and short-eared owl. All the trees at Bear River were killed by floods in 1983, so now the raptors congregate on fence posts, power poles, and power lines—

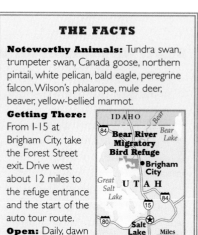

THE FACTS

Noteworthy Animals: Tundra swan, trumpeter swan, Canada goose, northern pintail, white pelican, bald eagle, peregrine falcon, Wilson's phalarope, mule deer, beaver, yellow-bellied marmot.

Getting There: From I-15 at Brigham City, take the Forest Street exit. Drive west about 12 miles to the refuge entrance and the start of the auto tour route.

Open: Daily, dawn to dusk, year-round.

Best Times to Visit: October through May.

Visitor Information: Bear River Migratory Bird Refuge, Brigham City office (801-723-5887), open Monday through Friday, 8 a.m.-4:30 p.m., year-round. An on-site visitor center is in the planning stages.

Entrance Fees: None.

Disabled Access: None.

Camping: None on-site.

anything that can provide a decent perch for scanning the terrain.

The lack of trees, save for willow thickets, somewhat restricts the diversity of mammal species. Still, the species that are found here tend to have fairly large populations. Look for mule deer, beaver, muskrat, coyote, red fox, striped skunk, white-tailed and black-tailed jackrabbits, and Nuttall's cottontail. Yellow-bellied marmot, a species that usually prefers alpine meadows, is also resident here.

Portions of the refuge are restricted at various times of the year to protect the birds, and some hunting is allowed in the fall and winter. Free access is generally allowed only along an established 12-mile route, which is suitable for driving, biking, or hiking. It provides excellent wildlife viewing.

Scott M. Matheson Wetlands Preserve

These wetlands in the heart of red-rock country are a stronghold of the great blue heron and related wading birds.

SITE 27 Moab, a small town in the heart of Utah's red-rock country, sits in one of the most dramatic landscapes in North America. The vast, encompassing Colorado Plateau and its fantastic sandstone formations are awe inspiring. They are also bone dry. The Scott M. Matheson Wetlands Preserve, which is the only significant wetland along the Colorado River in the state of Utah, attracts almost 200 species of birds and harbors mammals and amphibians not generally associated with the southwestern desert.

The Moab slough, a rare desert swamp, was used by early settlers as a grazing commons, a source of succulent fodder for local livestock. Later attempts were made to drain it to make room for orchards and row crops. But in 1983 and 1984 the Colorado River

reclaimed the slough in great floods. Recognizing that the resurrected wetland represented a great conservation opportunity, the Nature Conservancy of Utah and the Utah Division of Wildlife Resources began acquiring land for a preserve in 1990. That preserve now stands at 875 acres: a green oasis of bulrush marsh, flooded bottomland, and riparian forest in the vast, dry expanse of red slickrock.

Aquatic birds, obviously, are a significant attraction here. Their numbers are highest in spring, when they nest and raise their young, and again in fall, when they stop to rest and feed before heading off to warmer climes. An immense great blue heron rookery is located in a secluded section of the preserve, and these huge, rapier-billed birds are quite easily spotted as they feed in the marshes or along the edges of willow and Russian olive thickets. Other waders are here in lesser numbers—green-backed heron, white-faced ibis, and snowy egret are occasionally seen; black-crowned night-heron and Virginia rail less often.

Though the preserve isn't on a major migration route, large numbers of ducks and geese nevertheless make their way here. In spring look for nesting Canada geese, distinctive birds with black necks and heads and white chin straps. Common goldeneyes, ruddy ducks,

River otters are not disturbed by humans, as long as a discreet distance is maintained.

Wetland marshes provide well-stocked fishing grounds for the great blue heron.

buffleheads, canvasbacks, and northern shovelers also pass through in the spring. Mallards and American coots nest at the preserve.

Springtime brings migrating shorebirds. One visitor is the common snipe, a reclusive, long-billed marsh bird that flushes with a sharp "peep." Other species to look for include the solitary sandpiper, killdeer, American avocet, black-necked stilt, Wilson's phalarope, long-billed dowitcher, and greater yellowlegs. Pied-billed grebe, Virginia rail, and spotted sandpiper nest at the refuge.

The abundant water and excellent woodland cover draw great numbers of songbirds. Red-winged blackbirds, which have become something of an emblem for the marsh, are most visible during the spring nesting season, when they aggressively defend their nesting territories in the cattails. Five species of wrens—rock, marsh, canyon, Bewick's, and house—live here. Wood warblers are present in abundance; documented sightings range from the quite commonly seen yellow-rumped warbler to the equally rare yellow-breasted chat.

Flycatchers, swallows, and swifts feast on the plentiful insects in and around the marsh. In the skies over the wetland areas, particularly in the late afternoon, look for ash-throated flycatcher, gray flycatcher, western kingbird, violet-green swallow, barn swallow, northern rough-winged swallow, cliff swallow, Vaux's swift, and white-throated swift. Other noteworthy songbird species include the western tanager, warbling vireo, rufous-sided towhee, mountain bluebird, and great-tailed grackle. Bats—western pipistrelle, hoary, and pallid—are also drawn by the teeming insects of the marsh; look for them at twilight.

Golden eagles are often seen in and around the preserve, and migrating bald eagles sometimes drop by in the winter. Northern harriers, prairie falcons, American kestrels, and merlins can be seen soaring high above, or sometimes perching in, the trees. Good hunting also makes the marsh inviting to owls. Long-eared, short-eared, and western screech-owls might be seen at twilight as they begin their rounds.

Mammal species are typical for this arid part of the country, but their populations are unusually high as a result of the lush habitat. It's hard to miss mule deer, which weigh up to 400 pounds, cropping the rich sedges and young brush. Muskrats and river otters frequent the water and shore. Porcupine, coyote, raccoon, striped skunk, desert cottontail, and rock squirrel are all commonly seen. As always, chances of sightings are best at dawn or dusk.

The northern leopard frog, recognizable by its lovely spots and graceful frame, is of particular interest. Although rare, it may be found in the shallow, grassy portions of the marsh. Bullfrogs are exceedingly common. Woodhouse's toads and red-spotted toads may also be found wherever the soil is moist and abundant cover exists. Snakes, including striped whipsnake, gopher snake, and western yellow-bellied racer, live mostly at the margins of the preserve.

Although the Matheson Wetlands are located in a rather remote region of the West (the nearest large airport is in Grand Junction, Colorado, about 100 miles away), it makes a great side trip for anyone visiting the Moab area, and is a particularly pleasant place to while away a warm spring or fall day. Amateur photographers will want to stock up on film to take full advantage of a wildlife photography blind. The preserve is also ideally suited for children: Trails total only about a mile in length, and a boardwalk and an outdoor classroom site are available for students and teachers. Every Saturday from March through October, Conservancy staffers host morning nature walks; no reservations are necessary.

Haro Strait

Whale-watchers, on land or in a boat, are sure to catch sight of the orcas that range off Washington's San Juan Island.

 SITE 28 Scientists have learned something remarkable about orcas in the last few years: These killer whales, as they are sometimes called, have highly developed cultures, including their own language. It has also been determined that there are two distinct types of orcas, at least in the Pacific Northwest, that are divided not only by genetics (they live side by side but do not interbreed) but by the way they relate to the world.

Transient orcas travel in small groups, hunt and eat marine mammals, and speak only a rudimentary language of basic clicks and squeals. Resident orcas, on the other hand, travel in large pods, or groups, of 5 to 50 individuals that are dominated by alpha matriarchs, grandmothers, and great-grandmothers from 45 to 80 years of age. Residents subsist on fish—salmon, primarily. They stick to relatively discrete territories. And they are loquacious: Their vocalizations are rich and varied, and they jabber almost constantly.

In the simplest terms, transients are

Orcas, joined together in super pods, follow schools of salmon off the Washington coast.

stealthy hunters; they range far and wide, seeking seals and whales. They stay silent because their calls can alert their prey. Residents, on the other hand, behave more like herders. They follow the great schools of salmon and herring that swarm off the Washington and British Columbia coasts, and they communicate readily—their chatterings don't dis-

Humpback whales pass through Haro Strait on their migration along the Pacific coast.

turb the fish particularly, and they apparently direct one another vocally to areas where the prey is abundant.

Transients can be hard to find, patrolling as they do remote and far-flung regions. Residents, however, are easily observed—at least from San Juan Island, between the Washington mainland and Canada's Vancouver Island. More than 90 orcas in three separate pods range here, much to the delight of both scientists and amateur whale enthusiasts.

The pods—prosaically named J, K, and L—keep slightly different sched-

ules. J pod remains within the inland waters throughout the year. K pod ranges seaward for the winter, returning to the vicinity of San Juan Island by late May. L pod tends to be the most peripatetic, usually spending several months entirely at sea, not returning until a month or so after K pod. By June, however, all three pods are patrolling close to the island, working the salmon that have congregated in the Haro Strait prior to entering regional rivers to spawn. From June through August, the three pods often conjoin to form a super pod for extensive socialization and feeding that may last from a few hours to a few days. The sight of a meeting between pods is remarkable. The orcas go through an elaborate greeting ceremony, chattering, breaching, and frolicking in what can only be described (however anthropomorphically) as rapture at being reunited with old friends.

The whales often work very close to the shore. One of the favorite whale-watching sites on the island is Lime Kiln Point State Park, located due west of the town of Friday Harbor. Here the orcas sometimes patrol within a few feet of the rocky outcrops that comprise the shore—almost close enough to touch. They often forage between 30 and 100 yards offshore, spending a good deal of time inside and along the edges of the kelp forests, which grow in water that is only 20 feet deep.

The whales also patrol the deep

waters in mid-channel, sometimes diving up to 1,000 feet or more. They can still be observed from land at this distance (with good binoculars), but it's far better to view them from a boat—or rather, a kayak. Sea kayaks are silent, unobtrusive, and by far the best craft for encountering orca pods. If a discreet distance is maintained, the whales aren't bothered in the slightest by paddlers. Several outfitters offer whale-watching kayak trips from a half day to five days in duration.

Orcas aren't the only marine mammals apt to be spotted during a day of paddling the San Juan area. Minke whales also feed here. Dall's porpoises (which look like miniature orcas) and harbor porpoises are extremely common. Harbor seals are ubiquitous. From fall through spring, California sea lions and northern sea lions are often seen. Other occasional visitors include elephant seals, Pacific white-sided dolphins, gray whales, and humpback whales.

Raptors and marine birds are a lovely ancillary to any San Juan orca quest. Bald eagles, golden eagles, ospreys, red-tailed and sharp-shinned hawks, and peregrine falcons are year-round residents and nest in the San Juan Islands. Double-crested and pelagic cormorants breed here, too; they, along with Brandt's cormorants, are also present year-round.

Winter brings great numbers of migratory waterbirds into the area. Four species of loons—red-throated, Pacific, common, and yellow-billed—overwinter here, as do various grebes, scoters, and mergansers.

The San Juan archipelago, a group of 83 islands in northern Puget

THE FACTS

Noteworthy Animals: Orca, minke whale, harbor porpoise, Dall's porpoise, harbor seal, California sea lion, northern sea lion, bald eagle, golden eagle, osprey.

Getting There: San Juan Island is the main island of the San Juan archipelago, located halfway between the Washington mainland and Canada's Vancouver Island. Ferries operate from Bellingham, Anacortes, Port Townsend, and Seattle. For information call Washington State Ferries (206-464-6400 or 800-84-FERRY).
Open: Daily, 24 hours, year-round.
Best Times to Visit: June through September.
Visitor Information: No visitor center but tour operators and scientist guides can provide detailed information.
Entrance Fees: None.
Outfitters and/or Guide Services: Sea Quest Kayak Expeditions (360-378-5767), all trips led by marine biologists or environmental scientists; San Juan Kayak Expeditions (360-378-4436); Fair Weather Tours (360-378-2826). Fees for guided trips range from about $60-$100 a day; reserve in advance.
Disabled Access: Lime Kiln Point State Park has some wheelchair-accessible overlooks for whale watching.
Camping: Primitive sites on San Juan Island; no fees or reservations. Developed campsites at Moran State Park on Orcas Island, and at Spencer Spit State Park on Lopez Island; both have fees and require reservations. Call Washington State Parks (800-233-0321) for information.

Sound, is one of the premier recreational destinations in the Pacific Northwest. Sailing, kayaking, fishing, clamming, hiking, and bicycling are all favored pursuits.

North Cascades National Park Service Complex

The high mountain peaks of this rugged land are the domain of mountain goats, golden eagles, and adventurous backpackers.

SITE 29 About 45 miles east of northern Puget Sound is a mountain fastness of precipitous canyons, primeval forest, high rock, and ice. On maps the area is known as North Cascades National Park, Ross Lake National Recreation Area, and Lake Chelan National Recreation Area—together called the Park Service Complex. Here manifold species of wildlife have followed their timeless rhythms since the glaciers retreated at the end of the last Ice Age.

The complex's pristine condition can be attributed partly to its federal protected status, partly to its extremely rugged terrain. Make no mistake: This is not easy country to explore. Unlike the Sierra Nevada and the Rocky Mountains, which are characterized by long cordilleras that allow for relatively painless high-elevation hiking, the North Cascades consist primarily of freestanding peaks separated by deep valleys. Park biologists acknowledge that their wildlife surveys are scanty simply because the data are so hard to collect in such steep, densely forested, remote country.

Still, the rewards are lavish for those who manage to penetrate this vast 1,069-square-mile complex. Of the resident species of "charismatic megafauna," black bear and mule deer are the most common. Mountain lions are also doing well, as are mountain goats. Grizzly bears and gray wolves are known to use the complex, and elk—extirpated from the area in the early decades of this century—have been reintroduced from the Rocky Mountain states to different portions of the North Cascades with varying degrees of success.

The tiny pika, a relative of the rabbits and hares, thrives in this mountain habitat. These diligent lagomorphs harvest grass and dry it in front of their burrows for use during the long winter. Also look for bobcat, coyote, red fox, river otter, ermine, long-tailed weasel, mink, western spotted skunk, Douglas' squirrel, and snowshoe hare. Wolverine and fisher are known to inhabit the complex but are seldom seen because of their secretive ways.

The Skagit River, which flows through the complex, supports one of the greatest winter concentrations of bald eagles in the state. Up to 600 eagles gather along a 10-mile section of river just outside the park's western boundary. Within the park it's not uncommon to see gatherings of 80 or more eagles along the riverside. Golden eagles cruise the high alpine meadows in quest of hoary marmots, a favorite prey. The piercing cry of a startled "whistlepig" when an eagle is in the area is familiar to any experienced North Cascades backpacker.

Eagles are only two of the more than 200 different bird species that have been recorded here. Northern goshawks, rare across most of their range, are found in the deep forests of

The rocky freestanding peaks of the North Cascades seem custom-made for mountain goats.

Douglas-fir, red cedar, and western hemlock. Ospreys forage and nest along the Skagit and its tributaries. This is also the home of the northern spotted owl, a threatened species.

Gallinaceous birds are particularly well represented: ruffed grouse and blue grouse in the lower elevations, white-tailed ptarmigan above timberline, spruce grouse in the high

THE FACTS

Noteworthy Animals: Black bear, mule deer, mountain goat, elk, mountain lion, bobcat, wolverine, fisher, river otter, hoary marmot, pika, snowshoe hare, bald eagle, osprey, white-tailed ptarmigan.

Getting There: From the I-5 turnoff near Burlington, Wash. 20 provides easy access to North Cascades National Park and Ross Lake National Recreation Area—simply drive east for 40 miles and watch for signs. Wash. 20 bisects both the park and the recreation area. To reach the Lake Chelan National Recreation Area, take the ferry from Chelan on US 97; the recreation area is at the end of the lake, about 45 miles northwest.

Open: Daily, 24 hours, year-round. Sections of Wash. 20 closed from approximately November to mid-April.

Best Times to Visit: June through September.

Visitor Information: National Park Service Headquarters in Sedro Woolley (360-856-5700) on Wash. 20, open daily, 8 a.m.-4:30 p.m., from Memorial Day through mid-October. North Cascades Visitor Center in Newhalem (206-386-4495) open daily, 8:30 a.m.-6 p.m., July through Labor Day. Golden West Visitor Center in Stehekin (360-856-5700 ext. 340) open daily, 8 a.m.-4:30 p.m., spring through fall. Lake Chelan Ferry (509-682-2224).

Entrance Fees: None.

Disabled Access: Sterling Munro boardwalk, River Loop Trail, Newhalem Rockshelter Trail (all near North Cascades Visitor Center, Newhalem), and Happy Creek Forest Walk (Milepost 134) are wheelchair accessible.

Camping: Primitive camping; permit required; no fees. Several developed campsites along Wash. 20; fees; no reservations.

subalpine meadows. Listen for the muted booming of the cocks as they sit on their perches, surveying their mountain haven.

The gray jay, a sassy bird known by the accurate nickname of "camp robber," will boldly snatch food and shiny items from human encampments, as will Clark's nutcracker. Other prominent species include evening and pine grosbeaks—thick-billed finches of the forest—western tanager, red crossbill, and pine siskin. Warbler species include Townsend's, orange-crowned, yellow, yellow-rumped, and black-throated gray warblers.

The only way to thoroughly explore the complex is with a backpack and at least a week of time. Don't embark on such an undertaking lightly. Fitness and outdoor experience are prerequisites for an extended trip into the complex; climbing skills are helpful. Those who aren't sure of their endurance or skills can take advantage of the auto turnouts on Wash. 20 (especially good places to observe bald eagles), short hiking trails near the North Cascades Visitor Center, and some easier routes in the Lake Chelan National Recreation Area. Plan trips for late June through early September, when much of the snow is gone from the high country.

Winters are wet and frigid, and backcountry travel is highly inadvisable. But one of the most pleasant ways to see mountain goats and mule deer is possible at that time: Take the Lake Chelan ferry from Chelan to Stehekin at the upper end of the lake. The goats and deer overwinter near the lakeshore in the Stehekin region and are easily spotted.

National Elk Refuge

A wintertime sleigh ride through this Wyoming sanctuary offers a wonderful way to see huge herds of Rocky Mountain elk.

SITE 30

If there is a success story for an American wildlife species, it has to be the wapiti, which is better known as the elk. By the early 1900s, fewer than 90,000 elk remained in North America. In the eastern portion of the continent, they had been completely wiped out. But these magnificent animals have staged a dramatic comeback in recent years and now number nearly a million individuals. Roosevelt and Rocky Mountain elk have been reintroduced into mountainous portions of the eastern United States, and tule elk have been established at several sites throughout California; their populations are growing.

In the Rocky Mountain states, elk populations have exploded. In the greater Yellowstone area of Wyoming alone, their numbers are estimated to be at least 100,000. Each winter about 8,000 to 10,000 of them end up at the National Elk Refuge. This 24,700-acre preserve was established in 1912 to help stop the dwindling of the region's great elk herds, a result of several consecutive hard winters. Today protected winter range and supplemental feedings of hay by the U.S. Fish and Wildlife Service help thousands of elk endure the harsh Wyoming winters—and incidentally provide some of the best wildlife viewing in North America. In winter huge herds of elk can be observed by driving along the frontage roads adjacent to the feeding and grazing areas, but the best way to see them is on horse-drawn sleigh rides, available from late December through March.

The golden eagle has a dark body with light, or golden, highlights on the crown and neck.

In winter, you can see herds of elk from the roads surrounding the National Elk Refuge.

Located in one of the wildest areas of the continental United States, the refuge supports other animals as well. Bison, mule deer, badger, coyote, beaver, yellow-bellied marmot, long-tailed weasel, porcupine, Uinta ground squirrel, and several species of bats and shrews either live here or pass through. Rocky Mountain bighorn sheep, moose, river otter, and pronghorn are occasionally sighted. Managers expect that the expanding numbers of gray wolves (the result of recent relocations to nearby Yellowstone National Park) will ultimately result in wolf sightings. In all likelihood the wolves will be drawn to an area that offers such an abundance of their natural prey—old, infirm, very young, and injured elk.

Abundant wetlands and riparian habitat attract large numbers of migrating and nesting waterfowl. The largest trumpeter swan overwintering ground in the state is here; the heaviest concentration of these elegant birds is in November. Other waterfowl

include green-winged, blue-winged, and cinnamon teal; northern pintail; gadwall; common and Barrow's goldeneyes; and common merganser.

Resident and migratory songbirds include northern orioles, ruby-crowned kinglets, chipping sparrows, western and mountain bluebirds, and western tanagers. Five species of swallows—the violet-green, northern rough-winged, bank, barn, and cliff—are found here.

Birds of prey include bald and golden eagles, ospreys, peregrine and prairie falcons, northern goshawks, rough-legged and red-tailed hawks, and American kestrels. Owls are plentiful; species include great horned, northern pygmy-, long-eared, and northern saw-whet owls.

The refuge is busiest in the winter, when the crowds come to see the elk. But it's worth a visit at any time of year. Summer visitors to Grand Teton National Park, which is adjacent to the refuge, and Yellowstone (see p. 106), which is about 50 miles north, would do well to consider adding a visit to the National Elk Refuge to their itineraries.

Tensleep Preserve

Mountain lions still stalk elk and mule deer on this ancient Native American hunting ground in the Bighorn Mountains.

SITE 31

The Tensleep Preserve has been esteemed for its wildlife for a very long time indeed. Ancient pictographs at the site show Native Americans stalking bison and other game. And while the vast herds of bison no longer roam Tensleep— thought to be named by the Crow Indians because it was "ten sleeps" distance from both Fort Laramie and Yellowstone—it is still one of the richest wildlife habitats in the West.

Tensleep is a vast, rugged wilderness of canyons and gorges carved out of the sandstone and limestone formations of northern Wyoming's Bighorn range. A great diversity of habitats is found in the 8,500-acre preserve core, managed by the Nature Conservancy, and the 5,000 acres of privately owned lands under conservation easements that serve as buffer zones.

The canyon bottoms, lush with stands of cottonwood and box elder, are particularly significant because only 2 percent of Wyoming consists of such riverine habitats, but 80 percent of the state's wildlife species need them at some point in their life cycles. The northern slopes of the canyons are covered by Douglas-fir and lodgepole pine forests, and the higher elevations are cloaked by aspen and Englemann spruce groves. Extensive stands of ponderosa pine, juniper, sagebrush, and grassland are found along the plateaus.

This is a little-explored part of the West, and wildlife thrives. The Tensleep area is thought to have the highest density of mountain lions in the state. The primary reason for such a concentration of mountain lions is the abundance of prey, particularly mule deer and Rocky Mountain elk, both of which winter here. White-tailed deer, once rare in this part of Wyoming, are experiencing a population boom in the bottomlands, where they find abundant forage.

Black bears, which actually range in color from coal black to cinnamon, are quite common. Bobcat, coyote, badger, marten, mink, long-tailed weasel, short-tailed weasel (or ermine), white-tailed jackrabbit, snowshoe hare, and black-tailed prairie dog are other confirmed residents of Tensleep. Lynx are known to inhabit the Bighorn Range and are assumed to

Tensleep Preserve has the highest concentration of mountain lions in Wyoming.

pass through the refuge. At least ten species of bats, including three rare species—spotted, Townsend's big-eared, and pallid—live here.

The rugged country and the abundance of small prey make Tensleep a raptor haven. Golden eagles nest in the canyons, and bald eagles migrate through in the fall and winter. Prairie falcons are regular visitors. Tensleep was seriously considered as a hack site (a place where artificially propagated birds of prey are released into the wild) for peregrines, but the idea was rejected when it was discovered that too many golden eagles—which will prey on peregrines—inhabit the area. American kestrels and merlins, as well as red-tailed, Cooper's, rough-legged, and sharp-shinned hawks, hunt and breed here. Though declining over much of its range, the northern goshawk, a fierce, red-eyed accipiter of the deep woods, is holding its own at Tensleep. Great horned owls and northern pygmy-owls are also well distributed throughout the preserve.

Common nighthawks swarm the twilight sky in tremendous numbers, giving voice to their sharp cries as they scour the air for flying insects. This is also a good place to observe western songbirds. First among peers is the western tanager, a bright yellow bird which is both extraordinarily beautiful and very common. Also look for green-tailed towhee, American redstart, lazuli bunting, canyon wren, warbling vireo, MacGillivray's warbler, common yellowthroat, Say's phoebe, and Townsend's solitaire.

Woodpeckers seem to be everywhere. Species that have been noted include red-naped sapsucker; hairy,

---

THE FACTS

Noteworthy Animals: Mountain lion, black bear, Rocky Mountain elk, mule deer, white-tailed deer, bobcat, coyote, black-tailed prairie dog, golden eagle, rough-legged hawk, western tanager.

Getting There: From the town of Ten Sleep, go 3 miles east on US 16, to Wyo. 436 south. Follow Wyo. 436 for 11 miles, then turn left through a marked gate. Follow the signs to the office.

Open: Daily, dawn to dusk, Memorial Day through mid-September.

Best Times to Visit: June through August.

Visitor Information: Tensleep Preserve office (307-366-2671) open daily, 8 a.m.-5 p.m., mid-April through December. The Nature Conservancy, Lander office (307-332-2971), open Monday through Friday, 9 a.m.-5 p.m., year-round.

Entrance Fees: None.

Disabled Access: Limited. The preserve office is fully accessible. Additional facilities are planned.

Camping: Walled tents, hot showers, and full kitchen facilities are available at the preserve. Program fee is about $400 per week; reservations required. The facilities are also available for other groups and individuals; call 307-366-2671 for rates.

---

downy, and three-toed woodpeckers; and northern flicker.

The best way to see Tensleep is through one of the programs that are offered at the preserve. Guests stay in walled tents, eat hearty meals in the dining lodge, and help visiting naturalists with their research projects. Participants may find themselves digging up invasive exotic weeds or participating in bird inventories, to name just two possible activities. Plenty of time is left for exploring, and naturalists offer guided hikes.

Yellowstone National Park

Shaggy bison share the vast landscape of America's most famous wildlife refuge with grizzly bears, moose, wolves—and human observers.

SITE 32 After more than a century as the premier wildlife park in the lower 48 states, Yellowstone still takes the laurels—particularly for glamorous mammals. Nearly all of North America's western megafauna are found in this singular 2,221,766-acre landscape: bison, elk, moose, bighorn sheep, mule deer, grizzly bears, black bears, and most recently (thanks to reintroduction programs), gray wolves. Lynx, fisher, and wolverine are also known to live in Yellowstone, though their numbers are probably few; this is at the far southern edge of their range.

The 142-mile Grand Loop Road, which connects all five entrances, provides the primary access through the park. Animals that live or forage near roads have become acclimated to humans, so roadside viewing is always a viable option. But the rewards of getting into the backcountry and seeing the animals on their own terms are great. More than 1,000 miles of trails wind through the park; information and advice on various trails are available at all Visitor Centers.

Justifiably famous for its geological wonders—hot springs, geysers, and fumaroles among them—Yellowstone is also noteworthy for its healthy populations of continentally rare species. Bison herds are thought to number about 2,500 animals, down from past years because of severe winterkill. Look for these great shaggy beasts on Fountain Flat. It is estimated that any-

where from 250 to 610 grizzly bears now live in Yellowstone, and their numbers have been expanding at a rate of about 4 percent each year for the past decade.

Gray wolves, established just a few years ago, are rapidly expanding both in range and in numbers. This is not particularly surprising, given the fecundity of the species and the fact that so many elk and deer live in the park, constituting an enormous reservoir of prey. It is estimated that 50 to 60 of these superlatively efficient canid predators now range in and around Yellowstone, and the number grows annually. Because the elk often gather in large meadows near Gibbon Canyon, it is assumed that the wolves also favor this area.

Smaller mammals abound throughout Yellowstone's reaches. Coyotes hunt for mice and voles near the margins of forests. Bobcats, ermines, long-tailed weasels, red squirrels, northern flying squirrels, and snowshoe hares haunt the deep woodlands. River otters, mink, and beavers thrive in the myriad rivers, creeks, and lakes. White-tailed jackrabbits, Nuttall's cottontails, yellow-bellied marmots, Richardson's ground squirrels, and northern pocket gophers may be fleetingly spotted as they make their way through meadowlands, the smaller mammals trying to avoid the eyes of

The hope of seeing a grizzly bear draws many people to Yellowstone National Park.

Shy snowshoe hares inhabit heavily wooded areas with good cover.

predators, particularly golden eagles.

More than 300 bird species breed in or migrate through the park. Bald eagles overwinter in great congregations along the Yellowstone River corridor. Ospreys are abundant along Yellowstone Lake, where they are frequently seen snagging fish from the water's surface. Northern goshawks hunt in the deep woods, as do Cooper's and sharp-shinned hawks. Owls abound; watch for them just as the day's light is about to fail completely. Resident species include great gray, long-eared, short-eared, great horned, common barn-, western screech-, northern pygmy-, and northern saw-whet owls.

In the meadowlands and along woodland edges, look for large birds of prey, such as peregrine and prairie falcons; northern harriers; sharp-shinned, Cooper's, Swainson's, red-tailed, ferruginous, and rough-legged hawks; American kestrels; and merlins.

In the deep woods, look for black-capped and mountain chickadees, red-breasted and white-breasted nuthatches, and brown creepers. Rock wrens and canyon wrens frequent the gorges and other rugged areas. American dippers are abundant along all the streams, where they leap into the current to forage for aquatic insects. Nesting western wood warblers, thrushes, and vireos teem in the park's forested regions in the spring and summer months.

Among the bolder birds are the gray jay, which is known as the "camp robber" for its food-stealing skills, and Clark's nutcracker, which will also raid camps when the opportunity arises. Particularly beautiful songbirds here include western tanager, lazuli bunting, rufous-sided towhee, yellow-headed blackbird, northern oriole, pine grosbeak, red crossbill, and evening grosbeak.

The predatory loggerhead shrike and the northern shrike are found in Yellowstone in some abundance. Look for these handsome gray-and-white birds perching on branches—also look for their prey, impaled on thorns or barbed wire for later consumption.

Yellowstone welcomes nearly three million visitors annually, most of them in July and August, which makes for a short but intense tourist season. It's not a bad idea to plan a visit at another time of year. In May and June, the snow may still be on the ground, but it's possible to see newborn animals. A September or October visit generally offers blue skies, moderate temperatures, and a great deal more elbow room—for visitors and for the wildlife, most of which are actively foraging at this time. In winter the North Entrance Road, which runs through important winter range, remains open. Heated snow coaches ferry visitors to steaming hot springs and beyond, and snowmobiles are permitted the run of the unplowed roads.

THE FACTS

Noteworthy Animals: Grizzly bear, gray wolf, bobcat, lynx, wolverine, bison, elk, moose, bighorn sheep, mule deer, river otter, golden eagle, prairie falcon.

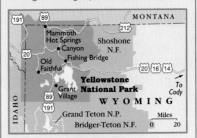

Getting There: There are five entrances to Yellowstone. To reach the North (main) Entrance and Park Headquarters from Bozeman, Montana, take I-90 east to US 89 south and drive about 30 miles to Gardiner. Call for other directions.

Open: Daily, 24 hours, year-round. Most roads close November through April; North Entrance Road, from Gardiner to Cooke City, Montana, is open year-round.

Best Times to Visit: May and June; September and October.

Visitor Information: Yellowstone National Park (307-344-7381) has five Visitor Centers: Mammoth Hot Springs, Old Faithful, Fishing Bridge, Grant Village, and Canyon. Mammoth Hot Springs Visitor Center is open daily, 9 a.m.-4:30 p.m., year-round.

Entrance Fees: $20 per vehicle; $15 per motorcycle or snowmobile; $10 per individual entry by bike, foot, or ski. All good for seven days; all include Grand Teton National Park.

Disabled Access: Numerous fully accessible features. For information, contact the Accessibility Coordinator (307-344-2018).

Camping: Twelve developed campgrounds; only five accept reservations. Call 307-344-7311 for fees and reservations. Backcountry camping allowed with permit only; no fees; apply at any ranger station 48 hours in advance.

Accommodations: Call AmFac Parks & Resorts (307-344-7311) for information and reservations in hotels, lodges, and cabins within Yellowstone.

CENTRAL STATES

Arkansas

Illinois

Indiana

Iowa

Kansas

Louisiana

Michigan

Minnesota

Missouri

Nebraska

North Dakota

Ohio

Oklahoma

South Dakota

Texas

Wisconsin

Bison on the vast
midwestern plains

Ouachita National Forest

Creatures both great and small—including bears, bats, armadillos, and salamanders—inhabit this expansive, but little-known, woodland.

SITE 33 A vast forest stretches across west-central Arkansas into southeastern Oklahoma, comprising one of the best preserved expanses of woodland in the United States. Although it covers 1.7 million acres, Ouachita National Forest is not very well known outside its home states. This is one place where visitors don't have to worry about crowds—the animals outnumber the people.

Ouachita encompasses a variety of woodland habitats, from old-growth hardwood forests to shortleaf pine glades. Much of the forest is mature, with trees averaging 80 years or older. The number and diversity of wildlife found here are truly impressive. Small creatures such as the red fox, gray fox, opossum, gray squirrel, and fox squirrel are all extremely common. Armadillos forage for insects and invertebrates along the roadsides, a habit that often leads to fatal encounters with automobiles.

Look for white-tailed deer, black bears, and predators such as bobcats and coyotes at the margins of woodlands and meadows. River otters, mink, and raccoons are quite often observed along the riverbanks. Even mountain lions have been occasionally spotted, although biologists haven't determined if they are truly wild or escapees from captivity.

The dense forests of Ouachita are a haven for woodland bats, a happy exception to their shrinking habitat elsewhere on the continent. Species include red bat, silver-haired bat, and the eastern pipistrelle. Watch for them swooping by at dusk, particularly near water and in small meadows.

This huge swatch of woodland is also a critical refuge for neotropical migrant songbirds (warblers and other birds that nest in North America and winter in South America). Most notable of these migrating songbirds is the cerulean warbler. This intensely

blue bird is declining across its range because of loss of its preferred habitat, old-growth deciduous forests. Other species found here are ovenbird, wood thrush, eastern bluebird, common yellowthroat, prairie and yellow warblers, northern parula, yellow-breasted chat, white-eyed and red-eyed vireos, American redstart, and summer tanager. Northern cardinals are resident and abundant, and the forest also supports a small population of the endangered red-cockaded woodpecker.

The excellent cover and abundant prey makes Ouachita very attractive to raptors, especially woodland accipiters like Cooper's and sharp-shinned hawks. Also look for Mississippi kites, as well as broad-winged, red-tailed, and red-shouldered hawks, and the occasional Swainson's hawk. Great horned, common barn-, eastern screech-, barred, and short-eared owls are here in large numbers.

Ouachita contains some of the country's richest amphibian habitat, particularly for salamanders. Three endemic salamanders are found here:

Spanish conquistadores named the armadillo—"little man in armor."

handsomely marked spotted and marbled salamanders; and amphiuma, a snakelike salamander with vestigial legs. Among the resident frogs are bullfrogs and leopard frogs. Green treefrogs, gray treefrogs, spring peepers, and upland chorus frogs fill the spring and summer evenings with their songs.

Snakes that find Ouachita hospitable include an anomalous population of western diamondback rattlesnakes. Other species include timber rattlesnake, copperhead, cottonmouth, black rat snake, rough green snake, eastern hognose snake, scarlet snake, southern black racer, northern water snake, plain-bellied water snake, garter snake, and red-bellied snake.

Virtually any place in Ouachita is excellent wildlife habitat. For visitors with some time, however, the Ouachita National Recreation Trail is well worth exploring, in part or in full. This 192-mile route begins in Talimena State Park in Oklahoma and extends into Arkansas along Ark. 9, south of Perryville and just west of Little Rock. The trail meanders through some of the loveliest and wildest country in Ouachita, some of it truly primeval. Early spring and fall are the best times for extensive hiking—temperatures are mild, and bird migrations are in full swing.

Ouachita also lends itself to car touring. There are several scenic routes, particularly US 270 west from Hot Springs to the forest's edge; Ark. 248 north from Mena to Abbott; Ark. 27 north from Mount Ida to Rover; Arkansas Scenic 7 Byway, north of Hot Springs; and the Talimena Scenic Byway from Talihina, Oklahoma, to Mena, Arkansas.

the Caddo Mountain, Rich Mountain, and Fourche Mountain salamanders. Other notables include lesser siren, a particularly large aquatic species; the

White River National Wildlife Refuge

The Arkansas black bear, a species native to the eastern part of the state, makes its home in this flooded forestland.

SITE 34 Every year the White River crests above its banks, abandons its channel, and spreads out across its broad, thickly forested floodplain. In the process it creates some of the richest wildlife habitat in the South: a paradise of woods and seasonal wetland. The trees in this lush 156,000-acre forest preserve are primarily mast-bearing species: Nuttall oak, overcup oak, and bitter pecan. Hackberry and bald cypress are also extremely common. This abundance of wild nuts and fruit allows for high concentrations of wildlife.

Of all the creatures that inhabit the preserve, the Arkansas black bear is the most renowned. A species endemic to the eastern part of the state, this bear was once reduced to a few dozen individuals. Thanks to careful management and game law enforcement, it has rebounded dramatically in recent years. The refuge is now the bear's stronghold, and populations are even expanding to outlying areas. Refuge managers are conducting DNA tests on the bears to determine whether they are a northern race of the endangered Louisiana black bear or a genetically distinct race. Like all black bears, they are shy, but every year a few are glimpsed by wildlife-watchers.

Other commonly observed mammals include white-tailed deer, which are particularly visible during flood times, when they herd together on the uplands. Look for river otter,

mink, swamp rabbit, muskrat, and beaver in or near water. As much as 90 percent of the refuge may be underwater during and after heavy spring rains. During these dramatic submersions, wildlife of all types seek high ground. Bobcat, coyote, and red and gray foxes frequent the timber and heavy underbrush. Gray and fox squirrels chatter away in the forest canopies.

White River was originally established by the U.S. Fish and Wildlife Service as a refuge for migrating waterfowl, and ducks and geese remain premier species of interest. Anywhere from 100,000 to 300,000 of them reside here each winter. One species, the American black duck, is seriously declining in numbers because of competition from and hybridization with mallards, which also frequent White River. Other species regularly spotted include wood duck, green-winged teal, blue-winged teal, northern pintail, northern shoveler, gadwall, ring-necked duck, lesser scaup, common goldeneye, bufflehead, and hooded merganser. The refuge also hosts a sizable population of overwintering Canada geese, sometimes numbering up to 5,000 individuals.

Woodland raptors, most notably sharp-shinned and Cooper's hawks, thrive here. Mississippi kites and bald eagles—both species of concern—have established nesting populations on the refuge. Look for eagles along the river; kites may be seen hunting over brushy areas and rangelands, dipping,

You can identify the male hooded merganser by its jaunty black-and-white crest.

hovering, and swooping in a distinctive manner. Other likely sightings include red-tailed, red-shouldered, and broad-winged hawks and the occasional osprey.

The expansive forests of this bottomland preserve constitute some of the best habitat for neotropical migrant songbirds in the United States. Prothonotary warblers—bold, brilliantly yellow denizens of flooded forests—thrive in the dense understory. Other wood warbler species to look for include orange-crowned, cerulean, magnolia, and yellow-rumped warblers; northern parula; American redstart; common yellowthroat; and yellow-breasted chat.

Other songbirds include the summer tanager, the males sporting brilliant scarlet plumage and the females clad in green and yellow. Golden-crowned and ruby-crowned kinglets,

blue-gray gnatcatchers, eastern phoebes, and eastern kingbirds are often seen foraging for bugs. A flash of blue could be a blue grosbeak, an indigo bunting, or an eastern bluebird. Other species here include hermit thrush and solitary, warbling, and red-eyed vireos. The ardent gobblings of wild turkey toms resound throughout the wooded areas during the spring breeding season.

Warm weather, abundant water, and the prime condition of the habitat make the refuge an excellent place for reptiles and amphibians. Alligators live here but are not particularly common, since the refuge is at the far northern edge of their range. Snakes, however, are extremely common, including venomous species such as copperhead, cottonmouth, and canebrake rattlesnake. Exercise reasonable caution when hiking or canoeing. In or around water, look for plain-bellied water snake, southern water snake, diamondback water snake, green water snake, and garter snake. The extremely handsome rat snake, and the kingsnake and milk snake favor the drier, upland areas. Other resident species include ribbon snake, brown snake, red-bellied snake, ringneck snake, hognose snake, rough green snake, and southern black racer.

Look for turtles sunning themselves along the banks or on logs. Species include common snapping and alligator snapping turtles; musk, map, chicken, smooth softshell, spiny softshell, and box turtles; and Missouri slider. Skinks—smooth-scaled, shiny, exceptionally active lizards, with somewhat snakelike bodies—are well represented. Species include five-lined, broad-headed, and ground skinks.

Amphibians, too, find the refuge agreeable. Look (and listen) for bullfrogs, green treefrogs, gray treefrogs, chorus frogs, spring peepers, cricket frogs, green frogs, leopard frogs, pickerel frogs, American toads, and Woodhouse's toads. Salamanders may be found both in water and in the leaf mold and woody detritus of the forest floor. Species include lesser siren, three-toed amphiuma, eastern newt, and spotted salamander.

Though White River is worth a visit at any season, fall is perhaps the best time to see it. The heat and humidity of summer have passed, the leaves are changing color, the ducks are arriving in force, and the mammals are active and aggressively foraging. Be aware, however, that wildlife-watchers must share the refuge with hunters from October through

January. While the refuge may be explored by foot, there is no maintained trail system—you follow paths that have been established by hikers, hunters, and wildlife.

Cars and boats are the best modes of transport here—especially boats. Roads wind throughout the refuge, providing good auto touring and giving boat access to the river and myriad oxbow lakes. Boats can be rented in Stuttgart (about 30 miles west) or Helena (the same distance east). In order to best plot your itinerary, ask at Refuge Headquarters for recent wildlife sightings.

Cache River Wetlands

The ancient bald cypress trees at this enormous preserve provide cozy homes for herons, wood ducks, snow geese, and owls.

SITE 35

It's hard not to perceive the bald cypresses of the Cache River Wetlands as sentinels somehow, standing guard over their magnificent redoubt. More accurately, they are witnesses: At least 1,000 years old, these huge trees are the oldest living things east of the Mississippi. They were here hundreds of years before Columbus landed. They have seen the seasonal flux of wild things across the middle span of the continent for a millennium, and they are still here.

The trees are the first thing noticed by the visitor to this remarkable 60,000-acre preserve, a joint project involving private conservation groups and government agencies.

As in the Big Thicket National Preserve in Texas (see p. 181), several distinct biomes intersect at the Cache River Wetlands. For example, cactuses typical of the southern central plains can be found growing just a few feet away from stands of bald cypress, trees associated with the Deep South.

But Cache River is more than an ecological anomaly—it's one of the richest sites in the Midwest for viewing wetland species. Twenty-three state and federal threatened and endangered species inhabit the preserve, including rare water-associated species such as the orange-footed pearly mussel and the dusky salamander.

Snow geese pass through here by the thousands during the fall migration, as do ducks of various species:

The brilliant yellow coloration of the prothonotary warbler makes this bird easy to spot.

blue-winged teal, canvasback, redhead, mallard, lesser scaup, gadwall, common and hooded mergansers, and common goldeneye. Wood ducks nest throughout the refuge.

Songbirds—most notably warblers, song sparrows, tanagers, flycatchers, gnatcatchers, and thrushes—nest in considerable numbers. The increasingly rare prothonotary warbler, a lovely, sunshine yellow bird, is also found at Cache River, typically haunting the foliage of the ancient cypresses.

The Heron Pond region in the northern section of the preserve is one of the crown jewels of the complex. Rare yellow-crowned night-herons nest here, as do black-crowned night-herons, great blue herons, green-backed herons, great egrets, American bitterns, least bitterns, common moorhens, soras, and Virginia rail.

Raptors include American kestrels and a variety of hawks—Cooper's, red-tailed, red-shouldered, and marsh. Owls are abundant; species include great horned, barred, short-eared, and the common barn-owl. At least one pair of bald eagles is known to nest at Cache River.

The largest and most commonly seen mammal is the white-tailed deer. River otter, bobcat, mink, raccoon, and opossum also live here, although it will take luck (and stealth) to spot one of them along the water's edge. Frogs, turtles, and snakes abound, including the bird-voiced treefrog, an uncommon species that is usually found much farther south. When near water, visitors should watch out for cottonmouths, big venomous black or brown snakes that can be quite aggressive. Copperheads and timber rattlesnakes

THE FACTS

Noteworthy Animals: Yellow-crowned night-heron, snow goose, wood duck, prothonotary warbler, marsh hawk, white-tailed deer.

Getting There: From Carbondale, take US 51 south for 20 miles to Ill. 146. Proceed east for 5 miles to junction with I-57 south; alternately, follow Ill. 146 for 15 miles to Ill. 37 south. Both routes skirt the site and give access to the preserve at about the 5-mile point. (The signs on I-57 are more clearly marked.)

Open: Daily, 24 hours, year-round.

Best Times to Visit: April through November.

Visitor Information: The Nature Conservancy of Illinois, Ullin office (618-634-2524), open Monday through Friday, 8 a.m.-4 p.m. year-round. Cache River State Natural Area, Bellnap office (618-634-9678), open daily, 7 a.m.-3 p.m. in summer. No on-site visitor center; information kiosks outside Bellnap office and at Heron Pond.

Entrance Fees: None.

Disabled Access: None.

Camping: None on-site.

are present in drier areas, so it's a good idea to walk carefully through areas of underbrush and give any snakes plenty of room for escape.

About 15 miles of trails meander through this stunning wetland, including a quarter-mile floating boardwalk. But perhaps the best way to experience the wetlands is from a canoe. There is a rental outlet at Perks Bridge in the Buttonland Swamp (central) portion of the refuge. Pack a compass and pick up a map at the canoe rental agency; the refuge's labyrinthine waterways can be disorienting.

Shawnee National Forest

You can observe an impressive array of birds, mammals, and amphibians in this midwestern woodland.

SITE 36 At 275,000 acres, Shawnee isn't particularly large as national forests go. But its significance far outweighs its size. Bounded by the Mississippi River to the west and the Ohio River to the east, Shawnee is Illinois' only national forest—a domain of hardwood forests and scattered pine groves that harbor some of the densest concentrations of wildlife in the Midwest.

One of the forest's chief attractions may seem anomalous for a woodland: ducks. Tens of thousands of them. Each

Furbearing mammals, such as the gray fox, thrive in Illinois' only national forest.

year forest managers flood an area in the northwest sector of the forest known as Oakwood Bottoms, creating a vast "green-tree reservoir," a seasonal forested wetland. By spring this shallow flooded woodland is burgeoning with small invertebrates—precisely the kind of high-energy food waterfowl need for the northward migration to their breeding grounds.

Once the timber is flooded, the ducks pour into the 3,200-acre bottoms in huge flights, gorging on the smorgasbord of small crustaceans,

insect larvae, and worms. Most of the birds are mallards, but gadwall, wood duck, and northern shoveler are also well represented. A network of levees provides access for car travelers and day hikers. You might want to bring earplugs: The cacophony of feeding birds during the height of the spring migration can be almost deafening.

Mammals are particularly numerous in and around seasonally flooded bottomlands. Species include white-tailed deer, eastern cottontail, swamp rabbit, woodchuck, raccoon, opossum, striped skunk, and long-tailed weasel. Furbearing mammals are doing extraordinarily well in Shawnee, thanks to the excellent habitat (and also to the fact that fur prices have been depressed for the past several years). Beavers, coyotes, red and gray foxes, mink, and muskrats are all thriving. Bobcats, which are on the state's threatened species list, are expanding their range throughout the forest and their numbers are growing.

Shawnee is particularly rich in wood warblers. Some extremely rare birds are found here, including the cerulean warbler, with its brilliant blue plumage. The cerulean warbler is rare across its range because of its need for large, mature timber for nesting sites, which have all but disappeared in the eastern United States. But the thriving hardwoods of Shawnee are a haven for this species, which is known to nest here.

A great many other eastern wood warblers also nest here. Birders will want to look for prothonotary, myrtle, worm-eating, yellow, yellow-throated, hooded, and Kentucky warblers; common yellowthroat; northern parula;

ovenbird; yellow-breasted chat; and Louisiana waterthrush.

A number of other songbirds can be seen flying through the forest canopies or scurrying through the underbrush. Keep an eye out for eastern phoebe and eastern kingbird, two flycatchers that flit from their perches to snatch insects in mid-flight. Swallows include purple martin, and northern rough-winged and barn swallows. The red-breasted nuthatch and white-breasted nuthatch creep along the branches and trunks of larger trees. The vibrant colors of the eastern bluebird, summer tanager, northern cardinal, and northern oriole make these birds relatively easy to spot. Other species that thrive in the forest include cedar waxwing, warbling vireo, red-eyed vireo, blue grosbeak, indigo bunting, and rufous-sided towhee. Sparrows abound; species include American tree, chipping, field, vesper, lark, song, and white-throated sparrows.

The forest is also excellent habitat for woodpeckers, which reap a rich harvest of grubs and insects from dead and dying timber. Listen for their spirited hammerings in the deeper woodlands. Notable species include pileated, red-headed, downy, and hairy woodpeckers; northern flicker; and yellow-bellied sapsucker.

Among the woodland-associated raptors that thrive in Shawnee are red-shouldered, sharp-shinned, and Cooper's hawks. Red-tailed hawks, northern harriers, northern goshawks, and American kestrels are relatively common, and bald eagles are beginning to nest in various locations within and around the forest. Resident species of owls are barred, common barn-, great horned, long-eared, and short-eared. Nightjars—specifically, common nighthawks, whippoorwills, and chuck-will's-widows—are frequently seen plying the skies at twilight. Mississippi kites are starting to appear along the Mississippi River.

Shawnee contains some wonderful snake habitat, particularly in the LaRue Pine Hills, where the U.S. Forest Service closes roads in the

The brightly colored male wood duck almost looks like a painted decoy.

bites with their sharp mandibles, so they should be approached with care.

Resident amphibians include the impressively large (though somewhat drab) hellbender, mudpuppy, and lesser siren. They are aquatic species, as is their smaller and more brightly colored relative, the eastern newt. Terrestrial salamander species include mole, small-mouthed, tiger, spotted, marbled, slimy, two-lined, cave, and long-tailed salamanders. They are often found on the forest floor, burrowing in soil or leaf mold.

Eastern spadefoots and Fowler's toads can be found on the damper portions of the forest floor. Terrestrial frogs include the enthusiastically vocal green treefrog, bird-voiced and gray treefrogs, chorus and cricket frogs, and spring peeper. Green frogs, bullfrogs, and pickerel frogs are common in the Shawnee's streams and ponds.

Spring is probably the best time to visit—mammals are actively foraging, duck populations are at their peak, and the high humidity and temperatures of summer haven't begun. Hiking at any time of the year is worthwhile. There are about 250 miles of developed trails in the forest, so finding good routes for day hikes or backpacking trips is hardly a problem. The truly ambitious backpacker might want to consider the River-to-River Trail, which runs 176 miles from the Ohio River west to the Mississippi. The rivers also offer a variety of aquatic pursuits, from pleasure boating to waterskiing to fishing.

autumn and spring to protect cottonmouths, copperheads, and timber rattlesnakes as they migrate between upland wintering den sites and lowland areas. Other terrestrial species include the handsomely marked rat snake, black and speckled kingsnakes, milk snake, red-bellied snake, smooth earth snake, ringneck snake, eastern hognose snake, rough green snake, and southern black racer. Snakes found in and near water include northern water and plain-bellied water snake, garter snake, western ribbon snake, mud snake, and brown snake.

The Shawnee's turtles and amphibians likewise demonstrate impressive diversity. Look for common snapping, musk, mud, map, and painted turtles resting on pond and riverbanks and sunning on midstream logs. Box turtles, which favor drier woodlands, are also found here. Smooth softshell and spiny softshell turtles, which have round leathery shells, are also abundant. These turtles can inflict serious

Muscatatuck National Wildlife Refuge

Until they were successfully reintroduced at this sanctuary in 1995, river otters had not lived in Indiana since the 1940s.

Bounded by the meandering river that shares its name, Muscatatuck National Wildlife Refuge is Indiana's largest wildlife sanctuary; it's also the best site in this intensively agricultural state for wildlife observation. The refuge, managed by the U.S. Fish and Wildlife Service, supports a variety of prime habitats: 3,000 acres of forest, 1,500 acres of permanent or seasonal wetlands, and 2,400 acres of old farms that are reverting to forested upland.

Because it is an island of wildness surrounded by a sea of cropland, Muscatatuck draws wildlife like a magnet—particularly birds. More than 250 different species of birds visit the refuge annually, and the number appears to be growing. As many as 15,000 ducks are on the refuge in March, during the peak of the spring migration. Sandhill cranes also drop by. Species that nest locally are great blue heron, Canada goose, mallard, and wood duck. Wood ducks, in fact, were once at a critically low ebb in southeastern Indiana, but because Muscatatuck seasonally floods large tracts of woodland and thus provides prime nesting grounds, these exceedingly colorful birds have staged a dramatic comeback. The fall migration is also impressive, with up to 20,000 waterfowl visiting the refuge in November and December.

Summer means songbirds. Among the frequently observed species are blue-gray gnatcatcher, eastern wood-pewee, wood thrush, gray catbird,

Nearly decimated by habitat destruction and trapping, river otters are prospering again.

red-eyed vireo, and blue-winged, yellow, yellow-rumped, and palm warblers. Look for the eastern kingbird, an aggressive, black-headed flycatcher and the only eastern songbird with a white-tipped tail. Woodpeckers—red-bellied, red-headed, downy, and hairy—inhabit the woodlands. Wild turkeys are in residence year-round.

Because Muscatatuck provides the best hunting opportunities for miles around, raptors such as red-tailed hawks, northern harriers, American kestrels, and turkey vultures are drawn to it. Great horned owls and barred owls are year-round residents. Other birds of prey that are sometimes sighted by diligent birders include osprey, Cooper's hawk, and bald eagle.

The river otter is the undisputed mammalian star of the sanctuary. Once common throughout Indiana, these playful mustelids were extirpated by the early 1940s. In 1995 Muscatatuck was selected as the state's first site for the reintroduction of the species. Otters from the marshes of Louisiana have been released, and several were outfitted with radio transmitters to help gauge the long-term success of the program. Current data indicate that the otters are expanding in range and numbers. Other mammals that live in the refuge include white-tailed deer, red fox, coyote, beaver, muskrat, and eastern cottontail.

Several species of reptiles inhabit Muscatatuck, including the copper-bellied water snake, which is extremely rare across most of its range, but quite common on the refuge. A sighting of this handsome snake with a black back and reddish belly is a good possibility, especially during spring

and fall, when the snakes move between lowland and upland areas.

The refuge is open from sunrise to sunset; not coincidentally, dawn and dusk are the best times to see wildlife. Get there very early or stay until just before dark. March and November are the best times to observe migratory waterfowl; songbird migrations usually peak in May. A 3-mile auto tour route is marked with numbered signs that correspond to an informational brochure for identifying points of natural significance. Eight hiking trails allow visitors a view of all the refuge's primary habitats—pick up a map from the Visitor Center.

THE FACTS

Noteworthy Animals: Wood duck, mallard, great blue heron, red-tailed hawk, great horned owl, eastern kingbird, red-bellied woodpecker, red-eyed vireo, river otter, muskrat, white-tailed deer.

Getting There: From Indianapolis, take I-65 south for 60 miles to US 50 near Seymour. (Louisville, Kentucky is about the same distance away, to the south, on I-65.) The refuge is on US 50, about 3 miles east of the I-65/US 50 junction.

Open: Daily, dawn to dusk, year-round.
Best Times to Visit: March through May; September through November.
Visitor Information: Muscatatuck National Wildlife Refuge Visitor Center (812-522-4352) open daily, 12:30 p.m.-4:30 p.m., year-round.
Entrance fees: None.
Disabled Access: Visitor Center, nearby nature trail, auto tour, and two fishing piers (Stanfield Lake and Lake Linda) are wheelchair accessible.
Camping: None on-site.

Yellow River State Forest

Rugged, tree-lined bluffs along the Mississippi River elate hikers
with stunning scenery and glimpses of deer and wild turkeys.

SITE 38

While Iowa is characterized as a land of flat-as-a-tabletop vistas of corn and soybeans, the state's northeast plateau is a dramatic exception. The local sobriquet of Iowa's Little Switzerland may be an exaggeration, but the rugged, heavily wooded bluffs along the Mississippi River do provide both stunning vistas and excellent wildlife habitat.

For the wildlife enthusiast, the best place to visit in this region is Yellow River State Forest. At 9,000

Badgers find sustenance, like this bountiful supply of birds' eggs, at Yellow River.

acres of tree-covered bluffs and deep declivities, it's the largest block of contiguous woodland in the state. Pines are the dominant tree, the result of large government plantings in the 1950s and 1960s for erosion control and timber. Logging continues under tight controls and rigorous replanting schedules. A healthy mix of native hardwoods keeps the forest from being a monoculture, and the deciduous trees provide the most colorful display of autumn foliage in the state.

This forest is not on a list of must-see destinations for a glimpse of a single species of extreme rarity. Rather, it is a patch of wildness in the tame Midwest that can provide a weekend or more of rewarding exploration and some worthwhile sightings. Primitive campsites and 25 miles of trails make it one of the best backpacking destinations in Iowa. This is a place of ecotones—diverse ecological niches caused by changes in vegetation and geographic features. Many of the ecotones are created by human intervention, such as logging or the farming of adjacent croplands.

The largest animal in the forest is the white-tailed deer, which thrives in areas where forest and cropland meet. The deer are seen year-round but are especially observable in the late autumn rut when the bucks are particularly bold. The fox squirrel is another notable forest resident. The nation's largest tree squirrel, these rodents can reach 30 inches long and weigh more than three pounds. Several other types of squirrels—southern flying, red, and gray—are also commonly seen. Eastern cottontail, red fox, long-tailed weasel, least weasel, badger, mink, and even the occasional bobcat also reside in the forest.

At least 56 bird species nest in or migrate through the forest. Look for the male rose-breasted grosbeak, which has a red breast and underwings, black hood, and white underbelly. The female is also handsome, with yellow underwings and a speckled brown-and-white breast. Other species include the cerulean warbler, eastern wood-pewee, rufous-sided towhee, scarlet tanager, American redstart, ovenbird, indigo bunting, Kentucky warbler, veery, pileated woodpecker, and yellow-bellied sapsucker.

The forest has the highest raptor concentration in the state. Species include Cooper's hawk, a handsome gray-white-and-brown accipiter. The broad-winged hawk, red-shouldered hawk, red-tailed hawk, and American kestrel are here as well. Owls include the common barn-, great horned, and barred owl.

Wild turkeys are commonplace, their gobbles and "perts" often heard in the coverts. Quiet progress through the forest may reward the hiker with a sighting of these majestic birds, especially during the spring, when the toms are busy displaying for the hens. Or, a hiker might flush a ruffed

grouse, a chicken-size groundbird with finely barred reddish plumage.

Hiking the Back Pack Trail is probably the best way to see and appreciate resident wildlife. This 25-mile trail traverses some of Iowa's most rugged country, wending its way up and down 350-foot bluffs. The trailhead is located near the forest's headquarters building. Though no point on the trail is more than a mile from a road or fence, the dense vegetation makes it advisable to take a compass. Nature lovers who spend some time in this forest and along the adjacent Mississippi River, which still supports surprising populations of wildlife, will find that every hour is well rewarded.

Cheyenne Bottoms Preserve

Take a driving tour of this internationally acclaimed wetland to see the shorebirds and waterfowl that visit it.

In the words of one biologist, Cheyenne Bottoms is "Kansas' Galapagos, its Amazonia, its Serengeti all in one." A strong statement, certainly, but by all accounts one that's on the mark. This 41,000-acre seasonal wetland has been given the highest priority for preservation by the Kansas Natural Heritage Foundation and has been designated a "wetland of international importance" through an international treaty adopted by 92 sovereign signatories, including the United States.

Why all the fuss? Simply because there is no other place exactly like it. Admittedly, the Bottoms does not comprise a majestic landscape. Essentially, it is mudflats hemmed in

The dunlin is one of the many sandpipers that stop at Cheyenne Bottoms to rest and refuel.

by agricultural fields. But the strategic location, coupled with an abundance of muck-dwelling midge larvae that birds find irresistible, have made it a critical staging area for shorebirds and waterfowl for at least 100,000 years. Despite all the changes on the continent, the birds still stop off at the Bottoms for food and rest during their annual migrations from the wintering grounds of the southern states and Central and South America to the breeding territory of the Arctic and Canadian pothole country.

The International Shorebird Survey recently concluded that Cheyenne Bottoms is the top shorebird springtime migration staging area in the lower 48 states. During the peak of the spring migration, more than 500,000 shorebirds and 250,000 ducks and geese may be actively foraging at the Bottoms. More than half of the Bottoms' acreage has been preserved so far: 20,000 acres are administered as a wildlife management area by the state of Kansas, and 6,700 acres are managed as a preserve by the Nature Conservancy.

Typical waterfowl sightings include mallard, northern pintail, greenwinged teal, blue-winged teal, gadwall, canvasback, redhead, common goldeneye, bufflehead, lesser scaup, snow goose, and Canada goose.

The Bottoms also hosts one of the rarest of North American avian rarities, the whooping crane. Several whoopers usually show up each year

The whooping crane, America's tallest bird, stands over four feet.

during the spring migration, as do representatives from two other endangered bird species: peregrine falcon and least tern.

While the whoopers are the most flamboyant visitors to Cheyenne Bottoms, they are not necessarily the most significant from the naturalists' point of view. This is crucial habitat for nine species of small sandpipers, known collectively and fondly as "peeps" by birders: western, spotted, pectoral, buff-breasted, solitary, white-rumped, semipalmated, least, and Baird's sandpipers.

Other shorebirds in great variety join the sandpipers at the Bottoms during the spring migration. Common sightings include the long-billed dowitcher, snowy plover, and piping plover, black-necked stilt, American avocet, greater yellow-legs, killdeer, long-billed curlew, marbled godwit, dunlin, common snipe, and Wilson's phalarope. Without the Bottoms, mid-continental and eastern populations of shorebirds would surely decline significantly. It is the most critical stop for shorebirds migrating along the central flyway—without it, they would starve.

Unlike most wildlife refuges, the Bottoms is best seen by car. A driving tour has been laid out along a gravel road that traverses Conservancy and state lands, affording numerous overlooks of the mudflats, as well as an upland area that supports a black-tailed prairie dog town. The road becomes impassable after a heavy rain, however; then hiking the levees around the refuge is the only option.

The peak time to observe migrating ducks is late March and early April; the peak time for shorebirds is late April to early May. The autumn migration is less dramatic, but as long as there is water, there will be birds. The numbers vary with water levels—generally speaking, the wetter the year, the better the birding.

Visitors will also want to investigate Quivira National Wildlife Refuge, 20 miles southeast of the Bottoms, which has another well-planned wildlife drive. Quivira's creatures include 270 bird species and many mammals, such as white-tailed deer, raccoon, badger, and black-tailed prairie dog.

Cypress Island Preserve

As thousands of herons and egrets feed and breed in this Louisiana swampland, big bull alligators prowl the ponds.

SITE 40 Not so long ago, most of Louisiana was a vast wetland teeming with wildlife. Much of its stunning natural diversity has been lost—but not all of it. Cypress Island Preserve, managed by the Nature Conservancy of Louisiana, is a 2,600-acre tract of cypress-tupelo swamp, ridges covered with old-growth live oak forest, and mixed hardwood bottomlands. It is a slice of the old, wild Louisiana, primeval and burgeoning with wild creatures.

American alligators have staged a big comeback in Louisiana's wetlands, and at no place is that more obvious than at Cypress Island. Some of the biggest alligators in the country live here; preserve managers have identified several bulls that are 14 feet or more in length. Look for gators partially submerged in ponds and sloughs, resembling floating logs, with only their snouts and eyes visible; these prehistoric-looking predators become most active toward evening.

But while alligators are a major attraction, the most significant reason for visiting is to see wading birds. The preserve's star attraction is a huge rookery where 20,000 or more pairs nest every year. Individual species include many herons—tricolored, great blue, little blue, green-backed—and black-crowned night-herons, American and least bitterns, great and snowy egrets, and white ibis. A visit to Cypress Island in mid-spring, when thousands of herons and egrets are raucously breeding, squabbling over territory, and feeding young, is one of the continent's most satisfying wildlife-viewing experiences.

As many as a dozen pairs of roseate spoonbills—large, rare, fantastically pink, platter-billed filter-feeders—nest here. They may be seen in the shallow wetlands that surround the island, straining water and silt through their impressively large bills to capture crustaceans and other small aquatic species. The anhinga, a waterbird that thrives in the freshwater swamps of

You might see an anhinga perching on a snag and stretching out its wings to dry.

Roseate spoonbills and great egrets are highly visible at Cypress Island Preserve.

the South, is often visible swimming with only its snakelike head and neck above water, or perched on a snag with wings spread to dry.

In the spring and summer, the island's trees are filled with neotropical migrant songbirds. Among the many visitors are solitary, warbling, and red-eyed vireos; orange-crowned, protho-notary, and cerulean warblers; northern parula; common yellowthroat; yellow-breasted chat; summer tanager; blue grosbeak; and indigo bunting.

Birds of prey at Cypress Island include red-shouldered hawks and barred owls, both of which are year-round residents. Broad-winged hawks are relatively abundant during the autumn migration, and great horned owls and eastern screech-owls reside here during the winter.

During the autumn months many waterfowl also flock to the preserve. Common sightings include northern pintail, blue-winged teal, gadwall, northern shoveler, ring-necked duck, and snow goose. Wood ducks are year-round residents.

Snakes and turtles are well distributed throughout this rich habitat; look for them along the margins of swampy areas. Turtle species include cooter and mud, box, painted, snapping, and alligator snapping turtles. Resident snakes include cottonmouth; green, diamondback, and plain-bellied water snakes. Among the amphibians are lesser siren, marbled salamander, and eastern newt.

Mammals are common, though furtive, and sightings of most species are rare. Exceptions to that rule are nutria—big, bucktoothed, aquatic rodents naturalized from South America—and muskrats, swamp rabbits, and white-tailed deer. Mink, river otter, red fox, coyote, striped skunk, raccoon, and opossum might be spotted at dusk. Southern flying, gray, and fox squirrels inhabit the hardwood canopies, and are best located by listening for their rasping cries.

A levee surrounding Lake Martin is the starting point for 3 miles of trails that wind through the swamp and the dense bottomland forests of oak and other hardwoods. Time your visit for spring or winter—the high temperatures and humidity of summer and autumn make the wildlife, and their human observers, sluggish.

Little Pecan Island

The rare roseate spoonbill and other wading birds inhabit the heavily wooded marshes and swamps of this island preserve.

SITE 41 Like many unique habitats, Louisiana's cheniers are in trouble. Dry, low-lying ridges distributed throughout the state's coastal marshes, cheniers once were typically covered with thick hardwood forests, adding greatly to the biodiversity of the surrounding wetlands.

Progress has not been kind to the cheniers. Most have been logged, grazed, contoured, or otherwise irredeemably degraded. But some have survived intact—most notably Little Pecan Island. At 7 feet above sea level, it is one of the highest points in all of Cameron Parish. This 1,800-acre preserve, managed by the Nature Conservancy, encompasses a wholly unspoiled 400-acre chenier, a lake, a cypress swamp, and abundant freshwater marshes. Such a felicitous conjunction of different habitats has made this relatively small preserve, which is accessible only by boat, one of the best places in Louisiana to see wildlife.

The marsh and swamp are paradise for wading birds, including the rare roseate spoonbill and white-faced ibis. Also look for American and least bitterns; great blue, tricolored, and little blue herons; black-crowned nightherons; great, snowy, and cattle egrets; and sora. The island is also home to the purple gallinule; a relative of the coot and moorhen, the gallinule has a brilliant purplish blue breast, greenish back, and red bill. Most of the waders inhabit the refuge year-round.

The mottled duck, which is vari-ously thought to be a subspecies of mallard or of American black duck, breeds here. Other duck species that might be seen include green-winged and blue-winged teal and American wigeon. The olivaceous cormorant, rare in North America, is here, as is the related double-crested cormorant, and the anhinga.

Even more significant than the marsh, however, is the chenier. Little Pecan Island is situated right at the conjunction of the central and Mississippi flyways. Being heavily wooded, it draws a variety of songbirds, especially warblers, thrushes, and flycatchers, with numbers rising in the spring and fall. Look for magnolia warblers, handsome birds with black-striped yellow breasts. Other warblers include the black-and-white, orange-crowned, and yellow-rumped warblers. The northern parula is recognizable by its bright yellow throat, blue-gray back, and white eye ring. Swainson's thrush; vermilion and scissor-tailed flycatchers; eastern phoebe; American redstart; and eastern kingbird are also found on the island.

Other common songbird sightings include tree and barn swallows; marsh wren; ruby-crowned kinglet; red-eyed and solitary vireos; blue-gray gnatcatcher; hermit thrush; and indigo bunting. The male painted bunting, with a blue head, red breast, and chartreuse back, is perhaps the most brilliantly hued of all American songbirds. Also look for the northern

The American alligator also lives in the marshes and swamps of Little Pecan Island.

mockingbird, gray catbird, and American pipit. Sparrows—field, chipping, vesper, savannah, fox, song, Lincoln's, and white-throated—are quite common.

Several types of raptors haunt Little Pecan Island and surrounding marshlands. Great horned owls are abundant in the woods and are often seen at dusk. Ospreys hunt the open water. Northern harriers, and Cooper's, red-shouldered, red-tailed, and sharp-shinned hawks can be seen perching motionless on snags.

Wetland mammals, reptiles, and amphibians are abundant. White-tailed

is at ease foraging either on land or in water. As always, mammal sightings are most likely at dawn and dusk.

The American alligator dominates Little Pecan Island's marshlands and cypress swamps. The alligators are usually spotted around dusk, and the roaring of the bulls is often heard throughout the night, sending a chill down the spine of all but the most jaded wildlife enthusiasts.

Bullfrogs are also impressively noisy in the evenings. Other resident amphibians include the cricket frog, green treefrog, pig frog, green frog, leopard frog, Gulf Coast toad, and three-toed amphiuma.

A variety of turtles inhabits the area: Look for alligator snapping and common snapping turtles; spiny soft-shells; mud, musk, and box turtles; cooters; and pond sliders. Snakes—most notably cottonmouth, green water snake, and plain-bellied water snake—are seen sliding through the water or sunning on logs. On drier ground watch for speckled king-snakes, large nonvenomous snakes with a salt-and-pepper pattern.

Little Pecan Island is not the place for a casual stopover. First, the only way to visit is with a guided Nature Conservancy tour, the shortest of which is two days in duration. Second, these tours are offered only in April and October, and reservations should be made at least six months in advance. Once visitors are on the island, they can strike off and explore on their own. Trails run throughout the woodlands and much of the surrounding swamp and marsh, and canoes are available for extended paddles in nearby bayous and canals.

deer, river otter, nutria, muskrat, armadillo, bobcat, raccoon, coyote, red fox, and mink all live here. The swamp rabbit, another island resident,

Sabine National Wildlife Refuge

Flocks of snow geese, mottled ducks, and mallards blanket the skies above this Louisiana wetland near the Gulf of Mexico.

SITE 42 The snow goose is one of the most far-ranging of North American waterfowl, breeding in the Arctic and migrating in the winter to far-flung refuges in California and the southern states. On the central flyway these beautiful geese head for the national wildlife refuges of Louisiana—particularly Sabine NWR, located by the Gulf of Mexico on the Texas border.

Sabine is one of Louisiana's greatest wetlands. It is gigantic—an amazing 124,511 acres of brackish, intermediate, and freshwater marsh—and it's surrounded by privately owned marshlands of similar dimensions, which further enhance its ecological significance (not to mention its appeal to geese). About 300,000 snow geese overwinter in southwest Louisiana each year. In December, during the height of the migration, it is not uncommon to see flocks of "snows" numbering 10,000 strong, a brilliant banner of white that spans the sky from horizon to horizon.

Migratory ducks are also extremely numerous at Sabine. Common species include blue-winged and green-winged teal, mallard, American wigeon, northern pintail, and wood duck. Mottled duck is a hallmark species of this preserve. Olivaceous cormorants, rare in North America, also maintain a rookery here. Look for these dark birds with serpentine necks clustered in trees.

Sabine is rich in wading birds.

White ibis; great blue, little blue, and tricolored herons; black-crowned night-herons; and great and snowy egrets are among the species that breed here. The noisy (and sometimes noisome) rookeries of these waders are the sites of spectacular springtime mating and territorial displays. Glossy ibis and roseate spoonbills are other common sightings. Belted kingfishers also frequent the refuge in considerable numbers, their cries heralding their presence in raucous and clattering fashion.

Sabine is at the heart of the continent's major migration corridor for neotropical migrants, songbirds that

Introduced into Louisiana in the 1930s as furbearers, the nutria escaped and multiplied.

nest in North America and winter in Mexico, Central America, or South America. Birders can add extensively to their life lists here; common species include marsh wren, common yellowthroat, yellow-billed cuckoo, orchard oriole, myrtle warbler, swamp sparrow, northern cardinal, and the brilliantly colored painted bunting.

Regularly observed birds of prey include red-tailed and broad-winged hawks, osprey, and common barn-owl. Northern harriers take particular advantage of the limited waterfowl hunting allowed on the preserve by preying on ducks and geese that are wounded by gunfire.

Sabine supports healthy populations of mammals, too. It's possible to see white-tailed deer, armadillo, swamp rabbit, and red fox. Muskrat and nutria—an introduced species that looks somewhat like an extremely large muskrat—are undergoing population explosions, apparently because of a collapse in the fur market. While the native muskrats are causing no problems, the naturalized and voracious nutrias are damaging large portions of the preserve by devouring much of the vegetation.

Bobcats, once thought expunged from the refuge, have been spotted

Springtime brings magnificent territorial displays of great blue herons and great egrets.

increasingly over the past few years and apparently are making a strong comeback, although these small cats are unlikely to be seen by a casual visitor.

Sabine's coyotes, which are more likely to be spotted by visitors, may not be true coyotes at all. Many biologists think they are hybrids, a result of matings between coyotes and red wolves, which are now extinct in the region. Studies to determine their genetic antecedents are underway.

The American alligator is the most notable of Sabine's reptiles. With as many as 9,000 gators living throughout the refuge, some are bound to be visible from the boardwalk. Snakes are abundant. Watch out for cottonmouths, the most common venomous snake on the refuge. These heavy, dark brown to black snakes have triangular heads and nasty dispositions. Other snakes that might be seen sunning themselves on exposed banks are speckled kingsnake; southern black racer; and diamondback, broad-banded, plain-bellied, glossy crayfish, and green water snakes.

This is also turtle country; look for Gulf Coast box turtle, spiny softshell turtle, pond slider, diamondback terrapin, and common snapping turtle. The alligator snapping turtle, which has a huge head, long tail, and can weigh up to 150 pounds, is unmistakable.

Given its watery nature, Sabine is best observed by means of a small outboard

THE FACTS

Noteworthy Animals: Snow goose, mottled duck, olivaceous cormorant, roseate spoonbill, white ibis, great blue heron, great egret, bobcat, muskrat, nutria, American alligator.

Getting There: From Lake Charles, take I-10 west about 5 miles to La. 27 at Sulphur. Take La. 27 south about 20 miles to the refuge entrance.
Open: Daily, dawn to dusk, year-round.
Best Times to Visit: March through May, September through November.
Visitor Information: Sabine National Wildlife Refuge. Visitor Center (318-762-3816) open Monday through Friday, 7 a.m.-4 p.m.; weekends, 12 p.m.-4p.m.; year-round.
Entrance Fees: None.
Disabled Access: Visitor Center and nature trail are wheelchair accessible.
Camping: None on-site.

motorboat. Bring your own or rent one (with trailer) at Lake Charles or Port Arthur, Texas. The boating season runs from mid-spring through early fall; in winter the refuge is closed to boats to protect the birds.

Earthbound visitors can enjoy a day at Sabine, too. There are public-use areas along La. 27, an observation tower, and an all-weather 1.5-mile nature trail. The trail, which includes a wooden boardwalk through a freshwater marsh, provides good handicapped access. Marshes yield their best wildlife viewing during dawn or dusk, so it's best to be there early or just before dark.

Hiawatha National Forest

Rare fishers and marten are among the 52 species of mammals you might see in this midwestern woodland.

SITE 43

Michigan's Upper Peninsula is still much as it was when Ernest Hemingway wrote about it in the 1920s—pristine, sparsely populated, and burgeoning with fish and wildlife. Amend that: There's probably more wildlife here than when Hemingway fished the big Two Hearted River. Efforts by the U.S. Forest Service to improve habitat and protect threatened species have yielded tremendous dividends.

Hiawatha National Forest covers a good portion of the peninsula—roughly one million acres divided into two units between Lake Superior and Lake Michigan. Though 75 miles separate the two units, they support the same habitats. About one-half of Hiawatha is forested; the trees are a mix of northern hardwoods (sugar maple, American beech, and yellow birch) and boreal conifers (black spruce, tamarack, and northern white cedar). The remainder of the forest is wetland—a stunning 500,000 acres of marshes, lakes, and patterned fens. (Unique to the region, patterned fens are wetlands characterized by a neutral pH, slight to moderate terrain gradient, and "flarks"—numerous little pools of water from 1 foot to several feet in diameter.)

This varied habitat supports a tremendous diversity of mammals—52 different species live here. White-tailed deer are visible foraging in second-growth forests and areas where woodlands, brushlands, and meadows meet. Moose favor bogs and marshes, which support abundant aquatic plants, their favorite fodder. Black bears are often seen at the margins of woodlands or in meadows.

Thanks to the superb cover and abundance of prey, timber (gray) wolves are numerous but seldom seen. Their tracks and scat, however, are often noted, particularly along riverbanks and lakeshores. Bobcats are another common predator in Hiawatha but, like wolves, they are furtive. Chances of a sighting are best near forest edges and game trails. Badgers inhabit the more open areas of the forest. Look for their burrows, which are somewhat larger than those excavated by woodchucks. Marten and fishers are expanding in range and numbers as the result of an ambitious reintroduction program and committed support from local residents. It takes luck to see one of these big, secretive mustelids; the best places for a sighting are groves of old-growth timber near dusk or dawn.

The most commonly observed woodland mammals include porcupine, snowshoe hare, eastern cottontail, woodchuck, and gray, red, and northern flying squirrels. River otter, mink, beaver, and muskrat are usually spotted in or around Hiawatha's waterways. Coyote, red and gray foxes, ermine, least and long-tailed weasels, and raccoon might be spotted in any and all habitats.

Woodland bats, including Keen's

White-tailed deer can be observed browsing for vegetation at the edges of the forest.

myotis, silver-haired bat, big brown bat, red bat, and hoary bat, are abundant. Look for them cleaving the skies at dusk or curled up in tree cavities during the day.

Hiawatha's vast wetlands draw significant numbers of breeding waterfowl, most notably trumpeter swans. During the fall migration, huge flocks of snow geese stop at the forest to feed and rest. Species that brood in the forest include blue-winged and green-winged teal, Canada goose, mallard, northern pintail, American wigeon, ring-necked duck, common goldeneye, and common, hooded,

and red-breasted mergansers.

In the spring large numbers of migratory shorebirds may be found foraging in the marshes and fens, particularly greater and lesser yellowlegs.

Thanks to its vast expanses of intact forests, Michigan's Upper Peninsula is known as the richest site in the United States for woodland neotropical migrant songbirds. Dainty, melodious wood warblers nest at Hiawatha in particularly extravagant numbers.

Among the 24 different species of warbler to watch for are magnolia, black-and-white, black-throated blue, black-throated green, chestnut-sided,

THE FACTS

Noteworthy Animals: Black bear, timber wolf, moose, white-tailed deer, marten, fisher, bobcat, coyote, beaver, river otter, porcupine, trumpeter swan, sharp-tailed grouse, ruffed grouse, spruce grouse.

Getting There: There are two units to the forest, located about 75 miles apart on Michigan's Upper Peninsula. The eastern unit is near Sault Ste. Marie; the western near Marquette. Both are accessible by US 2 and Mich. 28.

Open: Daily, 24 hours, year-round.

Best Times to Visit: Year-round.

Visitor Information: The U.S. Forest Service maintains Visitor Centers throughout the forest, some jointly administered with other agencies. Eastern section: St. Ignace (906-643-7900), just off I-75 at the beginning of the Upper Peninsula, open daily, 8 a.m.-6:30 p.m., May through October; Monday through Friday in winter. Western section: Munising (906-387-3700), off Mich. 28 near Grand Island, same hours as above.

Entrance Fees: None.

Disabled Access: Visitor Centers and portions of some trails accessible.

Camping: Primitive camping; no permit or fees. Semiprimitive camping (with pump or outhouse) in certain areas; permit required; fees. Developed campgrounds; fees; no reservations.

palm, pine, bay-breasted, yellow, and prairie warblers.

Raptors include bald eagles and all the usual woodland hawks: northern goshawk and broad-winged, red-shouldered, Cooper's, and sharp-shinned hawks. Owls are especially plentiful; breeding species include long-eared, great horned, barred, short-eared, and northern saw-whet owl. In winter snowy owls, boreal owls, northern hawk-owls, and great gray owls haunt the forest, searching for shrews, voles, mice, and lemmings.

Three species of grouse live in Hiawatha: the extremely common ruffed grouse, as well as the rarer sharp-tailed grouse and spruce grouse. All are large, dramatically marked birds that leave a significant impression on the wildlife enthusiast when they burst from the coverts with a wild thrumming of wings.

The vast wetlands teem with frogs and toads. Their evening choruses can be almost overwhelming, ranging from throbbing basso profundos to shrill sopranos. Species heard and seen include the American toad, gray tree-frog, green frog, bullfrog, wood frog, spring peeper, northern leopard frog, and pickerel frog.

This is a huge forest, and it takes some time to explore thoroughly. Three or four days are good—a week is better. Developed campsites can serve as bases for day hikes and canoeing on the Sturgeon River, Lake Michigan, and Lake Superior. Scenic motor routes through the eastern unit include Mich. 28, Mich. 123, and County Road H40; try US 2, Mich. 28, Mich. 94, and County Road H13 in the western unit.

Hiawatha is a four-season destination. Summer days are typically warm and beautiful, although sometimes humid. Spring and autumn tend to be cool to truly cold, but marked by periods of absolutely spectacular, clear weather. Winters are cold and snowy, but the snowshoeing and ice fishing are excellent.

Isle Royale National Park

Wolves and moose engage in their age-old struggle of predator and prey on this remote island in Lake Superior, Michigan.

SITE 44 A mysterious island set in an azure ocean, cloaked in primeval forest, and abounding with exotic wildlife: Madagascar? Palau? Papua New Guinea? Look a little bit closer to home—to the midwestern state of Michigan, in fact. Isle Royale, located in the freshwater inland sea of Lake Superior, remains both remote and untouched. Its 571,000 acres and 165 miles of hiking trails assure visitors a true wilderness experience, and it also provides something few places in the continental United States can match: a chance to glimpse one of North America's most majestic predators pursuing its natural prey in its natural habitat.

Among animal behaviorists, Isle Royale is renowned for its eastern timber wolf (a subspecies of gray wolf) and moose populations. Landlocked on the island, the two species dance a fascinating minuet with each other: Sometimes the wolves are up and the moose are down—sometimes it's the other way around.

Moose have been on Isle Royale since the turn of the century, but the wolves are relative newcomers. Every wolf on the island, in fact, is descended from a single pair that migrated across the ice in the winter of 1948-49. Their relatively recent arrival, coupled with the enforced isolation of the island habitat, continues to provide new insights into the dynamics of predator-prey relationships.

Populations of both species rotate continually, if unpredictably. In the early 1980s, it was feared that the wolves were doomed to extinction; their numbers had crashed from 50 down to 14. Theories on the decline abounded, including genetic entropy—some scientists thought that the animals were so inbred that they couldn't reproduce successfully. It now appears that the problem was a combination of a canine parvovirus and a moose population that was both relatively small and anomalously youthful. Even in the most favorable of circumstances, wolves are seldom able to kill healthy, robust moose—old, crippled, sick, or very young moose (calves) are their typical prey.

Today the moose community stands at 500, including elderly and ill animals, giving the wolves ample hunting opportunities. And the ravages of the virus appear to have passed. Isle Royale's wolf population has risen to 24, and successful reproduction is expected to continue for the foreseeable future.

Wolf sightings are admittedly rare, not only because of the natural shyness of the animals but also because the island is covered with dense vegetation—boreal spruce and fir on the northeastern end and northern hardwoods elsewhere. But a few fortunate visitors do manage to spot some of the wary canids each season, and wolf scat and tracks are commonly found. In autumn the wolves howl in the evening and early morning, treating

The moose population on Isle Royale currently numbers about 500.

lucky campers to deliciously eerie serenades as they lie snug in their sleeping bags.

Given the density of the moose population, sightings are relatively common. These huge ungulates are most often glimpsed browsing in the brush or dredging for aquatic vegetation in the ponds and streams.

Only 16 mammal species are indigenous to Isle Royale, including red fox, river otter, beaver, mink, ermine, and three different species of bats. Black bears have never made it across the ice. White-tailed deer were introduced to the island in the 1930s, but they never prospered.

Birds, however, are numerous, affording diligent birders an excellent opportunity to add to their life lists. More than 200 different species frequent Isle Royale. Look for common loons on the lake and bald eagles and ospreys perching on large snags. Shorebirds, such as spotted sandpipers and greater yellowlegs, are common during spring and fall, and the bogs and thickets harbor many migrating

neotropical songbirds. Sharp-tailed grouse may also be here, although the lack of recent sightings has led to the assumption that they have disappeared from the island. Diving ducks, such as the ruddy duck and lesser scaup, are often seen on Lake Superior or the island's interior lakes and ponds during the spring and summer.

The greatest difficulty involved in visiting Isle Royale is simply getting there. It is, after all, a remote island located in the continent's largest lake. By ferry the trip can take nearly seven hours; seaplane takes only 30 minutes but costs considerably more. Whatever mode of transportation you choose, be aware that changeable weather can make schedules unreliable, and visitors sometimes have to hold over for a few days under inclement conditions. The island is accessible only from mid-April through October.

Once on the island, plan to spend at least four days to unwind and fully appreciate its subtle beauties. A 165-mile network of trails covers the 45-mile length of the island, providing chances for good wildlife sightings all along the way. There are a number of developed campgrounds and there is also a rustic lodge for those who prefer to enjoy their wilderness experiences in conjunction with some creature comforts.

THE FACTS

Noteworthy Animals: Eastern timber wolf, moose, ermine, mink, river otter, common loon, bald eagle, osprey.

Getting There: Isle Royale is accessible by ferry or seaplane; no cars permitted on the island. Round-trip ferry tickets cost $60-$92; reservations recommended. Ferries: *Ranger* (6.5 hours; Houghton, Michigan, 906-482-0984); *Isle Royale Queen III* (4.5 hours; Copper Harbor, Michigan, 906-289-4437 in summer; 906-482-4950 in winter); *Voyager II* and *Wenonah* (2.5 hours; depart Grand Portage, Minnesota; office in Superior, Wisconsin, 715-392-2100). Round-trip seaplane fares run about $200; reservations required. Seaplane: Isle Royale Seaplane Service (30 to 40 minutes; Houghton, 906-482-8850 in summer; P.O. Box 371, Houghton, MI 49931, in winter).

Open: Daily, 24 hours, mid-April through October.

Best Times to Visit: Mid-April through October.

Visitor Information: Isle Royale National Park, Houghton Visitor Center (906-482-0984), open Monday through Friday, 8 a.m.-4:30 p.m., year-round.

Entrance Fees: None.

Disabled Access: None.

Camping: Primitive camping sites with shelters; permit required; $4 per person per day, children under 12 free; reservations required for groups.

Accommodations: Rock Harbor Lodge (906-337-4993 mid-May through September; 502-773-2191 from October through mid-May) is the only lodging on the island: Main building (60 rooms; meals included; about $250 per night, double occupancy) or ten cabins (kitchenettes; meals not included; $150 per night, double occupancy).

Bluestem Prairie Scientific and Natural Area

A chance to witness the courtship dance of the greater prairie-chicken is the main draw at this restored grassland.

SITE 45 If any bird was common on the Great Plains a century ago, it was the greater prairie-chicken. These large grouse provided many a meal for hungry pioneers and Native Americans alike. Chickenlike in appearance, with grayish barred feathers and a mild manner, this species was best known for the distinctive booming calls of the males during the mating season. Their numbers plummeted during the early decades of the 20th century, primarily as a result of mechanized agriculture, which stripped the land of cover. Today the greater prairie-chicken thrives only in those areas where ample native cover still exists.

The 3,258-acre Bluestem Prairie Scientific and Natural Area is just such a place. Here the native northern tallgrass prairie hasn't merely hung on because of benign neglect—it has been actively augmented and restored through reseeding, controlled burns, and removal of invasive nonnative plants. A cooperative project of the Nature Conservancy and the Minnesota Department of Natural Resources, the natural area enjoys tremendous regional support.

Small wonder, then, that it is one of the best places on earth to see the greater prairie-chicken in all its strutting splendor. Each dawn throughout much of the spring, at least 40 cocks display their long black neck plumes and bright yellow air sacs as they per-

form intricate dances on ancient courtship grounds, called leks. Their booming calls resound across the prairie, attracting the drab-colored hens, who apparently make their choice of mates based on the male's dance. The staff maintains a number of blinds at the leks, providing bird buffs and photographers unparalleled

opportunities for capturing arresting images of these courtship rites.

Several other rare prairie birds nest at Bluestem. To locate loggerhead shrikes look for small rodents or grasshoppers impaled on thorns or barbed wire—thrifty predators, the shrikes cache excess food when the hunting is good. Upland sandpipers (one of the nation's largest sandpipers) brood at the preserve; occasionally Henslow's sparrows do, too.

In total, about 70 species of birds have been recorded here. Other commonly observed birds include aquatic species such as marbled godwit, sandhill crane, and common snipe. Look for them in the spring. The cranes are merely stopping over on their way to their breeding grounds in Canada; the godwits and snipes will nest.

Watch for birds of prey soaring high above the prairie. Red-tailed and rough-legged hawks can be sometimes seen pouncing on rodents. American kestrels and Swainson's hawks are

In an effort to attract females, a male prairie-chicken inflates its brightly colored air sacs.

THE FACTS

Noteworthy Animals: Greater prairie-chicken, loggerhead shrike, marbled godwit, upland sandpiper, Dakota skipper, Poweshiek skipperling, regal fritillary.

Getting There: From Moorhead, drive east about 14 miles on US 10 to the intersection with Minn. 9. Go south for 1.5 miles, and then turn east on an unnumbered gravel road (follow the signs) and drive 1.5 miles to the parking lot.

Open: Daily, dawn to dusk, year-round.

Best Times to Visit: March through May; July and August.

Visitor Information: The Nature Conservancy of Minnesota, Minneapolis office (612-331-0750). Northern Tallgrass Prairie Ecoregion Office, Glyndon (218-498-2679). Both open Monday through Friday, 8:30 a.m.-4:30 p.m., year-round. No on-site visitor center.

Entrance Fees: None.

Disabled Access: None.

Camping: None on-site. Developed campsites available at adjacent Buffalo River State Park (218-498-2124).

more commonly observed chasing grasshoppers, one of their favorite foods. Great horned and short-eared owls are also resident; look for them at dusk, when they become active. Other commonly observed birds include common nighthawk, horned lark, western meadowlark, eastern and western kingbirds, rose-breasted grosbeak, indigo bunting, dickcissel, and grasshopper, vesper, and lark sparrows.

The coyote, the hardy little "song dog" that has prospered throughout the continent despite the unrelenting ire of ranchers and farmers, makes its home here. Other mammals representative of the wild northern prairie that are found at Bluestem include the badger, red fox, striped skunk, long-tailed weasel, white-tailed deer, plains pocket mouse, northern grasshopper mouse, and prairie vole. They all are most active at dawn and dusk.

Some of the natural area's most noteworthy species are also the most ephemeral: butterflies. Three extremely rare butterflies are found at Bluestem—the Dakota skipper, Poweshiek skipperling, and regal fritillary. Skippers and skipperlings are relatively dowdy, but fritillaries are lovely orange and silvery butterflies with dark filigreed markings. They can survive only in environs that support flowering herbaceous plants endemic to the northern prairies. Look for them from late spring through summer.

Spring is the best time to see the natural area. Not only is the deep freeze of winter past, but spring is when the prairie-chickens dance. Reservations are necessary for the blinds; call for details. In high summer the prairie is in full flower, and the butterflies are in full force. Restoration programs are ongoing, and volunteers are welcome. Tasks include everything from counting prairie-chickens to removing nonnative plants.

The wide-open aspect of the prairie makes hiking easy. Combine a visit with an exploration of Buffalo River State Park, which comprises the natural area's northern border. At roughly half the size of the natural area, the park contains a sizable component of tallgrass prairie as well as some excellent riparian habitat.

Sandy Island Eagle Sanctuary

In the cold winter months, bald eagles fish along these Missouri
River dams and perform their intricate courting rituals in the sky.

SITE 46 What do Missouri and
Alaska have in common?
Bald eagles, for one thing.
Alaska's spectacular concentrations of
our national bird are well known, but
the Show Me State's populations are
almost as impressive and have gone
largely unsung.

More than 2,000 bald eagles over-
wintered in Missouri in 1996—
double the number in 1986. That
makes Missouri second only to

Washington State in the number of
overwintering balds in the lower 48
states. At least 13 pairs of eagles now
nest in the state, the highest number
in five decades.

This is not mere happenstance.
In the 1980s federal and state officials
released 74 young bald eagles taken
from nests in the Gulf states in hopes
of reestablishing a nesting population
in Missouri. Simultaneously, they
made efforts to improve winter

The bald eagle, America's national bird, has recently rebounded from near extinction.

habitat along the state's waterways.

Human engineering has helped Missouri's eagles in another way. Bald eagles love fish—preferably dead fish that they can scavenge. Dams along the Mississippi River have functioned as veritable supermarkets for the big raptors. Fish that are swept over the dams are stunned or killed outright in the tailwaters, making for easy pickings. The 30 miles of river course between Lock and Dam 24 and Lock and Dam 25 (Lock 24 is about 40 miles north of St. Louis) are particularly productive grounds for eagles and for eagle-watchers. From December through February, several hundred eagles forage here, putting on weight to sustain them for their journey to the Gulf states, where they breed.

The best place to see the eagles along this stretch of the river is a large two-level platform constructed next to the Sandy Island Eagle Sanctuary at Lock and Dam 25. As many as 200 eagles may be seen roosting in the cottonwoods overlooking the dam's tailwaters. Bring a camera, plenty of film, and enough patience to spend a day or more waiting for the right shot. The platform is one of the very best places in North America to capture close-up images of feeding eagles, and many top wildlife photographers have logged time here.

In late February the eagles begin their courting displays preparatory to breeding. The aerial acrobatics can be spectacular—birds locking talons with each other and tumbling end over end as they plummet toward the earth—followed by spirited games of tag involving the passing of sticks from one eagle to another. These displays can often be seen even without the aid of binoculars.

Bundle up, because the viewing is often best when the weather is coldest. Ice-ups can affect large portions of the Mississippi during cold spells, but the tailwaters usually stay open, drawing eagles from miles around.

An adjacent slough also offers the opportunity for some excellent waterfowl viewing. Hundreds of ducks pile in here during the winter migration, especially mallards, the drakes gorgeous in their vibrant winter plumage and bright orange feet. Other species seen on the winter flight south include gadwall, northern pintail, blue-winged teal, and green-winged teal.

Lillian Annette Rowe Sanctuary

Whooping cranes and shorebirds come to rest and feed along the banks of the Platte River, restored by this Nebraska refuge.

SITE 47 Prior to the 20th century, the Platte River was a changeable beast. It raged in the late winter and spring, swollen with rain and snowmelt. By summer's end it diminished to a wide, shallow stream. The bed the Platte carved out of the prairie was broad and barren, providing optimum habitat for vast numbers of migratory aquatic birds—most notably sandhill and whooping cranes—which enjoyed the vast expanses of secure territory for resting and congregating.

But by the 1930s, several dams had been built along the Platte River, mitigating the river's great variations. With a steady course of water flowing down the system, the river channel narrowed, and forests of cottonwood, cedar, and mulberry took root on the formerly bare gravel and sand flats. With this loss of crucial staging territory—combined with the continental loss of wetlands—the cranes' fortunes plummeted.

Thanks to a number of ambitious habitat restoration programs in recent decades, however, the cranes have rallied; their continental population now stands at about 600,000. Of all the programs associated with their resurgence, none is more significant than the Lillian Annette Rowe Sanctuary. Comprising 1,150 acres owned by the National Audubon Society and an adjacent 450 acres of privately owned land managed for wildlife habitat through conservation easements, the sanctuary extends along 5 miles of the Platte River and supports up to 60,000 cranes during the peak of the spring migration.

Preserve managers have recreated the historic Platte barrens by removing riparian growth from the riverbed through fire and mechanical means. This intensively groomed expanse of river bottom gives cranes and migrating waterfowl a safe place to rest and, incidentally, provides nature lovers with an opportunity to observe one of the greatest migratory bird stagings on the continent.

The spring migration lasts from mid-February to mid-April, peaking in mid-March. During the peak time it's possible to see 2,000 or 3,000 cranes foraging in one of the many cornfields that neighbor the preserve. That's impressive enough, certainly. But even more dramatic are the dawn flights, when the cranes leave the preserve en masse to fly to their feeding grounds. At this time more than 30,000 airborne sandhills may be seen—and heard—simultaneously. The entire vault of the broad plains sky is alive with the huge but graceful birds, and their soft, throaty chortles combine into an awesome crescendo.

The spring also brings an influx of shorebirds as they journey to their breeding grounds in the northern Midwest and Canada. Among the diverse spring visitors are American avocet, willet, spotted sandpiper, upland sandpiper, and common snipe.

During the fall, ducks and geese on their way south pass through the sanctuary in significant numbers. Greater white-fronted geese and Canada geese sometimes gather in the tens of thousands. Other species that pass through at this time are green-winged and blue-winged teal, mallard, northern pintail, northern shoveler, gadwall, American wigeon, lesser scaup, and common merganser.

Raptors also benefit from the sanctuary. Numerous bald eagles are present from November through March; prairie falcons and peregrine falcons are relatively common. Swainson's and red-tailed hawks, northern harriers, American kestrels, and short-eared owls may be seen on their hunting flights over the river flats or the adjacent prairie. Sharp-shinned hawks and Cooper's hawks favor the riverine forest adjacent to the refuge, while great horned owls and eastern screech-owls haunt the trees.

The development of woodlands along the Platte has not been completely negative for wildlife, of course. Some species have benefited from the change, most notably migratory songbirds. Wood warblers—yellow, yellow-rumped, and orange-crowned warblers and common yellowthroat—are quite abundant. Look for flycatchers—willow and least flycatchers and western and eastern kingbirds—along stands of brush near the river channel. Other commonly observed songbirds include horned lark, indigo bunting, rufous-sided towhee, dickcissel, lark bunting, bobolink, western meadow-

Even at a distance, you can tell an American avocet by its bill and long legs.

THE FACTS

Noteworthy Animals: Sandhill crane, whooping crane, greater white-fronted goose, Canada goose, northern pintail, bald eagle, great horned owl, American avocet, dickcissel.

Getting There: Access is through private properties, and permission to enter the sanctuary is required; call in advance for instructions. From Kearney, take I-80 east about 15 miles to the Gibbon exit. Following the signs to the refuge, go 2 miles south and then 2 miles west on Elm Island Road.

Open: Daily, dawn to dusk, year-round.

Best Times to Visit: January through May; mid-March through mid-April for cranes.

Visitor Information: Lillian Annette Rowe Sanctuary office (308-468-5282) open Monday through Friday, 9 a.m.-5 p.m.; open daily, 8 a.m.-6 p.m., in March. During crane season, reservations required for viewing blinds.

Entrance Fees: None.

Disabled Access: The viewing blind is wheelchair accessible.

Camping: None on-site.

---

lark, and red-winged and yellow-headed blackbirds. Many sparrow species—American tree, chipping, vesper, lark, savannah, grasshopper, and song sparrows—may be observed foraging in the coverts and grasslands.

County and state roads that front the refuge provide surprisingly good viewing of the cranes and other waterfowl. There's also a fine viewing blind, and preserve managers have recently opened a trail that traverses all the river's major habitats.

Niobrara Valley Preserve

Pronghorn and mule deer roam freely in the diverse
habitat provided by this sanctuary on the Great Plains.

SITE 48 Pure stands of short-grass and tallgrass prairie are not the only Great Plains habitats that have greatly diminished over the decades. Transition zones—those areas where woodlands meet the prairie, creating a diversity of habitats that support a wide variety of species—have met the same fate. The 55,000-acre Niobrara Valley Preserve in Nebraska's remote Sand Hills country is one of the best remaining examples of such mixed grass-woodland ecosystems.

Administered by the Nature Conservancy of Nebraska, the preserve is located along the Niobrara River, one of the last free-flowing rivers on the Great Plains.

Here extensive riparian forests meet expansive grasslands. The woodlands comprise a unique combination of western and eastern species. Along the

Their large size, high antlers, and prominent black tails make mule deer relatively easy to spot.

river the ponderosa pine of the West grows next to the basswood and burr oak of the East. The Springbranch Canyon area, with groves of aspen and paper birch, is more typical of northern boreal forests.

Most of the major animal species associated with the Great Plains are thriving at Niobrara, a result of the preserve's isolation and the richness of the varied habitats. Pronghorn crop the prairie, stopping periodically to gaze about for possible sources of danger. Both mule deer (the classic deer of the West) and white-tailed deer (typically associated with the farmlands and second-growth forests of the East) are found here. Wildlife popula-

tions are always in flux, and it appears that the whitetails are gaining the upper hand on the "mulies," at least for now. Both species are frequently spotted by visitors.

Beavers are common along the Niobrara River and are most often seen at dawn. Coyotes and white-tailed jackrabbits are plentiful, although they move pretty fast and may disappear before you have had a chance to figure out what you glimpsed.

Black-tailed prairie dogs are here, as are two attendant species: badgers, which prey voraciously on the little rodents, and burrowing owls, a rare long-legged bird of prey that favors abandoned prairie dog burrows as domiciles. Quiet observation of a prairie dog colony—possible only from a distance with the aid of binoculars—may result in sightings of either or both species.

In addition to burrowing owls, other raptors frequent the preserve. Look for golden eagles, Swainson's hawks (in the spring), red-tailed, ferruginous, and rough-legged hawks, American kestrels, merlins, northern harriers, and great horned owls.

Two big gallinaceous birds are dramatically apparent on the preserve: the wild turkey and the ring-necked pheasant. The tom turkeys noisily challenge one another in the spring. Blinds are set up to give visitors a better chance of seeing them perform their courtship rituals of strutting in front of the hens, rattling their feathers, and puffing up their wattles. The calls of cock pheasants are heard throughout the preserve, especially from brushy coverts. They have a disconcerting habit of launching themselves

THE FACTS

Noteworthy Animals: Pronghorn, mule deer, badger, black-tailed prairie dog, burrowing owl, golden eagle, ferruginous hawk, rose-breasted grosbeak, chestnut-collared longspur, wild turkey.

Getting There: From Omaha, take US 275 northwest about 160 miles, connecting with US 20 near Ewing. Drive another 90 miles to Johnstown, then proceed 16 miles north on the county road toward Norden to the preserve. From North Platte, about 140 miles to the south, take US 83 north, connecting with US 20 near Valentine. Follow US 20 east to Johnstown and continue as above. Call ahead to check on road conditions.

Open: Daily, dawn to dusk, year-round.

Best Times to Visit: April through October.

Visitor Information: The Nature Conservancy of Nebraska, Omaha office (402-342-0282), open Monday through Friday, 9 a.m.-5 p.m., year-round. Niobrara Valley Preserve Outreach Center (402-722-4440) open Monday through Friday, 8 a.m.-5 p.m., year-round; not always staffed, call ahead. On-site Visitor Center open in summer only.

Entrance Fees: None.

Disabled Access: Visitor Center is fully accessible.

Camping: None on-site.

northern oriole, rufous-sided towhee, lazuli bunting, common yellowthroat, yellow warbler, loggerhead shrike, eastern bluebird, horned lark, and eastern kingbird. Sparrow species include clay-colored, chipping, and field.

During the fall and spring migrations, black-bellied plover, spotted sandpipers, willet, Wilson's phalaropes, and lesser yellowlegs may be seen along the river's sandbars. Like most shorebirds, they are wary and best observed with binoculars. The vibrant yellow color of the lesser yellowlegs' limbs stands out markedly from a distance, making identification easy.

Niobrara features two hiking trails, each about 2 miles long and each with good opportunities for seeing most resident species. While the hiking is easy at Niobrara, the same can't be said for getting there. Although the road connecting US 20 to the preserve can be traversed by a car with two-wheel-drive (preferably one with good shocks and high clearance), it turns into a quagmire when wet and becomes impassable to any and all motorized vehicles. Call ahead to make sure the road is open.

A herd of 300 bison roams a 7,000-acre quadrant of the preserve that is not open to the public. The Nature Conservancy will soon establish a second herd made up of animals from another region to assure a wider genetic base. Bison can be observed, however, by taking the drive-through route at Fort Niobrara National Wildlife Refuge (about 30 miles away). Fort Niobrara also offers the chance to see Texas longhorn cattle, a living legacy from the cattle drives of the Old West.

skyward just as hikers are about to stumble on them.

Look for the chestnut-collared longspur, a sparrow-like bird of the plains that sports a beautiful chestnut brown nape. Other songbirds include rose-breasted and black-headed grosbeaks,

Cross Ranch Nature Preserve

Resident bison graze this North Dakota prairie, a nesting spot for rare and threatened birds, including Baird's sparrow and piping plover.

SITE 49 Cross Ranch is a 6,000-acre preserve that contains some of the best preserved rolling prairie and floodplain woodland left in the Midwest. That's impressive in its own right. But what's even more remarkable about this lovely preserve is the way it has been enhanced and maintained: with bison and fire.

Before settlement the prairie remained the prairie in large part because fire burned across it regularly and because millions of bison grazed the resulting new growth intensively. Both phenomena encouraged the proliferation of native bunchgrasses. At the present time about 80 bison graze at Cross Ranch. The administering agency, the Nature Conservancy of the Dakotas, plans to expand the herd to 200 animals, the sustainable maximum. Conservancy staffers also set fires in the spring and fall to burn off the old grass, thereby returning critical nutrients to the soil in the form of ash.

The high grass of Cross Ranch offers cover and food for white-tailed jackrabbits.

The Nature Conservancy preserve lies along the Missouri River and contains one of the finest stretches of riparian forest in the Great Plains. Cross Ranch State Park, adjacent to the preserve, extends the habitat by 500 acres. About 6 miles of river frontage are forested, primarily in cottonwood. The combination of high-quality grassland and woodland cover has translated into burgeoning wildlife populations. In addition to the bison, visitors can expect to see white-tailed deer, mule deer, coyotes, raccoons, striped skunks, red foxes, and white-tailed jackrabbits. Beavers and badgers are also common, and pronghorn and bobcats move through the preserve regularly.

THE FACTS

Noteworthy Animals: Bison, mule deer, white-tailed jackrabbit, burrowing owl, bald eagle, Baird's sparrow, Sprague's pipit, least tern, piping plover.

Getting There: From Bismarck, take I-94 west for about 12 miles to Mandan and then connect to N. Dak. 25 north. Stay on N. Dak. 25 for 30 miles and follow the signs for Cross Ranch.

Open: Daily, 24 hours, year-round.

Best Times to Visit: Year-round.

Visitor Information: The Nature Conservancy of the Dakotas, Fargo office (701-293-5343), open Monday through Friday, 9 a.m.-5 p.m., year-round. Cross Ranch State Park Visitor Center (701-794-3731) open daily in summer.

Outfitters: Canoes or kayaks are for rent at the Lewis and Clark Cafe (701-462-3668) in Washburn.

Entrance Fees: $3 per vehicle.

Disabled Access: Visitor Center and many trails are wheelchair accessible.

Camping: Developed campsites at state park; fees; reservations required only on Labor Day weekend.

Several reptiles, including bullsnakes, common snapping turtles, and painted turtles, are well distributed throughout the prairie.

Two rare birds endemic to prairie ecosystems, Baird's sparrow and Sprague's pipit, nest here. Federally endangered least terns and threatened piping plover nest on sandbars in the Missouri. This is also the haunt of the northern shrike, a predacious bird that looks somewhat like a mockingbird. The shrike impales its prey (grasshoppers, rodents, or small birds) on thorns or barbed wire for later consumption. Common summer songbirds include bobolink, sage thrasher, mountain bluebird, yellow warbler, warbling and red-eyed vireos, American redstart, common yellowthroat, lazuli bunting, vesper sparrow, lark bunting, and chestnut-collared longspur.

During the spring a variety of aquatic birds may be seen at the refuge. One of the most conspicuous is the long-billed curlew, a large brownish shorebird with an exceedingly long down-curved bill. Other species include the white pelican, double-crested cormorant, sandhill crane, marbled godwit, willet, American avocet, spotted sandpiper, upland sandpiper, short-billed dowitcher, killdeer, common snipe, mallard, northern pintail, green-winged teal, blue-winged teal, northern shoveler, and redhead.

Birds of prey that might be seen include burrowing owl, bald eagle, northern harrier, red-tailed hawk, American kestrel, and merlin.

Fourteen miles of trails run through the woodlands and prairie of Cross Ranch. None of the routes are strenuous, and visitors don't necessarily have to stick to the trails; overland hiking is easy. Winter visitors can take advantage of well-maintained cross-country ski trails. Don't enter the fenced-in areas of the bison pasture; the animals are unpredictable and dangerous. It's also possible to boat or canoe on the Missouri River. Launch boats at the town of Washburn, about 3 miles upriver from the preserve.

One final note: Cross Ranch is the site of numerous ongoing wildlife studies. Plastic flags and colored markers are used to indicate areas employed in such research and should not be disturbed.

Edward M. Brigham III
Alkali Lake Sanctuary

This accessible North Dakota preserve is one of the best places in the country to see the mating dance of the sharp-tailed grouse.

SITE 50 A century ago the Great Plains were characterized by endless expanses of native grass. The magnificent sameness of the landscape was the essence of its grandeur. But there were little anomalies on the prairie, places where geography and water conspired to create different habitats. Here the wildlife was—and is—particularly abundant.

The National Audubon Society's Edward M. Brigham III Alkali Lake Sanctuary is one such place: a 500-acre permanent lake surrounded by 1,850 acres of upland. The habitats run the gamut from open water to seasonal marsh and mudflats, from native prairie to riparian woodland.

The preserve's name notwithstanding, the lake is not truly alkaline—it's brackish. Water that is neither totally fresh nor totally salty is agreeable to a wide range of planktonic species, forming the basis for a rich food web that supports everything from minute crustaceans to migratory waterfowl. Thousands and thousands of waterfowl, to be more accurate. During the peak of the fall migration in November and December, as many as 10,000 giant Canada geese (the largest of the numerous Canada races), 15,000 snow geese, 20,000 ducks of various species, and several hundred tundra swans may crowd into the refuge, cacophonously competing for food and space.

The refuge also counts about 70 potholes within its borders. These are the small evanescent ponds and lakes of the upper plains that are favored brood areas for the continent's ducks. During good precipitation years several hundred nestlings fledge at the preserve; species include mallard, gadwall, blue-winged and green-winged teal, northern pintail, northern shoveler, redhead, and canvasback. Mother ducks, fledglings in tow, are commonly seen paddling about the potholes or foraging at the water's edge.

The preserve is also critical foraging habitat for white pelicans. They fly in daily from Chase Lake (about 50 miles to the west), the nation's largest nesting colony for this species. In the spring Alkali Lake swarms with tiger salamanders, protein-rich creatures that are a favorite food of pelicans, young and old. The adult pelicans fill their crops with the abundant amphibians, partially digest them, then fly back to their nests to feed them to their young. Without Alkali Lake and its salamanders, pelican populations at Chase Lake would crash.

The prairie portions of the preserve also serve as essential brood habitat. Upland sandpipers, one of the nation's largest sandpipers and a species significantly depleted by modern agricultural practices, breed in the grassland areas. Other nesting shorebirds include American avocet, spotted sandpiper, willet, and Wilson's phalarope. Several other species of shorebirds visit during the spring and

Mallards mate before the fall migration, when the pairs head for the female's birthplace.

fall migrations, most notably the rare golden plover. Also look for pectoral sandpiper and western sandpiper.

Brigham is also one of the best sites in the country for viewing sharp-tailed grouse. A long-established lek is located within the preserve, and in the spring up to 30 males compete there for the attention of the females. The birds dance at dawn, and care must be taken to avoid disturbing them. Ask at preserve headquarters for details.

This is also an excellent place to observe raptors. In the winter bald eagles often haunt the waterfowl staging areas, picking off the weak and the ill. Swainson's hawks are very common, as are red-tailed hawks. Look for both species perched on fence posts and telephone poles or soaring on the thermals, scanning the ground for prey. Other commonly noted species include ferruginous, rough-legged, Cooper's, and sharp-shinned hawks, northern harrier, American kestrel, and the occasional prairie falcon.

Though not the primary reason for

a visit, several mammal species are common, most notably white-tailed deer, beaver, muskrat, mink, coyote, red fox, raccoon, and striped skunk. All are apt to be seen around the margins of the lake.

The northern leopard frog is another noteworthy species. Declining over much of its range, this lovely spotted frog is more than holding its own here. Chorus frogs are also common. Reptiles include the plains garter snake, smooth green snake, and painted turtle. The turtles are often seen around road margins in spring, laying their eggs in the soft loam.

Some of the preserve's most interesting attractions are archaeological. There are several well-worn tepee rings on high ground; the tribes favored such overlooks because they were exposed to the wind (which kept mosquitoes to a minimum) and because the vantage allowed them to survey the plains for game or enemies. There are also two "rubbing rocks," large boulders that have been polished smooth over the millennia by bison seeking to relieve the itch of their irritated hides. The ground immediately around the boulders has been pounded 2 to 3 feet below the surrounding prairie by the hooves of successive generations of bison crowding to scratch themselves.

Although the preserve is open year-round, the climate is extreme and

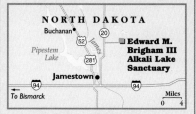
variable. Winter temperatures often fall below zero for extended periods of time, and summer temperatures can exceed 100°F. Spring and autumn are the most pleasant seasons for a visit. Access to the preserve is excellent. Several roads transect it, allowing visitors to view wildlife without leaving the car. For those inclined to hoof it, cross-country hiking is easy. Preserve managers maintain photography blinds at the sharp-tailed grouse leks and at the lake during the appropriate seasons. Horseback riding is also permitted, but you have to bring your own mount.

Little Missouri National Grassland and Theodore Roosevelt National Park

These adjacent parks on the Great Plains provide homes for wildlife of all sizes, from bison to black-tailed prairie dogs.

SITE 51 The two units of Theodore Roosevelt National Park are enfolded by the Little Missouri National Grassland. So while two different agencies oversee these holdings—the National Park Service administers the park, and the U.S. Forest Service handles the grasslands—from an ecological point of view, they constitute a single parcel. And a vast chunk of wildland it is: well over a million acres in all. There is, obviously, much to see—entire weeks can be spent here profitably.

The terrain is characterized by many different habitats, including open prairie, riparian woodlands and breaks, wooded draws, and rugged badlands. It can be explored either by foot or by car; a combination of both is ideal. The Little Missouri National Grassland has established a 58-mile round-trip auto tour that begins and ends in Medora. Posted signs and overlooks identify ten sites that offer a wide range of wildlife-watching opportunities, including golden eagle nests, sharp-tailed grouse dancing grounds, and black-tailed prairie dog towns. Get out and hike wherever the country looks promising.

Bison have been reintroduced in Theodore Roosevelt National Park and are doing exceedingly well. The two herds—one in the North Unit, one in the South Unit—have about 300 animals each. Finding them in the vast landscape can be a bit of a challenge but makes the final reward all the more exciting. The Visitor Center in Medora provides up-to-date information on the latest known locations of the herds.

Bighorn sheep have also been introduced and seem to be holding

their own. (Mortality has been high, but sheep populations often fluctuate wildly.) The herd on the Moody Plateau (in the southern portion of the grasslands) seems to be doing particularly well; individuals can usually be seen from East River Road, which leads south from Medora. Historically, this region was populated by the Audubon bighorn, a subspecies once common along the breaks of the

Missouri and Little Missouri Rivers. The last individual of that species in this area was shot in 1905 near the mouth of Magpie Creek in McKenzie County. Today's bighorns are descendants of the California subspecies, transplanted from British Columbia.

Three other prairie-associated ungulates—pronghorn, mule deer, and white-tailed deer—are quite numerous and very likely to be seen on any

Bison herds roam freely in the vast landscape of Theodore Roosevelt National Park.

THE FACTS

Noteworthy Animals: Bison, bighorn sheep, pronghorn, mule deer, white-tailed deer, black-tailed prairie dog, badger, white-tailed jackrabbit, coyote, sharp-tailed grouse, golden eagle.

Getting There: From Bismark, take I-94 west 135 miles, through Little Missouri National Grassland, to Theodore Roosevelt National Park Headquarters in Medora.
Open: Daily, dawn to dusk, year-round.
Best Times to Visit: May through September.
Visitor Information: Little Missouri National Grassland: U.S. Forest Service, Dickinson (701-225-5151); no on-site visitor center. Theodore Roosevelt National Park Visitor Center in Medora (701-623-4466) open daily, 8 a.m.-8 p.m., in summer; until 4 p.m. the remainder of the year. Satellite Visitor Centers in Painted Canyon (7 miles east of Medora) and in the North Unit (15 miles south of Watford City).
Entrance Fees: Little Missouri NG: None. Theodore Roosevelt NP: $5 per person, with a maximum of $10 per carload, good for 7 days.
Disabled Access: Visitor Centers, some trails, and campgrounds are wheelchair accessible.
Camping: Little Missouri NG: Primitive camping; no permit or fees. Theodore Roosevelt NP: Developed campgrounds; fees; no reservations.

given drive or hike. White-tailed jackrabbits, least chipmunks, and porcupines are also commonly seen. Wild horses and elk are occasionally sighted in the South Unit of Theodore Roosevelt National Park.

Birds, most notably gallinaceous species, are abundant. Three introduced species, ring-necked pheasant, gray partridge, and wild turkey, are the most populous. Sharp-tailed grouse, native birds that are rare across most of their range, are fairly common here. During their mating season, which runs from late March to mid-May, the birds occupy several dancing grounds, or leks. The sight of sharptails dancing in the breaking dawn is a memory every nature lover will cherish.

Black-tailed prairie dogs—once ubiquitous throughout the plains but now greatly reduced in range—maintain several towns throughout the region. In addition to the little rodents themselves, some other animals may be observed around the towns. Coyotes, badgers, and long-tailed weasels hunt the prairie dogs, while burrowing owls, prairie rattlesnakes, and cottontails use their burrows for homes.

Local raptors include golden eagles, northern harriers, turkey vultures, merlins, and American kestrels. Rare sightings of prairie falcons also have been reported.

From early spring through summer, look for long-billed curlews, black-billed magpies, northern flickers, red-headed woodpeckers, rufous-sided towhees, mountain bluebirds, meadowlarks, horned larks, and black-capped chickadees.

The best times to view wildlife are early in the morning and late in the afternoon, extending into dusk. Whenever you visit, be prepared for inclement weather. On the plains temperatures tend toward extremes. The mercury often drops well below zero in the winter and rises above 100°F in the summer.

Wayne National Forest

White-tailed deer, red foxes, and woodchucks are among the diverse residents of this expanding forest in southeastern Ohio.

SITE 52 Wayne National Forest currently comprises 227,053 acres of forest distributed in three units across southeastern Ohio. The U.S. Forest Service is actively expanding Wayne, acquiring and reforesting abandoned strip mines and eroded farmlands throughout southeastern Ohio. Investments are also being made in restoring marshlands, stabilizing stream banks, and replanting native grasses.

Like all nonwilderness-designated national forest lands, Wayne is predicated on the multiple-use concept. In fact, hunting and off-road vehicle activities are the top two draws; logging and grazing take place, too. It's a tribute to Wayne that it is able to sustain these activities yet still provide the best wildlife-viewing in the state.

One of the finest places to explore is the Wildcat Hollow backpack trail (near Corning, in the Athens Unit). This trail skirts stream bottoms, open meadows and ridgetops, pine plantations, and rock outcroppings. At 15 miles in length, it's ideal for a weekend trip. The North Country Trail (in the Marietta Unit) offers more of a wilderness experience. Its 41 miles lead through rolling hills, along streams, and over a natural bridge. Depending on the season, it's possible to traverse a good bit of it in relative solitude.

Mammals that might be spotted include white-tailed deer, eastern cottontail, least weasel, ermine, mink, raccoon, opossum, striped skunk, and woodchuck. River otters, beavers, and muskrats are more likely to be seen in streams or along the Ohio River. Gray, fox, and southern flying squirrels are commonly seen scurrying throughout the forest. Although red foxes and coyotes are known to inhabit the area, sightings are rare.

There are a number of good horse trails as well (bring your own horse). In the Marietta Unit, the 22-mile Stone Church Horse Trail is one of the most popular rides. The Ironton Unit has Vesuvius Horse Trail, which traverses 46 miles, eventually connecting to the neighboring Dean State Forest.

Extensive woodlands interspersed with meadows and farmlands make Wayne some of the best songbird country in the Midwest. The cerulean warbler, which is declining in population nationally, is abundant here. Other common warblers include the yellow

A woodchuck, or groundhog, will never travel far from the security of its den.

chat, northern cardinal, rufous-sided towhee, eastern kingbird, and blue-gray gnatcatcher.

Raptors generally have not fared well in Ohio, where centuries of intensive agriculture, industry, and mining have decimated their habitat. But birds of prey are still holding their own in Wayne, as a result of the abundant cover and a steady supply of meadow voles and southern bog lemmings. Look for American kestrels and red-tailed hawks. Sharp-shinned and Cooper's hawks are almost identical in markings and coloration, with gray backs, reddish breasts, and banded tails. The sharp-shinned hawks, however, are considerably smaller. Barred owls, great horned owls, and turkey vultures are fairly common.

The largest and most visually dramatic bird in the forest is the wild turkey, which is thriving. Listen for their distinctive gobbles during the spring mating season. When hiking, look for them skulking through the underbrush. They will run if pressed, sometimes flushing with a great thrumming of the pinions.

Unlike most of Ohio, Wayne is quite rich in reptiles. Snakes include copperhead, rat snake, and milk snake. Turtles are found along ponds, creeks, and the Ohio River; species include common snapping, box, map, painted, spiny softshell, and smooth softshell.

As national forests go, Wayne is by no means the most spectacular. There are no pristine alpine vistas, no vast wildernesses inhabited by rare animals. Wayne is a reclaimed forest—a wildland wrested back from agriculture and industry. That alone makes it a national treasure.

warbler, a handsome golden bird with russet streaks on its breast, and the American redstart, a lovely variegated orange-and-black songbird. Other species include the eastern bluebird, common yellowthroat, yellow-breasted

Arkansas River Least Tern Preserve

In the heart of downtown Tulsa, Oklahoma, colonies of endangered least terns nest along riverine sandbars and fish for minnows.

SITE 53

Least terns have not had it easy during the past hundred years. In the 1890s they were all the vogue—or rather, their skins and feathers were. The smallest of the terns—as dramatically marked as it is dainty—the least was almost exterminated by professional hunters supplying the American millinery trade. For several years fully mounted skins were de rigueur for high-fashion ladies' hats. Luckily, protections ended this dubious practice while a few terns still survived, and the population has slowly recovered. Least terns are still endangered, however, so any site they visit is extremely significant.

And one place they visit—and even nest in—is downtown Tulsa. Unlike most terns, least terns don't require remote terrain for their nests. But they do require riverine sandbars—which the Arkansas River in and downstream from Tulsa has in abundance. About 1,400 acres of prime nesting habitat have been protected in this preserve, which stretches along 9 miles of river corridor. Approximately 143 acres are in Tulsa itself; two prime viewing sites are at 15th and 81st Streets on the east side of the river. About 40 to 50 pairs of terns brood along the preserve annually. They usually start arriving in late April and early May and leave in September with their fully fledged young for the autumn migration to South America.

Least terns are colony nesters, so

A least tern lays its eggs in unlined scrapes on gravel beaches or pebbled sandbars.

THE FACTS

Noteworthy Animals: Least tern, bald eagle, peregrine falcon, osprey, great blue heron, little blue heron.

Getting There: From I-44, take the Riverside exit to Tulsa for views of some of the best nesting sites.
Open: Daily, dawn to dusk, year-round. Terns present only in summer.
Best Times to Visit: May through August.
Visitor Information: The Nature Conservancy of Oklahoma, Tulsa office (918-585-1117), open Monday through Friday, 9 a.m.-5 p.m., year-round. No on-site visitor center.
Entrance Fees: None.
Disabled Access: A developed river walk is wheelchair accessible.
Camping: None on-site. Public campsites available at Walnut Creek State Park (918-242-3362) and Keystone State Park (918-865-4477) at Keystone Lake, about 10 miles west of Tulsa.

where you see one bird you'll probably see more. Look for them nestled along the broadest part of the sand flats adjacent to the river. Foraging adults are easy to spot, as they hover over the river before folding their wings and diving for small fish.

Like many terns, least terns are susceptible to nest destruction from flooding. For species that brood on ocean beaches, the danger is from storms or very high tides. For inland-breeding least terns, the problem is high water due to dam releases or spring snowmelt. Inopportune releases from Keystone Dam upstream from Tulsa have flooded out tern nests many times in the past, but recent negotiations between preserve managers and dam operators appear to have ameliorated the problem.

Bald eagles use the preserve as well, patrolling the river downstream in their quest for fish. About 30 eagles overwinter in the area; most leave in the spring to nest in the Gulf states. At least one pair of eagles is nesting in the area, however, and local birders are hoping that more will establish themselves as year-round residents. Ospreys and peregrine falcons also transit the preserve. Passing peregrines raise great havoc with the nesting terns, which with good reason associate the shadow of the fierce little hawk with imminent danger.

Aquatic birds that visit the preserve include ring-billed gull, herring gull, great blue heron, and little blue heron. Portions of the river support cottonwood stands, which comprise some of the better songbird habitat in the greater Tulsa metropolitan area. Possible sightings include eastern phoebe, eastern kingbird, scissor-tailed flycatcher, horned lark, house wren, cedar waxwing, summer tanager, and grasshopper sparrow.

Tulsa is at the edge of the huge Osage Indian Reservation, which offers various outdoor recreational opportunities, including wildlife viewing. Several nearby reservoirs—Keystone Lake, Oologah Lake, Lake O' The Cherokees, Fort Gibson Lake, Tenkiller Lake, and Robert S. Kerr Lake—provide good fishing and pleasure boating. An added bonus is the close proximity of the Tallgrass Prairie Preserve (see p. 169).

Tallgrass Prairie Preserve

In addition to dazzling wildflower displays, a spring visit to this huge Oklahoma preserve may yield sightings of bison and prairie-chickens.

SITE 54 The tallgrass prairie once covered more than 142 million acres, spreading out over 14 states. It was an exceptionally rich ecosystem that was capable of supporting a vast array of species. It was also the heart of the range for the continent's bison and served as the homeland of the Osage and other prominent Plains tribes.

As a functioning ecosystem, the tallgrass prairie has virtually disappeared. Only about 10 percent remains, scattered in isolated pockets around Kansas and Oklahoma. Of the remnants that survive, the Nature Conservancy's Tallgrass Prairie Preserve in Oklahoma is the largest and most significant. At 37,500 acres, it is a virtually intact microcosm of the vast plains ecosystem of old. Visit Tallgrass Prairie Preserve and you're visiting the past.

The most spectacular species, of course, is the bison. In 1993 the Conservancy stocked the preserve with 300 bison, and plans call for the herd to expand to 2,200 head by 2003. The bison currently range in an 8,600-acre area in the western section of the preserve and can easily be seen by either motorists or hikers. As the population expands, managers are removing interior fences to give the bison more room to roam; eventually the animals will be allowed to roam freely. So, as the herd grows and has access to more remote areas, it will be tougher for visitors to spot them. In short, the sooner you go, the better.

While bison consume the tallgrass, they also sustain it. The historic grazing patterns of bison—thousands or millions of animals closely cropping a specific area, fertilizing it with their dung and urine, then moving on—stimulated the native big bluestem grass, Indian grass, switchgrass, and little bluestem grass that are the basis of the ecosystem.

Since Tallgrass Prairie Preserve's bison herd isn't yet of sufficient size to graze the entire refuge, cattle are being used on a temporary basis to augment their role. The result is a prairie that is becoming increasingly like the plains of old with each passing year.

The preserve positively teems with wildlife—more than 300 species of birds and

The prairie kingsnake spends most of the day curled up in the grass or under rocks.

The bison at Tallgrass Prairie Preserve have a limited range and are easily seen by visitors.

80 species of mammals are found here. White-tailed deer, armadillos, coyotes, and woodchucks are common sights. Beavers, bobcats, and badgers are also abundant but less likely to be seen, given their secretive ways.

The prairie is also home to—what else?—prairie-chickens. During the spring breeding season, their booming calls echo throughout the preserve. Two other ground birds—northern bobwhite quail and wild turkey— are also plentiful. Tallgrass provides rich hunting for raptors; expect to see bald eagles, northern harriers, American kestrels, and rough-legged, red-tailed, and red-shouldered hawks. Great horned and short-eared owls are also common.

Songbirds are all around. Look and listen for eastern meadowlark, eastern horned lark, golden-crowned kinglet,

eastern bluebird, summer tanager, and indigo bunting. Cliff swallows and barn swallows nest here. The lucky birder may spot a loggerhead shrike, one of our rarer birds, or a scissor-tailed flycatcher.

Nonvenomous snakes, including prairie kingsnake, common kingsnake, rat snake, and rough green snake, are numerous. Venomous copperheads and rattlesnakes are also present but, like most snakes, they are retiring and will retreat given the slightest opportunity.

All seasons show a different side of the preserve, but late spring is a particularly dramatic time to visit. The prairie is covered in wildflowers, and the grass is a vibrant green. The bison calve at this time, and the prairie-chickens engage in mating dances, their calls resounding over the plain. Also, temperatures haven't yet reached the torrid zenith of summer.

Much of Tallgrass can be viewed by car, but the best way to see it is on foot. Two self-guided hiking trails provide easy access even in September, when the grasses are at their maximum height—in some places, up to 10 feet.

Buffalo Gap National Grassland

This vast area provides critical nesting habitat for many rare birds, including ferruginous hawks and burrowing owls.

The great prairie is gone. The vast inland sea of grass has disappeared. Or has it? Gradually, step-by-step, portions of the prairie are being brought back to life. Sometimes the process is undertaken by private conservancy groups, sometimes by government agencies, sometimes by cooperative efforts involving both. At Buffalo Gap National Grassland, it's the federal government that's taking the lead.

This is no little jewel-like parcel. Faced with 591,000 acres, the visitor is apt to feel small and insignificant—a sentiment that was often expressed by the first settlers to cross the plains. Much of this land was settled by pioneers, or "sodbusters," who learned that the plains were not amenable to the plow. Many homesteads were eventually abandoned, but not before the deep-rooted native bunchgrass sod was destroyed, exposing the soil to the ravages of severe wind and water erosion. Today the U.S. Forest Service is trying to rehabilitate Buffalo Gap, balancing the relatively neutral effects of controlled cattle grazing with programs to revive the living plains. This is not a wildlife refuge in the strict sense of the word. Rather, it is a multiple-use tract that includes pasturage for ranchers and recreational opportunities for outdoor enthusiasts. Badlands National Park, an additional 244,300 acres, is enfolded by the national grassland.

Buffalo Gap offers a rich diversity of habitats, from open grassland to lush riparian corridors, juniper breaks, scrub, and wooded draws. It supports many colonies, or towns, of black-tailed prairie dogs. Buffalo Gap, in fact, is one of the few areas where these small, sociable rodents are still truly numerous—a fact that makes it an ideal site for reestablishing a population of the endangered black-footed ferret. Prairie dogs are the favorite food source for the ferret, the nation's

rarest mustelid. Efforts are underway to reintroduce these beautiful black-masked little predators at Buffalo Gap's prairie dog towns. Other mammals that visitors might see include pronghorn, mule deer, white-tailed deer, swift fox, coyote, and badger.

Birdlife is particularly rich, and the careful birder will identify many rare, threatened, and endangered species. First and foremost, this is raptor country. Bald eagles and golden eagles soar the wide, empty skies, searching for prey. So do 14 types of hawks, including such rare species as pere-grine falcon, prairie falcon, ferruginous hawk, and Swainson's hawk. Turkey vultures, which live off carrion, are here. Seven species of owls are residents of or migratory visitors to the refuge, including the burrowing owl, which nests in abandoned prairie dog burrows. The grassland is also home to several gallinaceous birds, most notably sage grouse, sharp-tailed grouse, and wild turkey.

The creeks, reservoirs, ponds, and seasonal wetlands sustain a great many migrating birds. Spring brings shore-birds, such as the long-billed curlew,

The endangered black-footed ferret is the rarest mustelid in North America.

Baird's sandpiper, greater and lesser yellowlegs, Wilson's phalarope, marbled godwit, and semipalmated plover. White pelicans and double-crested cormorants also frequent Buffalo Gap then, as do seven species of gulls and terns, including Forster's tern, a black-capped tern with a gray mantle and silvery wings. Autumn is the season for waterfowl, including trumpeter swan, snow and Canada geese, lesser scaup, hooded merganser, ruddy duck, horned and western grebes, redhead, green-winged and blue-winged teal, and gadwall.

Loggerhead and northern shrikes also frequent Buffalo Gap. Summer songbirds include mountain bluebird, Say's phoebe, chestnut-collared longspur, least flycatcher, Swainson's thrush, Townsend's solitaire, warbling vireo, orange-crowned warbler, and Wilson's warbler.

Plan to spend at least a couple of days at Buffalo Gap. The Grassland is easily explored by foot, thanks to the openness of the country—but first do some driving. A few hours in a car will help with general orientation and usually results in some excellent wildlife sightings. A network of gravel and dirt roads wind through the grassland, providing easy access.

Late spring is the best time to visit: Temperatures are moderate, bird migrations are underway, and the wildflowers are in riotous bloom. More than 2,000 different species of flowering plants are found at Buffalo Gap National Grassland.

So are the fossils of long-extinct Pleistocene epoch animals that once roamed these lands. While it's permissible to take invertebrate fossils (clams, snails, and such), vertebrate fossils must be left in place. Careless collectors have despoiled a number of prime beds, so be sure to ask for advice from the staff. Abundant artifacts of Paleo-Indians and their descendants who hunted big game on the plains are also here. Leave all flint and obsidian points, cutting edges, hand axes, and other artifacts where you find them.

Samuel H. Ordway, Jr., Memorial Prairie Preserve

This South Dakota sanctuary takes care of the prairie, and the prairie takes care of the wildlife, including bison and deer.

SITE 56 Historically, there were three basic types of Great Plains ecosystems: the tallgrass of the northern regions, the short-grass of the south, and the mixed grass in an expansive transition zone between the tallgrass and the short-grass. The mixed-grass ecosystem had its own unique aspects of flora and fauna, and it also combined significant elements of the other two systems. Today very few examples of this singular biome

are left. Among them, the Nature Conservancy's 7,800-acre Samuel H. Ordway, Jr., Memorial Prairie Preserve is perhaps the best example.

The preserve is managed for eco-type rather than for any specific animal species. By taking care of the prairie, it is reasoned, the prairie will take care of the wildlife. A great deal of effort is put into mimicking the natural forces that maintained the original mixed-grass prairie, such as seasonal wildfire

As populations expand eastward, mule deer are increasingly common at Ordway Preserve.

A coyote stands out against Ordway Preserve's white winter landscape.

and intensive grazing by bison.

Prescribed burning is regularly conducted in the spring, and a herd of 165 bison is rotated through the preserve. The herd will eventually expand to 220 animals, with cattle augmenting their numbers as needed. Intensive grazing of short duration favors the native big bluestem grass, Indian grass, switchgrass, buffalo grass, and blue grama grass and discourages the exotic grasses and plants that accompanied white settlers in the westward migration.

A trail transverses the huge bison pasture, giving visitors the chance to see the huge beasts roaming their native habitat. Ordway's bison, some of which weigh close to a ton, have not been acclimated to human beings. This is a deliberate effort to preserve their natural behavior. In addition to being skittish, they are dangerous animals, so don't even think of approaching them.

Many other mammals typical of the Great Plains thrive here. White-tailed deer are common sights, and mule deer have lately been moving in from the west. Other species include red fox, thirteen-lined ground squirrel, Franklin's ground squirrel, coyote, badger, striped skunk, and white-tailed jackrabbit. Two shrews occur at the preserve that are at the far southern limits of their range—the pygmy shrew and the arctic shrew. Expect to see no more than a glimpse if you see them at all, as they skitter about with almost manic zeal; they usually are found near water, where insects and worms are abundant.

Ordway lies in the heart of prairie pothole country—a region of the plains that is the continent's greatest nursery for waterfowl because of the existence of thousands of small evanescent ponds. There are about 400 potholes here, and they shelter more than a thousand pairs of brooding ducks annually. Northern shoveler, blue-winged teal, and gadwall are particularly numerous. Most of the pothole water has evaporated by early summer, leaving mudflats that shorebirds find extremely inviting. Visiting species include upland plover, killdeer, common snipe, long-billed curlew, willet, spotted sandpiper, marbled godwit, and Wilson's phalarope.

Ordway also has a substantial population of sharp-tailed grouse, the continent's second largest grouse. Like prairie-chickens and the bigger sage grouse, sharptails stage elaborate courtship rituals on long-established leks, or dancing grounds. In the spring the males gather on the leks at dawn to challenge one another and dance before the critical eyes of the hens.

Northern harriers are often seen flying low to the ground, trying to flush prey. Ferruginous hawks and Swainson's hawks are here, too; look for them perched on fence posts and telephone poles. Burrowing owls are sometimes observed standing solemnly in front of ground squirrel burrows that they have commandeered for nesting sites.

Large numbers of plains songbirds can be found at the preserve, including the threatened Sprague's pipit and Baird's sparrow. Other species include Henslow's, lark, clay-colored, savannah, field, and song sparrows; Lapland and chestnut-collared longspurs; lark bunting; dickcissel; western meadowlark; horned lark; and bobolink.

Spring usually witnesses the emergence of frogs and toads. Their disparate croaks and peeps blend into euphonious refrains each evening—music that is all the more profound

because of the overwhelming solitude and silence that characterize this remote part of the plains. Species include Woodhouse's toad, Great Plains toad, chorus frog, and leopard frog.

Open all year, the preserve is an ideal day-trip destination. A good self-guided hiking trail with three loops provides access. The weather is extreme and typical for the Great Plains: frigid in winter, blazing hot in summer. From late spring through early fall, dawn and dusk are the best times to visit; heat either drives prairie species underground or makes them somnolent. They are most active before or after the sun is at its zenith.

songbirds, especially from March through May. Neotropical migrants pass through in great numbers and variety, and many are extremely rare or nonexistent elsewhere in the country. Species of particular interest include the scissor-tailed flycatcher and painted bunting. Aransas is also

excellent raptor country. Black and turkey vultures—identifiable by their unfeathered heads—are the most commonly sighted birds of prey; other species include crested caracara, pere-grine falcon, osprey, American kestrel, merlin, and Swainson's, red-tailed, and red-shouldered hawks.

While mammals are not the prima-ry attraction for wildlife enthusiasts visiting Aransas, they are certainly here in abundance. White-tailed deer are very common and are likely to be seen as soon as you drive onto the refuge grounds. Collared peccaries (also called javelinas), the doughty lit-tle wild hog native to the Southwest, thrive here. Bobcat, coyote, and gray fox are present, but seldom are seen by the casual visitor. Armadillos, which are usually oblivious to humans because of their poor eye-sight, are more likely to be spotted by hikers or motorists.

The American alligator population claims about 250 individuals, which are commonly seen in freshwater and brackish marshlands. Snakes—including venomous species such as Texas coral snake, western diamond-back rattlesnake, and broad-banded cottonmouth—are relatively abun-dant, although encounters with them are rare. Among the nonvenomous species are Texas rat snake, kingsnake, eastern yellow-bellied racer, eastern hognose snake, coachwhip, and dia-mondback water snake.

The proximity of the intercoastal waterway, Matagorda Island National Wildlife Refuge and State Park, and Padre Island National Seashore offers the additional attractions of birding, boating, and beachcombing.

Big Thicket National Preserve

Bobcats, coyotes, alligators, and marbled salamanders make their home in this protected land in southeast Texas.

SITE 58 Because four distinct ecosystems converge here—southwestern desert, central plains, eastern forest, and southeastern wetland—Big Thicket National Preserve has been called the biological crossroads of the continent. Such recognition is, in fact, official in the highest degree: In 1981 this 86,000-acre refuge was declared an international biosphere preserve by the United Nations. Such a designation means an area is an irreplaceable repository of wild fauna and flora unique to the planet. Recent acquisitions have expanded the protected area to 96,000 acres.

Big Thicket boasts some of the greatest wildlife diversity in North America. That's not to say it is crawling with observable animals. Most species that live here are nocturnal, and the vegetation is heavy. Throw in heat and humidity (both debilitating factors for much of the year) and several species of poisonous snakes, and it's readily apparent that this is not a preserve for the novice wildlife-watcher. It takes time, patience, and a willingness to endure a little discomfort to truly appreciate Big Thicket, but the rewards are extravagant. About 215 different species of birds live or migrate through Big Thicket's 14 separate units, which are scattered north and northwest of Beaumont in eastern Texas. Birders can add substantially to their life lists here, assuming they're persistent—and lucky. The scissor-tailed flycatcher, with fantastically

The bobcat's wide vocal repertoire ranges from deep growls to high-pitched screams.

pepper coat and a russet face is here; so is the related red fox.

There are two convenient ways to see Big Thicket—by foot or by canoe. Four of the preserve's units have well-maintained trail systems, ranging in length from under a mile to almost 20 miles. One of the most popular routes is the Turkey Creek Trail, which starts from the Visitor Center at the Turkey Creek Unit and covers about 18 miles; pick up the trail at either Hickbaugh or Gore State Road.

Most of the trails wind through three to four distinct plant communities with their attendant wildlife species. The terrain is flat and the walking easy. Keep an eye out for poisonous reptiles—rattlesnakes, cottonmouths, copperheads, and coral snakes—and give them a wide berth. Bring plenty of insect repellent for the ticks, chiggers, and mosquitoes, and watch out for fire ant mounds. As its name implies, a fire ant's bite is painful. Take plenty of potable water, and don't hike when the temperature is over 90°F.

Big Thicket is crisscrossed with rivers, creeks, sloughs, and bayous, making a canoe tour both practical and pleasant. Canoe camping, which necessitates familiarity with both primitive camping practices and paddling, is allowed by permit. (Several local vendors rent canoes and can provide all ancillary equipment, including maps.) There are three primary routes: the Neches River (39 to 54 miles), Pine Island Bayou (49 miles), and Village Creek (37 miles). All offer dramatic tours of cypress swamps and hardwood forests and can be paddled with minimal difficulty.

long tail plumes and pink wing linings, is one possible sighting; the yellow-billed cuckoo, painted bunting, and vermilion flycatcher are others.

There are 63 types of reptiles at Big Thicket, including the American alligator and the massive alligator snapping turtle, which can weigh in excess of 150 pounds. Amphibians abound; look for the lesser siren, marbled salamander, Woodhouse's toad, green treefrog, and cricket frog.

Resident mammals include the ubiquitous white-tailed deer, coyote, bobcat, and armadillo. The gray fox, a dainty little canid with a salt-and-

Eckert James River Bat Cave

In a spectacular display, millions of Mexican free-tailed bats take
wing from this Texas cave on twilight food-finding flights.

SITE 59 Bats have a bad reputation. Historically, their detractors characterized them as rats with wings, vermin that sucked blood, became entangled in coiffures, and carried a host of unpleasant diseases.

Happily, these retiring little mammals have undergone a major public relations rehabilitation in the past ten years or so. North American members of the order Chiroptera are now widely recognized as benign predators that pollinate flowering plants and ingest tons of pesky and destructive bugs. Bats have gone from being actively persecuted to zealously protected—even promoted. Large colonies have become tourist attractions, wowing visitors with twilight displays of millions of bats zooming skyward for their evening meal. Their newfound popularity couldn't have come at a more propitious time. Bats have experienced a drastic diminution across the continent in recent years because of habitat destruction, pesticides, and vandalism of colony sites.

There are about ten major bat caves in Texas. Of them, the Eckert James River Bat Cave is probably the most significant maternity colony, a gigantic nursery where bats give birth to their young. Mexican free-tailed bats, like many songbirds, are neotropical migrants: They arrive from Mexico in spring and leave for warmer climes in the fall. And, like migrating birds, they are extremely vulnerable to habitat disturbance.

The Eckert James cave is uniquely well suited as a brood area. It's small, so it retains body heat—a prime necessity for these subtropical bats. It also has a northern exposure, so sunlight seldom penetrates; bats, being nocturnal, detest sunlight. When the time for the fall migration rolls around, the cave's bat population expands greatly. Between two to four million Mexican free-tailed bats (and about 50,000 other bats) enter the cave in spring; between three and six million Mexican free-tails head south in the fall.

The cave was donated by a prominent local ranching family to the Nature Conservancy of Texas, with the proviso that the public be granted controlled access. For more than a century, area residents enjoyed the nightly bat display as informal guests of the ranch's proprietors; now the public at large may participate in the experience.

The nightly exit of bats from the cave is spectacular, as awesome in its own way as the vast stagings of snow geese in California's Central Valley or the caribou migrations on Alaska's North Slope. The managers of this 9-acre preserve have established a small seating and interpretive area near the cave's mouth. (It is essential for observers to remain as unobtrusive as possible; the bats are disturbed by human activity.) As the sun begins to set, the bats issue forth, sometimes in one explosive stream, sometimes in

When Mexican free-tailed bats exit their cave, they form a dark cloud visible for miles.

several short bursts. As they climb for the sky, the bats are literally inches away from visitors. It seldom takes more than 20 or 30 minutes for the millions of resident bats to exit the cave. Unlike the various bat species commonly seen by people sitting on their back porches at twilight, the Mexican free-tailed bats do not forage close to the ground, slurping up mosquitoes. They prefer altitudes of 2,500 to 10,000 feet, where they prey on flying agricultural pests such as corn borer moths.

There is another basic, and primal, element of this nightly demonstration. Raccoons, peregrine falcons, great horned owls, and coachwhip snakes lurk around the cave entrance at dusk and dawn; the raccoons and snakes pounce on bats that become entangled in vegetation at the cave's mouth, while the falcons and owls snag bats in flight. At least one raccoon has taken to actively foraging for bats in the cave. Researchers know it by sight because its coat has been bleached white by the ammonia from a constant rain of guano.

A naturalist is at the cave throughout the maternity season, from May through October. Public access is restricted to four nights a week to give the bats some relief from intensive human observation. Due to the tremendous popularity of the cave, further restrictions may soon be necessary.

Laguna Atascosa National Wildlife Refuge

On a hike through this Rio Grande retreat, the patient observer may catch sight of a bobcat, a mountain lion, or even an ocelot.

SITE 60 The lower Rio Grande Valley was once a favored haunt for tropical felines: jaguar, jaguarundi, and ocelot. The jaguar essentially has been extirpated from the United States, though there have been isolated reports of lone individuals in extremely remote portions of New Mexico and Arizona. The jaguarundi is a fantastically rare will-o'-the-wisp, framed fleetingly once in a great while in the headlights of nocturnal motorists cruising along remote south Texas roads near the Mexican border. The ocelot is another matter. It is by no means common—at most, there are only 50 to 100 of these beautiful spotted cats living wild and free north of the Rio Grande. But their populations are stable, and recent efforts to restore riparian forest and scrubland (critical foraging habitat for ocelots) in south Texas bode well for their future. With any luck, the ocelot could be on its way to a modest (though still significant) recovery.

The northern homeland for the ocelot is Laguna Atascosa National Wildlife Refuge, a 45,000-acre expanse of thornbush upland, freshwater wetland, evanescent lakes, salt marsh, and open bay waters about 30 miles north of Brownsville. If you want to see ocelots, this refuge, managed by the U.S. Fish and Wildlife Service, is the place to go: The largest breeding population of ocelots in the United States is here.

Candidly, the odds of a sighting are not favorable; ocelots are nocturnal and secretive. But patience and luck can pay big dividends. Every year a significant number of first-time visitors report sightings. Hiking the refuge's excellent trail system near sunrise or sunset is the best way to catch a glimpse of an ocelot—and a lot of other rare animals as well, for

that matter. This is also one of the best places in the country to see bobcats. These bobtailed, tuft-eared felines are quite common here, and many visitors mistake them for ocelots.

Acre for acre, Laguna Atascosa is one of the richest wildlife sites on the continent. A number of other nationally rare mammals are found here, including collared peccaries, mountain lions, and nilgai. The nilgai is a huge antelope weighing up to a thousand pounds, with a tiny head and small spike horns. Naturalized from the Indian subcontinent, nilgai are a favorite game species offered on the sprawling "hunting ranches" common throughout Texas. Occasionally they stray onto the refuge, so if you see something that looks like a pinheaded elk browsing among the refuge's abundant white-tailed deer, don't be alarmed. Other common mammals here include coyote, badger, raccoon, opossum, armadillo, black-tailed jackrabbit, eastern cottontail, Mexican ground squirrel, long-tailed weasel, and striped skunk.

Laguna Atascosa has the most recorded bird species of all the country's

While nilgai are not full-time residents of Laguna Atascosa, you can sometimes see them.

Probably no more than a hundred ocelots still inhabit the United States.

federal refuges—402 at last count. Knowledgeable birders flock here from around the country to add to their life lists. Plain chachalacas—hefty chickenlike birds typically associated with South American locales—are quite common and might be seen skulking around the refuge's headquarters during the early morning hours. At least two pairs of Aplomado falcons (even rarer than peregrine falcons, which are also found here) are known to utilize the refuge. Ospreys are commonly seen at the refuge, especially in the winter. Other unusual birds include white-tailed hawk, black-shouldered kite, crested caracara, Harris' hawk, great kiskadee, scissor-tailed flycatcher, green jay, painted bunting, varied bunting, Botteri's sparrow, curve-billed thrasher, and Chihuahuan raven.

Migratory waterfowl, shorebirds, and wading birds are especially abundant. Up to 700,000 ducks and geese are on the refuge during the height of the winter migration. About 80 percent of the continent's redhead ducks overwinter here and in the adjacent Laguna Madre, as does a sizable cohort of the related canvasback ducks. Fulvous whistling-duck, black-bellied whistling-duck, and rare masked duck have been sighted as well. Other duck species include northern pintail, blue-winged teal, northern shoveler, gadwall, American wigeon, ring-necked duck, lesser scaup, red-breasted merganser, and ruddy duck. Snow, Canada, and greater white-fronted geese flock to the refuge in the fall and winter, foraging together in huge flocks.

Black skimmers, common loons, brown pelicans, and eared grebes frequent the open bay waters. Look for shorebirds along the refuge's extensive tidal flats and lagoons, particularly in late winter and early spring, when the migrations are underway and water levels are most likely to be high. The piping plover, a small, pale gray-and-white plover that is threatened throughout most of its range, is here. Other species to look for include black-bellied, semipalmated, and snowy plover; killdeer; black-necked stilt; American avocet; greater and lesser yellowlegs; spotted, western, and least sandpipers; dunlin; long-billed dowitcher; long-billed curlew; whimbrel; marbled godwit; ruddy turnstone; and common snipe.

Wading birds can be seen everywhere there is water, probing the lagoons and exposed tidal areas for fish and crustaceans. Look for the sandhill crane; white-faced ibis; tricolored, green-backed, great blue, and little blue herons; black-crowned night-heron; great, snowy, cattle, and reddish egrets; American and least bitterns; clapper and Virginia rail; and sora.

This is at the westernmost range limits for American alligators, which are usually seen in open bodies of water, with only their eyes and nostrils visible. Other reptiles of note include the Texas indigo snake, Texas horned lizard, and Texas tortoise (all on the state's endangered or threatened list). Coral snakes and western diamondback rattlesnakes also find the habitat agreeable, so visitors should exercise appropriate caution while hiking, particularly in areas of dense vegetation.

Visitors can hike or drive through the refuge. Two good auto tour routes have been established: Lakeside Drive starts at the refuge's headquarters and dead-ends a mile later at the lake from which the refuge takes its name; Bayside Drive makes a 15-mile loop through all the refuge's major habitats.

THE FACTS

Noteworthy Animals: Ocelot, collared peccary, mountain lion, bobcat, nilgai, white-tailed hawk, black-shouldered kite, plain chachalaca, Aplomado falcon, painted bunting, Chihuahuan raven, American alligator, Texas tortoise.

Getting There: From Brownsville, take North Paredes Line Road (Rte. 1847) for about 20 miles, driving through Los Fresnos. Turn right at Rte. 106 and drive 10 miles to a "T" dead end; turn left, then drive 3 miles to the Visitor Center. From Harlingen, take Rte. 106 and proceed as above.

Open: Daily, dawn to dusk, year-round.

Best Times to Visit: October through May.

Visitor Information: Laguna Atascosa National Wildlife Refuge (956-748-3607) Visitor Center open daily, 10 a.m.-4 p.m., November through April; weekends, 10 a.m.-4 p.m. June through September; schedule varies rest of year, call for hours.

Entrance Fees: $2 per vehicle per day.

Disabled Access: Visitor Center is wheelchair accessible.

Camping: None on-site.

Laguna Atascosa presents a variety of miens depending on the season and the year. Sometimes it is dry as a husk; the wildlife congregates at available water like the teeming animals of the African veldt. After heavy rains it is a verdant web of marshlands burgeoning with migratory aquatic birds of every description. Call ahead for conditions, and try to visit the refuge at different times to fully appreciate its myriad and shifting aspects.

Horicon Marsh National Wildlife Refuge

In the fall, thousands of ducks and geese, representing more than 20 different species, congregate in this marsh outside Milwaukee.

SITE 61 The largest freshwater cattail marsh in the United States, Horicon Marsh has been designated a "wetland of international importance" by the Ramsar Convention, an international conference that identified marshes and swamps of global significance. It's easy to see why: During seasonal migrations hundreds of thousands of ducks and geese congregate here, providing one of the most dramatic waterfowl stagings in the Midwest. More than 20 different species of ducks—including northern pintail, American wigeon, blue-winged and green-winged teal, lesser scaup, northern shoveler, and mallard—pass through. Canada geese and sandhill cranes also stop by. At dawn the birds fill the sky as they lift off in great waves, heading to their feeding grounds.

But the marsh is more than a rest stop on the Mississippi flyway. The 32,000 acres of this national wildlife refuge, administered by the U.S. Forest Service, are home to a panoply of species of great interest to the wildlife enthusiast. Wetland-associated birds are beleaguered across most of

Large flocks of Canada geese congregate at Horicon Marsh NWR in November and December.

their range, but they are thriving in this near-pristine marsh. Soras, Virginia rail, and common moorhens nest here, as does the yellow-headed blackbird, a marsh-loving bird that is declining over much of its range.

The largest heron and egret rookery in the state is here at Four Mile Island, a kind of refuge-within-a-refuge. Scores of these obstreperous birds breed at the rookery, raucously contending for nesting territory. Although the rookery is off-limits to visitors in order to protect the breeding birds, large numbers of stately great blue herons, green-backed herons, and great egrets may be seen wading throughout shallows of the surrounding marsh.

Although mammals are not the primary attraction for visitors to Horicon Marsh, they thrive here nonetheless. Muskrats are important architects of the marsh, using the cattails for food and shelter and opening up more areas for the birds. River otters scour the quieter backwaters for fish, amphibians, and crayfish. Mink, raccoon, and opossum are nocturnal species and if seen at all, will be observed at twilight or dawn. White-tailed deer are common and may be glimpsed at most times of the day, browsing among the sedges and willows.

Turtles, aquatic snakes, and amphibians are abundant. Frequently seen species include common snapping and painted turtles, garter and northern water snakes, spotted salamander, American toad, chorus frog, green frog, bullfrog, northern leopard frog, pickerel frog, and wood frog.

Located only about 40 miles from Milwaukee, Horicon Marsh is a pop-

ular day-trip destination for urban wildlife enthusiasts. There is a variety of interpretive nature programs offered from spring through fall. Several road overlooks provide good birdwatching, and 6 miles of trails offer fine hiking and, in winter, cross-country skiing. Portions of the marsh can be explored by canoe; bring your own or rent one at Horicon Marsh. Dedicated birders might want to visit at the same time the birds do—late October through mid-November, when the migrations are at their peak.

Lower Wisconsin State Riverway

Viewed from land or water, this stretch of the Wisconsin River may yield sightings of ospreys, wood warblers, and river otters.

SITE 62 While it's true that the Wisconsin River has more hydroelectric dams than any other river in the country, its last 92 miles run unimpeded to its confluence with the Mississippi. This portion of the Wisconsin, in fact, constitutes the longest free-flowing stretch of river in the Midwest. For people willing to undertake a little paddling, the riverway offers superb wildlife viewing combined with some of the finest river scenery east of the Rockies. Good frontage roads and numerous access points allow boaters to plan trips of varying lengths—from a single afternoon to a week. Wildlife viewing is also possible from shore; Wis. 60 and Wis. 133 skirt the riverway, providing numerous access points and overviews.

The riverway begins at the village of Prairie du Sac, just below the Wisconsin's last dam. This is one of the finest sites in the continental United States for observing overwintering bald eagles. Fish are plentiful in the ice-free tailwaters below the dam, and the eagles gather in large numbers to prey on them. Up to 200 eagles settle in Prairie du Sac's riverine zone from December through February, and the town has constructed a special viewing area complete with spotting scope so that residents and visitors can keep convenient tabs on the majestic birds.

The terrain below the dam is relatively rugged and lushly forested;

habitats range from southern hardwoods to open prairie. Both ospreys and bald eagles brood along the river; look for their large unkempt nests atop large snags. Rough-legged hawks—big, mottled-breasted buteos with wingspans of 4 feet or more—are here. Some other raptors that may be encountered include American kestrels and sharp-shinned, Cooper's, red-shouldered, and red-tailed hawks. Gyrfalcons occur here only rarely. Owl species include great horned, barred, long-eared, short-eared, and

northern saw-whet. The riverway is at the southernmost range for snowy, boreal, northern hawk-, and great gray owls, and it is not at all unlikely for sightings of any of these species to occur during the winter.

The riverway's high-quality riparian woodlands have made it one of the most significant places in the state for neotropical migrant songbirds. This is wood warbler habitat par excellence, and a drifting canoe is certainly a superior platform for viewing these retiring birds. Look for black-and-white, prothonotary, golden-winged, blue-winged, Nashville, yellow, cerulean, chestnut-sided, and pine warblers, as well as northern parula, ovenbird, and Louisiana waterthrush.

Other songbirds also flock to this lush riparian habitat. The northern oriole builds its distinctive hanging nests here. Other nesting birds include the eastern bluebird, veery, bobolink, yellow-headed blackbird, Acadian flycatcher, rose-breasted grosbeak, indigo bunting, and rufous-sided towhee. Vireos (warbling, yellow-throated, and red-eyed) are plentiful, as are sparrows (Henslow's, chipping, American tree, vesper, lark, grasshopper, and song).

Pileated and red-headed woodpeckers nest in riverside snags; look for them in the spring, flying to their

Tundra swans pass through the Lower Wisconsin River on their way northward in the fall.

THE FACTS

Noteworthy Animals: Bald eagle, osprey, tundra swan, northern parula, great blue heron, American bittern, beaver, mink, river otter, red fox, white-tailed deer.

Getting There: From Madison, take US 12 about 15 miles north to Prairie du Sac, where the riverway begins. Wis. 60 and US 14 (north bank) and Wis. 133 (south bank) skirt most of its length.
Open: Daily, 6 a.m.-11 p.m., year-round. Winter boating usually impractical.
Best Times to Visit: December through February for eagles; May through September for canoeing.
Visitor Information: Tower Hill State Park, about 35 miles west of Madison, off US 14 near Spring Green (608-588-9128), open daily, 8 a.m.-4:30 p.m., May through October. No on-site visitor center.
Outfitters and/or Guide Services: For listings, call the Chambers of Commerce in Spring Green (608-588-2042 or 800-588-2042), Boscobel (608-375-2672), or Muscoda (608-537-2338).
Entrance Fees: None.
Disabled Access: None.
Camping: Developed camping at Tower Hill State Park and Wyalusing State Park (608-996-2261) along the riverway and at nearby Governor Dodge State Park (608-935-2315) and Blue Mound State Park (608-437-5711); fees; no reservations.

nests with bills crammed with tasty grubs for their fledglings. Game birds, most notably ruffed grouse, wild turkey, and American woodcock, are numerous, and a walk through the riverside brush may flush a few.

Waterbirds in great variety use the riverway. Look for them on the many sandbars, foraging or resting. Canada goose, wood duck, blue-winged teal, mallard, common goldeneye, and hooded merganser all nest locally and might well be seen during fall southward migrations. Shorebirds include the upland sandpiper, which nests here in the spring. Wading birds, such as the black-crowned night-heron, green and great blue herons, and American and least bitterns, are visible in the spring. Tundra swans are often seen overhead during the fall migration.

Also keep an eye out for turtles along the banks and sandbars, especially during the summer. Species to look for include spiny softshell and smooth softshell, common snapping, common musk, map, wood, Blanding's, and painted turtles.

Since it's best to explore the riverway by means of canoe, kayak, or raft, the chance of seeing resident mammals is good. Paddle craft are usually of little concern to wildlife, and most mammals actively forage along the river. Look for white-tailed deer, river otters, mink, beavers, and muskrats along the water's edge. Coyotes, bobcats, red and gray foxes, gray and fox squirrels, northern flying squirrel, and eastern cottontails are among the smaller resident mammals. Bats—eastern pipistrelle, Keen's myotis, silver-haired, big brown, red, and hoary—appear over the river snatching up insects as the day dies.

The Wisconsin is not a particularly difficult or dangerous river, but it deserves respect. Water levels can rise quickly, so don't head out if the water is running high. If you are a novice boater, make sure your paddling partner is experienced and competent. Above all, always wear a life preserver.

St. Croix National Scenic Riverway

Take an easy canoe trip down this unspoiled Wisconsin river to spot raccoons, black bears, and striped skunks.

SITE 63

While the Lower Wisconsin State Riverway (see p. 192) offers excellent wildlife-viewing opportunities within a few miles of downtown Madison, the St. Croix National Scenic Riverway represents wildness of an entirely different magnitude. Here it's entirely likely that paddlers may spot animals of the true wilderness, especially black bears. And because there are three different gray wolf packs that range in and around the riverway, a shoreside sighting of a wolf, or at least its scat or tracks, is not impossible.

This pristine system, which includes the entire Namekagon River and most of the St. Croix River, presents a variety of habitats along its 252-mile length. The streams join near Danbury, becoming the St. Croix. As it meanders along to its confluence with the Mississippi, the river penetrates extensive bogs and marsh, passing by steep bluffs and through croplands interspersed with hardwood copses and brushy bottomlands.

Such a rich diversity of habitats translates into an extraordinary abundance of wildlife. Four mustelids are common, but they are furtive and usually seen only in glimpses: ermine, mink, least weasel, and long-tailed weasel. In recent years fishers have been reintroduced along the riverway. Tracks of this large, dark-furred,

Raccoons prowl riverbanks and streams in search of fish, frogs, and turtle eggs.

Black bears use shaggy-barked trees to rub away loose fur and relieve itching.

riverbank. Striped skunks are apt to be found along the shore, especially at dusk; their more playful cousins, spotted skunks, are seen more rarely. Eastern cottontails, badgers, and woodchucks favor meadow areas. Look for white-tailed deer, bobcat, coyote, red fox, gray fox, raccoon, snowshoe hare, and porcupine in the deep woodland.

The abundance of mast-rich trees has made the St. Croix one of the richest regions in the country for squirrels. Fox, gray, red, northern flying, and thirteen-lined ground squirrels abound. Woodland bats—including Keen's myotis, and big brown, silver-haired, hoary, and red bats—are also thriving in the deep woods.

Bald eagles and ospreys nest along the riverway, and the woodlands are known to harbor healthy populations of northern goshawks. American kestrels and northern harriers hunt where the river borders meadows. Broad-winged, red-tailed, red-shouldered, and rough-legged hawks are distinguished by their stocky bodies and long wing surfaces. Sharp-shinned and Cooper's hawks also thrive here. Barred, great horned, northern hawk-, long-eared, short-eared, and northern saw-whet owls are resident. Snowy, great gray, and boreal owls are seen in the winter. Riverside coverts hide ruffed

secretive woodland mustelid are now fairly common on the banks of the upper river, and the extraordinarily lucky paddler may catch a glimpse of one at dusk or dawn.

River otters and beavers are most often seen swimming close to the grouse, sharp-tailed grouse, and American woodcock.

Below its confluence with the Namekagon, the St. Croix flows through extensive marshes and fens that support a great number of aquatic birds. Trumpeter swans nest near the river. During the fall migration, sightings of Canada goose, mallard, northern pintail, blue-winged teal, common goldeneye, hooded and common mergansers, common loon, wood duck, and pied-billed grebe are regularly reported. Also look for American and least bitterns, great blue herons, Virginia rail, and soras along the shore or sometimes in nests and rookeries.

The lush forests of the St. Croix riverway make it one of the best places in Wisconsin for sighting songbirds, especially wood warblers and sparrows, which are particularly evident during the fall and spring migrations. Among the many notable species are American redstart, yellow-rumped warbler, scarlet tanager, snow bunting, and Lincoln's sparrow.

Spiny softshell turtles and painted turtles are found throughout the riverway, while gray treefrogs, chorus frogs, spring peepers, mink frogs, green frogs, northern leopard frogs, pickerel frogs, and wood frogs abound in the marshes and bogs.

There is road access to the riverway at several points; Wis. 63, in fact, skirts about 40 miles of the upper Namekagon. And in winter the cross-country skiing is quite good. But the only truly satisfactory way to see this splendid natural marvel is by canoe. There are a smattering of Class I and II rapids, and a couple of portages

around dams, but canoeists of even moderate ability should have few, if any, problems. There are four Visitor Centers on the river—at St. Croix Falls, Trego, Pine City, and Stillwater. All have excellent exhibits on local wildlife and provide pertinent information on access and trip logistics.

THE FACTS

Noteworthy Animals: Gray wolf, black bear, river otter, raccoon, fisher, bald eagle, osprey, northern goshawk, trumpeter swan, snowy owl.

Getting There: From Minneapolis/St. Paul, Minnesota, take I-35 north 20 miles. Pick up US 8 east for 20 miles to Riverway headquarters in St. Croix Falls. Or take I-35 north for 50 miles to Minn./Wis. 70 east, which crosses the riverway at Grantsburg, an excellent access point.

Open: Daily, 24 hours, year-round.

Best Times to Visit: May through September.

Visitor Information: St. Croix National Scenic Riverway, St. Croix Falls Headquarters (715-483-3284), open Monday through Friday, 9 a.m.-5 p.m., year-round. Visitor Centers—at Trego, Wisconsin (715-635-8346), Pine City, Minnesota (320-629-2148), and Stillwater, Minnesota (612-430-1938), have seasonal hours; call ahead.

Outfitters and/or Guide Services: Each Visitor Center maintains a list of canoe rental companies.

Entrance Fees: None.

Disabled Access: All Visitor Centers are fully accessible.

Camping: Primitive camping; no fees or reservations.

EASTERN STATES

Alabama

Connecticut

Delaware

Florida

Georgia

Kentucky

Maine

Maryland

Massachusetts

Mississippi

New Hampshire

New Jersey

New York

North Carolina

Pennsylvania

Rhode Island

South Carolina

Tennessee

Vermont

Virginia

West Virginia

A wild horse on the
Virginia dunes

Dauphin Island Audubon Sanctuary

Spring brings blue-winged warblers, reddish egrets, scarlet tanagers, and other brightly colored birds to this island's beaches.

SITE 64 Dauphin Island lies at the mouth of Mobile Bay, like the extruded tongue of a frog, seemingly ready to lap something up. And, in fact, the island is extraordinarily good at catching things—birds, to be precise. Comprising some of the last landfall before the Gulf of Mexico, the island draws at least 210 species of birds, which congregate here during the migrations simply because there is no other place to rest before making the big leap to Central America.

To be sure, great pains have been taken to make the island as inviting as possible to avian visitors. Although the eastern portion of Dauphin is largely residential, it is also home to the 164-acre Audubon sanctuary. This parcel contains some of the choicest habitat on the island, a combination of beaches and maritime forests of live oak, magnolia, longleaf pine, and loblolly pine. The western part of the island is a long, narrow barrier island consisting mostly of sand dunes.

Late March through early June is the best time for a visit to Dauphin Island—both for the balmy weather and the songbird migration. (The fall migration is also significant, but more compressed in duration.) Dauphin's extravagant spring songbird displays draw birders from all over the country. The woods positively teem with birds, and the mix of species is constantly in flux. Although the entire island is a bird sanctuary, the Audubon sanctuary is locally acknowledged as the choicest site for birding. Other recommended spots include the Shell Mound (an ancient Indian shell midden with pre-Columbian live oaks), Pelican Point, West End, the airport, and the causeway to the mainland.

Wood warblers, resplendent in their brilliant breeding plumage, are the springtime stars. Look for bright yellow prothonotary warblers flitting through the foliage of large trees near the marshlands. Swainson's warbler, an extremely rare buff-breasted warbler of southern wetlands, is here as well. Among the many other warblers that might be spotted are Wilson's, black-and-white, blue-winged, and orange-crowned warblers; northern parula; yellow, hooded, and cerulean warblers; magnolia and blackpoll warblers; black-throated green and yellow-throated warblers; ovenbird; pine, prairie, and palm warblers; northern and Louisiana waterthrushes; Kentucky, Connecticut, Nashville, and Canada warblers; yellow-breasted chat; mourning and worm-eating warblers; and American redstart.

Other spring visitors include the brilliantly colored scarlet and summer tanagers, rose-breasted and blue grosbeaks, and indigo and painted buntings. Wood and hermit thrushes; golden-crowned and ruby-crowned kinglets; American pipits; white-eyed, solitary, red-eyed, yellow-throated, and warbling vireos; black-headed

The mudflats and salt marshes of Dauphin Island attract tricolored herons.

grosbeaks; and dickcissels are also regularly observed. Dauphin Island also gets an occasional vagrant species during the migrations; recent sightings have included a scissor-tailed flycatcher and a common redpoll—the first a bird of the tropics, the latter a resident of the far north.

Because the sound (north) shore of the island is a high-quality salt marsh and the Gulf (south) shore is primarily dunes and flat beach, the island is an excellent place to observe aquatic birds. Look for reddish egrets, a rare species with only about 2,000 breeding pairs in the United States. Other wading birds include glossy ibis; great blue, little blue, green-backed, and tri-colored herons; black-crowned and yellow-crowned night-herons; and great and snowy egrets. Look for them stalking the shallows for fish and crustaceans. Virginia rail, American and least bitterns, common moorhen, and purple gallinule are more timid; look for them lurking in or near thick aquatic vegetation.

In spring at low tide, both marsh and beach are filled with masses of shorebirds probing the sand for burrowing crustaceans. Semipalmated, snowy, piping, and black-bellied plover can be identified by their swollen bill tips, a characteristic of the plover family. Willet, which on the ground look very similar to both greater and

Dauphin's salt marsh is a magnet for ducks on their fall migration. Dabblers, such as northern pintail, American black and mottled ducks, mallards, green-winged and blue-winged teal, wood ducks, fulvous whistling-ducks, American wigeon, and northern shovelers, are often seen bottom side up as they forage for vegetation at the bottom of the marsh. Redheads, canvasbacks, common goldeneyes, buffleheads, greater and lesser scaup, ring-necked ducks, and hooded mergansers are found in deeper water.

Ospreys nest on a nearby island and bald eagles occasionally pass through. Other raptors that are known to visit include Mississippi and swallow-tailed kites; peregrine falcons; broad-winged, red-shouldered, red-tailed, Cooper's, and sharp-shinned hawks; merlins; and American kestrels. Northern harriers are winter residents of the marshes.

Dauphin Island also provides critical habitat for the Gulf of Mexico's endangered marine turtles. Both loggerhead and Atlantic Ridley sea turtles nest on the Gulfside beaches during spring with moderate success. The best chances of a sighting are in the evening or right at dawn. Don't approach nesting turtles—they are vulnerable to disturbance. Galliard Lake, a 5-acre pond on the west end of the sanctuary, is inhabited by American alligators; look for their distinctive low-lying silhouettes at dawn and dusk.

A good trail system winds through the Audubon sanctuary. The miles of beach on the Gulf offer excellent opportunities for birding, beachcombing, and surf-fishing.

lesser yellowlegs, are distinguished by a bold black-and-white pattern on the underwings. Black skimmers might be observed flying just above the water, with their long lower bills trailing through the water. American oystercatchers are most likely to be seen patiently stalking in mudflats and marshes. Other species include killdeer; ruddy turnstone; Baird's, spotted, solitary, least, pectoral, stilt, semipalmated, and western sandpipers; sanderling; red knot; dunlin; short-billed and long-billed dowitchers; marbled godwit; and black-necked stilt.

Sharon Audubon Center

Monarch butterflies and ruby-throated hummingbirds flock to the flowered gardens of this lovely Connecticut preserve.

SITE 65 The Sharon Audubon Center in northwestern Connecticut is proof positive that good things come in small packages. At 758 acres, this is no sprawling refuge embracing an entire ecosystem. It is a natural jewel, a singular amalgam of preserve and interpretive center that has something to offer everyone from budding nature enthusiast to experienced birder.

For such a small place, there's a lot to see. Several different natural communities are represented at the preserve: pond and stream, deep hardwood and hemlock forests, wetlands, and forest-and-field ecotones ("edge" areas comprising numerous habitat niches). Eleven miles of hiking trails allow thorough exploration.

White-tailed deer are the largest mammal resident here, and they are plentiful. Smaller species that may be seen include bobcat, beaver, river otter, muskrat, raccoon, and woodchuck. More commonly spotted are "little critters" such as eastern chipmunk, fox squirrel, red squirrel, and gray squirrel.

Appropriately for a refuge managed by the National Audubon Society, the Sharon center is particularly rich in birds. Neotropical migrants, including Blackburnian and Cape May warblers and northern parula, pass through in April and May and again in September and October.

The preserve also serves as a nesting site for many other songbirds, including the scarlet tanager, northern oriole, eastern bluebird, Louisiana waterthrush, American redstart, yellow warbler, and black-throated green warbler. White-throated sparrows can be seen in November and December, and dark-eyed juncos migrate from higher latitudes to spend the winter. Two of the resident woodpecker species are the pileated woodpecker and the yellow-bellied sapsucker.

Thanks to a special garden maintained by the staff, the center is positively abuzz with ruby-throated hummingbirds from the late spring through the fall, particularly at the plots planted with bee balm. Tubular-shaped red flowers are especially attractive to hummingbirds. The garden also enjoys justifiable local renown for its butterflies, including

Ruby-throated hummingbirds extract nectar and tiny insects from tubular red flowers.

reptiles and amphibians, including painted turtle, northern water snake, and two-lined salamander.

Several species of owl and hawk hunt at the preserve. Common sightings include great horned owl, barred owl, eastern screech-owl, red-tailed hawk, and sharp-shinned hawk. Other, less common raptors are the northern saw-whet owl, Cooper's hawk, and red-shouldered hawk.

The center maintains a wild bird rehabilitation program that specializes in treating injured raptors, most of which are the victims of collisions with automobiles. The goal of the program is to return all the birds to the wild. Some, however, are injured too severely to be released, and these individuals are used to educate visitors about birds of prey. Orphaned songbird young are also given a second chance. They are raised lovingly and returned to their natural habitats.

There are seven trails at the sanctuary, offering surprising diversity in length, relative ruggedness, and habitats. The Lucy Harvey Trail is short (0.3 mile) and appropriate for handicapped nature lovers. At 2.3 miles, the Woodchuck Trail is the longest and offers lovely views of open fields and deciduous forest.

The sanctuary also sponsors a summer camp for children as well as regular nature walks led by staff naturalists. The Adventure Center in the interpretive complex affords young children an exciting hands-on, self-explanatory nature tour. For adults there are regularly scheduled lectures and seminars on a wide range of topics—everything from birdbanding techniques to tree identification.

monarchs, black swallowtails, and tiger swallowtails.

The center's two ponds and riverine habitat support diverse waterfowl. Canada geese brood their young here. Duck species include mallard, wood duck, American wigeon, lesser scaup, and ring-necked duck. The wetland habitats also teem with a variety of

Port Mahon Preserve

Each spring thousands of horseshoe crabs swarm ashore on the protected beaches of this Delaware Bay sanctuary.

SITE 66 A remarkable series of federal refuges, state parks, and private preserves extends along the shore of Delaware Bay, providing food and shelter for a great array of birds and marine invertebrates. At the heart of this complex is the Nature Conservancy's Port Mahon Preserve, a 341-acre salt marsh surrounded on the north, west, and south by refuge lands and bordered to the east by the bay.

What makes this preserve special? A very humble creature indeed— the horseshoe crab. These ancient

Horseshoe crabs are not crabs at all but close relatives of scorpions and spiders.

You can identify a red knot in flight by its whitish rump finely barred with gray.

animals, virtually unchanged for 500 million years, have long delighted children with their fantastic armament and scuttling gait. Phylogenetically, horseshoe crabs are as far removed from true crabs as lobsters are from grasshoppers; among their other unique characteristics, they have blue blood.

For the last 400 million years or so, horseshoe crabs have carried on their annual mating ritual. Each spring during new-moon high tides, thousands of them swarm ashore on the beach and mudflats to lay their eggs in the sand and silt. This is one of the great marine spectacles on the planet and it is easily observed at Port Mahon. During this time the density of crabs on the shore can be incredibly thick:

up to 30 of them per square yard of shore. They lay eggs by the hundreds of millions, though relatively few eggs develop to maturity.

Impressive as the crab's breeding cycle is, it's not merely an interesting reproductive phenomenon left over from an ancient era. For the more than one million migratory shorebirds that fly along the East Coast, horseshoe crab eggs are an essential food source, a veritable groaning board of rich fat and protein. During the spring migrations, the Delaware Bay shore is the primary staging area for eastern shorebirds on their way to Arctic breeding grounds from their winter homes in Central and South America. Many species fly nonstop from the tropics over a four- to seven-day period and arrive at Port Mahon totally exhausted and nutritionally depleted. During the course of a week's stay at the refuge, a bird can literally double its weight on horseshoe crab eggs before resuming its journey.

Among the migratory shorebirds that visit the preserve are ruddy turnstone, dunlin, black-bellied plover, killdeer, willet, common snipe, black-necked stilt, American avocet, semi-palmated sandpiper, and spotted sandpiper. Look for the red knot, a plump, chestnut-breasted bird that is declining over most of its range, in mixed flocks with sanderlings and short-billed dowitchers. Wading birds frequent the preserve's salt marshes and numerous ponds. Look for the great blue heron and the related little blue heron, a lovely diminutive heron with a gray body and a purplish head. Other waders include American bittern and great and snowy egrets.

Red-throated and common loons, and pied-billed, horned, and red-necked grebes prefer areas of open water. Mallards, blue-winged and green-winged teal, northern pintail, greater scaup, gadwalls, American wigeon, canvasbacks, redheads, common goldeneyes, buffleheads, red-breasted mergansers, American black ducks, and ruddy ducks also pass through in significant numbers.

Port Mahon lies along the East Coast's primary fall migration route for raptors; each year thousands of birds of prey funnel down the eastern seaboard on their way to their wintering grounds in the southern states and Latin America. Bald eagles and peregrine falcons are often seen in the

THE FACTS

Noteworthy Animals: Horseshoe crab, red knot, sanderling, great blue heron, red-throated loon, horned grebe, bald eagle, peregrine falcon.

Getting There: The nearest city is Dover, about 5 miles west. From Dover, take Del. 8 east to Del. 9 south and proceed to Port Mahon Road. Turn left and follow it to the end. The preserve is on the left side of the road.

Open: Daily, dawn to dusk, year-round.

Best Times to Visit: March through May; September through November.

Visitor Information: The Nature Conservancy, Delaware field office (302-369-4144), open Monday through Friday, 9 a.m.-5 p.m., year-round. No on-site visitor center.

Entrance Fees: None.

Disabled Access: Excellent; most viewing can be done from cars or the road.

Camping: None on-site.

winter months, so are ospreys; northern harriers; sharp-shinned, red-tailed, red-shouldered, and rough-legged hawks; American kestrels; and merlins.

This is an ideal refuge for children and elderly or handicapped travelers. Port Mahon Road runs adjacent to the preserve, and a great deal of the wildlife viewing is typically conducted from cars and roadside viewing areas (the marsh is mucky, inappropriate for hiking). The marsh is on one side of the road and the bay shore, where the crabs spawn, is on the other. Port Mahon offers a relatively passive wildlife-viewing experience, but there's usually plenty to see in the course of a day. Spring and fall are the best times for a visit: spring for horseshoe crabs and shorebirds, fall for the raptors.

Blowing Rocks Preserve

Volunteers get hands-on experience with endangered, nesting
sea turtles on the beaches of this popular refuge.

SITE 67 Sea turtles are almost exclusively denizens of tropic seas (with the exception of the leatherback, which sometimes strays into cold water), and they nest on beaches that are located in the planet's warmest latitudes. Little wonder, then, that they are not usually associated with the continental United States. At one time, however, sea turtles nested in great numbers in Florida, drawn by the pristine sandy beaches and tropical climate. Sadly, their fortunes turned with the advent of the state's construction boom; brooding turtles now stand at a fraction of their former population.

There are still a few places—very few, dotted along the coast from Florida to Virginia—where these magnificent reptiles crawl ashore each spring and summer to lay their eggs in cavities dug out in the warm and inviting sand: Foremost among them is Jupiter Island's Blowing Rocks Preserve. Depending on the year, between 500 to 1,000 turtles lay their eggs at the refuge, helping ensure that sea turtles will forever remain a part of Florida's marine ecosystem. Three different species of sea turtles nest here: the leatherback, green, and loggerhead. All three are endangered.

Blowing Rocks Preserve contains a 73-acre nesting beach on Jupiter Island, as well as a 5-acre preserve of rare tropical vegetation 3 miles north on the mainland. The managing agency, the Nature Conservancy of Florida, is also actively restoring the tidal areas of the adjacent Indian River Lagoon, one of the most biologically diverse estuarine systems in the Northern Hemisphere.

Turtles nest and hatch at Blowing Rocks Preserve from March through November, and guided tours are held regularly at this time. Visitors can have a hands-on experience with these marvelous marine reptiles by signing

up for the preserve's rescue program. Jupiter Island is characterized by limestone outcroppings and fissures that can trap gravid sea turtles; during the nesting season, volunteers patrol the area daily, freeing any turtles that become ensnared.

While sea turtles are the primary draw, Blowing Rocks is also rich in other animals that are characteristic of South Florida. Four different ecological communities characterize the preserve: mangrove swamp, coastal strand, beach-dune, and maritime hammock.

This mix of habitats supports an astounding array of species. In addition to sea turtles, resident reptiles include the green anole eastern coral snake, and the threatened eastern indigo snake. Manatees regularly visit Blowing Rocks and are the most notable mammal for wildlife enthusiasts. Bobcats, foxes, raccoons, and opossums also enjoy the protection of the refuge. As always, mammal sightings are most likely in or near areas of heavy vegetation.

Birds are exceedingly abundant,

An adult loggerhead sea turtle can be four feet long and weigh 350 pounds or more.

particularly aquatic birds. The brown pelican is a continentally rare species, but a relatively common sight here. Once threatened with extinction because of DDT and other pesticides, the brown pelican is now on the rebound. Wading birds—great blue and green-backed herons and great and snowy egrets—are often seen searching around mangrove roots for prey. Black skimmers; Pomarine jaegers; laughing, Bonaparte's, ring-billed, and herring gulls; and gull-billed, Caspian, common, Forster's, and least terns may be observed diligently patrolling nearshore waters for fish or clustered along the strand resting.

Shorebirds are everywhere water meets sand or silt. Short-billed and long-billed dowitchers, stocky birds with reddish breasts and long stiletto-like bills, feed together in flocks with red knots. Other species include semi-palmated plover, black-necked stilt, American avocet, ruddy turnstone, dunlin, and common snipe. Tiny "peeps"—spotted, western, and least sandpipers—are here in abundance.

Migratory songbirds favor the vegetated portions of the preserve. Overwintering flycatchers love it here, specifically eastern phoebe, eastern kingbird, and scissor-tailed flycatcher. Other wintering migrants include many warblers (myrtle, orange-crowned, palm, and pine warblers; northern parula, ovenbird, common yellowthroat) and sparrows (vesper, Bachman's, white-crowned, and fox). Sightings of white-eyed vireos, eastern bluebirds, hermit thrushes, gray catbirds, Carolina wrens, and ruby-crowned kinglets are reported regularly. Also look for purple martins, tree swallows, and northern rough-winged swallows. Year-round residents include the blue jay, northern mockingbird, and northern cardinal.

Birds of prey that may be seen include ospreys, bald eagles, northern harriers, merlins, and American kestrels. Sightings of Cooper's, red-shouldered, and red-tailed hawks are also possible.

A beach trail and a boardwalk make the wildlife-watching exceptionally easy and accessible. The biggest difficulty is just getting in. Blowing Rocks is one of the most popular nature preserves in Florida, a state that is just about saturated with visitors. The guided walks and the turtle rescue programs in particular fill up quickly, so call ahead for reservations.

Crystal River National Wildlife Refuge and Chassahowitzka National Wildlife Refuge

The endangered manatee feasts on the abundant muskgrass and swims in the warm, sheltered waters of this Florida sanctuary.

SITE 68 Florida's western coast has undergone an intensive development boom in the last 30 years that has proved incredibly destructive to its native wildlife. Foremost among the affected species is the manatee, a gentle, herbivorous aquatic giant of a mammal that may reach 13 feet in length and weigh up to 3,000 pounds. Manatees were once abundant throughout Florida, and common in much of the maritime Deep South. Today, only about 2,000 survive, finding sanctuary in Florida's diminished estuarine waterways and rivers.

The best place to see these endangered animals is the federal Crystal River-Chassahowitzka wildlife refuge complex. Here, in one of the last sizable expanses of intact estuarine wetland left in western Florida, the manatee has endured, providing a glimpse into Florida's wild and unspoiled past.

At 46 acres spread over nine islands and encompassing waterways, Crystal River isn't particularly large but it is essential to the manatee's survival. It was founded in 1983 specifically for the protection of the manatee. About 15 percent of Florida's manatees—more than 200 animals—may winter here, seeking the warm water flowing from the springs that charge the Crystal River. Manatees cannot tolerate temperatures below 68°F for any sustained period of time, so the 72°F water of the Crystal River is perfectly

suited for their biological requirements. The best months to see these retiring behemoths at Crystal River are from November through March.

As the Gulf waters warm, the manatees gradually leave Crystal River and mosey south about 10 miles to the Chassahowitzka refuge, a 30,500-acre network of saltwater bays and inlets, estuaries, brackish marshes, and hardwood swamps. Though it was founded in 1943 as a refuge for migratory waterfowl, it has since been recognized as a critical spring, summer, and fall habitat for manatees as well. Here they loll in the water, foraging on muskgrass, wigeon grass, water milfoil, and other aquatic plants. They need a lot to sustain them—an 800-pound manatee will consume about 32 pounds of plants daily.

The best way to observe manatees is to explore slowly in a boat, watching the surface of the water closely. Manatees make a unique circular disturbance on the surface of the water with their tails. They are sometimes seen basking on the water's surface. Note that boat collisions are the single greatest source of manatee mortality; when in their territory, proceed very slowly and carefully.

In addition to the manatee, about 250 species of birds, 50 species of reptiles and amphibians, and at least 20 other species of mammals throng these refuges.

Visitors are likely to see such

Navigate with care—at Crystal River, boat accidents are the top cause of manatee mortality.

distinctly Floridian wading birds as the wood stork and white-faced ibis. Look for them stalking the tidal flats or perched in trees. Wood storks will also be seen soaring high on afternoon thermals. Other waders inhabiting the refuges include tricolored heron, great blue heron, snowy egret, great egret, sora, Virginia rail, black rail, least bittern, American bittern, and purple gallinule. Also be on the lookout for the anhinga, or "snakebird" perching on a snag, its long wings and serpentine neck extended to speed up the drying of its feathers after a dive for fish.

The brown pelican, currently on the rebound after nearly suffering extinction from chlorinated hydrocarbon pesticides, forages here, and is often joined by white pelicans; black skimmers; red-throated and common loons; and gull-billed, Caspian, least, and common terns.

Birds of prey include the crested caracara, the strikingly handsome raptor more typically associated with Mexico. It is identified by its distinctive red face, black crest, streaked white breast, black wings and back, and long, yellow legs. Other resident species are osprey; bald eagle; sharp-shinned, Cooper's, red-shouldered, and red-tailed hawks; and barred, short-eared,

and great horned owls.

Crystal River and Chassahowitzka are rich in songbirds. The crimson-colored summer tanager (the female is yellow-green) is often spotted here. Red-winged blackbirds nest in waterside vegetation. Look also for yellow-billed cuckoos, eastern bluebirds, pileated woodpeckers, and yellow-bellied sapsuckers.

The refuge has transient populations of two of Florida's rarest large mammals—black bear and bobcat. River otter, raccoon, opossum, and white-tailed deer are permanent residents and are fairly common; look for them by scanning the shoreline with good binoculars from a slow-moving boat.

Reptiles are extremely common, with the American alligator getting top billing. They are commonly seen in the backwaters, especially near dawn and dusk. Snakes are found in great diversity and considerable numbers, among them handsomely patterned terrestrial species such as the Florida pine snake, corn snake, milk snake, common kingsnake, and scarlet snake. Venomous species are also abundant, including eastern coral snake, cottonmouth, copperhead, water moccasin, and diamondback rattlesnake; maintain appropriate caution in heavy vegetation. Turtles are often observed sunning themselves along banks or on partially submerged logs. Look for Florida box turtles, Florida softshell turtles, Suwanee cooters, alligator

snapping turtles, and mud turtles.

Both refuges are accessible only by boat. Rentals, full- or half-day charters, or guided trips can be arranged at nearby Homosassa Springs, Chassahowitzka, or Crystal River. Signs are posted throughout the refuge to denote favored manatee habitat, and boaters must reduce speed accordingly. Boats account for considerable injuries and mortality among Florida manatees each year.

Everglades National Park and Big Cypress National Preserve

One of the world's great natural wonders, the Everglades harbors American alligators, wading birds, and the rare Florida panther.

SITE 69 Sadly, the Everglades is much degraded. How could it be otherwise, given Florida's booming population and a vast agricultural district sucking up water like a sponge north of the legendary "river of grass"? But there is reason to hope that the worst is over. With the 1996 passage of ambitious federal legislation aimed at restoring the greater Everglades, as well as ongoing cooperative ventures on the state and local levels, it seems that the region could well be on its way to a significant, if partial, ecological recovery.

Approximately 50 percent of the historic Everglades survives today. The Everglades complex—particularly Everglades National Park and Big Cypress National Preserve—constitutes one of the great natural wonders of the world. It is hard to describe this region in anything less than superlatives. It contains the largest continuous stand of saw-grass prairie in North America, the largest mangrove ecosystem in the Western Hemisphere, and the largest designated wilderness in the Southeast. It is home to 14 threatened and endangered species, contains the largest breeding grounds for tropical wading birds in North America, and is the only subtropical preserve on the North American continent.

It is also huge. Together, the park and preserve constitute about 4,500 square miles of wetland, hardwood hammock, and mangrove swamp at the southern tip of Florida. For wildlife enthusiasts, the Everglades is comparable to Alaska: Sooner or later you have to go.

What will you see? Depending on the site and the season, likely sightings include American alligators and anhingas, bald eagles, and ospreys—even manatees. With some luck, the diligent observer will spot the endangered snail kite. These square-tailed, long-winged raptors live only in southern Florida and only about 500 of them still survive. Other birds of prey include American swallow-tailed kites and barred owls.

Large aggregates of wading birds, either in rookeries or at favored feeding areas, are common sights. Endangered wood storks are still found in considerable numbers here, although their long-term future remains very much in doubt because of the ongoing destruction of the wetlands that are essential to their survival. Faring better are roseate spoonbills; great and snowy egrets; tricolored, great blue, and little blue herons; least and American bitterns; and white ibis. Also look for Virginia rail, sora, common moorhen, and American coot. Flamingos, which are probably naturalized escapees from various zoos or amusement parks, are occasionally seen.

Even in the Everglades, it's unlikely you'll see the endangered Florida panther.

This region also constitutes a critical habitat for migrant songbirds. Among the species that pass through are the eastern phoebe, eastern kingbird, scissor-tailed flycatcher, purple martin, northern rough-winged and tree swallows, marsh wren, ruby-crowned kinglet, hermit thrush,

The population of snail kites has been seriously reduced by the draining of wetlands.

American pipit, summer tanager, indigo and painted buntings, and northern cardinal. Orange-crowned, Nashville, magnolia, Cape May, and cerulean warblers; solitary vireo, northern parula, American redstart, and common yellowthroat are numerous. Birders may also spot mangrove cuckoos, which in North America are found only in South Florida.

In the dense vegetation of the Everglades, it is much harder to see mammals than birds. Still, some—such as white-tailed deer, raccoon, opossum, and marsh rabbit—will likely be spotted by the casual visitor, especially toward dawn or dusk. River otters and bobcats are possible sightings in Everglades National Park; feral hogs and the indigenous Big Cypress fox squirrel may be seen at Big Cypress. Sightings of the endangered Florida panther, a mountain lion subspecies, are another matter entirely. Only about 50 still survive in the state. Although a good percentage of those live in the Everglades, rangers and biologists can spend their entire careers in the field without ever catching a glimpse of this elusive and beleaguered feline.

This is the world's greatest stronghold for the once endangered American alligator, that ultimate swamp predator. The survival of the American crocodile, a species that was declared endangered in 1975, still remains questionable. A small population of crocodiles is known to live in the southernmost area of the Everglades.

Other reptiles are doing quite well. Snake species include southern black racer, cottonmouth, ribbon snake, southern ringneck, mud snake, and eastern coral snake. Common snapping, musk, and mud turtles, and diamondback terrapins are thriving. Three endemic turtle species—

Florida softshell, Florida red-bellied, and Florida box turtles—are also commonly seen. Loggerhead sea turtles inhabit Florida Bay and appear to be profiting from strict protections.

The Everglades is one of the most popular natural areas in the Southeast, and is well equipped for visitors. It's possible to see the complex by car, foot, boat, or a combination of all three. Drivers can cruise US 41 (Tamiami Trail), Turner River Road, and Fla. 94 through Big Cypress, and the main park road through the Everglades for a good overview of the system. Developed trails—including the Anhinga Trail, Gumbo-Limbo Trail, and Coastal Prairie Trail in the Everglades and the Tree Snail Hammock Trail in Big Cypress—wind through various habitats. Visitors can hike on their own, but wildlife sightings are usually better on one of the many ranger-led walks (they know where to look). And a 15-mile tram tour from the Shark Valley Visitor Center offers fine opportunities for viewing birds and alligators.

To really understand a wetland, however, you have to get on the water. There are manifold opportunities for that at the Everglades. The National Park Service and licensed concessionaires offer guided boat tours from Flamingo and Everglades City. For independent travelers, the Nine-Mile Pond Canoe Trail, West Lake Canoe Trail, Hells Bay Canoe Trail, and Bear Lake Canoe Trail offer excellent short to moderate-length paddles. For an extended trip, the 99-mile Wilderness Waterway, which winds through the western section of the park, is open to motorboats and canoes.

THE FACTS

Noteworthy Animals: American alligator, manatee, Florida panther, wood stork, white ibis, roseate spoonbill, snail kite, American swallow-tailed kite, mangrove cuckoo, loggerhead sea turtle.

Getting There: Big Cypress National Preserve: From Miami, take US 41 west for 35 miles to the preserve's entrance. Everglades National Park: From Miami, take Florida Turnpike or US 1 35 miles south to Florida City. Turn right on Palm Drive and follow the signs to Fla. 9336 and the main park entrance in Homestead. Or take US 41 (as for Big Cypress) west for about 30 miles to the Shark Valley Visitor Center. From Naples, take US 41 east for 30 miles to Fla. 29. Follow that south for 5 miles to the Everglades City entrance.

Open: Daily, dawn to dusk, year-round.

Best Times to Visit: October through April.

Visitor Information: Big Cypress National Preserve Visitor Center (941-695-4111) open daily, 8:30 a.m.-4:30 p.m., year-round. Everglades National Park Visitor Center (305-242-7700) open daily, 8:30 a.m.-5 p.m., year-round.

Entrance Fees: Big Cypress: None. Everglades NP: $10 per vehicle per week at main entrance; $8 at other entrances.

Charter and/or Guide Services: Everglades NP (305-242-7700); Everglades City (941-695-2591); Flamingo Marina (941-695-3101).

Disabled Access: Big Cypress: Visitor Center is handicapped accessible. Everglades NP: Main Visitor Center, several trails, and Shark Valley Tram are wheelchair accessible.

Camping: Big Cypress: Primitive camping; no fees or reservations. Everglades NP: Developed campsites and primitive camping; fees for sites; no reservations required.

Florida Keys National Wildlife Refuges

There's more to the keys than margaritas. American crocodiles and Key deer are among the animals found here.

SITE 70 The Florida Keys are experiencing one of the longest sustained building booms in the United States. It began in earnest in the 1970s and shows no signs of abating. But while the proliferating developments and hordes of visitors have greatly enriched state coffers, the region's wildlife has been stuck with the tab. There was never much terrestrial habitat in the keys to begin with, and there's less every passing year.

Some of it, happily, will be preserved forever, come what may. The four refuges comprising the Florida Keys National Wildlife Refuges—Key West National Wildlife Refuge, Crocodile Lake National Wildlife Refuge, Great White Heron National Wildlife Refuge, and the National Key Deer Refuge—encompass 26,000 acres of islands spread over 1,400 square miles of water. On these keys, at least, Margaritaville has been held at bay. Three of the four refuges are open to visitation; only Crocodile Lake is off-limits, a restriction necessary for maintaining its population of endangered American crocodiles.

The National Key Deer Refuge harbors the most charismatic of the keys' endangered species—the Key deer. Of the 33 known subspecies of white-tailed deer, this is the smallest. (Another subspecies, which inhabits several islands off Panama, is roughly comparable in size.) Bucks seldom reach one hundred pounds, and most does weigh in at about 50 pounds—

no heavier than a moderately large dog. The Key deer inhabit several keys and are most numerous on Big Pine Key and No Name Key, where the chances of a sighting are best. Resist the urge to approach, pet, or feed Key deer—interaction with humans can result in behavior modifications that will be fatal to the animals. Big Pine Key boasts the Watson Nature Trail, a short loop through pine stands and freshwater marsh; a 700-foot spur providing wheelchair accessibility has just been added.

Aquatic birds are doing quite well in the keys, including the namesake great white heron of the Great White Heron National Wildlife Refuge. A year-round resident, the heron is best seen by slowly boating through the mangrove inlets. This stunning white bird is now considered a color phase of the great blue heron by most ornithologists. Another remarkable bird, seen most often at the Key West and Great White Heron refuges, is the appropriately named magnificent frigatebird; adults typically have wingspans that exceed 7 feet. Male frigatebirds sport bright scarlet throat pouches, which inflate to alarming size during the spring, when they breed. Frigatebirds are opportunistic to the extreme and are sometimes seen chivying brown and masked boobies, robbing them of their prey.

Wading birds abound, including great blue heron, little blue heron, tricolored heron, green-backed heron, black-crowned night-heron, great egret, snowy egret, and reddish egret. Look for the waders wherever water and land meet.

The skies resound with the cries of terns and gulls. Regularly observed species include royal terns (distinctive because of their full cockade), least, Caspian, Forster's, gull-billed, and common terns, and laughing and ring-billed gulls.

Fulvous whistling-ducks, tropical long-legged ducks that perch in trees, are seen in the mangroves and hammocks. Other common ducks include blue-winged teal, American wigeon,

In the Florida Keys, that floating log might be an American alligator.

and red-breasted merganser.

A variety of shorebirds winter in the keys, and most favor mangrove inlets. Look for semipalmated plover, black-necked stilts, American avocets, whimbrels, marbled godwits, ruddy turnstones, red knots, sanderlings, dunlins, and short-billed dowitchers. The rare piping plover and four species of sandpipers—western, spotted, least, and stilt—are here in significant numbers.

The fall migrations of raptors are exceptional. While the bald eagle is the undisputed star, turkey and black vultures are abundant. American kestrels, peregrine falcons, and Swainson's, short-tailed, broad-winged, and sharp-shinned hawks are also common. Ospreys are well-distributed year-round residents and are frequently observed snatching fish from the water.

Because of the extreme isolation of the western keys, terrestrial birds are not too common but there are several species of note. White-crowned pigeons migrate through the refuges in the spring and summer and are often seen in poisonwood groves, gorging on fruit. The secretive mangrove cuckoo haunts the lush tropical hammock that characterizes the undeveloped keys. Palm warblers and gray kingbirds are relatively abundant. Summer evenings in and around the complex are enriched by large flights of Antillean nighthawks; seldom seen on the mainland, this beautiful

THE FACTS

Noteworthy Animals: Key deer, great white heron, magnificent frigatebird, mangrove cuckoo, black-crowned night-heron, American alligator, American crocodile, loggerhead sea turtle.

Getting There: From Miami, take US 1. For the National Key Deer Refuge, go to the 30-mile milepost, then turn right onto Big Pine Key. (Key West is at mile 0 about 165 miles south of Miami.) The refuges are clustered north, northwest, and west of the highway.

Open: Daily, dawn to dusk, year-round.

Best Times to Visit: September through April.

Visitor Information: National Key Deer Refuge, Big Pine Key (305-872-2239), provides information on all four refuges. Open Monday through Friday, 8 a.m.- 5 p.m., year-round.

Outfitters and/or Guide Services: Call the Key West Chamber of Commerce (305-294-2587) for canoe rental agencies and guide services.

Entrance Fees: None.

Disabled Access: National Key Deer Refuge headquarters wheelchair-accessible. The Blue Hole and Watson Nature Trail are also wheelchair accessible.

Camping: Developed campsites at Big Pine Key Fishing Lodge (305-872-2351). Developed campsites at Long Key State Recreation Area (305-664-4815) and John Pennekamp Coral Reef State Park (305-451-1202) on Key Largo; fees; reservations.

neotropical migrant songbirds such as the blue-gray gnatcatcher, white-eyed vireo, yellow-rumped warbler, prairie warbler, northern parula, northern waterthrush, yellow-throated warbler, black-throated blue warbler, blackpoll warbler, black-and-white warbler, American redstart, ovenbird, and common yellowthroat.

The National Key Deer Refuge is home to the Stock Island tree snail, an endangered mollusk. Hawksbill and loggerhead sea turtles, which are also endangered, inhabit the complex; they may be seen plying the waters of the Great White Heron and Key Deer refuges, and they nest on some of the islands in the Key West refuge. The National Key Deer Refuge is also the site of the locally famed Blue Hole, a rock quarry filled with salt water and topped with a thick layer of fresh water. The hole teems with fish and turtles and supports a healthy population of American alligators.

As beleaguered as the keys themselves are, the waters that surround them are still fantastically productive, in large part because of the relatively good health of the mangrove thickets and turtle-grass flats that serve as nurseries for a great variety of fish and shellfish. Ichthyologists say that the keys contain the greatest diversity of marine fish in the world, thanks to these rich nursery areas and the fact that the islands straddle the utmost limits for both tropical Gulf species and cold-water Atlantic species.

US 1 leads straight from Miami to Key West, where it's possible to charter a boat or hire a guide and set off to prowl the turquoise bays and inlets of the refuges at leisure.

nightjar is noted for its distinctive complex call. Other birds of this region include yellow-billed cuckoo, scissor-tailed flycatcher, and Bahama mockingbird.

During the winter months, look for

Cumberland Island National Seashore

This Georgia barrier island is a birder's paradise. Look for the white-faced ibis, least bittern, tricolored heron, and anhinga.

 During the past several hundred years, Cumberland Island—the largest of Georgia's barrier islands—has been in a constant state of flux. Prior to the arrival of the Europeans, it was a rich hunting and fishing ground for the Timucuan Indians. Excavated potsherds indicate that Spanish soldiers and missionaries established base camps here as early as the mid-1500s.

By the 18th century, the British-held island supported two military forts—one on the southern shore to defend against the Spaniards, another on the northern shore to deter colonial rebels. It was not long before a large plantation was established and worked by slaves, whose cabin ruins can still be seen today.

In the 1880s Thomas Carnegie, brother of steel magnate Andrew Carnegie, and his wife, Lucy Coleman, built a palatial mansion here called Dungeness. The Carnegies had seven children, some of whose descendants are the island's only inhabitants today. After the Civil War, some of the freed plantation slaves moved to the north end of the island, where they established a free community simply called the Settlement.

The plantation and settlement were abandoned long ago, and some of the Carnegie estate was donated to the National Park Service. Cumberland Island has been gradually returning to a more natural state since it was declared a national seashore in 1971.

Today its marshes, dunes, and maritime forest are preserved for wild things and the people who come to visit them.

Eighteen miles long and 0.5 to 3 miles wide, the island is accessible only by ferry from the town of St. Marys; hiking trails and a road span most of its length. Its northern half is a designated wilderness area. A system of unsullied beaches, dunes, and freshwater ponds dominates the eastern shore, and the interior is cloaked in a lush hardwood forest. The western shore is characterized by expansive salt marshes, the largest of which are formed by the inlets and oxbows of the Brick Kiln River, which abuts the wilderness area.

Of the island's three major ecosystems, the salt marshes are undoubtedly the richest. With the ebb of each tide and the resulting exposure of the mudflats, fiddler crabs emerge from their burrows. Mullet, redfish, and many other fish species teem in the inlets and bays. More than 300 kinds of birds frequent the island, and many of them can be seen on the marshes at low tide, probing the mudflats for small crustaceans or foraging for fish in the shallows. Bring binoculars and a field guide when you visit—this is a birding paradise.

There are several bird rookeries on the island, including some that support endangered wood storks, huge wading birds with dark unfeathered heads and heavy downturned bills. Also

White-tailed deer enjoy the wide open spaces of Cumberland Island.

look for other birds that are associated with fresh and brackish water, such as white-faced ibis; tricolored, great blue, little blue, and green-backed herons; black-crowned and yellow-crowned night-herons; snowy, great, and cattle egrets; American and least bitterns; and anhinga.

Four species of terns—least, royal, Caspian, and gull-billed—are found here. These spritely black-capped birds are commonly seen diving into the water for small fish. Among the other notable marine birds are double-crested cormorant, black skimmer, Bonaparte's gull, and laughing gull.

Shorebirds visit Cumberland in great number and variety. Look for

provide good nesting sites for a substantial number of wood ducks. The extensive woodlands also swarm with songbirds, both resident and migratory. The bright red, blue, and green feathers of the male painted bunting can only be fully appreciated when the bird is seen in full sun; in poor light the nation's most colorful songbird appears quite drab. Listen for northern mockingbirds, which voice their calls in a seemingly endless cascade of notes that can last well beyond nightfall. Additional species include yellow-billed cuckoo, yellow-rumped warbler, yellow-breasted chat, yellow-throated warbler, northern parula, summer tanager, indigo bunting, eastern phoebe, Carolina wren, and gray catbird.

Raptors are drawn to Cumberland by the abundance of small prey. Ospreys, patient and diligent fish-hunters, are often robbed of their catch by bald eagles. Cooper's hawk, sharp-shinned hawk, peregrine falcon, American kestrel, merlin, great horned owl, barred owl, eastern screech-owl, and short-eared owl hunt in the woods of the island's interior. Pileated woodpeckers are frequently seen flapping through the maritime forest, hooting raucously.

long-billed and short-billed dowitchers, least sandpipers, sanderlings, ruddy turnstones, marbled godwits, whimbrels, and willet. Greater yellowlegs and lesser yellowlegs, which are readily identified by their long, brilliant yellow limbs, overwinter on the island. American avocets, black-necked stilts, and black-bellied and semipalmated plovers are frequently seen.

Cumberland Island's many trees

The most charismatic of the island's mammals are not indigenous. Both feral horses and feral hogs are numerous, to the delight of many visitors. Park supervisors, however, are not so charmed, given the damage inflicted on Cumberland's delicate habitats by these large, robust, and earnestly fecund beasts. The horses may be spotted at any time of the day, in any habitat. They resemble their barnyard

counterparts, of course, but tend to be smaller and have rougher coats.

Bobcats have been reintroduced to the island with some success. Other resident mammals here include white-tailed deer, armadillo, marsh rabbit, and raccoon. Manatees visit in spring and summer, and the lucky visitor may see them foraging in sub-

merged portions of the salt marshes.

Reptiles are abundant, including eastern rattlesnakes, eastern coral snakes, and cottonmouths, so exercise reasonable caution when hiking. The star reptiles at the national seashore, however, are American alligators and loggerhead sea turtles. The deep, basso profundo drummings of the bull gators are common spring evening concerts. Endangered loggerhead sea turtles crawl up from the sea to lay their eggs on the island's seaward beaches on spring and summer nights; lucky visitors may spot some nests.

Among the frog species croaking exuberantly through the night are pig, southern leopard, southern cricket, and little grass frogs; pine woods, barking, squirrel, green, and gray treefrogs. Toad species include eastern spadefoot, oak, and southern toad.

Spring and fall are the best times to visit Cumberland Island; the weather is usually balmy, bugs are at a minimum, and migrating birds are active and singing. The island makes an excellent destination for a day trip; the birding can be combined with fishing, beachcombing, and casual hiking. There are no stores on the island, so bring your own food and drink (water is available), and don't forget sunscreen, insect repellent, a good hat, and sunglasses.

While it is all too common to see wildland transformed into a developed tract of houses and malls, Cumberland Island provides the rare opportunity to witness the process in reverse. Once dominated by forts and mansions, it is now the domain of alligators, manatees, and shorebirds. They live here; we are just passing through.

Okefenokee National Wildlife Refuge

The highlight of a springtime canoe trip through this lush
Georgia wetland might be spotting a black bear or white ibis.

SITE 72 There are wetlands and there are wetlands, and then there's the Okefenokee. It has no peer other than, perhaps, the Everglades. With 395,085 acres—that's 617 square miles—visitors never feel crowded. This is some of the wildest country in the East—a huge parcel of lush forested wetland in southeastern Georgia and northern Florida that is the most significant remnant of the vast swamps that covered much of the area. Managed by the U.S. Fish and Wildlife Service, the Okefenokee is not untouched, but it remains the crown jewel of the Southeast's heritage wetlands and one of the nation's great wildlife bastions.

Several different habitat types are encompassed within the refuge's borders: There is bald cypress and tupelo blackwater swamp, open "prairie" marsh, upland longleaf and slash pine forests, scrub-shrub, and hardwood hammocks. Such rich habitat diversity provides niches for a wide range of species, from the thoroughly aquatic to those resolute about keeping their feet dry.

The refuge contains one of the South's largest black bear populations (perhaps as many as 500 individuals), a result of the abundant elbow room and ample forage. Canoeists regularly spot the bears traversing the prairie marshlands and moving through the upland habitats. Bobcats live here as well, favoring heavily wooded tracts; sightings are unusual and will be prized by wildlife enthusiasts.

Look for river otters disporting in the water, especially in the cooler months when the alligators are not active. The otters are not shy about

You can quickly identify a white ibis by its bright red bills and, in breeding season, red legs.

fishing or playing near humans, as long as a reasonable distance is maintained. The Okefenokee's mammal species are quite diverse, including coyote, red fox, and gray fox, as well as opossum, raccoon, white-tailed deer, marsh rabbit, fox squirrel, gray squirrel, southern flying squirrel, and armadillo. Staffers occasionally receive reports of panther (mountain lion) sightings, but none have been confirmed. The refuge's mature, cavity-rich trees support excellent populations of woodland bats: hoary, evening, red, and Rafinesque's big-eared bat.

Populations of aquatic birds have declined in recent years, whether because of natural fluctuations or more ominous factors is unclear. But the numbers are still impressive, particularly for wading birds. Wood storks and white ibis are often seen feeding in the shallow marshes and expansive cypress swamp along the Suwanee River, which flows through the center of the refuge. Roseate spoonbills occasionally pass through. Sandhill cranes forage in the prairies. It's not uncommon to spot an anhinga perching on a snag, spreading its wings to dry between dives for fish.

The tricolored heron, the quintessential heron of the Deep South, is very much in evidence. Somewhat smaller than the related great blue heron, the tricolored is blue-gray overall, with a white belly and a reddish neck and upper wings. Other commonly sighted waders include great blue, little blue, and green-backed herons; black-crowned and yellow-crowned night-herons; great, snowy, and cattle egrets; American bitterns; and purple gallinules. During the spring breeding season, the herons and egrets demonstrate aggressive mating and territorial displays. Wood ducks are year-round residents, and are often seen along the boat trails, preening their brilliant purple-blue-and-green plumage.

About 32,000 acres of the refuge are covered with pine, hardwood, and scrub, affording wonderful habitat for a great many upland birds. The long-leaf pine woods are a redoubt of the endangered red-cockaded woodpecker. In fact, the entire refuge is something of a woodpecker paradise, since the abundant timber harbors a banquet of insects and grubs. In addition to the red-cockaded, look for pileated, red-bellied, red-headed, hairy, and downy woodpeckers, northern flickers, and yellow-bellied sapsuckers.

Songbirds like the Okefenokee, too. Neotropical migrants, particularly wetland-loving wood warblers such as prothonotary and yellow-throated warblers and the northern parula, are frequent visitors. Look for them in the cypress and tupelo swamps.

Resident raptors include swallow-tailed kites and ospreys. In the winter migrating bald eagles may be seen. Also look for northern harriers, red-shouldered, sharp-shinned, and Cooper's hawks. Owl species include barred, long-eared, and great horned owls, and eastern screech-owl.

Among the turtles that are found in the Okefenokee are alligator snapping and common snapping turtles, and musk, mud, chicken, box, and Florida softshell turtles. Look for them paddling in quiet water.

Several of the nonvenomous snakes

inhabiting drier portions of the refuge are particularly handsome. Keep an eye out for Florida pine, indigo, rat, eastern milk snakes, and kingsnakes. Venomous snakes are also abundant, specifically eastern coral snakes, cottonmouths, and rattle-snakes—pigmy, timber, and eastern diamondback. Exercise caution while hiking and boating.

The night is filled with the chorus of the many frogs and toads that thrive here. In woodland areas, look (and listen) for the aptly named spring peepers and treefrogs—green, pine woods, barking, squirrel, and gray—as well as eastern narrow-mouthed, southern, spadefoot, and oak toads. Marshlands and water meadows are the favored habitats of such frogs as the chorus, little grass, cricket, river, green, leopard, pig, carpenter, and bullfrog.

The best way to explore the Okefenokee is by canoe, which affords vistas of all the major habitats. Canoes can be rented at the east and west entrances to the refuge, and a canoe trail system connects seven overnight camping shelters. Typical trips range from two to five days; high demand in March and April limits trips to three days. Reservations for the shelters are absolutely essential and are accepted two months in advance.

It's also possible to hike or drive through portions of the refuge. The Visitor Center at the east entrance maintains a boardwalk through the swamp and an observation tower. The Suwanee Canal Recreation Area on the refuge's east side has a hiking trail and an auto tour route that traverse prime red-cockaded wood-

pecker habitat. Stephen C. Foster State Park, located at the end of a peninsula that extends into the refuge, features a boardwalk, museum, and camping facilities.

Ballard Wildlife Management Area

This refuge's boardwalk, auto tour route, and camera blind offer good vantage points for observing birds, mammals, and reptiles.

SITE 73 Two hundred years ago Kentucky was a vastly different place than it is today. Woodland bison greeted the first white trappers who explored the expansive virgin hardwood forests. Settlers followed the trappers in the usual pattern, and the great oaks and hickories were felled in order to create farmland. Today the bison are long gone, and thoroughbred horses are the animals most associated with the Bluegrass State.

In one particular corner of the state, however, wild animals are doing just fine. The Ballard Wildlife Management

The gray fox favors the brushy transition zones between woodland and meadow.

Area consists of 8,373 acres of hard-wood bottomlands, riverine forests, sloughs, and oxbow lakes hard by the Ohio River. By any measure, it is one of the best wildlife-viewing areas—and one of the most accessible—in the state. Most of Kentucky's native species are found here, many in significant numbers.

Located on the Mississippi flyway, Ballard is a major stopover for migratory waterfowl, particularly geese. Most of the refuge is closed from mid-October to mid-March to protect the birds, but a boardwalk, 2-mile auto loop, camera blind, and observation post remain open throughout the year. These features afford excellent and easily accessible vantage points from which to observe migratory bird displays.

As many as 100,000 Canada geese and 200,000 snow geese stage at the refuge during the height of their fall migration in November and December, and it's not uncommon to witness a cacophonous flock numbering in the thousands settling on a field to feed or rest.

As many as 20,000 ducks congregrate here as well. Mallards are the most numerous species, but significant numbers of green-winged and blue-winged teal, northern pintail, and gadwalls also pass through. (Wood ducks are in residence year-round.)

The fall migration attracts a large complement of bald eagles. At that time as many as 50 eagles hang out at the wildlife management area, picking off birds that have been crippled by hunters in the shooting areas. There are also at least two pairs of bald eagles that nest at the refuge. Other birds of prey that hunt here include the Mississippi kite, northern harrier, Cooper's hawk, sharp-shinned hawk, and red-tailed hawk.

The spring and summer months are the best times to check out the sloughs and oxbows for wading and diving birds. In addition to great blue and green-backed herons, black-crowned night-herons, great egrets, American and least bitterns, and double-crested cormorants, Ballard is one of the northernmost sites for anhinga, the "snakebird" typically associated with the extreme southern states. Sandhill cranes also migrate through in moderate numbers and are most often seen foraging in meadows and fields.

The muddy banks of Ballard's backwaters are a major regional attraction for migrating shorebirds in the springtime. The common snipe, a rotund little shorebird with a small head and a long bill, is often seen some distance away from the water; it has a habit of suddenly launching up from the ground in an erratic zigzag flight. Killdeer and three species of sandpipers—spotted, Baird's, and least—may be seen puttering around the water's edge.

Ballard's conjunction of water and hardwood forest is very attractive to a great many songbirds. The Louisiana waterthrush, a brown warbler with a brown-and-white streaked breast,

forages boldly along the waterways. Other notable species include scarlet tanager, summer tanager, Kentucky warbler, the rare Swainson's warbler, northern parula, yellow warbler, yellow-throated warbler, warbling vireo, red-eyed vireo, northern oriole, and northern cardinal.

The mammals that live in the management area are notable for their robust populations. Gray squirrels and fox squirrels race through the tree canopies. Raccoons forage along the lake and riverbanks, particularly in the evening. River otters, beavers, and muskrats are often seen cleaving the water, with only their heads visible. Transition zones between woodland and meadows are the places to watch for white-tailed deer, coyote, gray fox, red fox, opossum, striped skunk, and eastern cottontail. Deep timber provides good cover for the bobcat; although this species is relatively abundant at Ballard, it will take a particularly alert visitor to catch a glimpse of one.

With all this water, turtles and water snakes are inevitable. Resident species include common snapping turtle, the exquisitely marked painted turtle (look for congregations of this species sunning on logs), diamondback water snake, northern water snake, yellow-bellied water snake, and Mississippi green water snake.

Frogs and toads are abundant and vocal. The beautiful gray treefrog, which is difficult to see because of its camouflaged coloration, inhabits the upper branches of trees in or near water. Other notable species include dwarf American toad, Fowler's toad, green treefrog, bird-voiced treefrog, chorus frog, spring peeper, southern leopard frog, and bullfrog.

Ballard is open year-round. The heaviest waterfowl concentrations occur in the fall and winter. Although access is somewhat limited at that time, the auto tour route, boardwalk, and observation post continue to provide good birdwatching opportunities. Spring and summer visitors have the added option of fishing or hiking their way to see shorebirds, songbirds, and frogs.

Daniel Boone National Forest

The "watchable wildlife" at this easily accessible forest includes raccoons, wood ducks, and every fish native to Kentucky.

SITE 74 With 680,000 acres distributed throughout the rugged eastern regions of Kentucky, Daniel Boone National Forest offers recreational possibilities and wildlife-watching that are unavailable anywhere else in the Bluegrass State.

Lakes are rare in Kentucky, so the existing ones act as virtual magnets for wildlife, providing reliable sources of water and forage for a wide array of species. This is the case at the man-made 8,270-acre Cave Run Lake, which is located near Morehead and surrounded by the heavily wooded wildlands of Boone. In recent years, the U.S. Forest Service has created more than 120 wetlands near Cave Run Lake.

Recognizing the importance of Boone to animals and humans, the Forest Service has embarked on an ambitious program to enhance its wildlife resources and to help visitors learn about and appreciate their furred and feathered friends. The centerpiece of the "watchable wildlife" program is the Shallow Flats Wildlife Viewing Area. Directly off Ky. 801, near Morehead, a paved viewing area with spotting scope and raised observation platform overlooks the lake, wetlands, mowed meadows, and woodlands. Because of the remarkably easy access, it's an ideal destination for very young children or people with limited mobility.

Kentucky is not the Serengeti or Alaska's North Slope, and so it isn't the place to observe charismatic megafauna. What visitors do see at Shallow Flats is a stable and healthy wildlife habitat that is well populated with species typical of the region: white-tailed deer, gray squirrels, woodchucks, striped skunks, raccoons, opossums, wild turkeys, and even the occasional coyote or red fox. In 1992

Wild turkeys, once nearly wiped out by overhunting, have made a strong comeback.

because of an active restoration program, their numbers have grown dramatically. In fact, they are now the most commonly observed species here. In the third week of June, the Forest Service bands the geese as part of a monitoring program. Volunteers are welcome to participate; call for dates and information.

The woodlands of the surrounding area provide some of the best habitat in Kentucky for songbirds, including a large population of eastern bluebirds that raise their young in artificial nest boxes. Other forest residents include rufous-sided towhee, indigo bunting, summer tanager, Louisiana waterthrush, cerulean warbler, American redstart, and warbling vireo.

Kentucky's largest warm-water fish hatchery is just north of Shallow Flats, near Cave Run Dam on Ky. 801. The Minor E. Clark Fish Hatchery contains a large viewing pool stocked with every fish native to Kentucky, including exceptionally large specimens of muskellunge, one of North America's noblest game fish, and garfish, an ancient group of predatory fish with long toothy jaws and heavy armorlike scales. In winter bald eagles congregate at the foot of the dam, drawn by gizzard shad that have been stunned by downriver water releases. As many as 15 eagles might be seen hunting in the tailwaters of the dam at one time.

In addition to offering educational programs and guided walks, the Forest Service has developed two excellent interpretive nature trails complete with stations and signs that describe the various habitats and identify areas where sightings are most probable.

river otters were successfully reintroduced into the forest.

The local population of wood ducks is booming, thanks to a nesting box program sponsored by the Forest Service. Hooded mergansers and mallards are also year-round residents, as are many wading birds, including great blue and green-backed herons. Twenty years ago Canada geese were quite rare in eastern Kentucky, but

Acadia National Park

The many aquatic species in the waters off Maine's Mount Desert Island include fin whales, harbor seals, and harlequin ducks.

SITE 75 Biological diversity is usually determined by ecological diversity—the number of different niches to wildlife in a given area. Ecological diversity, in turn, is created by the convergence of different habitats, creating abundant "edges," or ecotones.

Acadia National Park—certainly one of the richest wildlife sites in all of the Northeast—is a veritable cornucopia of ecotones, a 35,000-acre archipelago characterized by boreal coniferous forest, deciduous temperate forest, coastal peatlands, riverine thickets, granite palisades, freshwater lakes, brackish ponds, protected estuaries, and rocky coastline. Acadia is not, however, a remote wilderness. It shares Mount Desert Island with the good-size town of Bar Harbor and smaller towns and hosts two million visitors annually. It also supports a vast array of wild species in a great variety of habitats.

There are at least 44 terrestrial mammals that live in the park. White-tailed deer are the most common large mammal, and they might be seen anywhere along roads and trails.

You will often see fin whales on a summertime whale-watching expedition from Acadia.

River otters, mink, and beavers haunt the park's ponds and streams. Red foxes and striped skunks prowl along the riverbanks and hunt in brushy areas and meadows. Fishers and marten, the rarest of the continent's deep-forest mustelids, also favor the deep woods. They are known to live in the park but are considered rare.

Of as much interest as the land-dwelling mammals are their marine brethren. The waters surrounding the park support an abundance of pinnipeds and cetaceans. Park Service and private boat trips are regularly scheduled from spring through fall, and commonly observed species include fin whales (the world's second largest animal, after blue whales), minke whales, sei whales, humpback whales, Atlantic white-sided dolphins, harbor seals, and gray seals. Right whales are also seen with relative frequency. As of 1997, federal regulations require vessels to keep a quarter mile away from right whales. Lately harp seals, a species usually associated with more northern latitudes, have been seen in and around the park during the winter months.

Acadia is also phenomenally rich in birds—at least 335 species have been recorded within its borders or immediately offshore. Flocks of marine birds offer some stunning displays, slashing nearshore schools of baitfish during the spring and summer. Black guillemots and common eiders are often seen on and around the headlands. Other nearshore marine birds that are sighted regularly include brant; red-necked and horned grebes; Bonaparte's, laughing, and herring gulls; common tern; double-crested

and great cormorants; and common loon. Offshore birds are sometimes present in mind-boggling numbers from late spring through early fall; species include Atlantic puffin, northern gannet, northern fulmar, sooty shearwater, and Wilson's storm-petrel.

Perhaps the most unusual aquatic bird at Acadia is the harlequin duck. Though relatively common in Alaska and the Rocky Mountains, these handsome diving ducks—dramatically marked in russet, gray, black, and white—are extremely rare in the Northeast. A small population that ranges from Baffin Island on the Arctic Circle to Maine is thought to be a subspecies or race separate from the western group. About 500 harlequin ducks spend the winter at Acadia's Isle au Haut, braving the tumultuous surf for mussels and chitons. In spring they fly north to forage and breed on swift-flowing streams in northern Atlantic Canada.

Raptors are another major attraction at Acadia. There are at least six pairs of bald eagles and three pairs of peregrine falcons that nest within the park's borders. The concentration of peregrines might seem unusual, except for two important factors: the abundance of sheer granite cliffs (a favored peregrine nesting site) and the throngs of seabirds and songbirds, which peregrines relish. The National Park Service maintains observation platforms on the Precipice Hiking Trail, one of the peregrine nesting sites.

Ospreys also nest in Acadia, as do northern goshawks, sharp-shinned hawks, and northern harriers. Snowy owls might be seen in the winter, and great horned, barred, and northern saw-whet owls reside in the park throughout the year.

Acadia's forests also shelter a great many songbirds, most notably wood warblers and other neotropical migrants. More than 20 individual warbler species are consistently recorded in the park. Birders delight in the spring migrations when the birds are active and in their most vibrant plumage phase. In deep old-growth woods, look for Blackburnian, black-and-white, Tennessee, and Nashville warblers. Near rivers, ponds, and wetlands, the likely species include common yellowthroat, northern parula, northern waterthrush, and yellow, palm, bay-breasted, Canada, and black-throated blue warblers. Second-growth groves, mixed woodlands, and scrublands are the places to look for magnolia, black-throated green, and chestnut-sided warblers; ovenbird; and American redstart.

Other notable passerines include solitary and red-eyed vireos, hermit thrushes, and wood thrushes. Handsome songbirds such as golden-crowned and ruby-crowned kinglets, scarlet tanager, rose-breasted and evening grosbeaks, purple finch, pine siskin, common redpoll, and white-winged crossbill are consistently sighted.

Perhaps the best recommendation for Acadia is that there are so many different ways to see it. Good paved roads provide fine car access. Park boat tours afford fantastic overviews of the coastline, while sea kayaks allow for more intimate exploration. Acadia has 45 miles of carriage roads that are off-limits to cars. Mountain bikers, hikers, and horseback riders use them in the snowless months, and

THE FACTS

Noteworthy Animals: Fin whale, minke whale, right whale, harbor seal, gray seal, white-tailed deer, river otter, beaver, peregrine falcon, osprey, snowy owl, harlequin duck, purple finch.

Getting There: From US 1 at Ellsworth, pick up Maine 3 south for about 10 miles to the park Information Center.

Open: Daily, 24 hours, year-round.

Best Times to Visit: Year-round.

Visitor Information: Acadia National Park Headquarters near Eagle Lake (207-288-3338) open daily, 8 a.m.-4:30 p.m., November to mid-April; Monday through Friday rest of year. A Visitor Center (no phone) southeast of Hull's Cove is open daily, 8 a.m.-4:30 p.m., mid-April through October; until 6 p.m. in July and August.

Outfitters and/or Guide Services: Guides can be hired and sea kayaks and mountain bikes can be rented from Acadia Bike and Coastal Kayaking (207-288-9605) and the Acadia National Park Outdoor Activity Center (207-288-0342).

Entrance Fees: $5 per vehicle for one day; $10 per vehicle for four days.

Disabled Access: The Visitor Centers are fully accessible.

Camping: Blackwoods Campgrounds: fees; reservations required; Seawall Campgrounds: fees; no reservations; (call DESTINET 800-365-2267).

Accommodations: Bar Harbor offers a full range of accommodations. Call the Chamber of Commerce (207-288-5103 or 800-288-5103) for information.

cross-country skiers employ them in the winter. Regardless of the time of year, Acadia has much to offer both the outdoor recreationalist and the serious wildlife enthusiast.

Allagash Wilderness Waterway

A floating canoe makes a fine platform for observing the black bears and white-tailed deer that live along this remote river.

SITE 76 The Allagash River flows north from Chamberlain Lake into Quebec, traversing about three million acres of northern coniferous and hardwood forest. This is legendary trout-fishing country as well as one of the finest wildlife venues in the Northeast. A float down the Allagash will yield memories that will last a lifetime: ospreys snagging fish in front of the canoe; bald eagles keening overhead at sunrise; moose foraging in the shallows, framed by a backdrop of black spruce and balsam fir; legions of trout breaking the water during an insect hatch.

This state-managed wilderness consists of 92 miles of waterway roughly divided between headwater lakes and river, and a canoe trip is the only way to see it. There are several requisite portages and some mild white water

Black bear cubs, born in January or February, quickly learn the art of tree-climbing.

in the river sections—Class II at the highest. Still, even Class II rapids can present problems for a fully loaded canoe, especially if it is manned by novice paddlers. This is a genuinely remote part of the East, so exercise reasonable care and precautions when making the trip.

The Allagash is a haven for the region's megafauna. Black bears are probably as numerous here as they are anywhere in the Northeast. They're often seen foraging along the shore, particularly in the fall when they are fattening up for the winter hibernation. Moose are extremely common and can be found wherever there is succulent herbage bordering the river or abundant aquatic plants. The Allagash is also a primary wintering area for white-tailed deer, which feast on the bountiful white cedar along the river's corridor.

Furbearers are abundant: fisher, marten, red fox, bobcat, coyote, ermine, and mink. Seeing them is strictly a matter of being in the right place at the right time, but canoes are ideal platforms for surreptitious wildlife observation. River otters and beavers are also common, and riverside hardwoods often bear evidence of the beavers' not-so-tender ministrations. Some lynx have been spotted as well but are considered rare. Also keep an eye out for the "little critters"—red squirrels, fox squirrels, muskrats, snowshoe hares, and woodchucks.

Birds of prey are very much in evidence along the river. In addition to bald eagles and ospreys, look for northern goshawks, the biggest and most aggressive of the continent's woodland raptors. Sharp-shinned and Cooper's hawks also hunt the woods. American kestrels, merlins, and red-shouldered and broad-winged hawks favor the more open areas along the river. Great horned and northern saw-whet owls are sighted regularly. Long-eared owls are sometimes found in large groups in conifer groves, and snowy owls hunt along the river's corridor in the winter months.

Two types of grouse occur here—the common mottled-brown ruffed grouse and the rarer blue-gray spruce grouse. Both favor brushy coverts and generally are not seen unless they are flushed from cover. American woodcocks probe for earthworms in the moist soil of hardwood groves. The dipsy-doodle flight pattern of these snipelike birds is distinctive.

The Allagash system is a major brood area for aquatic birds, particularly ducks and gulls. A large herring gull rookery on the appropriately named Gull Island is used by locals as an indicator for the river's ice-out in spring. The first gulls typically show up about 30 days before the ice runs. Common loons appear shortly after the ice goes, nesting and hooting along the system's lakes and backwaters. Brooding ducks include the American black duck, ring-necked duck, and common goldeneye. This is also good breeding territory for mergansers, the "fish ducks" known for their serrated bills, colorful plumage, and fish-eating proclivities. All three

species of North America's mergansers—common, hooded, and red-breasted—nest here.

The Allagash also serves as a vast flyway and brooding area for songbirds. Flycatchers, including the great crested flycatcher, alder flycatcher, yellow-bellied flycatcher, and eastern phoebe, are all quite common. In the spring, look for wood warblers nesting in the riverside trees. In addition to the Tennessee warbler, a small bird with a yellowish breast and green back that is particularly abundant during outbreaks of spruce budworm, species include Nashville, yellow, magnolia, Cape May, myrtle, chestnut-sided, blackpoll, and Wilson's warblers; ovenbird; American redstart; and northern waterthrush. In the deep woods, be on the watch for eastern wood-pewee, red-breasted nuthatch, hermit thrush, Swainson's thrush, and veery. Ruby-crowned and golden-crowned kinglets are active, tiny birds that can be recognized by their brightly colored heads. Other significant species include blue-gray gnatcatcher; solitary and red-eyed vireos; rose-breasted, evening, and pine grosbeaks; and hoary and common redpolls. Pine siskins, red crossbills, and white-winged crossbills will often be spied in the conifers.

The Allagash system is especially rich in fish and amphibians. In addition to abundant brook trout in the river and lake trout and landlocked salmon in the headwater lakes, species include whitefish, burbot, and white sucker. Frogs are abundant along the river, particularly in quiet backwaters and marshy shorelines. Of particular note are the beautifully spotted northern leopard frog and the pickerel frog and mink frog. Bullfrogs and green frogs also live along the river. In the woods and grassy areas, wood frogs—attractive little frogs with cunning black eye masks—may be found. At night all these amphibians raise their myriad voices in earnest chorus, providing a lovely accompaniment to the moon and stars.

Terrestrial salamanders are common but not often seen, as they usually bury themselves in leaf mold or soil.

Moose calves feed in the shallows of the Allagash River.

Resident species include blue-spotted, spotted, northern dusky, northern two-lined, and red-backed salamander.

Until a couple of decades ago, a float down the Allagash was more an expedition than a mere trip, requiring strenuous lake crossings, arduous portages, and a minimum of two week's time. Now good roads provide sufficient access to the river to make three- and four-day float trips feasible; the entire river course can be run in a week.

Blustery winds on the headwater lakes can swamp full canoes, so watch the weather and exercise appropriate caution. Inexperienced canoeists should always travel with a seasoned veteran and plan trips late in the season, when the water isn't high. This isn't a place for novice paddlers to explore solo. The most challenging white water on the trip is Chase Rapids, a 9-mile stretch of Class II white water between Churchill Dam and Umsaskis Lake. A portage service is available for those who wish to avoid the run. Keep an eye out for the mandatory portage around Allagash Falls near the end of the trip; running the falls could prove fatal.

The blackfly season usually runs throughout the summer. These vicious little insects can be maddening so pack insect repellent and netting. The system's lakes are a popular winter destination for ice fishermen, cross-country skiers, and snowmobilers. Fishermen should beware of thin ice, and recreationalists of all stripes must keep an eye out for inclement weather. With the exception of a single trail to Chamberlain Lake, no winter access routes are maintained.

Blackwater National Wildlife Refuge

This Chesapeake Bay sanctuary boasts growing numbers of breeding bald eagles. Golden eagles, rare in the East, also pass through.

SITE 77 Most of the land that borders Chesapeake Bay once resembled the Blackwater National Wildlife Refuge—a biologically rich maze of brackish marsh, freshwater marsh, tidal creeks, and mixed woodlands. Today the bay and its critical wetland resources are under siege, seriously threatened by pollution and development. But the Blackwater refuge, at least, has remained relatively unspoiled. At over 23,000 acres, it contains the best terrestrial habitat left on the bay. And with further acquisitions planned, it serves as an anchor for an ambitious regional restoration program that may help the Chesapeake region regain some of its former glory.

Managed by the U.S. Fish and Wildlife Service, Blackwater is perhaps best known for its population of breeding bald eagles. In 1996, 12 pairs of eagles nested at Blackwater, and an additional 15 pairs nested in adjacent environs. A total of 80 fledglings were raised from these nests—a stunning wildlife success story by any measure. Look for the eagles in spring and early summer, when they are raising their fledglings. (Ask at Refuge Headquarters about nest locations.) Winter populations of these majestic birds can exceed 200 birds.

Golden eagles (raptors typically associated with the West) are also seen at the refuge, usually from November through March. Ospreys are also common from spring through early fall and are often seen cruising above the tidal waters, looking for fish, or tending their young on nesting platforms erected by the refuge. Other common birds of prey include northern harriers—typically seen flying low over the marshlands—and red-tailed hawks, rough-legged hawks, and American kestrels, which use trees, telephone poles, and fence posts as vantage points. Great horned owls, common barn owls, and short-eared owls may be seen at dusk, when they launch themselves on silent pinions for the hunt.

Given its location, it should come as no surprise that Blackwater supports large populations of migratory waterfowl. Up to 35,000 Canada geese, 5,000 snow geese, 20,000 ducks, and 1,500 tundra swans may be found here by late autumn or early winter. The geese mass in large congregations at different points throughout the refuge; ask at headquarters for good viewing sites. Puddle ducks such as mallard, blue-winged and green-winged teal, and American wigeon favor backwaters that are out of the direct wind. Northern pintail like open "sheet" water in the middle of large tidal ponds and inlets, as do diving ducks such as canvasback, redhead, greater scaup, lesser scaup, common goldeneye, bufflehead, hooded merganser, and red-breasted merganser.

Shorebirds flock to the refuge in the spring, when staffers create extensive mudflats by drawing down freshwater

Sika deer, naturalized from Asia, have prospered in Blackwater's mixed woodlands.

ponds. Look for semipalmated plover, killdeer, common snipe, spotted sandpiper, willet, greater yellowlegs, lesser yellowlegs, red knot, dunlin, sanderling, long-billed dowitcher, and short-billed dowitcher. Wading birds are likely to be seen at the junctions of land and water. Species include American bittern, great blue heron, little blue heron, great egret, snowy egret, cattle egret, green-backed heron, black-crowned night-heron, and glossy ibis.

The refuge is excellent songbird country, particularly for wetland-associated species. In spring and autumn, look for warblers in wooded or brushy areas, most notably prothonotary warbler, northern parula, yellow warbler, Louisiana waterthrush, common yellowthroat, Canada warbler, and American redstart. Red-winged blackbirds are common in the reeds and sedges, the males defining and defending their nesting territories by aggressively displaying their bright crimson shoulder patches. Flycatchers can often be spotted flitting high up into the air from a bush or fence post to snag bugs; individual species include eastern phoebe, Acadian flycatcher, willow flycatcher, least flycatcher, and eastern kingbird. Other songbirds often spotted in the marshes include tufted titmouse, marsh wren, veery, blue-gray gnatcatcher, golden-crowned kinglet, savannah sparrow, Henslow's sparrow, and seaside sparrow. Bluebird nest boxes on the refuge yield nearly a hundred young each year.

Mammals are plentiful. This is prime territory for the Delmarva Peninsula

fox squirrel, an endangered species once endemic to much of Maryland but greatly reduced in range in recent decades. Thanks to judicious habitat management, these large silver-colored squirrels are doing exceedingly well at Blackwater.

River otters disport in the ponds and creeks. Muskrats are omnipresent, largely because the refuge was once a fur farm where the bucktooth little furbearers were propagated. Nutrias are also common—too common, according to refuge managers. These voracious rodents are naturalized from South America, and they are exerting a negative impact on aquatic vegetation, destroying extensive areas of tidal marsh. White-tailed deer are common, as are sika deer, an exotic from Asia. Unlike nutrias, however, sika deer appear to be living within their means and are not considered pests. Look for them placidly browsing near the loop road and trails.

While the birds and mammals get all the attention, the refuge is most essential for what is under the water, not above it. Blackwater is one of the best shellfish and finfish nursery areas on the bay. Clams, oysters, crabs, and numerous species of fish depend on the refuge's sheltering marshes and estuaries; without Blackwater and its sister estuarine lands, Chesapeake Bay would be a biological desert.

The refuge is open year-round, but winters can be blustery and summers sultry. Come in the spring to catch the optimum populations of shorebirds, and in late autumn for ducks and geese. (Call first to check estimated populations.) The refuge maintains a tour route that affords good views of all the major habitats. It can be driven but is best explored by bicycle (bring your own). The loop is 6.5 miles long. Two hiking trails—the Woods Trail and the Marsh Edge Trail—provide excellent venues for observing songbirds. Fishing is allowed; anglers might want to try their luck for crappie and black sea bass in the Blackwater River in the upper reaches of the refuge.

Nassawango Creek Cypress Swamp Preserve

Easily explored on foot or by canoe, this Maryland sanctuary offers glimpses of wood warblers and river otters.

SITE 78 One of the continent's richest wildlife habitats, bald cypress swamps have been greatly reduced in range and acreage, drained for agriculture and development. Associated with the Deep South, they nevertheless penetrated as far north as Delaware and as far west as Illinois. The Nassawango Creek Cypress Swamp Preserve is one such anomaly. By any reckoning, it is one of the northernmost stands of bald cypress remaining on the continent, a living heirloom from the millennia following the last ice age, when the cypress swamps greatly expanded their range in response to the warming climate.

Owned and managed by the Nature Conservancy, the preserve packs a lot of biodiversity into its 3,000 acres. Thick forests border the swamplands surrounding Nassawango Creek, a meandering stream subject to tidal influence from nearby Chesapeake Bay. This confluence of upland and wetland habitats attracts a wide variety of wildlife species. Birds are very well represented at the preserve, most notably wetland-associated wood warblers, which dote on the combination of forest and swamp. At least 21 different species of warblers live in or migrate through the preserve, including the prothonotary warbler, a bold bird with dazzlingly yellow plumage that is associated with bald cypress swamplands. Also be on the lookout for Swainson's warbler, ovenbird, common yellowthroat, Kentucky warbler, northern parula, orange-crowned warbler, yellow warbler, yellow-rumped warbler, American redstart, and yellow-breasted chat.

Various flycatchers, including the willow flycatcher, eastern phoebe, and eastern kingbird, perch on branches from which they launch themselves for midair strikes against tasty insects. Both red-breasted and white-breasted nuthatches may be observed creeping up or down the trunks of the larger trees. Among the more colorful songbirds are the intensely orange-and-black northern oriole, and the summer tanager, northern cardinal, blue grosbeak, eastern bluebird, and indigo bunting. Also look for brown creeper, house and winter wrens, golden-crowned and ruby-crowned kinglets, blue-gray gnatcatcher, northern mockingbird, cedar waxwing, and warbling and red-eyed vireos. The many sparrow species include American tree, chipping, field, vesper, savannah, song, and white-throated.

Woodland-associated hawks and owls are often seen at the preserve, especially during the fall migration, which usually peaks in October. Look for Cooper's hawks, sharp-shinned hawks, and the occasional northern goshawk lurking in the trees; red-tailed hawks are often seen soaring over the open areas of the preserve. Barred owls and great horned owls likewise

THE FACTS

Noteworthy Animals: Prothonotary warbler, willow flycatcher, wood duck, red-breasted nuthatch, pileated woodpecker, Cooper's hawk, river otter.

Getting There: From Annapolis, take US 50 east to Salisbury, then proceed south on Md. 12 about 13 miles to Snow Hill. Turn right at Old Furnace Road and drive about a mile to the preserve's parking lot at the Furnace Town Village Store.
Open: Daily, dawn to dusk, year-round.
Best Times to Visit: March through November.
Visitor Information: The Nature Conservancy of Maryland/District of Columbia office (301-656-8673) open Monday through Friday, 9 a.m.-5 p.m., year-round. No visitor center on-site.
Entrance Fees: None.
Disabled Access: Paul Leifer Nature Trail is wheelchair accessible.
Camping: None on-site.

branches overhanging the water, chittering madly before diving for small fish. Resident waders include great blue, little blue, and green-backed herons; black-crowned night-herons; great and snowy egrets; and American bitterns.

The creek supports a thriving population of river otters. These fun-loving mustelids will usually tolerate discreet human observers, and the displays they stage in their pursuit of fish or recreation can be spectacular. White-tailed deer are very common and can often be seen browsing along woodland edges. Other common species include striped skunk, opossum, and raccoon.

Northern water snakes and painted turtles are common, though wary; silent exploration along the creek or through the swamp is requisite for seeing them. Nassawango Creek is also quite rich in fish and is an important spawning ground for striped bass, shad, and herring.

The Nature Conservancy maintains two short nature trails. The easiest one to find is the Paul Leifer Nature Trail, which is reached via Old Furnace Road. A canoe trip through the Nassawango is hugely rewarding. Canoes can be rented at the nearby town of Snow Hill; the bridge crossing at Red House Road is the traditional put-in. The 2-mile float to Nassawango Road makes for an easy half-day trip; more ambitious paddlers can continue another mile or so to the creek's confluence with the Pocomoke River, then proceed upstream to Snow Hill. It's wise to avoid periods of extreme low tides, as water levels can drop considerably.

haunt the trees, and ospreys fish along the Nassawango's course.

The abundance of trees, both dead and living, make the preserve a wood-pecker haven. Pileated woodpeckers—gaudy, crow-size, and noisy—are common here. Yellow-bellied sapsuckers, northern flickers, and downy, hairy, and red-headed woodpeckers are also present in the forest. On the ground, wild turkeys and American woodcocks populate the coverts.

Aquatic birds that may be spotted include American black duck, wood duck, and hooded merganser, a fish-eating duck with a marvelously bushy crest. Belted kingfishers perch on

The pileated woodpecker boasts a red cap and loud, ringing call.

Monomoy National Wildlife Refuge

During the spring and fall migrations, millions of shorebirds search for food in the tidal flats of these islands off Cape Cod.

SITE 79 The Monomoy Islands have the distinction of two designations: national wildlife refuge and federal wilderness. It's easy to see why such double-barrel status was bestowed on them. Dangling off Cape Cod's elbow, this 3,000-acre refuge looks much as it did before the Pilgrims arrived, with pristine dunes and marsh framed by the sparkling sea. About 250 different species of

birds have been logged at Monomoy, making it one of the richest birding sites in New England. Marine birds and shorebirds are the top attractions here, although waterfowl, raptors, and songbirds also turn up in impressive numbers.

The two islands—North and South Monomoy—were part of the mainland until 1958, when a fierce storm severed the sandspit from the

The Monomoy Islands offer space and peace for 250 species of birds, including the least tern.

mainland. In all likelihood, they will someday be rejoined with the continent, given the constant shifting of nearshore sands. For now, however, the breach heightens the sense of isolation visitors experience on exploring this beautiful seaside realm.

The only way to reach the refuge is by boat. A private ferry leaves from the beach in front of the Visitor Station (located on the mainland) regularly during daylight hours throughout the summer, and shuttles can be arranged at two marinas in the nearby village of Chatham. Transit time to North Monomoy is about 20 minutes, about double that for the south island.

The Western Hemisphere Shorebird Reserve Network has declared Monomoy to be a regionally significant shorebird staging area. During the spring and fall migrations, literally millions of shorebirds descend on the refuge's rich tidal flats to replenish themselves with nutritious invertebrates. This is a particulary good site to observe Hudsonian godwits—large, slender shorebirds with long bills and chestnut breasts.

The diversity of shorebirds at Monomoy can be mind-boggling. During the migrations, individuals from any or all of the following species may be seen commingling on the beaches, frantically probing the sand for invertebrates: piping and black-bellied plover; ruddy turnstone; long-billed and short-billed dowitchers; killdeer; willet; greater and lesser yellowlegs; and spotted, pectoral, least, western, and semipalmated sandpipers.

Monomoy supports one of the largest herring and great black-backed gull rookeries on the East Coast. In fact, far too many gulls nest here. No gull nests were recorded in 1960, but drawn by local garbage dumping (since restricted), the gulls moved in and multiplied with a vengeance. In 1995, 12,000 pairs of gulls nested here, to the great detriment of smaller and meeker shorebirds. The gulls have usurped most of the available brood areas on the refuge, and managers are contemplating control measures that will allow shorebirds to reclaim some of their nesting habitat.

Other commonly observed migratory marine birds include endangered roseate terns; northern gannets (often seen diving for fish after storms); ring-billed and Bonaparte's gulls; common, least, arctic, and Caspian terns; black skimmers; double-crested cormorants; red-throated loons; horned and red-necked grebes; sooty shearwaters; and northern fulmars. Wilson's storm-petrels, graceful soot gray birds, skim over the surface of the sea.

Most wading birds here—including great egret, great blue heron, and black-crowned night-heron—are relatively bold and can often be observed blithely stalking the shallows for fish and crustaceans. Green-backed herons and American bitterns are more timorous; look for them in quieter backwaters.

Brant, the small, dark goose of the continent's nearshore marine waters, are often seen in large flocks winging

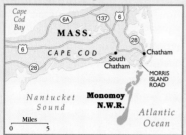
winter months, marine ducks are very common, most notably white-winged, surf, and black scoters. Common eiders, big sea ducks with sloped heads and heavy bills, overwinter here. Also look for male oldsquaw ducks, which have distinctive pink-striped bills and long tails.

Raptors are attracted to Monomoy because of the high-quality habitat and abundant prey. Sightings of ospreys, bald eagles, and peregrine falcons are regularly reported. Additional sightings include northern harrier, red-tailed hawk, rough-legged hawk, and American kestrel.

Mammals are not found in great numbers or variety, though a colony of white-tailed deer that were stranded on the islands after the 1958 storm continue to eke out an existence. Coyote scat has been found along the strand, though no sightings have been confirmed. It is thought that the opportunistic little canids are swimming over from the mainland to hunt the whitetails.

Monomoy's fisheries and shellfisheries are robust. Conservation measures have brought back striped bass and bluefish populations dramatically, and soft-shell clams and quahogs are found throughout the tidal flats. Angling and clamming (in season and with a state license) can pleasantly augment a day at the refuge.

Trails encircle both islands; transit from one island to another, obviously, must be accomplished by boat. Private camping is not allowed, but overnight camping and natural history excursions are sponsored by the Cape Cod Museum of Natural History and the Massachusetts Audubon Society.

over the water or grazing on tidal flats. Marshes and freshwater ponds on the southern end of South Monomoy support breeding mallards, American black ducks, blue-winged teal, and common mergansers. In the fall and

Pascagoula River Wildlife Management Area

The rare yellow-blotched map turtle is just one of the many species sustained by this lush riverine habitat, the best in Mississippi.

SITE 80 Mississippi is generally thought of as a rural patch-work of sleepy small towns and cotton fields. But there's some truly wild country here in the deepest heart of the Deep South—most notably, the corridor of the Pascagoula River. At 40,000 acres of hardwood bottomland, blackwater swamp, and remote oxbow lakes, it constitutes the finest wildlife habitat in the state.

The preserve was land originally owned by a local timber company. In a green version of a corporate takeover, the Nature Conservancy of Mississippi bought the firm and liquidated its assets, keeping the land and selling off the equipment. The land was then sold to the state of Mississippi; under the state's management the preserve has become one of the South's show-case refuges and recreation sites.

This is a land of lush vegetation. Along the river and its tributary creeks, bald cypress, water tupelo, and black gum thrive in primeval swamps. In upland areas where the seasonal flooding due to is shorter, mast-bearing species such as Nuttall oak, overcup oak, and water oak prevail. Hundreds of species of mammals, birds, reptiles, and amphibians make their homes here, affording visitors excellent viewing opportunities by

The cottonmouth, one of the pit viper family, should never be disturbed; its bite can be fatal.

Pascagoula's abundant lily pads serve as little rafts for the brilliant purple gallinule.

means of canoe, foot, or car.

This is stellar mammal habitat. White-tailed deer are exceedingly abundant. Black bears transit through the bottomlands. Sightings are not particularly common, but it is often possible to find tracks and scat. Bobcats are common and the lucky visitor may see one of these extremely shy felines at dawn or dusk. Look for river otters in the oxbows—the narrow lakes that form whenever the river breaches its banks during floods, then retreats. Mink also favor wetland areas. Gray foxes, long-tailed weasels, opossums, raccoons, striped skunks, swamp rabbits, and armadillos may be glimpsed dashing through the undergrowth. Look for gray, fox, and southern flying squirrels in the forest

canopies. Woodland bats—including eastern pipistrelle, hoary, red, evening, big brown, and Rafinesque's big-eared—are doing well. Look for them at dusk, when they glean the evening sky for flying insects.

Two rare raptors—the Mississippi kite and the swallow-tailed kite—maintain nesting populations here. Sharp-shinned hawks and Cooper's hawks nest in the woods. In open areas, soaring red-shouldered hawks, broad-winged hawks, American kestrels, and merlins are likely sightings. Bald eagles and ospreys occasionally pass through the Pascagoula. Great horned, barred, long-eared, and short-eared owls are resident.

Wading birds are well represented, sustained by the tremendous quantity of fish, amphibians, reptiles, freshwater crustaceans, and aquatic invertebrates available for the taking. In the backwaters, herons (tricolored, great blue, little blue, green-backed, and black-crowned night-heron) and great and snowy egrets are commonly seen by visitors. American and least bitterns, which are declining over their range due to habitat loss, are in residence but are seldom seen. These extremely shy brown-and-buff herons frequent marshy areas with thick reeds, where their excellent camouflage hides them from view. Glossy ibis, yellow rail, soras, and purple gallinules are much more visible.

The Pascagoula is also a major staging area for waterfowl using the Mississippi flyway during the fall and winter migrations. Mallards, American black ducks, gadwalls, blue-winged and green-winged teal, and northern shovelers all pass through. Wood ducks live here year-round, making their homes in the cavities of old trees and nesting boxes maintained by refuge staff and volunteers.

Neotropical migrant songbirds are also doing well along the Pascagoula. Two rare and gorgeous warblers, the bright yellow prothonotary and the brilliant blue cerulean, are sighted with regularity. The hooded warbler, another rare species, has also been noted. Other warblers include orange-crowned, Swainson's, myrtle, yellow-throated, pine, and Kentucky warblers; Louisiana waterthrush; common yellowthroat; northern parula; and yellow-breasted chat. Watch for them in spring, when they display vibrant breeding colors. Vireos, yellowish gray relatives of warblers, are

also well represented: yellow-throated, red-eyed, white-eyed, and solitary. Also be on the lookout for the brightly plumaged northern oriole, American goldfinch, summer tanager, eastern bluebird, blue grosbeak, indigo bunting, and painted bunting. Other noteworthy passerines include wood thrush, hermit thrush, blue-gray gnatcatcher, and American pipit.

The wildlife area is rich in native fishes, including the gigantic alligator gar, which can weigh 300 pounds. Rare Gulf sturgeons also swim here. Other fish species include spotted gar, short-nose gar, long-nose gar, bowfin, largemouth bass, spotted sunfish, white crappie, bluegill, and long-ear sunfish. Bring your tackle—the angling is great.

The Pascagoula is one of the best sites in the country for herptiles. The American alligator, of course, rules. Alligators are particularly numerous in the oxbows, where fish and turtles—their favored prey—are plentiful. Look for these fearsome reptiles at dusk, when they often cruise with only their eyes above water.

The yellow-blotched map turtle, endemic to the Pascagoula system, is on both the state and the federal threatened species lists. Gopher tortoises also live here and are sometimes spotted as they crawl along the forest floor. Other turtles include the alligator snapping turtle and common snapping turtle; mud, musk, and chicken turtles; river cooter; red-eared slider; and smooth softshell and spiny softshell. Look for them sunning on banks and logs.

Snakes, including venomous species, are very common. When in doubt

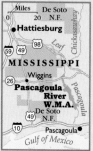
about a snake's species, give it a wide berth. Cottonmouths are found wherever there is water, as are eastern coral snakes. Eastern diamondback and pigmy rattlesnakes inhabit the drier areas. Nonvenomous water snakes such as southern and northern water snakes, plain-bellied and diamondback water snakes thrive. Particularly attractive terrestrial snakes include the black pine snake, rat snake, mole kingsnake, scarlet kingsnake, and speckled kingsnake, all of which display arresting

striped, speckled, or spotted skin patterns. Other resident snakes include queen, garter, eastern ribbon, earth, red-bellied, ringneck, smooth earth, eastern hognose, southern hognose, rainbow, scarlet, rough green, coachwhip, and southern black racer.

Amphibian diversity is likewise splendid, particularly where salamanders are concerned. Aquatic species include lesser siren, three-toed amphiuma, two-toed amphiuma, and eastern newt. Any or all of them may be observed along quiet waterways. Terrestrial salamanders are harder to spot, since they often burrow in the leaf mold and soil. Notable species are mole, small-mouthed, marbled, dwarf, and long-tailed salamander.

Frogs and toads are here in big numbers, but they are more often heard than seen; the twilight choruses can be most impressive. In the woods, southern, Woodhouse's, and oak toads; green, gray, barking, pine woods, squirrel, and bird-voiced treefrogs; and spring peeper, chorus, and cricket frogs are common. Aquatic frog species include pig, river, green, southern leopard, and bullfrog.

The refuge is open year-round, but be aware that summers are positively torrid, with both temperature and humidity often reaching the 100°F mark. Refuge access is excellent: Well-maintained roads lead to myriad trailheads for hikers and canoe put-ins. Seasonal water levels can affect both trail and waterway access, so check in at the Visitor Center before setting out. The Gulf of Mexico, only 20 miles to the south, is replete with opportunities for fishing, crabbing, and beachcombing.

Green Hills Preserve

Black bears roam this rugged New Hampshire sanctuary, devouring blueberries in preparation for winter hibernation.

SITE 81 Like much of New England, this 2,822-acre Nature Conservancy preserve is heavily forested. The usual upland northern hardwoods predominate, but there are also four regionally rare woodland communities: vernal woodland pools, hardwood swamps, rocky summit boreal spruce forests, and red pine ledge forests. These varied forest habitats, combined with a large pond that adjoins the preserve, have resulted in exceptional wildlife diversity.

New England's large mammals are particularly well represented here. Black bears are truly abundant. There are at least two active denning sites on the preserve, and large numbers of bears forage in the extensive blueberry patches and beech groves in late summer and fall, fattening up for winter on fruit and mast. Chances of spotting a bruin are good during this pre-hibernation feasting.

Moose are often seen in the boreal forests, and white-tailed deer are ubiquitous. The whitetails are so common, in fact, that hunting is not prohibited, as it usually is in a protected area. Without an annual cull, the deer would quickly overwhelm their available range.

Mammals include bobcats and coyotes, although sightings of these shy animals are rare. Look for red and gray foxes in meadows and scrubby areas. River otters and mink frequent ponds and wetlands, as do ermines, long-tailed weasels, striped skunks, and raccoons. Look up into the tree canopy for glimpses of gray, red, or northern flying squirrels. Fishers—big, rare, densely furred mustelids—are spotted with some regularity, particularly in stands of older timber.

The preserve's varied canopies and woodland types make it a haven for neotropical migrant songbirds, particularly warblers and especially in the spring. Older-growth groves, easily identified by the large size of the trees, are hot spots for birds. Look for Blackburnian warblers, northern parulas, and black-and-white warblers. Most warblers, however, prefer open forest areas. Commonly sighted species include Nashville, yellow, magnolia, Cape May, black-throated blue, black-throated green, myrtle, chestnut-sided, bay-breasted, blackpoll, Tennessee, pine, palm, mourning, Wilson's, and Canada warblers; ovenbird; northern waterthrush; and American redstart.

Vireos, those small gray birds of the understory, are also well represented. In spring yellow-throated, red-eyed, Philadelphia, solitary, and warbling vireos are all in residence. Several other songbirds are worth noting, particularly the intensely colored scarlet tanager, rose-breasted grosbeak, and indigo bunting; their names eloquently describe their hues. The evening grosbeak, colorfully arrayed in yellow, black, and white, is equally attractive.

Woodland raptors are quite common throughout the area. The

You'll often see white-tailed deer in the forests of Green Hills Preserve.

sharp-shinned hawk, a handsome gray-backed, russet-breasted accipiter, might be seen perching on snags or fences. Northern goshawks move through the woods on occasion; look for them in dense forest. Barred, great horned, long-eared, boreal, and northern saw-whet owls are very common and are sometimes spotted at their daytime perches in densest portions of the woods. Peregrine falcons cruise the sheer granite outcrops that characterize much of the preserve and, in spring and fall, migrating bald eagles and ospreys pass through.

The 100-acre pond that borders the preserve provides excellent habitat for wading birds and waterfowl; the birdwatching is especially good in the spring. A thriving great blue heron rookery is located here, and wood ducks brood in nesting boxes maintained by Conservancy volunteers. Nesting American black ducks and mallards are often seen along the pond's margins.

The preserve's vernal pools constitute some of the richest amphibian territory in the state. Among the noteworthy species to be aware of are the increasingly beleaguered northern leopard frog, a beautiful large frog with spotted skin, and the handsome blue-spotted salamander. Other resident species include American toad, gray treefrog, spring peeper, green frog, pickerel frog, wood frog, eastern newt, Jefferson salamander, spring salamander, red-backed salamander, and northern two-lined salamander.

An excellent multiuse trail system has been established at Green Hills, helping make it a favorite regional destination for hikers and mountain bikers. Located in the heart of New Hampshire's ski resort region, the preserve also attracts plenty of winter recreationalists; cross-country skiing and snowmobiling are both allowed. Green Hills is too big and rugged to be explored in a day—a weekend would be ideal.

William D. & Jane C. Blair, Jr., Cape May Migratory Bird Refuge

In the fall, this seaside sanctuary boasts the heaviest concentration of raptors—eagles, hawks, and ospreys—in the country.

SITE 82 Situated at the southernmost tip of New Jersey, Cape May separates Delaware Bay from the Atlantic Ocean. This unique geographic position makes it a kind of avian funnel; birds traveling up and down the eastern seaboard during the spring and fall migrations become concentrated here, incidentally creating some of the most spectacular birding on the continent.

This is one refuge where limited terrain works for rather than against the naturalist. At 187 acres, the Cape May Refuge is tiny as far as nature preserves go. Yet it is habitat of the highest quality, a combination of tidal flats, wetlands, dunes, and scrublands. Visitors don't need to walk long distances or stalk quietly for hours to see wildlife; the birds are everywhere.

The refuge is located on what was once the seaside resort town of South Cape May, incorporated in 1884. In the 1950s a huge storm blew in and inundated the town, which was abandoned. The site was used for farming and grazing until 1981, when it was acquired by the Nature Conservancy.

In autumn the refuge receives the largest concentration of raptors in the United States. Tens of thousands pass through on their southward migration. Both bald eagles and ospreys hunt the tidelands and marshes for fish, and visitors might see the opportunistic eagles bullying the hardworking ospreys into yielding their catch.

Other birds of prey that use the refuge include northern harriers, peregrine falcons, American kestrels, merlins, and Cooper's, sharp-shinned, and red-tailed hawks.

Migrating ducks and geese are also abundant in the fall. Sighting a tundra swan, America's most numerous swan, is almost a sure bet. Brant, Canada geese, mallards, and American black

ducks are also regularly seen. Eurasian and American wigeon, northern shovelers, and gadwalls feed in sheltered coves, while greater and lesser scaup, canvasback, redhead, king eider, common goldeneye, bufflehead, hooded merganser, ruddy duck, and black, surf, and white-winged scoters favor more open water.

Warblers are especially numerous at Cape May, both in numbers and species. In the fall, look for the Cape May warbler (of course). Any tree or shrub is likely to support an orange-crowned, yellow, yellow-rumped, Nashville, black-throated green, Tennessee, or worm-eating warbler, which despite its name, doesn't eat worms. Golden-winged and blue-winged warblers, two species that are increasingly hybridizing with each other, may also be seen. Other warbler species include chestnut-sided, bay-breasted, pine, prairie, palm, Kentucky, mourning, and hooded warblers; American redstart; common yellowthroat; and yellow-breasted chat. Other songbirds that flock to the

The tricolored heron's nest, constructed from sticks, can be found in trees or bushes.

THE FACTS

Noteworthy Animals: American kestrel, merlin, peregrine falcon, least tern, piping plover, tricolored heron, brant, Cape May warbler, monarch butterfly.

Getting There: From Atlantic City (about 100 miles north), take the Garden State Parkway south to its end, in the town of Cape May. Bear right at West Perry Street, which becomes Sunset Boulevard, and follow it for 1 mile. The refuge is on the left, just past Bayshore Drive.
Open: Daily, dawn to dusk, year-round.
Best Times to Visit: May and June; September through November.
Visitor Information: The Nature Conservancy of New Jersey, Morristown office (609-785-1735), open Monday through Friday, 9 a.m.-5 p.m, year-round. No visitor center on-site.
Disabled Access: One observation platform is wheelchair accessible.
Camping: None on-site.

ularly numerous along the tidal flats. Look for short-billed and long-billed dowitchers, black-bellied plover, black-necked stilts, greater and lesser yellowlegs, willet, spotted and least sandpipers, ruddy turnstones, red knots, sanderlings, and dunlins. Wading birds that nest locally include great blue, tricolored, and little blue herons; clapper, black, and Virginia rail; and American and least bitterns. During the spring breeding season great, snowy, and cattle egrets display the long delicate plumes that were so prized by milliners a century ago.

Cape May is also a rest stop for migratory insects, most notably monarch butterflies. Thousands of these beautiful orange-and-black butterflies pass through during their annual autumnal transcontinental flight to wintering grounds in Central America. Monarchs have declined dramatically over much of their range as a result of habitat destruction, so the significance of Cape May grows each passing year.

Located at the southernmost end of the Jersey Shore—one of the East Coast's primary tourist destinations—the Cape May refuge offers a welcome respite from the bustle of surrounding commercial developments. Plan to spend at least a day here. Trails traverse all parts of the refuge, and a kiosk provides maps and pamphlets. An interpretive center is in the planning stages. Remember, however, that this is an extremely popular preserve, and birds are thus vulnerable to disturbance. Stay on marked trails and cross dunes only at designated sites. Leave all pets, bicycles, horses, and motorized vehicles at home.

refuge during the fall migration are willow flycatcher, eastern phoebe, eastern bluebird, veery, summer tanager, blue grosbeak, and indigo bunting. The northern cardinal is a year-round resident.

Spring migrations are not as dramatic as their fall counterparts, though birds still move through in considerable numbers. The least tern and the piping plover nest at Cape May at that time. Both brood in the dune area of the preserve, so visitors are required to stick strictly to the paths to avoid disturbing these and other birds.

In the spring, shorebirds are partic-

Adirondack Park

The haunting cry of the loon echoes along the many waterways
that thread New York State's Adirondack Mountains.

SITE 83 Founded in 1892 with an
avowed purpose of remain-
ing forever wild, Adirondack
Park is huge by eastern standards—
some 120 miles north to south and 80
miles east to west. Most of the 2.7 million acres of public lands in the park
are designated as forest preserve; under
the state constitution they cannot be
sold, developed, or exploited in any
way. In 1972 the state approved the
Adirondack Park State Land Master
Plan, further toughening restrictions
on public land within the park area.
Four broad categories define usage—
wilderness, primitive, canoe, and wild
forest; for all practical purposes, all are
wilderness designations, and natural
resources are strictly protected.

Paradoxically, not all the land in the
park is public; in fact, more than half
of it is private. Running around and
through the pristine wilderness of the
park's public lands are large parcels of
private holdings, including ski resorts
and summer camps, scores of towns
and villages, and hundreds of miles of
paved highway. This successful partner-
ship between private and public inter-
ests shows that wildlife conservation
can be predicated on the coexistence
of human and wildland habitats.

It is no exaggeration to say that the
Adirondacks teem with wildlife. But
don't go there expecting to see rare
beasts parading before your car like
creatures in an animated movie. The
Adirondacks are heavily wooded

The Adirondacks' lakes and rivers provide ideal nesting spots for the common loon.

The shy red fox is very difficult to find.

mountains threaded with numerous waterways. In other words, this is rugged, densely vegetated terrain, and the animals that live here are true creatures of the forest—extremely wary and quite adept at evasion. But patience and stealth usually yield some good sightings. To increase your likelihood of success, follow the lead of the wildlife: Go to the lakes and streams close to dawn and dusk, when most mammals drink. Although the cover is thick, quiet observation is often rewarded.

There are many ways to explore this vast park: by foot, canoe, car, or combinations of the three. One of the best ways to observe the Adirondacks' wildlife is from a canoe. From Saranac Lake in the north-central region of the park, a chain of lakes and connecting streams runs 70 miles southwest, providing multiple routes. The canoeing is also excellent on the Raquette River Reservoir and the Cranberry Lake-Oswegatchie River area in the park's northwestern corner. Paddle slowly during the early morning or late afternoon hours, have your binoculars handy, and try to keep

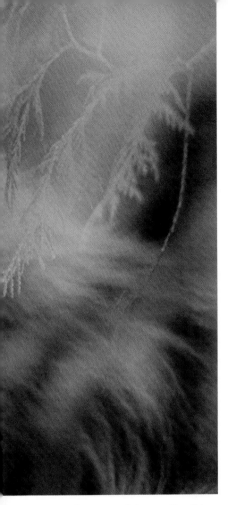

foliage is thinner (not to mention riotously colored), making observation easier. Also, bear and deer are feeding voraciously on mast and berries in anticipation of winter; they are more apt to be out and about during daylight hours than they are in the earlier seasons. Be aware, however, that hunting is allowed in this area; the season opens in mid-October.

Small predators are extremely common throughout most areas of the park; species include ermine, long-tailed weasel, striped skunk, raccoon, river otter, mink, gray fox, and red fox. Of particular interest to wildlife enthusiasts is the relative abundance of marten and fishers. These large deep-forest mustelids are generally rare throughout their continental range but are thriving here. They are difficult to observe, however, because of their reclusive nature and nocturnal habits. Chances are increased by frequenting undisturbed stands of old timber at dawn and twilight.

Other common mammals that are widely distributed throughout the park's reaches are beaver, porcupine, snowshoe hare, red squirrel, gray squirrel, northern flying squirrel, and several species of bats: eastern pipistrelle, big brown, silver-haired, and hoary bats; little brown, small-footed, Keen's, and Indiana myotis.

More than 30 species of reptiles and amphibians have been logged in the park. During the summer the evening concert of spring peepers, bullfrogs, and pickerel, mink, leopard, green, chorus, and wood frogs can be stirring indeed. The park boasts notable diversity in newt and salamander species: ten in all, including the mudpuppy,

conversation to a minimum. Possible sightings could include black bear, white-tailed deer, moose, coyote, and perhaps even a bobcat.

Backpacking is another popular activity. Lovely day-hiking routes are scattered throughout the park; the High Peak area southeast of Saranac Lake is particularly popular, but has suffered damage from overuse. Greater solitude might be found at the Tongue Mountain trail complex near Lake George in the southeast park, or the Goodnow Mountain trail system near Newcomb. Trailside sightings of large mammals are more likely during the fall than in spring or summer. The

eastern newt, and spotted, mountain, red-backed, two-lined, and four-toed salamanders. Look for amphibians, as well as common snapping turtles and painted turtles, along any pond or lakeshore or in quiet backwaters of streams, creeks, and marshes. Ring-

Although fishers are primarily nocturnal, some are active during the day.

neck, smooth green, and milk snakes are found in upland areas; timber rattlesnakes are found only in the Lake George basin.

Birds, not surprisingly, run heavily to woodland species, although numerous waterfowl and some wading birds frequent the lakes, streams, and fens during the spring. More than 20 types of warblers inhabit the park; frequently observed species include black-and-white, Tennessee, magnolia, black-throated blue, black-throated green, Cape May, and Blackburnian warblers.

Other songbirds likely to be seen are the hermit thrush, brown thrasher, least and yellow-bellied flycatchers, black-capped chickadee, brown creeper, golden-crowned and ruby-crowned kinglets, yellow-throated and solitary vireos, scarlet tanager, rose-breasted and evening grosbeaks, bobolink, American redstart, and song sparrow.

Common loons are so abundant that they have become an emblem for the lakes of the Adirondacks. Their cry, which John Muir described as "one of the wildest and most striking of all wilderness sounds," will indelibly mark the heart of anyone who hears it.

Other water-associated birds that frequent the Adirondacks during the fall migration and spring breeding season include Canada geese; American black, ring-necked, and wood ducks; mallards; green-winged and blue-winged teal; American wigeon; common and hooded mergansers; common goldeneyes; lesser scaup; green-backed and great blue herons; and American bitterns. In spring shorebirds such as killdeers; common snipes; semipalmated plover; spotted, solitary, and least sandpipers; and greater and lesser yellowlegs may be seen.

Woodland raptors are abundant, although they are typically seen only as flashes of plumage through the understory. Sharp-shinned, broad-winged, and Cooper's hawks hunt here; so does the threatened northern goshawk. American kestrels, ospreys, and merlins are fairly common, and there have been occasional sightings of bald eagles and peregrine falcons. Owls, including great horned, barred, common barn-, northern saw-whet, and long-eared, are plentiful. In spring and summer the evening sky blossoms with the aerial displays of common nighthawks and chimney swifts. The spring and summer months are also the best times to look for tree, bank, and barn swallows.

In addition to being one of the Northeast's most significant wildlife strongholds, the Adirondacks are a recreational wonderland. There is no finer place in the state for day hiking and camping. Scores of little resorts and motels make the park extremely popular for extended summer vacations. Summertime fishing for trout and landlocked salmon is superb. And the angling doesn't stop during the winter: The park's lakes are a favorite with local ice fishermen. Other popular winter pastimes include cross-country skiing, snow-shoeing, and snowmobiling. At Lake Placid, site of the 1932 and 1980 Winter Olympics, visitors can even try the luge or bobsled runs.

But with nearly three million acres to roam, it's impossible to pin down "best" areas for either wildlife or humans. For a first visit to the park, it's a good idea to call the New York State Department of Environmental Conservation for planning materials. Once there, don't be shy about asking registered Adirondack guides, park staff, locals, and other visitors about their favorite wildlife or recreation site—everyone has at least one.

THE FACTS

Noteworthy Animals: Black bear, red fox, marten, fisher, common loon, northern goshawk, Cooper's hawk, magnolia warbler, scarlet tanager, painted turtle.

Getting There: Adirondack Park covers one-fifth of upstate New York, and many large and small routes crisscross it, linking communities, campgrounds, and recreation areas spread out across it. Main access routes are I-87 north from Albany, N.Y. 12 north from Utica to N.Y. 8 and N.Y. 28 east, and N.Y. 3 east from Watertown. N.Y. 30 runs through the middle of the park from Malone to Mayfield.

Open: Daily, 24 hours, year-round.

Best Times to Visit: March through November.

Visitor Information: New York State Department of Environmental Conservation, Albany (518-897-1200). Visitor Centers in Newcomb (518-582-2000), on N.Y. 28 about 60 miles north of Old Forge, and Paul Smiths (518-327-3000), on N.Y. 30 about 15 miles north of Tupper Lake, provide information for the entire park. Both open daily, 9 a.m.-5 p.m., year-round. The Adirondack Regional Tourism Council (about 120 miles north of Glens Falls) open daily, 8 a.m.-5 p.m., year-round and will answer questions in person or by phone (518-846-8016 or 800-487-6867).

Entrance Fees: None.

Disabled Access: Visitor Centers at Paul Smiths and Newcomb are wheelchair accessible. Many developed observation points along lakes and rivers are accessible.

Camping: The N.Y.S. Department of Environmental Conservation operates 43 campgrounds in the park; call 800-456-2267 for reservations.

Accommodations: Consult the Visitor Centers or the Saranac Lake Chamber of Commerce (518-891-1990).

Mashomack Preserve

Winter is the ideal time to spot harbor seals swimming offshore or resting on the rocks of this Shelter Island sanctuary.

SITE 84 Only 90 miles from New York City, Shelter Island dominates Peconic Bay at the eastern end of Long Island. Used as an exclusive hunting club for generations, the 2,039-acre Mashomack Preserve now accounts for the entire southeastern third of the island. It was obtained by the Nature Conservancy in 1980, ensuring that the "jewel of the Peconic" will remain forever wild.

For the northeast's urban corridor, this is truly a huge refuge. When combined with Morton National Wildlife Refuge and other reserves on both the north and south forks of Long Island, it serves to protect one of the richest marine and estuarine environments on the eastern seaboard. There are 17 miles of trails at the Mashomack Preserve, spanning a multitude of different habitats: tidal marsh, freshwater and brackish wetlands, upland forest, meadow, and coastal strand. More than 80 species of birds have been recorded breeding here, and 56 different species overwinter.

If there is one species that is emblematic of Mashomack, it is the osprey. These magnificent hawks were almost extirpated by DDT and other chlorinated hydrocarbon pesticides in the 1950s and 1960s. Since the banning of these poisons, the osprey has made a stunning comeback at Mashomack. Several pairs nest at the preserve, and their annual springtime return from their wintering grounds

along the Gulf Coast is much heralded on Shelter Island. Local birds of prey include red-tailed hawks, American kestrels, merlins, eastern screech-owls, and great horned owls.

Another species of particular

interest is the ruby-throated hummingbird. Population fluctuations
among these birds have been linked
to the annual availability of Usnea
lichen, an epiphyte that grows on
some of the preserve's trees and
shrubs. The hummingbirds, it seems,
are extremely particular about the
materials they use to line their nests—
Usnea is by far the preferred choice.
So, the more Usnea, the more hummingbirds.

Other birds often seen in the upland
areas include scarlet tanagers, dazzling
red birds of the woodland canopy.
Northern orioles, rufous-sided towhees,
solitary vireos, northern parulas, yellow
warblers, yellow-rumped warblers,

Local birdwatchers rejoice in the spring, when ospreys return to Shelter Island to nest.

THE FACTS

Noteworthy Animals: Osprey, red-tailed hawk, ruby-throated hummingbird, hooded merganser, least tern, laughing gull, great horned owl, harbor seal, white-tailed deer, mink.

Getting There: From New York City, take the Long Island Expressway to the Manorville-Hampton Bays exit south to connect with N.Y. 27 east to Bridgehampton. From there take N.Y. 79 north about 5 miles to connect with N.Y. 114 in Sag Harbor. Turn left and proceed north about 3 miles to the Shelter Island Ferry. The ferry carries both cars and pedestrians and runs every ten minutes, daily, year-round, 6 a.m. to midnight; no reservations required. Once on the island, proceed north on N.Y. 114 for 1 mile to the preserve.

Open: Wednesday through Monday, 9 a.m.-5 p.m.; winter hours vary.

Best Times to Visit: December through February; late March through mid-June.

Visitor Information: Mashomack Preserve Visitor Center (516-749-1001) open Wednesday through Monday, 9 a.m.-5 p.m., Memorial Day through Columbus Day; open weekends only rest of year. Maps are always available.

Entrance Fees: Suggested donation is $1.50 for adults; $.50 for children under 12.

Disabled Access: Visitor Center is fully accessible, and one short trail has a wheelchair-accessible boardwalk.

Camping: None on-site.

rally attract a great many waterfowl, wading birds, and shorebirds. During the fall and winter months, American black ducks, greater scaup, white-winged scoters, common and Barrow's goldeneyes, buffleheads, hooded and red-breasted mergansers, and American wigeon shoal up on the open water. Double-crested cormorants perch on rock outcroppings between dives for fish. In spring and summer, great and snowy egrets; great blue, little blue, and tricolored herons; and black-crowned night-herons frequent the inlets and coves. Black-bellied plover, killdeers, willet, spotted sandpipers, ruddy turnstones, dunlins, and sanderlings teem on the tidal flats. Laughing, ring-billed, herring, and great black-backed gulls; and common, roseate, and least terns are abundant in the waters near shore.

Mammals are typical for this part of the East—white-tailed deer, mink, red fox, and raccoon. Winter is the best time to look for mammals; not only are they easier to see against the snow, but their abundant tracks are plainly visible. Harbor seals frequent the waters around Shelter Island and use some of the more remote areas for haul-outs (resting spots). The best places to see seals are on the rocks bordering the Gardiner's Bay Trail.

Mashomack makes an ideal day trip from New York City and the surrounding metropolitan area. Not only is it a place of superb natural beauty and impressive biodiversity, but it offers an extensive trail system that allows for a variety of hikes, from one-hour strolls to all-day marathons. A variety of guided walks is offered; call the Visitor Center for details.

American redstarts, northern cardinals, and indigo buntings are all common sightings in the spring and summer, when they join the resident chipping sparrows and American tree sparrows.

Shelter Island's rich wetlands natu-

Green Swamp Preserve

Red-cockaded, pileated, red-bellied, and downy woodpeckers pound on the dead wood at this North Carolina coastal preserve.

SITE 85 Red-cockaded woodpeckers are fastidious birds. They will nest only in the cavities of old-growth pines. There are plenty of pine trees in the South—the region's timber industry is booming, and new plantings go in all the time. But most trees are harvested before they start developing the capacious cavities—induced by disease, insects, or injury—that red-cockaded woodpeckers need to propagate. The result has been a precipitous decline in the species; until a few years ago, it seemed that the red-cockaded woodpecker would go the way of its cousin, the extinct ivory-billed woodpecker.

There is nothing particularly dramatic about the red-cockaded woodpecker's appearance. It is a small woodpecker with a buff breast and a red earpatch. It is gregarious, often gathering in groups of six or more. But these are canaries in the coal mine as much as they are woodpeckers in the pine woods. As they go, so go the ecological health and biodiversity of the region. Red-cockaded woodpeckers are not, so to speak, out of the woods yet. But projects like the

Green Swamp Preserve shelters a healthy population of red-bellied woodpeckers.

Nature Conservancy's 15,770-acre Green Swamp Preserve on North Carolina's coastal plain offer hope that the decline of this species can be halted and perhaps reversed.

The preserve is a combination of pocosin wetland and sandy ridges dominated by pine savannas. (Pocosin lands are characterized by deep, extremely acidic peat soils and shrubby vegetation.) The plant diversity of the savannas is tremendous. In some areas, there are more than one hundred species per square yard. Biologists consider Green Swamp and similar coastal plain wetlands second only to virgin tropical rain forests in biodiversity. Among the flora here, the most renowned species is the Venus flytrap, which grows only in a 70-mile radius from Wilmington. Pitcher plants, also carnivorous, are likewise common.

Red-cockaded woodpeckers are not the only tree pounders to find the swamp salubrious. Other species here include pileated, red-bellied, red-headed, hairy, and downy woodpeckers. They are likely to be found wherever there are standing dead trees. Aquatic birds are also common. White ibis, herons (great blue, yellow-crowned and black-crowned night-herons), and great and snowy egrets all have rookeries here. Tricolored herons, purple gallinules, and American and least bitterns may be seen hunting for fish and crustaceans in open areas of water.

The swamp is excellent songbird habitat. One of the great local success stories is that of the eastern bluebird, which has been in decline for years but is making a strong comeback in the preserve. The prothonotary warbler, the rare golden warbler of the deep eastern swamps, is also here. The hooded warbler (named for the male's black hood), another neotropical migrant that has undergone dramatic declines in recent decades, also nests in the swamp. The rare Bachman's sparrow is seen with some regularity. Look for the rare Swainson's warbler as well as the more common orange-crowned, yellow-throated, palm, and Kentucky warblers; common yellowthroat; yellow-breasted chat; wood and hermit thrushes; blue-gray gnatcatcher; golden-crowned and ruby-crowned kinglets; and red-eyed vireo. Northern bobwhite quail are fairly common in the upland areas; listen for their call in the spring.

Birds of prey include the broad-winged hawk. Chunky and somewhat sluggish, these bar-breasted hawks sometimes act truly tame, allowing for close observation. Watch for them perched near (or soaring over) water, where they hunt reptiles and amphibians. Other resident raptors are red-shouldered, Cooper's, sharp-shinned, and red-tailed hawks, and the occasional bald eagle or osprey.

Black bears are thriving in the swamp, a result of the abundant cover and ample food. An observation is most likely in June, when the blueberries are ripe. Bobcat, gray fox, mink, long-tailed weasel, striped skunk, raccoon, opossum, fox squirrel, and marsh rabbit also inhabit the thickets. Chances of a sighting are best at dawn and dusk. River otters are fairly numerous, particularly in the creeks that drain the swamp. Resident bats include little brown myotis and red, hoary, evening, and Rafinesque's big-eared bats.

As in most reasonably intact south-eastern wetlands, herptiles are diverse and numerous. The swamp is home to three species of glass lizards, which are legless lizards of subterranean habits. Many of the resident snakes inhabit the preserve's deepest coverts and are not likely to be seen. Still, chances of observation are increased by moving as quietly as possible. Heavy footfalls and snapping brush quickly convince snakes to move on. Some possible sightings include brown, rough green, pine, rat, and milk snake; kingsnake; pigmy and timber rattlesnakes; and southern black racer. Cottonmouths are very abundant in and around water; they are aggressive and venomous, so take appropriate measures to avoid them.

American alligators are regularly seen in a pond near the trailhead. Turtles, which are extremely sensitive to disturbance, are abundant wherever there is ample water. Look for common snapping turtles; mud, musk, spotted, box, and chicken turtles; cooters and river cooters; and sliders. Frogs are best appreciated at dusk, when their myriad croakings fill the air. Species include the southern leopard frog, a beautiful spotted frog that has declined significantly across much of its range in recent years. Also in residence are many species of tree-frogs—green, pine woods, barking, squirrel, and gray—and the related chorus, ornate chorus, little grass, cricket, carpenter, green, and gopher frogs; spring peepers; and bullfrogs.

Green Swamp is managed by the Nature Conservancy to protect the resident plants and animals. Because these communities are tremendously

THE FACTS

Noteworthy Animals: Red-cockaded woodpecker, red-bellied woodpecker, yellow-crowned night-heron, eastern bluebird, broad-winged hawk, black bear, bobcat, American alligator.

Getting There: From Wilmington, drive southwest on US 17 about 20 miles to the town of Supply. There, turn right onto N.C. 211 and drive north about 6 miles to the preserve's parking area.
Open: Daily, dawn to dusk, year-round.
Best Times to Visit: October through May.
Visitor Information: The Nature Conservancy of North Carolina, Durham office (919-403-8558); local stewardship office, Wilmington (910-762-6277); both open Monday through Friday, 9 a.m.-5 p.m., year-round. No visitor center or on-site facilities.
Entrance Fees: None.
Disabled Access: None.
Camping: None on-site.

vulnerable to human disturbance, a good portion of the preserve is not accessible to visitors. Right now only one trail exists (off N.C. 211, about 5.5 miles north of the town of Supply), and it's being overused, resulting in damage to the habitat. An expanded trail system is in the works, but in the interim, visitors are requested to call ahead for information about human density levels and alternative routes. With a good pair of binoculars, successful birdwatching is possible even from a car parked on the shoulder of N.C. 211, the road that skirts the preserve.

Pea Island National Wildlife Refuge

Vast numbers of birds, including oystercatchers, stilts, and skimmers, nest on the beaches of this barrier island refuge.

SITE 86 North Carolina's barrier islands are a haven for many oceanic and estuarine species, whether finned or feathered. And perhaps the best place to witness this panoply of marine life is Pea Island National Wildlife Refuge, a strategically located refuge on Hatteras Island that encompasses all the region's critical wildlife habitats—ocean beach and dunes, maritime scrublands, salt marsh, brackish ponds, and estuaries.

Managed by the U.S. Fish and Wildlife Service, the refuge consists of 5,915 acres of land and salt marsh and 25,700 surface acres of water in Pamlico Sound, giving both wildlife and visitors ample room to stretch and explore. This is an ideal place for long walks; the terrain is easy, and good wildlife viewing is almost guaranteed. Aquatic birds are the main attraction here; at least 264 different species use the refuge as a nesting, wintering, or staging ground.

In spring large nesting colonies of black skimmers, common terns, and endangered least terns can be seen on the oceanside beaches. American oystercatchers—big, ploverlike birds with heavy, bright red bills—nest on the beaches and dunes. Also nesting here are black-necked stilts—tall, delicate shorebirds with exceptionally long legs and beautiful black-and-white markings. In 1996 a pair of threatened piping plover nested at the refuge, the first to do so in many years. Ospreys also nest in and around the refuge, as

do black-crowned night-herons and white ibis, which prefer to utilize shrubs at the edges of ponds. American black ducks and gadwalls also brood at Pea Island, though their nesting success is marred by the high population of common snapping turtles, which feed on the tender ducklings.

Shorebirds and waterfowl pass through in the thousands during both spring and fall migrations. Shorebirds, including greater and lesser yellowlegs, semipalmated and black-bellied plover, common snipes, killdeers, willet, red knots, and dunlins, are typically spotted along the beaches and estuaries at low tide. Least, semipalmated, and western sandpipers can be easily confused with one another since all three species display similar gray-white-and-brown plumage.

Tundra swans are the most dramatic waterfowl at the refuge. Look for them in the man-made ponds and the more remote parts of the estuaries. Snow geese and Canada geese throng here, as do mallards, northern pintail, green-winged and blue-winged teal, American wigeon, northern shovelers, redheads, canvasbacks, ring-necked ducks, greater and lesser scaup, common goldeneyes, buffleheads, ruddy ducks, and hooded, common, and red-breasted mergansers.

Many types of wading birds also frequent the estuaries and beaches at low tide. Species include tricolored heron, great blue heron, little blue heron, green-backed heron, yellow-crowned

The brown pelican is a familiar sight in the waters surrounding Pea Island NWR.

night-heron, American bittern, clapper rail, black rail, yellow rail, snowy egret, and great egret.

Marine birds crowd the beaches and nearshore waters. Brown pelicans are year-round residents. Northern gannets overwinter here and are often seen diving into nearshore waters for fish from considerable heights. Other commonly observed birds include double-crested cormorant, great black-backed gull, Bonaparte's gull, ring-billed gull, and Forster's tern.

In the fall large numbers of migrating raptors pass through the refuge. Bald eagles are seen occasionally, and peregrine falcons are reported regularly. The broad, open terrain of the refuge teems with rodents and small birds, which attract large numbers of hawks. Look for the big birds soaring or hovering over the beach and

estuaries or perching on fence posts, telephone poles, and snags. Noted species include red-shouldered, red-tailed, and broad-winged hawks, northern harrier, and merlin.

The refuge is one of the continent's northernmost nesting sites for loggerhead and green sea turtles. In an average year, about 10 to 15 nests are dug on the beaches. The sea turtles, zealously protected by a local corps of volunteers, appear to be making a moderate comeback along the barrier islands. Another success story at Pea Island is the diamondback terrapin. This saltwater and estuarine turtle was almost driven to extinction early in the 20th century because of the popularity of turtle soup.

The salt environment here is not particularly good for snakes but a few species manage to thrive. Southern black racers; eastern kingsnakes; northern water and brown water snakes; garter, brown, rough earth, rough green, and rat snakes are here. There are no venomous snakes, though cottonmouths and timber rattlesnakes are known to inhabit barrier island lands to the north and south.

The salt environment also minimizes mammal populations. Red foxes, raccoons, and opossums are abundant but reclusive; chances of seeing them are best at dusk. Nutrias and muskrats abound in the waterways and may be seen at any time; they, too, are most active at dawn and twilight.

The refuge is open year-round. Spring is the best time to see the seabird colonies and migrating shorebirds. Fall and winter are the seasons for observing migratory waterfowl. Well-maintained nature trails and observation towers make birding exceptionally easy. Pamlico Sound and the inshore Atlantic Ocean adjacent to the refuge comprise some of the richest fishing grounds off the continental United States. Bluefish, red drum, black drum, weakfish, blue crab, shrimp, and oysters inhabit these waters, and are sought enthusiastically by both locals and savvy visitors.

Allegheny National Forest

On an easy hike through this Pennsylvania forest, you might spot white-tailed deer and raccoons.

In 1900 there was no Allegheny National Forest. That's because all the trees had all been logged, leaving behind a vast panorama of brush and stumps. Today the forest is back, albeit in a modified form. While the primeval forest had been beech, maple, and eastern hemlock, the current mix runs toward transition species: oaks, white ash, yellow poplar, and most particularly, black cherry. The black cherries produce an abundance of fruit ("soft mast" in the vertebrate biologist's parlance) that many species of wildlife find delicious. Add acorns from the abundant oaks, and the result is a solid foundation for a rich food web.

White-tailed deer have perhaps taken undue advantage of all this excellent sustenance. Deer density at Allegheny is exceptionally high; apparently higher than any other large tract of wildland in the country. Their teeming numbers have literally transformed the forest. A hike at Allegheny is like a stroll through a manicured woodland park: beautiful open stands of hardwoods carpeted at their roots with ferns. There is little or no shrubby undergrowth because the deer have eaten it all. This simplification of woodland structure has made this 500,000-acre forest easy to hike, and easy to spot the deer, but has also reduced the available niches for

Although raccoons are quite sedentary, a male will travel miles in search of a mate.

A porcupine has an average of 30,000 protective quills.

many species of wildlife.

Still, the species that are doing well are doing very well indeed. Like the deer, the black bears of Allegheny comprise one of the most robust populations east of the Mississippi. And given the forest's open structure, sightings are much more likely here than in most of the Northeast. Look for them in the late summer and fall, when the bruins are gorging on fruit and nuts in preparation for winter.

River otters are plentiful here, thanks to successful reintroduction programs. The first otters were stocked in 1990; they have since expanded their range dramatically and are successfully reproducing. In coming years, the sight of otters cavorting in the forest's clear clean streams should be relatively commonplace. The success of that program led, in 1997, to the reintroduction of fishers; although it is too soon to tell, all signs are that they, too, will thrive at Allegheny.

Mink, raccoons, beavers, and muskrats frequent streams and ponds. Look for them when the sun is either setting or rising; examine muddy riverbanks for their tracks, which are usually abundant. Red squirrels, gray squirrels, northern flying squirrels, and southern flying squirrels inhabit the forest canopy; walk quietly and look upward to see them. Porcupines might also be seen in the trees, eating bark, or on the forest floor, waddling from one tree to another. Other resident mammals include coyotes, red and gray foxes, and long-tailed weasels. All are most active at dawn and dusk, though coyotes may be spotted at any time of the day or night.

From a birder's perspective, Allegheny contains one of the continent's most important wildlife sites: Hearts Content, a tract of hardwoods that was somehow spared the frenzied logging of the last century. Some of the trees at Hearts Content are 500 years old: huge, hoary beeches and maples that rise majestically into the sky, providing shelter for rare old-growth-associated songbirds. For example, Blackburnian warbler densities at Hearts Content are 45 times greater than at any other known site in North America. Other species include cerulean warbler, black-and-white warbler, worm-eating warbler, black-throated green warbler, warbling vireo, wood thrush, hermit thrush, and Swainson's thrush. Two other old-growth groves—the Tionesta Scenic and Natural Area and Hickory Creek—also offer good birding for these species.

Allegheny's huge tracts of second-growth woodland serve the many species of warblers that prefer this kind of habitat, most notably chestnut-sided warblers. John James Audubon saw this species only once during his lifetime, presumably because most of the forests of his day had yet to see the logger's ax and crosscut saw. Today the chestnut-sided warbler is one of the most common songbirds at Allegheny; its populations have exploded in direct correlation to the increasing availability of its favored habitat. Other species likely to be seen in second-growth groves include golden-winged warbler, blue-winged warbler, Nashville warbler, yellow warbler, and ovenbird. Spring is the best time to look for these wood warblers.

The forest supports a diverse assemblage of woodland raptors, including red-shouldered hawks and northern goshawks. Ospreys fish at Allegheny Reservoir, a large impoundment on the northern end of the forest. At least two pairs of bald eagles nest at

THE FACTS

Noteworthy Animals: White-tailed deer, black bear, river otter, raccoon, beaver, porcupine, Blackburnian warbler, chestnut-sided warbler, cerulean warbler, bald eagle, osprey.

Getting There: Allegheny National Forest is primarily accessible by Pa. 66 off I-80, and US 62, which skirts the forest's western border. From Pittsburgh, take I-79 north for about 70 miles. Pick up I-80 east and follow it to Pa. 66 to reach the forest's borders.
Open: Daily, 24 hours, year-round.
Best Times to Visit: April through October.
Visitor Information: Allegheny National Forest, Warren headquarters (814-723-5150), open Monday through Friday, 7:30 a.m.-4:30 p.m., year-round. No visitor center, but maps and information available at headquarters and at district ranger stations in Ridgway, Bradford, and Marienville.
Entrance Fees: None.
Disabled Access: Disabled-accessible interpretive trails are located at Hearts Content and Twin Lakes.
Camping: Developed campsites; fees; no reservations required. Primitive camping; permit required.

Allegheny, and between 10 and 15 eagles hunt here.

Allegheny offers excellent backpacking and day hiking virtually anywhere within its borders. Good trout fishing may be had on the Tionesta, Kinuza, Bear, Big Mill, and East Hickory Rivers. Allegheny Reservoir is trophy water for muskellunge, pike, and walleye.

John Heinz National Wildlife Refuge at Tinicum

This patch of green in the heart of urban Philadelphia offers respite to more than 280 species of birds, from sparrows to eagles.

SITE 88 From the air, it's extremely easy to spot the John Heinz National Wildlife Refuge at Tinicum. As you make the final approach to Philadelphia International Airport, look down: Anything that isn't paved is the refuge. This 1,200-acre oasis, which contains the largest remnant freshwater tidal marsh in Pennsylvania, is a patch of true wilderness in the urban sprawl of greater Philadelphia, a haven for shorebirds and migratory waterfowl in a megalopolis of five million human beings. It makes an ideal day trip for anyone visiting metropolitan Philadelphia and its environs.

The original Tinicum Wildlife Preserve was established in the 1950s, when the Gulf Oil Company donated 150 acres to Philadelphia's Department of Recreation. Since then it has grown, bit by bit, parcel by parcel. In 1972 the site was placed under the management of the U.S. Fish and Wildlife Service. Given the profound development pressures that have borne in on it from all sides for well over a century, the refuge's success has made it a remarkable symbol of urban preservation and restoration.

There are bigger refuges; perhaps there are better refuges if quality of habitat and numbers of animals are the defining criteria. But there is certainly no refuge that is better loved. From high to low, Philadelphians have embraced Tinicum Marsh. The volunteers who participate in cleanup projects and lead guided walks run the social gamut from debutantes to gang members. Philly is a tough town, but it has a tender heart where its refuge is concerned.

More than 280 species of birds have been recorded at Tinicum, and at least 85 nest here. So critical is the refuge as a staging area and rest stop for everything from Canada geese to wood warblers that it was the first site designated by the National Audubon Society as an "important bird area," a designation that indicates a site of paramount importance to a region's resident and migratory bird populations.

The marsh provides a haven for scores of species of migrating songbirds, particularly vireos and wood warblers and especially during the spring migration. Look for vireos— solitary, warbling, white-eyed, red-eyed, and yellow-throated—flitting through dense foliage of trees and shrubs. Wetland-associated warblers, most notably northern parula, yellow-breasted chat, and yellow, Nashville, Kentucky, myrtle, and Canada warblers, may be found throughout the refuge. Even the rare hooded warbler has been recorded here.

Rufous-sided towhees nest in the thickets and coverts, their distinctive chestnut flanks making them fairly visible and instantly recognizable. Seven native sparrows are residents:

The sweet song of the northern cardinal may be heard at any time of the year.

Look for chipping, American tree, vesper, field, savannah, song, and white-throated sparrows. In the spring, red-winged blackbirds aggressively defend their nesting territories against all comers filling the air with their melodious song. Look for the males boldly displaying their crimson shoulder patches to intimidate rivals. Other commonly observed species include common grackle, eastern meadowlark, northern oriole, purple finch, house finch, pine siskin, and American goldfinch.

In spring the migrating shorebirds and wading birds arrive in force. Scan exposed mudbanks for feeding black-bellied plover, killdeers, greater yellow-legs, common snipes, and spotted and pectoral sandpipers. Search the quieter backwaters for American and least bitterns; great blue, little blue, and tricolored herons; black-crowned night-herons; great, snowy, and cattle egrets; Virginia rail; soras; and common moorhens.

In recent years refuge managers have constructed nesting towers, hoping to convince ospreys to brood at the marsh. So far they've had no luck; the birds have checked out the structures with interest, but none have made the commitment. Ospreys occasionally hunt at an impoundment on the preserve, however, and are a great favorite with local birders.

As autumn and winter approach, there is still plenty going on at Tinicum. Although northern cardinals live here year-round, their bright red plumage is a particularly cheery sight in the bleak winter landscape. The common redpoll, a species typically associated with the far north, also shows up in winter. Migrating bald eagles are eagerly awaited by regular visitors. Other raptors that may be seen then include northern harriers, American kestrels, and sharp-shinned, red-shouldered, red-tailed, and rough-legged hawks.

Winter also means the arrival of migratory waterfowl, which congregate at the refuge in impressive numbers. Canada geese, blue-winged and green-winged teal, mallards, gadwalls, and Eurasian and American wigeon favor the protected coves. Northern pintail, canvasbacks, redheads, ring-necked ducks, lesser scaup, common goldeneyes, and buffleheads paddle peacefully on the open water. Pied-billed grebes and common loons also favor areas of open water.

While the species diversity of resident mammals may not be particularly stunning, their populations are stable, even optimal, which is remarkable considering the miles of surrounding concrete. White-tailed deer, red fox, opossum, muskrat, eastern cottontail, and striped skunk are the largest of the lot. Look for them at daybreak and twilight along the edges of the waterways and near trees. Small mammals abound, particularly meadow voles, white-footed mice, short-tailed shrews, and eastern moles. While humans might never even notice these small animals, they're an important food source for great horned owls, barred owls, and other birds of prey.

Realizing that the success of the refuge depends on the goodwill of the surrounding urban population, Tinicum's managers have done everything possible to facilitate access while simultaneously protecting habitat. Nature trails and boardwalks wind through the majority of the property, and guided hikes and lectures are scheduled for most weekends throughout the year.

Block Island

Easily explored by foot or bicycle, this Rhode Island refuge offers spectacular ocean views as well as excellent birdwatching.

SITE 89 Just 12 miles off the coast of Rhode Island lies a chosen place of marshes and dunes, salt ponds, and grassy uplands, where the predominant sounds are the mewling of seabirds, the barking of seals, and the gentle susurrus of the sea. Block Island has escaped the mad rush toward development that has devoured much of the rest of the eastern seaboard; about 25 percent of its 6,400 acres is open space, protected by both private and public conservation groups, and the remaining land is rigorously guarded.

Ferries ply the waters daily from Point Judith, Rhode Island; in summer there is frequent ferry service from Newport, Rhode Island; New London, Connecticut; and Montauk, New York. Most dock in Old Harbor on the eastern shore. Whenever possible, leave the car at home. Block Island is best appreciated on foot, and the islanders like to keep automobiles to a minimum. First-time visitors will want to check in with the small Visitor Center at the ferry landing area for maps and advice.

Birds are what Block Island is all about—all kinds of birds, from hawks to hummingbirds. The island's few thousand acres comprise salt ponds, freshwater swamps, bluffs, grasslands, and scrublands, and all teem with life. Located on the Atlantic flyway, Block Island is a critical stopover point for first-year migratory birds. Savvy East

Harbor seals bask contentedly on secluded patches of sun-warmed beach or rocks.

Sanderlings run along the beach, following the outgoing tide and snatching up exposed mollusks.

Coast birders come here hoping to put rare songbirds on their life lists; they are often successful. One such sighting could be the golden-winged warbler, which is declining across its range but relatively common here.

The spring migration is fairly long, with birds trickling through until early summer. The fall migration is more compressed—typically running from early September through late October —and often affords the greatest concentration of birds. Autumn is also the best time for spotting vagrant species, as inexperienced fledglings are sometimes driven from their migration routes by prevailing winds. This is also a good time to sight raptors, including ospreys, peregrine falcons, northern harriers, and bald eagles.

Because the island is small, access to trails is easy. The ferry docks at Old Harbor, where bicycles and mopeds can be rented and taxis engaged. About a mile inland from Old Harbor, the Greenway affords a good overview of the various habitats. The Clay Head Trail complex on the north end of the island features spectacular ocean views, nesting sites for common barn- owls, and some excellent songbird-watching opportunities.

In the center of the island, the Great Salt Pond and its adjacent estuaries brim with waterfowl and shorebirds. Look for shorebirds in early May and again in August. Willet, spotted sandpipers, red knots, sanderlings, dunlins, and common snipes are all likely to be seen feeding avidly in the mud. In summer ruddy turnstones sport distinctive red-and-black back feathers, a rare flash of color.

Winter is the time for waterfowl sightings. Brant and Canada geese are commonly observed. A variety of estuarine-associated ducks are present, including greater and lesser scaup, common goldeneye, canvasback, red-head, American wigeon, oldsquaw, bufflehead, and ruddy duck.

Red-throated and common loons, in particular, flock to Block Island, as do common eiders and red-breasted mergansers. Northern gannets and thick-billed murres are often seen resting on the headlands or foraging in the offshore waters for fish. On the north end of the island, a very large herring and great black-backed gull rookery annually hosts thousands of raucously breeding pairs.

In the winter months marine mammals regularly frequent Block Island. Very lucky ferry passengers might catch a glimpse of pilot whales, common dolphins, and harbor porpoises. There are three popular haul-outs where seals like to rest and sun themselves—Old Harbor Point, the entrance to New Harbor, and Clay Head. Gray seals and harbor seals are the most commonly sighted species, although harp and hooded seals are occasionally spotted as well.

Finally, Block Island is one of the few sites in the world that supports the American burying beetle. Once common throughout the eastern United States, this globally endangered insect is now found only on Block Island, and in parts of Oklahoma, Nebraska, Arkansas, and Kansas.

Block Island makes an excellent

THE FACTS

Noteworthy Animals: Red-throated loon, common loon, thick-billed murre, great black-backed gull, herring gull, upland sandpiper, sanderling, gray seal, harbor seal, American burying beetle.

Getting There: To reach the Point Judith Ferry (401-783-4613) from Providence, take I-95 south for 12 miles to US 4. Proceed south to US 1, take the Narragansett exit for R.I. 108, then go 3 miles to the ferry exit. The ferry runs year-round. There is summer ferry service from Newport, R.I.; New London, Conn.; and Montauk, N.Y. Round-trip ferry tickets range from $10 to $30; cars cost an additional $20 each way (make reservations in advance). Block Island Airlines (800-411-3592) offers connections and chartered flights from a number of locations.

Open: Daily, 24 hours, year-round.

Best Times to Visit: March through November.

Visitor Information: The Nature Conservancy of Rhode Island, Block Island office (401-466-2129) and Visitor Center, open Monday through Friday, 9 a.m.-5 p.m., year-round.

Entrance Fees: None.

Disabled Access: Many birding spots are accessible by car or wheelchair.

Camping: None on-site.

Accommodations: Call the Chamber of Commerce (401-4466-2982) for a list of hotels and guesthouses.

day-trip destination for local wildlife enthusiasts, but it's also a great place for a weekend getaway or a summer vacation. Its many and varied attractions include long sandy beaches, country lanes, historical lighthouses, and scores of restaurants and shops.

Narragansett Bay National Estuarine Research Reserve

Hope, Patience, and Prudence Islands provide a rich harvest for scores of migrating shorebirds, seabirds, and waders.

SITE 90 For at least 8,000 years prior to European settlement, Native Americans reaped a plentiful harvest from Narragansett Bay's Prudence, Patience, and Hope Islands. The woods yielded an abundance of wild game, nuts, and berries; cleared meadowlands were planted for maize; estuaries teemed with bluefish, flounder, and striped bass. The bay's mudflats were just as rich as the islands' deep soil, and the encompassing blue waters supported a cornucopia of shellfish such as lobsters, blue crabs, quahogs, soft-shell clams, oysters, and mussels.

While the islands and bay haven't emerged completely unscathed from the last three centuries of progress, they have remained remarkably intact. And thanks to a strong preservationist sentiment among Rhode Island residents, they are likely to stay that way. The 4,300-acre Narragansett Bay National Estuarine Research Reserve (comprising all of Hope and Patience Islands, most of Prudence Island, and adjacent waters) serves as the linchpin for an ongoing effort to preserve this priceless northeastern estuary.

There are none of the charismatic species here that attract hordes of visitors to other refuges—no manatees, bison, or grizzly bears. The focal point at this reserve is the essential biological system, that great interconnecting web of life that makes estuaries one of the richest habitats on the planet.

The reserve isn't noted for easy access either, being made up of islands that can be reached only by boat. Still, getting there isn't an insurmountable problem. Landings are not allowed on Patience and Hope Islands, but Prudence Island is serviced regularly by ferries from Bristol. On Prudence, there are foot trails winding through most of the reserve's holdings.

Spring visitors can observe migratory shorebirds, nesting wading birds, and gulls. Fall is the best time for migratory waterfowl, songbirds, and raptors. Whatever the season, low tide is the best time to view the reserve, simply because there's more to see: more tidal flats and more foraging wildlife, to be precise. Great banks of mussels and slipper shells are exposed to view, and the flats teem with wading birds and shorebirds. Three species of egrets—great, snowy, and cattle—probe for fish and crustaceans on the flats, their white plumage and erect posture unmistakable. Herons share the same habitat and hunting inclinations; look for American bitterns, great blue, little blue, and tricolored herons, and black-crowned night-herons.

Killdeers, black-necked stilts, American oystercatchers, willet, spotted sandpipers, ruddy turnstones, red knots, sanderlings, dunlins, and common snipes flock to Narragansett Bay in the spring. Belted kingfishers; pied-billed, horned, and red-necked grebes;

In the breeding season, the great egret exhibits long lacy plumes.

and common and least terns arrive in spring and stay through fall. At least six species of gulls—Bonaparte's, ring-billed, glaucous, herring, and great and lesser black-backed—feed actively at low tides. King eiders, black scoters, surf scoters, and white-winged scoters—large sea ducks with bold black-and-white markings and heavy bills—are also common, typically keeping to the open water.

During the fall migration, waterfowl are extremely abundant. Look for northern pintail, American wigeon, and greater scaup rafted up on open water or hanging close to leeward shorelines during stiff winds or inclement weather. Tundra swans and snow geese both ply the reserve, and people sometimes confuse the two species. (The tundra swans are the ones with the extremely long necks and completely white wings; snow geese have black wingtips.)

Canada geese winter here in large numbers, as do ducks, most notably green-winged and blue-winged teal; mallard; gadwall; European wigeon; hooded, common, and red-breasted mergansers; canvasback; redhead; black and ring-necked ducks; lesser scaup; common goldeneye; and bufflehead. Red-throated and common loons also visit in the winter.

Moving inland, the shore gives way to a mix of scrub, woodland, and meadows that supports good songbird populations. Species are varied and

may include surprises; islands often pick up anomalous birds blown off-shore during migrations. In spring migrating flycatchers and warblers take up residence in the larger trees and thicker scrub. Alder and willow flycatchers, eastern phoebes, and eastern kingbirds perch on branches or fence wires, flitting up occasionally to snatch flying insects. American pipits, northern parulas, yellow warblers, American redstarts, northern water-thrushes, and common yellowthroats represent the myriad warbler species. Other notable visitors include eastern bluebirds, veeries, brown creepers, rose-breasted and blue grosbeaks, and indigo buntings. The reserve is good sparrow country; look for American tree, chipping, field, vesper, savannah, song, and white-throated sparrows along woodland margins and in meadows. Year-round residents include noisy blue jays, as well as northern cardinals and rufous-sided towhees. In winter, look for black-capped chickadees, dark-eyed juncos, snow buntings, and winter wrens.

Raptors, including bald eagles and peregrine falcons, use the island as a rest stop during the fall migration and are often seen soaring high above the woods, meadows, and beaches, searching for prey. Look for northern harriers swooping low over the meadowlands. Sharp-shinned and Cooper's hawks favor the trees, while American kestrels and red-shouldered, red-tailed, and rough-legged hawks are apt to be seen perching on snags or fence posts.

A variety of mammals inhabits the inland areas of Prudence Island. White-tailed deer are the most numerous. Too numerous, in fact. Their populations must be controlled, both to preserve habitat and mitigate deer ticks, which carry Lyme disease. Smaller residents include mink, red fox, eastern cottontail, and raccoon.

As in the past, the reserve's greatest natural resource remains its fisheries. Striped bass, bluefish, butterfish, sea trout, blackfish, lobster, and quahogs are sought by local anglers and commercial fishermen, who are among the reserve's biggest boosters.

Cape Romain National Wildlife Refuge

This coastal refuge in South Carolina harbors American alligators, wood storks, and the extremely rare red wolf.

SITE 91 Cape Romain National Wildlife Refuge, established in 1932, is the jewel in the crown of South Carolina's nearshore island system, which stretches 130 miles from Myrtle Beach to Hilton Head. Composed of three main islands and numerous smaller ones, the refuge itself runs along the central South Carolina coast for a full 20 miles, encompassing 34,229 acres of salt marsh and woodland and an additional 30,000 surface acres of open water. This rich saltwater and estuarine system is burgeoning with both terrestrial and marine wildlife. The refuge's centerpiece is its largest island, 5,018-acre Bull Island.

Much of Cape Romain can be explored only by boat, though there is a ferry that shuttles between Moore's Landing on the mainland and Bull Island. Once there, the visitor finds 16 miles of trails and roads traversing the heavily wooded island, which supports a beautiful mature forest of live oak, magnolia, pine, and palmetto. The forest also harbors one of the continent's great wildlife rarities: a breeding population of red wolves.

In the spring, American alligators roam in the creeks and ponds of Bull Island.

One of North America's endangered canids, red wolves fall roughly between coyotes and gray wolves in size, aggressiveness, and dietary proclivities. Ranging from 40 to 80 pounds, they are lighter in frame than gray wolves and sometimes display a distinctive russet overtone. Unlike gray wolves, red wolves don't form highly socialized packs, preferring to live alone or in pairs or occasionally in small, loosely associated groups.

Red wolves once roamed throughout the South and Southeast, but they have been extirpated throughout their range. Efforts are underway to reintroduce them, and the breeding stock on Bull Island (now about seven or eight animals) is critical to this project. Pups from the island have been used to re-establish the species at Alligator River Refuge in North Carolina and at Great Smoky Mountains National Park (see p. 290). Visitors probably won't see these reclusive animals but might find their spoor or scat. The incredibly lucky could catch a glimpse of one of these rare creatures as it skulks through the undergrowth or trots over a sand dune.

Other, more visible, mammals include white-tailed deer (including a subspecies found only on Bull Island), bobcat, river otter, long-tailed weasel, and gray and red foxes. The smaller creatures include seven species of indigenous mice and rats as well as six species of bats. Bottlenose dolphins are common in the tidal creeks, where they search for mullet and other small fish, and sometimes frolic openly in front of boats.

Birds of all feathers find Cape Romain a paradise, and more than 275 species visit regularly. During the spring and fall migrations, waterfowl by the thousands ply the marshes and ponds. Look for tundra swans, wood ducks, northern pintail, green-winged teal, American wigeon, and American black ducks. Shorebirds are particularly abundant in the spring. Commonly observed species include black-bellied, lesser, golden, and semipalmated plover; ruddy turnstones; greater yellowlegs; long-billed and short-billed dowitchers; American oystercatchers; laughing gulls; Caspian, royal, black, and least terns; and black skimmers.

Cape Romain's lush wetlands support an abundance of wading birds, including some of the largest populations of wood storks and white-faced and glossy ibis in the United States. Wood storks are currently declining across their range as the wetlands disappear. Other species that are found here include least bittern; great and snowy egrets; great blue, little blue, tricolored, and green-backed herons; and black-crowned night-heron.

Ospreys, northern harriers, and red-tailed and sharp-shinned hawks are regularly seen; bald and golden eagles and peregrine falcons are occasionally seen. There have also been confirmed sightings of Mississippi kites and swallow-tailed kites, delicate raptors that are known for their graceful flight patterns. Eastern screech-owls and great horned owls are abundant, often observed as they glide silently across the twilight sky. The same may be said of nightjars such as the common nighthawk and chuck-will's-widow.

Woodpeckers, vireos, thrushes, warblers, swallows, kinglets, gnatcatchers, nuthatches, flycatchers, tanagers, finches, titmice, wrens, and orioles: They're all here. Look and listen for them, and for other songbirds—indigo and painted buntings; orchard oriole; purple martin; northern cardinal; yellow-throated vireo; summer tanager; yellow-throated, yellow, and hooded warblers; golden-crowned kinglet; eastern phoebe; hermit thrush; and blue-gray gnatcatcher. A little patience and luck may reveal the rare prothonotary, Blackburnian, Cape May, and bay-breasted warblers.

Because most reptiles and amphibians are ill adapted to a saltwater environment, Cape Romain does not have great numbers of turtles, snakes, lizards, or frogs. Still, some are here, and most of them congregate around the tidal creeks. There are 11 species of frogs and toads, including the little spadefoot toad, southern leopard frog, and green treefrog. Marbled and slimy salamanders will also be found in frog habitat. Snakes include cottonmouth, yellow rat snake, and eastern kingsnake. The huge Atlantic loggerhead sea turtle is just one of the seven turtle species found here.

A single day isn't sufficient to enjoy Cape Romain. If possible, plan to spend at least a couple of days hiking the larger islands, and another day or two exploring the surrounding waterways. If you don't have a boat, rentals and charters are available in nearby Charleston.

Spring is an ideal time for a visit: Temperatures are moderate; the songbird migrations are at their peak; storks, egrets, and herons are nesting; and the local population of American alligators are active in the Jack's Creek and Upper Summerhouse Pond

THE FACTS

Noteworthy Animals: Red wolf, bottlenose dolphin, wood stork, glossy ibis, white-faced ibis, American oystercatcher, eastern screech-owl, Atlantic loggerhead sea turtle, American alligator.

Getting There: From Charleston, take the I-526 loop north to US 17, then drive about 14 miles to the turnoff for Moore's Landing and the Bull Island Ferry (803-795-2968). March through November, the ferry makes two trips on Tuesday, Friday, and Saturday and one trip on Thursday; December through February, it makes a single trip on Saturday only. Charter trips are available Monday, Wednesday, and Sunday year-round.
Open: Daily, dawn to dusk, year-round.
Best Times to Visit: February through May; September through November.
Visitor Information: Cape Romain National Wildlife Refuge Visitor Center (803-928-3368), on US 17 on the mainland, open Tuesday through Sunday, 9 a.m.-5 p.m., year-round.
Charter and/or Guide Services: For kayak rental and charter services, call Coastal Expeditions (803-881-4582).
Entrance Fees: None.
Disabled Access: None.
Camping: None on-site.

regions of Bull Island. But winter also has its pleasures: Waterfowl migration is at its peak, and most of the Atlantic Coast's American oystercatcher population is on the refuge. Those who try sportfishing will find the sheltered, nutrient-rich waters of the various bays and inlets that border the islands teeming with red drum, weakfish, bluefish, blue crab, and shrimp.

Francis Beidler Forest

This woodland, with the world's largest stand of virgin bald cypress, supports bats, birds, and bobcats.

SITE 92 A vast network of bald cypress and tupelo forest once dominated the South Carolina coastal plain, sustaining wildlife populations of great density and diversity. Most of it is gone now, but a few stunning remnants remain, the Francis Beidler Forest foremost among them. This 6,331-acre refuge is administered by the National Audubon Society and contains the largest remaining stand of virgin bald cypress and tupelo gum trees in the world. Many of these gigantic trees are more than a thousand years old.

This is a true blackwater swamp, with water levels fluctuating seasonally. In the summer and fall, the swamp shrinks to a series of shallow lakes and ponds connected by creeks. In the winter and spring, the entire 1.5-mile-wide floodplain may be awash, constituting a broad, sluggish river.

This is one of the continent's great refuges for neotropical songbirds, most notably the prothonotary warbler. This extremely vivid, sunshine yellow warbler is rare over most of its range but common here. It is not a shy bird and delights visitors with an amiable in-your-face attitude. Other songbirds include Kentucky, Swainson's, and hooded warblers; northern parula; and red-eyed, white-eyed, and yellow-throated vireos. Since Hurricane Hugo passed through in 1989, killing and damaging many trees, the forest has become a haven for woodpeckers, which nest in and forage on the dead wood. Look for pileated, red-headed, red-bellied, and downy woodpeckers, and yellow-bellied sapsuckers.

Many birds of prey are also associated with the mature cypress and pine woodlands typical of Beidler. Species known to nest here include Cooper's, red-shouldered, red-tailed, and sharp-shinned hawks; great horned and barred owls; and American kestrel.

The forest also provides a wonderful habitat for wading birds, including the endangered wood stork, as well as the white ibis; great blue, little blue, and green-backed herons; and great egret. There is a breeding population of the increasingly rare yellow-crowned night-heron here. During the breeding season these birds feed almost exclusively on crayfish, a resource in

The yellow-crowned night-heron's powerful bill is ideal for crushing crayfish shells.

which the forest is particularly rich. Their rookeries are typically found wherever the "mudbugs" are thickest. Other water-loving birds abundant in the forest include wood duck, hooded merganser, and belted kingfisher.

Steep bluffs provide an upland component to the forest, greatly increasing biodiversity. Mammals include bobcat, coyote, red and gray foxes, raccoon, opossum, river otter, mink, long-tailed weasel, white-tailed deer, marsh rabbit, eastern cottontail, and several species of bats. Mammals here, like mammals everywhere, tend to be secretive. To improve your chances for a sighting, take a quiet walk through the refuge in the late afternoon or sit quietly near obvious game trails.

Beidler is an especially good place to view water-associated reptiles, including cottonmouths; red-bellied and brown water snakes; common snapping, mud, and musk turtles; and Florida and river cooters. The American alligator has a special relationship with its fellow preserve resident, the long-nose gar, a large fish that inhabits the refuge's permanent lakes and streams. Gars tend to loll near the water's surface, a habit that makes them extremely vulnerable to hungry alligators. It's not unusual to see a gator suddenly attack this favored prey from beneath, seize it in its jaws, and rush up the bank with the flopping fish, where it can be devoured without chance of escape.

Another piscine resident of the forest deserves special mention: the bowfin. This large native fish has an ancient pedigree. It is a relative of the lungfishes and, like them, can tolerate stagnant water. In the spring and early

summer, the bowfin migrate up little creeks, where they brood their young in the shallows. A ten-pound bowfin sitting stolidly on its nest, guarding hundreds of tiny, squirming progeny, is an arresting sight.

The forest makes an excellent day-trip from Charleston. A 1.5-mile boardwalk allows visitors to penetrate the heart of the preserve and affords excellent wildlife viewing. A good way to gain a deeper appreciation of this unique habitat is to take one of the guided canoe tours, hikes, and night walks offered by the National Audubon Society.

Great Smoky Mountains National Park

Although it hosts nine million visitors a year, this Appalachian
refuge manages to remain wild, sustaining scores of wildlife.

SITE 93 No doubt about it: Great Smoky Mountains National Park has some problems. Most of them stem from the fact that people love it too much. It is the most popular national park—about nine million people visit it each year, more than visit Yosemite, Yellowstone, the Grand Canyon, or Glacier. Roads through the park can become seriously gridlocked during the height of the summer season.

But the congestion is somewhat illusory. Park staffers estimate that 95 percent of the visitors are car campers—people who seldom stray far, if at all, from their vehicles. The vast percentage of Great Smoky's 520,000 acres is lightly trod. There is much to appreciate here, but it's best to get out of the car to do it.

The park is noteworthy for its deep gorges, unique in the East. Lush stands of deciduous hardwoods blanket the low-lying coves (an Appalachian term for woodland valleys). Up at the 6,000-foot level, boreal forests of spruce and fir are found. Between these extremes are three other separate vegetative zones. Elevation often determines temperature in the park as well. The mercury will be at very different places at the two extremes of 800 and 6,000 feet. Still, on average, summers are generally warm and humid; spring and autumn are extremely pleasant; and winter temperatures are variable.

The wide range of elevation trans-lates into myriad biological niches—and hence, lots of different plants and animals. Simply put, the park is a brimming wildlife reservoir. This is especially true for black bears. Bruin populations are typically at their sustainable limit in the park, and bears are constantly moving out to outlying environs in their never-ending quest for food. It's estimated that 500 to 700 bears live in the park at any given time, making the chances of a sighting (even for car-bound visitors) fair to good—particularly in the fall, when vistas have opened up as the result of fallen leaves and because the bears are actively foraging in anticipation of the coming winter.

Great Smoky also contains one of the East's densest populations of white-tailed deer. Such an abundance of large herbivores has led biologists to promote the park as a release site for endangered red wolves, for whom the deer would be prey. Wolves have been released into the park each year since 1991. There have been setbacks, and the wolves' mortality rate is high. It remains to be seen how these rare canids will fare in the long run; they face manifold difficulties, including hybridization with coyotes. But people both in and out of the park are rooting for them. The red wolf release has engendered little controversy, unlike gray wolf releases in the

The Smoky Mountains support a large
population of black bears.

The yellow warbler is one of the most abundant and widespread warbler species.

West. Red wolves are smaller and less aggressive than gray wolves. And because livestock is not a major industry in the Appalachians, there is no resistance from local farmers. Although a red wolf sighting is unlikely, they have been reported, particularly in the Cades Cove area.

River otters are other beneficiaries of a release program. At least 135 of them have been released into the park's 730 miles of river course. They have taken well to their new home and are expanding their range, particularly in the lower elevations, where large warm-water fish provide abundant prey. The park service has also begun studies on restoring elk to Great Smoky; elk, as well as bison, lived in this region prior to extensive human settlement.

Other resident mammals include bobcat, red fox, and gray fox. Chances of a sighting are best at dawn and dusk, and the same is true for mink, long-tailed weasel, opossum, raccoon,

and striped skunk. Woodchucks are common in meadow areas, where they are often seen grazing or standing sentinel over their burrows. Eastern cottontails, which also favor open areas, are likely to be recognized only as a flash of white. The forest canopy supports thriving populations of fox, gray, and red squirrels as well as southern and northern flying squirrels. Woodland bats—including little brown myotis, eastern pipistrelle, silver-haired bat, hoary bat, red bat, evening bat, and Rafinesque's big-eared bat—flit over meadows and water at dusk.

Woodland raptors are common throughout this lushly forested park. Species include northern goshawk, which is at the southernmost limit of its range, and Cooper's, sharp-shinned, and red-shouldered hawks, which are often seen dodging through the trees, either in pursuit of prey or to avoid human visitors. There are healthy populations of red-tailed hawks and American kestrels. Golden eagles, which are more typically found in the West, also occur here. Bald eagles are sometimes spotted as they pass through on their winter migration to their breeding grounds on the Gulf of Mexico. Owls are abundant, and chances are good for seeing one at dusk, when they glide from their daytime hideaways to commence their nightly hunts. Among the species are barred, great horned, long-eared, northern saw-whet, common barn-owl, and eastern-screech owl.

Thanks to its high-quality woodlands, Great Smoky constitutes one of the most significant habitats for nesting neotropical migrant songbirds in the United States. Warblers are especially abundant—and especially dramatic in the springtime when they sport their vivid mating plumage. Species include such rare old-growth forest-dependent species as the cerulean warbler and the extremely rare Swainson's warbler. Also look for golden-winged, black-and-white, and blue-winged warblers; northern parula; yellow, black-throated blue, black-throated green, and yellow-throated warblers; ovenbird; Louisiana waterthrush; Kentucky and Canada warblers; yellow-breasted chat; chestnut-sided and pine warblers; and American redstart. Three species of vireo nest here: yellow-throated, solitary, and red-eyed. Other brilliantly plumaged species are the scarlet tanager, summer tanager, rose-breasted grosbeak, indigo bunting, and painted bunting.

With 27 species of resident salamanders, staff biologists claim without hyperbole that the park is the salamander capital of North America. These small, lizardlike amphibians are prime indicators for water, air, and soil purity, since they can't abide contaminated environments. Terrestrial frog and toad species include American toad, Fowler's toad, gray treefrog, wood frog, upland chorus frog, and spring peeper. Aquatic frogs are green frog, bullfrog, and pickerel frog. Snakes are also thriving: Look for northern water, queen, garter, red-bellied, ringneck, eastern hognose, rough green, rat, and milk snakes, as well as timber rattlesnakes and copperhead.

A fine trail system provides access to most parts of the park. One of the best places to see wildlife is at Cades

Cove, a 6,000-acre valley in the park's northwest quadrant. The cove was once cultivated and still supports open meadows. Wild mast and fruit are abundant, and so are bears, deer, and wild turkeys—particularly in the fall. Park staffers claim the cove is the best place to see large concentrations of wildlife east of the Rockies. A loop road provides viewing opportunities for car-bound travelers.

William B. Clark Conservation Area

Because much of this forest is often under water, it is especially attractive to frogs, turtles, snakes, and salamanders.

SITE 94 Take a forest. Apply water on a regular basis. The result: a marvelous array of wildlife. Any doubts about the reliability of this formula? Simply take a look at the William B. Clark Conservation Area. This 330-acre refuge, an expanse of bald cypress and tupelo bottomland forest, is subject to regular flooding from the adjacent Wolf River, a major tributary of the Mississippi. The deep woodland canopy and underlying wetlands fairly teem with wildlife of every description.

How you explore the preserve depends on whether it's wet or dry. From late fall through late spring, standing water covers most of the preserve, and canoes and kayaks are the only reasonable means of access. The higher ground usually dries out by midsummer, allowing for foot travel. The tupelo and cypress canopy keeps undergrowth to a minimum, making hiking easy. And although only about a quarter-mile of trail has been developed to date, an extensive boardwalk system is in the planning stages.

Resident mammals include the bobcat, rare throughout most of the Southeast. Lucky visitors may catch sight of one of these bobtail felines near dusk or dawn, along woodland margins, trails, or even roadways. Their tracks are easier to find; look along the banks of waterways and other muddy places. White-tailed deer are everywhere, often visible as they browse "edge" areas early and

late in the day. From late morning to midafternoon, they tend to hole up in the deeper parts of the forest.

As always, beavers and muskrats will be found in or near the water. Both of these aquatic rodents are extremely shy; the best chances of seeing one require stealthy canoeing or sitting patiently near a likely site. Sightings of river otters have been reported from Wolf River, and it is likely that they inhabit the refuge during the winter and spring high-water periods. Coyotes, which are plentiful and always on the prowl for prey, might be spotted unexpectedly at any time of day and at any place within the refuge. Red and gray foxes, opossums, striped skunks, and raccoons are also found here and are most likely to be seen near dusk or dawn. Look for eastern cottontails in open areas.

Short-tailed shrews and least shrews are found near water and may be seen scurrying through the leaf litter. Check out the forest canopy for gray, fox, and southern flying squirrels. Bats are common, including Keen's and Indiana myotis; eastern pipistrelle; and big brown, evening, silver-haired, hoary, and Rafinesque's big-eared bats. Look for them in the twilight sky.

This is a true haven for birds, particularly songbirds and most particularly cerulean warblers. These brilliant blue birds have been at a disadvantage in recent decades as forests and large woodlots have shrunk. But they are doing well at the Clark preserve

The great horned owl finds good hunting opportunities at the William B. Clark Conservation Area.

because of the abundant mature timber. Prothonotary warblers, another rare neotropical migrant, also thrive here. Other warbler species include Swainson's, worm-eating, yellow, myrtle, yellow-throated, pine, prairie, Kentucky, and hooded warblers, as well as ovenbird, Louisiana waterthrush, northern parula, yellow-breasted chat, and American redstart.

Many other songbirds are year-round residents or seasonal migrants. Northern orioles are stunningly beautiful in their spring breeding plumage; males are orange, black, and white, and females are an orange-red, olive, and white. Summer tanagers, blue grosbeaks, indigo buntings, and painted buntings are here, too. Great crested flycatchers, eastern phoebes,

and Acadian flycatchers snatch insects in midair. Look also for northern cardinals, rufous-sided towhees, eastern wood-pewees, eastern bluebirds, wood thrushes, blue-gray gnatcatchers, golden-crowned and ruby-crowned kinglets, and white-eyed, red-eyed, and warbling vireos.

The combination of excellent cover and abundant prey is very attractive to hawks and owls. Species include broad-winged hawk; look for them perched near water. Sharp-shinned, Cooper's, and red-shouldered hawks hunt in and around the woods. Northern harriers are often spotted cruising low to the ground, their distinctive white rump patch providing an easy identifying mark. Owls are often seen at dusk as they commence

THE FACTS

Noteworthy Animals: Cerulean warbler, northern oriole, great horned owl, pileated woodpecker, northern harrier, belted kingfisher, bobcat, coyote, red fox, eastern cottontail, painted turtle.

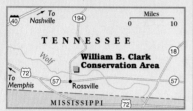

Getting There: From Memphis, take Tenn. 57 about 25 miles to Rossville, then go about 2 miles north on Route 194. Cross the first bridge on the Wolf River. Make an immediate right-hand turn into the parking lot. A boat ramp is located at the lot.

Open: Daily, 24 hours, year-round. At high-water times (late winter through early spring), not accessible by land.

Best Times to Visit: March through November.

Visitor Information: The Nature Conservancy of Tennessee, Nashville office (615-255-0303), open Monday through Friday, 9 a.m.-5 p.m., year-round. This office organizes canoe trips through the preserve, or call 901-877-3958 for canoe rentals. No on-site visitor center.

Entrance Fees: None.

Disabled Access: None.

Camping: None on-site.

their evening hunts; species include eastern screech-owl, great horned, barred, long-eared, short-eared, and northern saw-whet.

Another likely bird sighting is the pileated woodpecker. This large red-crested woodpecker calls attention to itself with its loud, lilting cries. Near water look for belted kingfishers; great blue, little blue, and green-backed herons; black-crowned night-herons; great egrets; American bitterns; king rail; and double-crested cormorants.

Not surprisingly, this is especially rich reptile and amphibian habitat. Keep an eye out for cottonmouths, fat-bodied, dark, ill-tempered venomous snakes that are common in the wetlands. Diamondback water snakes, plain-bellied water snakes, and mud snakes are other resident water-associated snakes. Rat snakes, kingsnakes, and milk snakes are three especially handsome terrestrial snakes, all of which display multicolored patterns on their scales. Other terrestrial species include ringneck, eastern hognose, scarlet, and rough green snakes.

Turtles—river cooter; slider; and common snapping, musk, mud, map, painted, box and spiny softshell turtles—are common in and along the Wolf River after the floods. Watch for them sunning on logs or swimming at the water's surface. Resident aquatic frogs are bullfrog, green frog, and southern leopard frog. Terrestrial frogs include green treefrog, gray treefrog, chorus frog, spring peeper, and cricket frog; look for them sitting motionless in the grass or on leaves, particularly after a rain. Aquatic salamanders include lesser siren, three-toed amphiuma, and eastern newt. Although their penchant for burrowing renders them difficult to find, a number of terrestrial salamanders, including the mole, small-mouthed, marbled, spotted, and two-lined, are here.

This portion of Tennessee is rural and picturesque, and the surrounding countryside allows for excellent car touring, especially along Tenn. 57, Tenn. 18, and Tenn. 100. Pickwick Lake, a reservoir on the Tennessee River about 70 miles east of the preserve, offers good boating and fishing.

Green Mountain National Forest

The Appalachian Trail gives hikers access to the interior of this rugged Vermont forest, where moose, bears, and deer roam.

SITE 95 At 350,000 acres, Green Mountain National Forest covers a full five percent of the state of Vermont. It is characterized by wide ranges in elevations, from deep valley bottoms to wind-scoured granite peaks. This is a lush forest of varied composition—eastern hardwoods primarily, but also red spruce and balsam fir. Tree species are distributed according to both elevation and slope exposure.

The region's two largest wildlife species—black bear and moose—are thriving. The forest's oaks and beeches yield abundant mast for the bears, and the heavily vegetated, rugged terrain provides them requisite cover. The bears are most easily observed in the fall, when they are actively rooting in the hardwood groves for beechnuts and acorns. Moose densities are increasing, approaching the forest's highest sustainable natural level. Interestingly, white-tailed deer numbers are low. This conforms with a well-accepted wildlife biologist's correlation: White-tailed deer and moose populations are directly obverse to each other. For whatever reason— food availability, disease, aggression— when the numbers of one are high, the numbers of the other are low.

Aquatic mammals are doing extremely well in the forest's rivers, streams, and wetlands. Beavers and mink are very abundant, and one of the heaviest concentrations of river otters in the Northeast is found here.

One of Green Mountain's great success stories is the fisher, which was wiped out from most of New England by the late 19th century. In the 1950s restocking began in an attempt to bring this deep woodland predator back to its home ground. Today fishers are well established throughout the forest, and the lucky hiker may catch sight of one of these large sinuous, mustelids toward dusk or dawn. Also listen for their cry: a high scream and a hiss. In recent years attempts have also been made to reintroduce the related marten to the forest, but it is still too early to determine if the program has been successful.

Bobcats also live here, but they favor the deep woods and are not likely to be seen by visitors. Smaller predators, however, are more easily spotted. Look for coyotes, gray and red foxes, ermines, long-tailed weasels,

Wood ducks frequent the wooded streambanks of Green Mountain.

The ermine is white only in winter; the rest of the year its fur is dark brown.

raccoons, striped skunks, and opossums. They all frequent "edge" areas between woodlands and more open habitats, particularly at dusk.

Eastern cottontails and woodchucks inhabit the meadows and scrubby areas. Red, gray, and northern flying squirrels are most likely to be sighted in hardwood canopies. Mice, voles, lemmings, and moles are present in all habitats. Watch for woodland bats, including small-footed, Keen's, and little brown myotis; eastern pipistrelle; and silver-haired, big brown, hoary, and red bats, at twilight in search of their evening meal of insects.

The forest is extremely rich in birds. Gamebirds such as ruffed grouse, wild turkey, and American woodcock congregate in bottomland coverts. Casual hikers will often flush them into the open. Wood ducks and American black ducks brood in the forest's wetlands, most of which are made by beaver flowages. Woodland raptors are thriving, particularly the rare northern goshawk. The forest is the state's stronghold for this beautiful blue-gray raptor, which is now expanding its range to areas outside the forest. Forest officials have also successfully released captive peregrines into the forest, and at least ten of them now hunt here. Red-shouldered, Cooper's, and sharp-shinned hawks are also here. Owls are very common, although they are usually glimpsed only at dusk or during the day when flushed from their deep woods redoubts. Species include eastern screech-owl, and barred, great horned, long-eared, northern saw-whet, and boreal owl. In winter snowy owls may be sighted as well.

Green Mountain is an actively managed forest, that is, it has been logged to one degree or another for a long time. The result of the ongoing harvest is a varied canopy ranging from old-growth behemoths to saplings. This, in turn, supports a great variety of songbirds; different birds require different canopies for optimal breeding. Many of the common eastern warblers and flycatchers are found in the forest; what you find depends on where you look. Blackburnian warblers favor old-growth conifers, black-throated green warblers prefer mixed woods and swampy areas, and chestnut-sided warblers are strictly birds of the second growth.

Late spring and summer evenings are enriched with the songs of gray treefrogs, spring peepers, green frogs, bullfrogs, pickerel frogs, and American toads. They can be found by shining a flashlight on ponds, rivers, or meadows where their songs are heard. Salamanders include eastern newt, dusky salamander, and northern two-lined salamander.

The abundant streams and ponds abound in game fish, particularly brook trout. The more remote streams, in fact, contain some of the best native brookie fisheries in the Northeast. Efforts to bring the noble Atlantic salmon back to the tributaries of the Connecticut River, several of which flow east from the forest, have

met with some success.

Green Mountain is Vermont's premier hiking and backpacking destination: Both the Appalachian Trail and the Long Trail (which runs from Vermont's northern to southern border) traverse the forest. Road access is also quite good, with Vt. 7A and Vt. 30 providing particularly scenic views. Auto touring may actually result in some excellent wildlife sightings, particularly at dawn or dusk. Generally speaking, though, you have to strike out on foot for optimal wildlife viewing.

THE FACTS

Noteworthy Animals: Black bear, moose, fisher, river otter, beaver, ermine, wood duck.

Getting There: There are two units to the forest; both are accessible by US 7, western Vermont's primary north-south thoroughfare.

Open: Daily, 24 hours, year-round.

Best Times to Visit: April through October.

Visitor Information: Green Mountain National Forest, Rutland Headquarters (802-747-6700), and district offices in Middlebury (802-388-4362) and Manchester (802-362-2307) are all open Monday through Friday, 8 a.m.-4:30 p.m., year-round. The Rochester district office (802-767-4261) is open on summer weekends.

Entrance Fees: None; fishing and hunting licenses required.

Disabled Access: The Robert Frost Wayside Trail traverses a wetland complex and beaver flowage and is completely accessible. Interpretive sites along the White River Travelway are also accessible.

Camping: Developed campsites; fees; no reservations. Primitive camping; no permit or fees.

Helen W. Buckner Memorial Preserve at Bald Mountain

In the highly developed Lake Champlain region, one of New England's finest wildlife habitats is being fiercely protected.

SITE 96 The Lake Champlain Valley is experiencing intense development pressure these days from swelling throngs of vacationers and retirees. But even as it faces increasing threats from suburbanization, sentiment is mounting to preserve the region's tremendous natural heritage. One of the most ambitious programs is the Helen W. Buckner Preserve at Bald Mountain. Created by the Nature Conservancy of Vermont, this pristine 3,100-acre preserve sits at Lake Champlain's south end, near the Poultney River confluence.

The preserve is significant from an eco-regional perspective because it is on the cusp of a major forest transition

A beaver can remain underwater for fifteen minutes before resurfacing for air.

zone. Most of the Lake Champlain area is covered by northern hardwood forests typical of the eastern Great Lakes region: birch, beech, and sugar maple. All of these trees are found at the preserve, but so are species associated with more southern forests, specifically oaks and hickory. The topography here is extremely rugged and geologically complex. The varied terrain, the conjunction of two different vegetation zones, the Poultney's well-preserved riparian corridor and wetlands, and the nearness of the lake all combine to make this one of New England's finest wildlife environments.

Canoes are an excellent means for viewing the preserve—and there's an easy put-in on the Poultney River just upstream from the project's boundary. There is some wonderful hiking here, but because the preserve is so new, trails are just beginning to be forged. The terrain remains relatively rough, and hiking here is not an undertaking for the novice backpacker.

Rewards can be significant for wildlife enthusiasts willing to undertake the effort to explore the preserve. In the spring the wetlands and river support nesting Canada geese, wood ducks, American bitterns, and American black ducks. Great blue herons feed in the area. White-tailed deer are common and are spotted regularly. River otters, beavers, muskrats, and mink live all along the river and in the wetlands and are most easily seen from a canoe. Coyotes, bobcats, gray and red squirrels, and northern flying squirrels are abundant in and around the woods; hike quietly in the early morning or late afternoon for the best chances of a sighting. Summer populations of woodland bats are high; a complete census has not been taken, but species are presumed to include little brown myotis and silver-haired, red, and hoary bats.

Sheer cliffs are scattered throughout the preserve, attracting nesting peregrine falcons; watch for them in the spring. Other birds of prey include bald eagles and ospreys, which hunt for fish at Lake Champlain and the Poultney River. Northern goshawks, as well as red-shouldered, Cooper's, and sharp-shinned hawks, keep mostly to the woods. Look for northern harriers cruising wetlands and open meadows for prey. American kestrels and merlins are often seen perching on fence wires or dead snags. Great horned and barred owls are often heard at dusk.

The riparian and upland forests attract numerous songbirds, both migratory and resident. Wood thrushes and hermit thrushes creep through the understory. In fall and winter, flocks of cedar waxwings—beautiful little birds with rose-gray-and-yellow plumage, peaked crests, and black eye stripes—careen across the gray skies. Rufous-sided towhees are year-round residents. Nesting warblers are common in the spring, when they display their handsome breeding plumage. Red-eyed and warbling vireos nest here, as do northern orioles, scarlet tanagers, and rose-breasted grosbeaks. Other regularly

observed species include evening grosbeak, common yellowthroat, American redstart, and northern parula. Also look for black-and-white, black-throated green, chestnut-sided, yellow, and mourning warblers. The ovenbird, a little warbler with a chestnut crest and a white breast streaked with black, wags its tail vigorously as it walks along the forest floor. Another groundwalker, the wild turkey, might also be seen.

Snakes generally have not fared well in New England but they are holding their own at the Champlain Valley preserve. Of particular interest are several timber rattlesnake dens—caves or deep crevices where the snakes congregate for winter hibernation. These are literally some of the last denning sites for rattlers in the state and thus comprise a natural legacy of priceless value. If you discover a den, be sure to give it a wide berth—not because the snakes are dangerous, but because they are exquisitely vulnerable to disturbance. Wild New England cannot afford to have a single denning site threatened.

Virtually all the other reptiles associated with New England are found here as well. Common snapping turtles and musk, map, and painted turtles sun themselves along the lake or river and swim in quiet backwaters. Common snake species include northern water, garter, red-bellied, ringneck, smooth green, and black rat snake; all are most active from late spring through early fall.

Amphibians are abundant. Look for eastern newts and northern two-lined salamanders in springs or creeks. Spotted salamanders, red-backed salamanders, and four-toed salamanders are more terrestrial (and subterranean) in habits. American toads, gray treefrogs, and wood frogs haunt the forests and meadows and are wildly vocal on warm spring evenings. Their songs join with those of green frogs, bullfrogs, northern leopard frogs, spring peepers, and pickerel frogs, which are found in and around water.

Buckner provides a glimpse of the old, wild New England. Here it's still possible to find rugged crags and deep forest, undeveloped and unpeopled. When you're ready for civilization, simply head for Lake Champlain, where recreational opportunities are readily available.

Back Bay National Wildlife Refuge

These Virginia wetlands provide food and shelter for such waterbirds as snow geese, tundra swans, and brown pelicans.

SITE 97 The mission of the Back Bay National Wildlife Refuge is simple—to provide food and rest for migratory waterbirds. This goal is accomplished admirably, thanks to the unique array of habitats found here and to the care of the U.S. Fish and Wildlife Service. As its name implies, this 7,700-acre refuge is located in Back Bay north of Currituck Sound, a 70-mile-long northern adjunct of Albemarle Sound.

Despite the fact that Currituck Sound is a saltwater estuary, the waters of Back Bay are fresh—not even brackish. This is due to the heavy inflow from the North Landing River (see p. 311) and several creeks. These freshwater wetlands provide a vast delicatessen of plants that waterfowl relish, including wigeongrass, milfoil, coontail, muskgrass, and wild celery. For ducks and geese battling their way down the Atlantic flyway to warmer climes in the fall and early winter, the bay is a welcome sight indeed—a secure sanctuary replete with nourishing foods.

The refuge also encompasses two other highly desirable habitats: a sizable tract of pristine barrier island that fronts the Atlantic Ocean and several freshwater impoundments or reservoirs. Just as the waterfowl flock to

Snow geese, in flocks that may number several thousand, winter at Back Bay.

A fledgling great blue heron reveals little of its future majestic adult visage.

Canada geese, mallards, ring-necked ducks, and both blue-winged and green-winged teal seek out smaller coves and backwaters; pintail, redheads, and canvasbacks prefer open water.

In the spring shorebirds flock to the refuge (although present in both spring and fall, their numbers are most concentrated in the spring). Sanderlings crowd the ocean strand by the teeming thousands. These white robin-size birds typically retreat up the beach just ahead of the breakers, then immediately turn and follow the retreating water to feed on the exposed crustaceans. Back Bay also supports small numbers of the threatened piping plover during migrations. Other shorebird species include ruddy turnstone, red knot, semipalmated and black-bellied plover, killdeer, black-necked stilt, American avocet, greater and lesser yellowlegs, willet, spotted sandpiper, dunlin, and common snipe.

Spring and summer are also the best times for observing wading birds. Check out the impoundments and bays for herons (great blue and little blue, tricolored, green-backed, and black-crowned night-heron), egrets (snowy, great, and cattle), American bittern, Virginia and clapper rail, and sora. A large heron rookery is located just beyond the refuge's boundary at Cedar Island and can be glimpsed from a boat.

Back Bay's beach frontage also draws large congregations of marine birds. Threatened brown pelicans—stately birds that glide in groups close to the ocean's surface, occasionally crashing into the water for fish—reside here in significant numbers. Northern gannets are often seen in the springtime,

the bay, so do migratory shorebirds descend by the thousands on the beach frontage, gorging on the rich trove of invertebrates living in the sand.

The reservoirs also attract great numbers of waterbirds seeking food and rest. Shorebirds probe the mud when the water levels are lowered in the spring; food plants grow on the exposed soils throughout the summer; and the water levels are raised again just before the fall waterfowl migration. Ducks and geese feed on the submerged plants throughout the autumn and winter.

Tundra swans and snow geese, in particular, favor Back Bay. In optimum years when the plant production has been especially high, up to 10,000 "snows" overwinter at the refuge in flocks that may number several thousand birds. It is stunning to see such an aggregation wheeling through the sky, their haunting cries filling the air, the sun glinting off their pure white feathers.

dive-bombing the sea for fish. Populations of red-throated and common loons are also substantial.

Refuge managers take great pride in the fact that a pair of bald eagles is now nesting at Back Bay. Between five and eight pairs of ospreys also nest here annually, utilizing artificial platforms constructed for that purpose. Peregrine falcons are frequently seen cruising the beachfront during the fall migration, seeking waterfowl and shorebirds. Other common raptors include northern harriers, sharpshinned hawks, merlins, and American kestrels. Barred owls and great horned owls are also residents.

Two of Back Bay's most common mammals are naturalized: nutria and feral hogs. Nutrias are large muskrat-like rodents from South America; they're frequently seen swimming in the bay. The hogs are descendants of domestic stock that took to the bush decades ago, and they display the characteristics of their wild brethren: lean, narrow frames, thick bristly coats, and impressively long tusks. Because they inflict considerable damage on the refuge's delicate habitats with their incessant rootings, staffers try to keep their numbers at tolerable levels by means of annual hunts.

Back Bay also supports a large population of river otters, thanks to the fine wetland habitat and abundant supply of fish. White-tailed deer are often seen browsing along the margins of the marshes and in scrubby areas. Striped skunks, opossums, raccoons, long-tailed weasels, and marsh rabbits are most often spotted toward evening.

An ideal day trip or weekend destination, the refuge has a good trail

THE FACTS

Noteworthy Animals: Snow goose; great blue heron, tundra swan, bald eagle, brown pelican, piping plover, red-throated loon, river otter, feral hog, nutria.

Getting There: From Virginia Beach take Va. 44 east to the Birdneck Road exit. Proceed south to General Booth Boulevard, turn right and go 3 miles to Princess Anne Road. Go left, then take another left onto Sandbridge Road. Take a right on Sandpiper Road and follow it 4 miles to the end of the road and the refuge.

Open: Daily, dawn to dusk, year-round. Partial closures during the spring and fall migrations to protect the birds and in the fall for hunting; call ahead for details.

Best Times to Visit: February through May; September through November.

Visitor Information: Back Bay National Wildlife Refuge Visitor Center (757-721-2412) open Monday through Friday, 8 a.m.-4 p.m.; weekends, 9 a.m.-4 p.m., spring through fall.

Outfitters and/or Guide Services: Ocean Rentals (757-721-6210 or 800-695-4212), Tidewater Adventures (757-480-1999).

Entrance Fees: $4 per vehicle; $2 each for hikers and bicyclists.

Disabled Access: The Visitor Center is fully accessible. Wheelchair-accessible nature trail and boardwalk.

Camping: None on-site. Primitive sites at False Cape State Park (757-426-7128 or 800-933-7275) and developed campsites at Seashore State Park (757-481-4836 or 800-933-7275); fees; reservations.

network that allows easy access to all three habitats. Try to supplement hiking with canoe exploration—the paddling is excellent. A canoe ramp is located near the Visitor Center, but boat trailers are forbidden; bring in canoes or kayaks by roof rack.

Great Dismal Swamp National Wildlife Refuge

A variety of wetland-loving species, from marsh rabbits to little grass frogs, make their homes in this swampy sanctuary.

Funny the difference in perspective 300 years can make. When surveying the boundaries between North Carolina and Virginia, William Byrd deemed this singular wetland "a vast body of dirt and nastiness." Byrd also tacked on the "dismal" to the swamp's name. While the swamp has retained its original appellation, today adjectives like "spectacular" are used to describe it. At 170 square miles—or about 107,000 acres—this heavily forested swamp has been greatly diminished from its original 2,200-square-mile expanse. But it is nevertheless one of the premier wetlands in the southeastern United States, and one of the great marsh-swamp complexes on the continent. The 3,100-acre freshwater Lake Drummond, Virginia's largest natural lake, is the centerpiece of the refuge. It teems with fish and birds and supports lovely stands of bald cypress.

The swamp is not particularly easy to penetrate, which in large part accounts for its marvelous array of wildlife. Great Dismal supports one of the East's largest populations of black bears—about 350 animals at last count. Though they typically haunt the swamp's deepest coverts, they are sometimes seen at the edges of lakes, ponds, or canals.

River otters, beavers, mink, and muskrats are also found wherever there is water. Marsh rabbits, relatives of the eastern cottontail, also prefer the wetlands. White-tailed deer are very abundant and can be seen browsing vegetation on the higher ground. Bobcats, raccoons, opossums, red foxes, and long-tailed weasels are the most common predators; when they are seen at all, it is in brief glimpses at dawn or dusk. Flying squirrels and gray squirrels keep to the trees. Listen for their chittering to locate them.

Bats, declining over most of their range, are thriving in the relative isolation of the swamp. Species include little brown myotis, eastern pipistrelle, and silver-haired, big brown, evening, hoary, Rafinesque's big-eared, and red bats. The bats typically emerge from their roosts in the early evening to begin their nightly harvest of the swamp's abundant insects.

The swamp is an excellent habitat for wading birds, of course. Species include glossy ibis, a dark, long-billed bird that is one of our rarer waders. Egrets—great, snowy, and cattle—stalk through the shallows, hunting for fish. Great blue and little blue herons and black-crowned night-herons fish along the water's edge. More diffident are green-backed herons, American bitterns, and soras. They keep to the reeds and bankside vegetation and are most often spotted when they are flushed by a passing canoe or hiker.

The abundant timber has made the swamp a haven for wood ducks, which are year-round residents. Look for them in the spring, preening along the banks or flying to and from their nests in tree cavities.

During the fall migration, thousands of tundra swans and snow geese congregate on Lake Drummond. Northern pintail, canvasbacks, redheads, and lesser scaup also prefer to raft up on big, open water. Canada geese, hooded mergansers, mallards, blue-winged and green-winged teal, gadwalls, northern shovelers, ringnecked and American black ducks, and American coots head for protected inlets and coves.

This is prime territory for passerine songbirds, especially during their fall and spring migrations. Rare warblers associated with old-growth forests are found here, most particularly the spectacularly yellow prothonotary warbler and the intensely blue cerulean warbler. Look for them in tree canopies. Other warblers that are consistently sighted include pine, prairie, yellow-rumped, and hooded warblers; American redstart; common yellowthroat; and yellow-breasted chat.

Red-winged blackbirds nest throughout the refuge, and their skirling songs are commonly heard in spring and summer. Summer tanagers, blue grosbeaks and indigo buntings are often spotted in the trees, their

As adept in water as on land, the marsh rabbit is found throughout the Great Dismal Swamp.

Although best known as graceful runners, white-tailed deer are also good swimmers.

colorful plumage drawing the eye. The Acadian flycatcher, eastern phoebe, and great crested flycatcher are also prominent, given their habit of perching on bare branches while scanning the air for insects.

Woodpeckers thrive, mining the abundant inventories of dead wood for grubs and insects. The most flamboyant species is the pileated woodpecker, easily recognized by its huge size, bright red crest, and hooting, boisterous call. Other species include yellow-bellied sapsucker, northern flicker, and downy, hairy, red-bellied, and red-headed woodpeckers.

Birds of prey are common and most are highly visible. Ospreys and bald eagles perch on trees near water. Cooper's, sharp-shinned, and red-shouldered hawks, being forest birds, are most often spotted in or near trees. Red-tailed hawks and American kestrels prefer open environs; look for them perched near open wetlands or meadows or soaring on the thermals.

Barred and great horned owls and eastern screech-owls are all swamp residents, and are sometimes noticeable at dusk when they begin their nighttime hunting.

Reptiles and amphibians? They're doing extremely well, thanks to the excellent habitat and warm climate. Water snakes are especially well represented. Look for them in any canal, slough, or pond, particularly near vegetation. Nonvenomous species include northern water snakes and red-bellied water snakes. The black rat snake, a beautiful serpent that shows a faint white speckling over a glossy black background, is terrestrial. Other land-based species include eastern king-snake, as well as garter, brown, rough earth, eastern hognose, scarlet, rough green, mud, and ringneck snakes. There are also plenty of venomous snakes here, so always place hands and feet with care, particularly in areas of dense vegetation. In and around water, watch for cottonmouths; on land, keep an eye peeled for copperheads and timber rattlesnakes.

Turtles are plentiful and they are usually seen sunning on logs or banks

Noteworthy Animals: Black bear, bobcat, red fox, river otter, white-tailed deer, marsh rabbit, glossy ibis, eastern screech-owl, diamondback terrapin, little grass frog.

Getting There: From Norfolk, take I-64 east to the junction with US 13/58/460. Proceed west for 6 miles and take the exit for downtown Suffolk. In Suffolk, turn left onto Va. 32 south and follow it for 5 miles to Cypress Chapel Road. Make a left and follow signs to the end of the road. Turn left onto White Marsh Road and go 7 miles to the Washington Ditch entrance on the right. One mile farther along White Marsh Road is Desert Road; turn left there and drive another 2 miles to the refuge office.

Open: Daily, dawn to dusk, year-round.

Best Times to Visit: March through May; September through November.

Visitor Information: Great Dismal Swamp National Wildlife Refuge, Suffolk Headquarters (757-986-3705), open Monday through Friday, 7:30 a.m.-4 p.m., year-round.

Entrance Fees: None.

Disabled Access: Wheelchair-accessible boardwalk at Washington Ditch.

Camping: Primitive camping; no fees or reservations.

amphiuma—both huge salamanders that can reach 30 inches in length. Other salamander species include eastern newt and tiger, marbled, many-lined, mud, slimy, southern red-backed, two-toed, and long-tailed. Look for them in quiet backwaters or on moist earth. Salamanders are very vulnerable to human disturbance, so don't bother them.

Toads and frogs populate the entire swamp, as demonstrated by their robust evening choruses. Southern toads and Fowler's toads and a variety of terrestrial frogs—spring peepers; green, pine woods, squirrel, and gray treefrogs; Brimley's chorus frogs; and southern cricket frogs—inhabit the upland portions. America's tiniest frog, the half-inch-long little grass frog, lives here, too. Resident aquatic frogs are carpenter, green, southern leopard, pickerel, and bullfrog.

For travelers, the heat, humidity, and insects that are part of any swamp experience can all be problematic. Spring and fall are the best times to visit—bird migrations are in full swing, and temperatures are moderate.

About 100 miles of old logging roads wind along the swamp's waterways, affording good pedestrian and mountain-bike access. Exploring by canoe, kayak, or other small boat provides the most intimate view of the swamp and its inhabitants. Bring your own boat or rent one from one of the recreational equipment rental agencies in the nearby Norfolk-Portsmouth metropolitan area. A public boat ramp is located about 10 miles south of Portsmouth on US 17 and is the best put-in for a visit to Lake Drummond.

or floating in the water with just their heads sticking above the surface. Species include common snapping turtles; box, musk, and mud turtles; diamondback terrapin; spotted and painted turtles; river cooter; and yellow-bellied pond slider.

Possible amphibian sightings include the greater siren and two-toed

North Landing River Preserve

Two beautiful diving ducks, the canvasback and the redhead,
find this urban marsh refuge in Virginia most inviting.

The city of Virginia Beach is big—310 square miles, to be exact. But it has only about 400,000 inhabitants, and half of it remains rural and undeveloped. Such an abundance of undeveloped land accounts for the presence of this singular urban refuge—10,000 acres of swamp, marshland, and riverine forest located right in the heart of a major municipality.

The North Landing River is short as rivers go, starting in the town of Chesapeake and terminating 15 miles to the south at Albemarle Sound. As it flows through Virginia Beach, 10 miles of its course are entirely protected, providing spectacular and easily accessible wildlife-viewing opportunities. The preserve straddles the northern and southern limits for the eastern seaboard's major plant communities, resulting in a rare mix of plant and animal species.

Like all the major intact marshes of the Southeast, North Landing River Preserve is a superb site for migratory waterfowl. Located in the heart of the Atlantic flyway, it's one of the first inviting habitats that southwardly migrating ducks and geese spy after leaving Chesapeake Bay. Snow geese and Canada geese arrive in significant numbers in the fall, as do American black ducks, mallards, green-winged and blue-winged teal, northern pintail, northern shovelers, gadwalls, European wigeon, and American wigeon. Even tundra swans

are occasionally spotted at that time. Diving ducks include the rust-pated, very large, and exceedingly handsome canvasback and its close relative, the redhead. Also look for lesser scaup, common goldeneyes, buffleheads, hooded and common mergansers, and ruddy ducks. Wood ducks, finding the abundant tree cavities agreeable for nesting, are year-round residents.

Numerous wading bird species nest at the preserve. Look for the large nests of great blue heron, great egret, and black-crowned night-heron in groves of trees. Least bittern, green-backed heron, and sora make their nests in cattails, reeds, and other dense streamside vegetation. They are shier than the egrets and herons, more subtly colored, and tougher to see.

The preserve's lush stands of bald cypress, Atlantic white cedar, red maple, and oak attract passerine songbirds by the thousands. The fall migration, which usually peaks in October and November, is particularly spectacular, and the diligent birder is apt to see scores of species—particularly wood warblers. However, warblers do sport uniformly drab plumage in the autumn and can be difficult to differentiate. Species include northern parula; yellow, yellow-rumped, prothonotary, cerulean, and orange-crowned warblers; common yellowthroat; yellow-breasted chat; and American redstart.

Exposed branches serve as perches for bug-loving flycatchers such as the

The great egret typically has a wingspan nearly five feet wide.

eastern phoebes and eastern kingbirds. Look for white-breasted nuthatches and brown creepers in the trees, as well as hermit thrushes and warbling and red-eyed vireos. Rufous-sided towhees, which are year-round residents, prefer the thickets. Marsh wrens and red-winged blackbirds haunt the reeds, cattails, and high grass. Watch for the brilliant blue plumage of east-ern bluebirds, blue grosbeaks, and indigo buntings, as well as the bright red of the male summer tanager and the brilliant yellow of the female summer tanager.

Ospreys and bald eagles will invariably be seen near water; with any luck, visitors might glimpse one or the other snagging a fish. Cooper's, red-shouldered, and sharp-shinned hawks

bers on dead snags.

Several species of woodpeckers nest and forage at North Landing; species include northern flicker, and pileated, red-headed, downy, hairy, and red-bellied woodpeckers. Also look for belted kingfishers, which typically hover or perch over water, chattering madly before diving for fish. Loggerhead shrikes are sometimes visible, and if they're not, their prey is—rodents or grasshoppers impaled on thorns or barbed wire.

The preserve harbors a good population of canebrake rattlesnakes, a state-endangered species. This large snake is not especially aggressive but its protective coloration makes it difficult to see, so watch your step. Caution is also warranted for two other resident venomous snakes, the cottonmouth and copperhead. Nonvenomous snakes are both abundant and diverse. Possible sightings of terrestrial snakes include black racers, and rough green, rough earth, red-bellied, worm, ringneck, eastern hognose, and mud snakes. Of particular interest are the milk snake, scarlet snake, and eastern kingsnake, all of which sport exceptionally handsome banded patterns.

Water snakes—northern, brown, and red-bellied—are likely to be seen during any extended visit to the preserve. Note that water snakes can be aggressive, delivering a nasty if nonvenomous bite. Don't molest them.

Common snapping turtles, which are distinctive for both their large size and massive jaws, are here. Diamondback terrapins, an estuarine species once driven almost to extinction for its succulent flesh, also live here. Yellow-bellied pond sliders and musk,

seek small birds and mammals in the woods. Look for big, white-rumped northern harriers gliding along meadows and marshlands in their search for prey. Red-tailed hawks and American kestrels are often seen perching stolidly on telephone lines and fence posts. Barred, great horned, and short-eared owls keep to the woods, coming out at dusk to hunt. Black vultures and turkey vultures are both abundant and apt to be seen perching in large num-

THE FACTS

Noteworthy Animals: Tundra swan, great egret, least bittern, eastern bluebird, muskrat, diamondback terrapin, canebrake rattlesnake, greater siren.

Getting There: From Virginia Beach, take I-64 to Indian River Road and go south for 8 miles. Turn right at North Landing Road, drive about 2 miles, then turn left at Fentress Airfield Road and follow it briefly, to connect with Blackwater Road. Go about 9 miles to DCR's entrance and boardwalk.

Open: Public boat access daily, 24 hours, year-round. Boardwalk open daily, 10 a.m.-5 p.m., October through April; 10 a.m.-7 p.m., May through September.

Best Times to Visit: March through May; September through November.

Visitor Information: The Nature Conservancy of Virginia, Charlottesville office (804-295-6106), open Monday through Friday, 9 a.m.-5 p.m. year-round. Virginia Department of Conservation and Recreation, First Landing office (757-481-2131), open daily, 9 a.m.-5 p.m., year-round. No on-site visitor center.

Outfitters and/or Guide Services: Ocean Rentals (757-721-6210 or 800-695-4212), Tidewater Adventures (757-480-1999).

Entrance Fees: None.

Disabled Access: Boardwalk is wheelchair accessible.

Camping: None on-site.

mud, spotted, and painted turtles are often spied sunning on logs or even crossing the boardwalks.

The preserve provides excellent habitat for amphibians. Bullfrogs and pickerel, green, and southern leopard frogs live in and near the water. The surrounding woods and meadows support little grass frogs, spring peep-ers, Brimley's chorus frogs, southern cricket frogs, and carpenter frogs. Southern toads, Fowler's toads, and eastern spadefoots are also terrestrial in habitat preference. It's easiest to find frogs and toads near dusk; shine a flashlight on areas where their songs are loudest.

Salamanders include greater sirens and two-toed amphiumas, both of which prefer aquatic environments. The greater siren is huge (up to 30 inches long) and has large, flowery external gills. Terrestrial salamander species include marbled, southern red-backed, mud, and slimy salamanders; they are usually found under logs and rocks or burrowed in leaf litter.

The largest mammal is the white-tailed deer, which is often seen grazing near the river. Mink, marsh rabbits, and muskrats are never far from the water (muskrats are usually in it). Red foxes and eastern cottontails frequent woodland edges and meadows. Tree bats—little brown myotis and hoary, red, big brown, evening, and silver-haired bats—are doing well and are often seen on summer evenings, swooping over the river as they snatch insects.

North Landing is jointly administered by the Nature Conservancy of Virginia and the Virginia Department of Conservation and Recreation (DCR). The only way to fully explore North Landing is by boat, preferably a canoe or other low-draft craft. There are public boat ramps at Blackwater Creek and Pocaty Creek and a DCR canoe launch area on Alton's Creek. Two boardwalks, complete with interpretive signs, accommodate the more earthbound visitor and provide surprisingly good viewing.

Cranesville Swamp Preserve

The terrain of this West Virginia refuge is always changing, thanks to the activities of an active beaver population.

SITE 100 During the last ice age, the glaciers never reached current-day West Virginia; they crept only as far south as Pennsylvania. Still, central Appalachia was a lot colder 12,000 years ago than it is now. It was a land of sphagnum bogs, alder scrub thickets, and boreal coniferous forests. In short, it looked a great deal like eastern Canada does today.

Today West Virginia is a temperate state cloaked in hardwood forests—with one exception. The 2,000-acre Cranesville Swamp Preserve is a small segment of Pleistocene West Virginia, preserved like an insect in amber. Here the larch, hemlock, and alder forests endure, as they have since the glaciers retreated north. That's because the swamp is a deep sink in a large valley surrounded by mountains. Cold air settles in, and the snow stays much longer than it does anywhere else in the state. At Cranesville Swamp, the ice age continues to linger, however tenuously.

The swamp is characterized by a complex mosaic of different habitats. Coniferous groves lie interspersed with alder thickets, ponds, and cranberry bogs. This unique environment is the work of active and aggressive engineering—but by beavers, not people. The preserve has a robust population of beavers, and they're constantly on the move. As they roam, they build new dams and abandon others. New territory is constantly being submerged while old ponds dry out as unmaintained dams leak and break.

More at home in water than on land, beavers build underwater entrances to their burrows.

Cranesville Swamp supports a breeding population of northern saw-whet owls.

The result is an abundance of eco-tones, providing a rich trove of wildlife niches. Beaver sightings are difficult, given the natural shyness of the animals and the heavy cover. The best bet is to wait quietly by a pond either at dawn or dusk.

As with the flora, some of the preserve's animal species are anomalously northern. The northern saw-whet owl is the most noteworthy example. There are a good number of nesting saw-whets at Cranesville, representing one of the most southerly breeding populations of this lovely little owl east of the Mississippi. Northern goshawks also visit the preserve, which is at the far southern margins of their range. Golden-winged warblers, black-throated green warblers, and black-throated blue warblers, which

typically favor more northern latitudes, are present at Cranesville. The preserve also supports several species of dragonflies and moths that are typically residents of New England or points north.

Cranesville also has good populations of mammals. White-tailed deer are the most likely to be seen, usually in the early morning hours as they browse. Bobcats and coyotes are much more wary but are sometimes glimpsed as they dash for the sanctuary of the trees and brush. Black bears regularly forage in the swamp. Smaller mammals include gray fox, raccoon, opossum, least weasel, mink, striped and eastern spotted skunks, and eastern cottontail; look for them near water at daybreak or twilight. Squirrels—gray, fox, red, and southern flying—keep to the trees. Walk quietly through the woods with an ear cocked for their vocalizations to locate them. Water shrews are often seen in winter diving through the ice in their incessant quest for prey.

Woodland raptors are common, particularly Cooper's, sharp-shinned, and red-shouldered hawks. Look for them perched in trees and listen for their high, keening cries. Broad-winged hawks—chunky, somewhat sluggish raptors—haunt the preserve for its abundant supply of insects, amphibians, reptiles, and rodents. Barred, and great horned owls and eastern screech-owls live here and are likely to be spotted at dusk as they leave their woodland perches to hunt; long-eared and short-eared owls are here as well, but sightings are much rarer. Wild turkeys, North America's largest gallinaceous birds, are abundant, as are wood ducks.

During the spring and fall migrations, most of Appalachia's songbirds pass through the refuge; many nest here. Some of the showier birds are scarlet tanager; rose-breasted, pine, evening, and blue grosbeaks; and indigo bunting. Rare, old-growth-associated wood warblers, such as the Blackburnian, hooded, and cerulean, may also be spotted here. Also look for wetland-loving warblers such as the Nashville warbler, Louisiana waterthrush, northern waterthrush, yellowthroat, yellow-breasted chat, Canada warbler, American redstart, northern parula, and yellow warbler.

On occasion birders have seen red crossbills or white-winged crossbills, notable for their distinctive specialized bills that allow them to pry open coni-

THE FACTS

Noteworthy Animals: Beaver, black bear, white-tailed deer, northern saw-whet owl, northern goshawk, scarlet tanager, water shrew, wild turkey.

Getting There: From I-68 in Maryland, take the Friendsville exit. Go south on Md. 42 and pick up Blooming Rose Road. Follow it for about 2 miles to Trap Run Road and follow it until it ends at White Rock Road. Turn left and drive 9 miles. When the road forks, keep right until Cranesville Road. Follow the road around the swamp and turn right on Lake Ford Road. Bear right at a "Y" intersection, and look for the preserve sign.

Open: Daily, dawn to dusk, year-round.

Best Times to Visit: Year-round.

Visitor Information: The Nature Conservancy of West Virginia, Charleston office (304-637-0160), open Monday through Friday, 8:30 a.m.-4:30 p.m., year-round. No visitor center, but a kiosk contains maps and pamphlets.

Entrance Fees: None.

Disabled Access: None.

Camping: None on-site.

fer cones for the nuts. Look for swamp, savannah, and song sparrows; alder, great crested, and Acadian flycatchers; and eastern wood-pewees. Northern cardinals, resplendent in their scarlet plumage, live here year-round.

Cranesville Swamp is one of the most user-friendly preserves in the country. While not a vast or pristine wilderness, it's a remarkably pleasant place to spend the day and is ideal for children. Four color-coded interpretive trails and a boardwalk take visitors through all the major habitats. The landscape is particularly arresting in winter when snow is on the ground.

A closer look
at 100 featured
creatures.

A red fox on the
alert in dense brush

throughout most of the continent. They will eat carrion, but bald eagles are mainly fish eaters and often rob ospreys of their catch. **See sites 1, 3, 9, 13, 14, 17, 19, 22, 23, 24, 25, 26, 27, 28, 29, 30, 31, 32, 34, 35, 36, 37, 43, 44, 46, 47, 49, 50, 53, 54, 55, 62, 63, 64, 66, 67, 68, 69, 70, 71, 72, 73, 74, 75, 76, 77, 79, 80, 81, 82, 83, 85, 86, 87, 88, 89, 90, 91, 93, 96, 97, 98, 99.**

Beaver

North American's largest rodent, the beaver (*Castor canadensis*) grows to 48 inches long, including a foot-long, flat, paddlelike tail. The average weight is between 45 and 60 pounds, although weights of 100 pounds have been documented. They are primarily nocturnal, but their work—dams of woven sticks, reeds, and saplings caulked with mud—is much in evidence. Beavers live along rivers, streams, and ponds; their lodges incorporate one or more underwater entrances. Valued for their dark brown heavy pelts, beavers were hunted to the point of extinction in the 19th century. They have regained most of their original range and are found throughout the United States, with the exception of Florida, Nevada, and southern California. **See sites 3, 9, 11, 13, 17, 20, 22, 23, 24, 25, 26, 30, 32, 34, 36, 37, 43, 44, 48, 49, 50, 52, 54, 62, 63, 65, 73, 75, 76, 83, 87, 94, 95, 96, 98, 100.**

Bighorn Sheep

Bighorn sheep (*Ovis canadensis*) are scattered throughout the West and are most common in the California Sierra, the Death Valley region, Yellowstone National Park, and Glacier National Park. Also called mountain sheep, or Rocky Mountain bighorn sheep, this husky ungulate is noted for its massive curling horns, thick neck, and white rump. It grows to 42 inches at the shoulder and weighs 250 pounds or more. Rams have huge horns that curve up and back over the ears, then back up over the cheeks in a curling C shape; ewes have small spiky horns. They favor high elevations and open, rocky country and meadows. Bighorns have suffered great reversals because of habitat destruction, overhunting, and disease. **See sites 4, 5, 6, 14, 18, 19, 21, 23, 30, 32, 51.**

Bison

There is no mistaking the bison, or buffalo, for any other beast. *Bison bison* stand 72 inches at the shoulder and may weigh a ton. Both sexes are horned and have huge heads, substantial humps, and short-furred flanks. The bulls are dark brown on the head, tail, and legs, with lighter fur on the shoulders. The cows are smaller and have a more even brown hue. Although this quintessential symbol of the Great Plains has narrowly escaped extinction, it still faces travails. Recently about one-third of Yellowstone National Park's bison were slaughtered when they straggled into Montana, inciting ranchers' fears that they might be vectors for a disease fatal to cattle. Bison are currently found in scattered parks, preserves, and private holdings in the Great Plains and Rocky Mountain West. **See sites 30, 32, 48, 49, 51, 54, 56.**

Black Bear

The black bear (*Ursus americanus*) is abundant throughout the Rocky Mountains, along the Pacific coast, and in much of the East. Its name notwithstanding, it displays a remarkable array of color phases, ranging from yellow to cinnamon to brown to jet black. The black bear is smaller than the grizzly bear, seldom exceeding 450 pounds. Black bears can become accustomed, even habituated, to human beings—in the latter case depending on them for garbage or picnic baskets. In the wild they will eat anything remotely resembling protein or carbohydrates, including rodents, reptiles, fish, injured or sick larger game, carrion, roots, berries, insects, grass, and tree bark. **See sites 1, 2, 3, 4, 12, 14, 17, 18, 19, 20, 23, 25, 29, 31, 32, 33, 34, 43, 63, 68, 72, 76, 80, 81, 83, 85, 87, 93, 95, 98, 100.**

Black-footed Ferret

North America's rarest mammal, the black-footed ferret (*Mustela nigripes*) once ranged throughout the Great Plains and the Southwest. Prairie dogs were its primary prey; as ranchers systematically poisoned the West's huge prairie dog colonies, the ferret plummeted almost to extinction. A few black-footed ferrets survive and breed in captivity, and tentative reintroduction programs have begun. This tawny weasel reaches 24 inches in length and has a white face set off with a black bandit mask, black feet, black tail tip, and yellowish fur. In addition to prairie dogs, it will eat mice, voles, gophers, ground squirrels, birds, snakes, and lizards. **See site 55.**

Bobcat

America's most common wild feline, the bobcat (*Felis rufus*) has rebounded from decades of excessive hunting and

trapping. Numerous in the western states, it is also faring well in New England, upstate New York, Appalachia, and parts of the Deep South. These stubby-tailed cats resemble their northern cousin, the lynx, except that they are smaller, more heavily spotted, and reddish brown to pale brown rather than buff or gray. They reach 35 inches in length and weigh up to 30 pounds. Bobcats are adept hunters and take a wide variety of prey, including rabbits, squirrels, mice, rats, voles—even porcupines. They adapt well to different habitats and can be found in deep forests, brushlands, wooded swamps, and even farmland. **See sites 4, 5, 6, 8, 11, 14, 18, 19, 20, 21, 29, 31, 32, 33, 34, 35, 36, 38, 41, 42, 43, 49, 54, 57, 58, 60, 62, 63, 65, 67, 68, 69, 71, 72, 73, 76, 80, 81, 83, 85, 91, 92, 93, 94, 95, 96, 98, 100.**

Brown Pelican

Almost wiped out by chlorinated hydrocarbon pesticides in the 1960s, the brown pelican (*Pelecanus occidentalis*) has staged a remarkable resurgence. Today individuals are found along the Atlantic and Gulf coasts from Florida to Texas and off the California coast. Stockier than the white pelican, the brown pelican typically reaches 55 inches in length, with a wingspan exceeding 84 inches. They are gray-brown overall, with a white neck; the head is yellow in winter and white in summer. Brown pelicans have truly gigantic bills, which they endeavor to fill with fish after diving headlong into the water. Flocks are often seen cruising in a long single-file line, just above the wave tops. **See sites 7, 11, 60, 67, 68, 86, 97.**

Bullfrog

North America's largest frog, the bullfrog (*Rana catesbeiana*) can reach a length of nine inches. Originally native to the East, it is now found throughout the country, with the exception of the northern Great Plains, the Great Basin, and most of the Rockies. A bullfrog may be green, olive, or brown; the belly is whitish or silvery, mottled with gray or light brown, with a yellow tinge at the chin and throat. The eardrums are large and conspicuous. Bullfrogs will inhabit virtually any permanent, relatively placid body of water, and will travel overland considerable distances from one pond to another. They sometimes show up in backyard goldfish ponds. Bullfrogs are voracious predators, and in addition to insects, they will eat small reptiles, fish, ducklings—anything they can cram down their huge maws. **See sites 27, 33, 34, 36, 41, 43, 61, 72, 73, 76, 80, 83, 85, 93, 94, 95, 96, 98, 99.**

Burrowing Owl

Active during the day, the burrowing owl (*Athene cunicularia*) is often seen balanced on one long leg, guarding its home in the ground. Burrowing owls usually live in small colonies, inhabiting several contiguous burrows that have been abandoned by prairie dogs, ground squirrels, or badgers. Burrowing owls typically reach nine inches in length. The back is spotted with brown and white; in adults, the breast is barred. They prefer open, semiarid country, particularly prairies; they will also nest at airports and golf courses. Although burrowing owls are found from North Dakota and Texas west to California, they are in serious decline because of habitat destruction and predation by coyotes and foxes. **See sites 5, 8, 9, 13, 23, 24, 48, 49, 51, 55, 56.**

California Sea Lion

The California sea lion (*Zalophus californianus*) is the trained seal seen in marine shows. Extremely vocal and inquisitive, this pinniped is also an exceptionally fast swimmer, reaching speeds of 25 miles per hour. Sea lions are dark brown but appear black when wet. Bulls can exceed 600 pounds, and the females may weigh up to 250 pounds. Extremely sociable, sea lions establish themselves in large rookeries along the coastline, usually in rocky areas, on breakwaters, or on floating docks. California is the heartland of their range, but males roam widely northward, sometimes to Canada. **See sites 7, 10, 11, 28.**

Caribou

Believed to be the same species as the reindeer of Europe and Asia, caribou (*Rangifer tarandus*) are the most migratory of mammals. These large deer range widely over the Arctic tundra, often in herds numbering in the tens of thousands. Caribou are found throughout northern Canada and in the far northern United States— Alaska, Washington, and Idaho. They reach 42 inches at the shoulder and weigh up to 400 pounds. Their fur is long and shaggy, with wide variations in color, from almost white to dark brown. Both sexes have antlers—those of the males are large, flattened, and somewhat palmate; females' antlers are smaller and thinner. Caribou are herbivorous, eating mushrooms, grass, twigs, even their own fallen antlers.

This species faces grave dangers from oil development and excessive hunting. **See sites 2, 3.**

Coati

A relative of the raccoon, the coati (*Nasua nasua*) sports a black mask similar to that of its more familiar cousin and has a banded tail, although its tail is long and semiprehensile, unlike the bushy raccoon tail. Coatis, or coatimundis as they are also called, can reach 50 inches in length; males are typically twice as large as females. Extremely social, they travel in troops of up to 25 members, usually comprising females and juveniles. Coatis are active daytime hunters of small prey, feasting on insects, scorpions, spiders (particularly tarantulas), ground-nesting birds and their eggs, lizards, and snakes; they will also root out grubs and tubers with their long, thick-skinned noses. Adept climbers, coatis prefer wooded slopes and gorges and are common in Mexico and points south; in the United States they are found only in parts of New Mexico, Arizona, and Texas. **See sites 4, 6, 23.**

Coho Salmon

One of the Pacific coast's five species of salmon, cohos (*Oncorhynchus kisutch*) are also known as silver salmon. They are smaller than the equally prized chinook (or king) salmon, reaching a maximum weight of 20 pounds. Cohos once constituted fully half of the West Coast's sport and commercial salmon catch, but the species has been devastated by the degradation of their spawning grounds. They spawn in small, cold streams in old-growth forests from southeast Alaska to northern California. Such timberlands have been excessively clear-cut in recent years, and cohos have declined accordingly. The coho is now listed as threatened under the federal Endangered Species Act. **See site 1.**

Collared Peccary

Also known as the javelina, the collared peccary (*Dicotyles tajacu*) roams the deserts of Texas and southern Arizona in large bands. Descended from wild pigs that lived more than 25 million years ago, these handsome little swine reach 18 inches at the shoulder and weights of up to 50 pounds. They have bristly brown coats frosted with white, a whitish collar, long snouts, muscular bodies, and dainty hooves. They are aggressive and omnivorous foragers, feeding on snakes, lizards, fledgling birds, rodents, insects, and herbaceous plants. Although javelinas have a reputation for ferocity, they will fight only if cornered. **See sites 4, 6, 23, 57, 60.**

Cottonmouth

The cottonmouth (*Agkistrodon piscivorus*) is an extremely venomous aquatic snake found throughout the Deep South, west into Texas, and north to Illinois. Anywhere from two to six feet long, a cottonmouth may be olive, brown, or blackish, with crossbands outlined by dark borders. Like rattlesnakes, they vibrate their tails when aroused and will often attack rather than flee. When greatly agitated, a cottonmouth will throw its head back and gape widely, revealing the white mouth that has given it its name. Cottonmouths are found wherever there is water—swamps, rivers, lakes, ponds, ditches, even rice fields. They prey on fish, amphibians, other snakes, young alligators, and aquatic birds. **See sites 33, 34, 35, 36, 40, 41, 42, 57, 58, 68, 69, 71, 72, 80, 85, 91, 92, 94, 98, 99.**

Coyote

The coyote (*Canis latrans*) may be the greatest wildlife success story on the continent—despite humans, who have tried to poison, shoot, and trap it into oblivion. Today coyotes number in the millions and are found in all states except Hawaii. They inhabit deep wilderness and suburbia alike. "Song dogs" (so called for their wild, yapping evening choruses) typically run to 27 inches at the shoulder and 55 inches in length, and weigh 50 pounds. They are buff to gray in color, with whitish underparts and rufous ears, feet, and legs. Prey consists of rodents, reptiles, and ground-dwelling birds, though coyotes will sometimes join forces to bring down a deer. In the wild, coyotes are sometimes mistaken for wolves; but wolves run with their tails held horizontally, while coyotes run with their tails down. **See sites 4, 5, 6, 8, 9, 11, 13, 14, 17, 19, 20, 21, 22, 23, 26, 27, 29, 30, 31, 32, 33, 34, 36, 37, 40, 41, 42, 43, 45, 48, 49, 50, 51, 52, 54, 55, 56, 57, 58, 60, 62, 63, 72, 73, 74, 76, 79, 81, 83, 87, 92, 93, 94, 95, 96, 100.**

Dall's Sheep

A resident of Alaska and the Yukon, the pure white Dall's sheep (*Ovis dalli*) reaches 42 inches at the shoulder and weighs approximately 150 pounds. A dark phase called the stone sheep occurs in the southern part of the range; color runs from silvery to black, with white rump, belly, and face. The horns of the ram are huge, although slighter than those of the bighorn sheep. Rams engage in impressive butting contests during the rut; the sound of horns colliding can be heard more than a mile away. Highly prized as game animals, Dall's sheep are fairly common over their range but extremely wary in areas where they are hunted. **See sites 2, 3.**

Desert Tortoise

The desert tortoise (*Gopherus agassizii*) reaches 14 inches in length and has a domed dark brown shell with prominent growth rings. The hind feet are stumpy, the forefeet are scraperlike, the tail short. The desert tortoise uses its forefeet to dig burrows in sandy soil for nesting and protection. The diet consists of fruit, flowers, and leaves. The three American species of the *Gopherus* genera (desert, gopher, and Texas tortoises) are widely separated and represent the far northern edge of their range; they are found, respectively, in Arizona, Florida, and Texas. **See sites 4, 5, 6.**

Eastern Coral Snake

The subject of an old mnemonic rhyme, "Red and yellow, kill a fellow, red and black, poison lack," the eastern coral snake (*Micrurus fulvius*) has red, yellow, and black rings encircling the body, with the red always bordered by yellow. (Look-alike species, such as milk snakes, have black rings separating the red and yellow rings.) Coral snakes are highly venomous but are not aggressive, often refusing to bite even when molested. Unlike North America's other venomous snakes, they are not pit vipers. They have short fangs and are related to cobras. Reaching 30 inches in length, they favor a variety of habitats ranging from dry pine woods to dense hammock. Eastern coral snakes are found from coastal Mississippi to southern North Carolina, including all of Florida. Related species inhabit Texas and Arizona. **See sites 4, 60, 67, 68, 69, 71, 72, 80.**

Eastern Newt

A member of the salamander family, the eastern newt (*Notophthalmus viridescens*) looks like a lizard, but is actually related to frogs and toads. Primarily aquatic, an eastern newt is born and lives the first few weeks of its life in water before transforming into a subadult form, called an eft, that lives on the forest floor for three to four years before returning to the water and assuming adult characteristics. Efts are about three inches long and orange-red to red-brown in color; various subspecies may have rings, spots, and stripes as well. They are most often seen on the forest floor after a rain shower. The newt favors ponds and quiet backwaters, and is found along the Atlantic coast from Canada to Florida and inland to Texas. **See sites 34, 36, 40, 80, 81, 83, 94, 95, 96, 98.**

Elephant Seal

The world's largest pinniped, the northern elephant seal (*Mirounga angustirostris*) bull may reach four tons; a cow may weigh up to a ton. They eat skates, stingrays, fish, small sharks, as well as squid. Elephant seals are sociable but territorial; the bulls spend much of their time in spring and summer fighting over the cows. The older bulls, or "beachmasters," inflate their huge snouts to amplify their sonorous bellows. If visual and auditory threats fail, chest-to-chest physical battle ensues. Elephant seals are found from Alaska to California; in recent years they have expanded their range in California, establishing at least two new colonies along the central coast. **See sites 7, 10, 11, 28.**

Fisher

The fisher (*Martes pennanti*) has a thin, low-slung body up to 40 inches long. Its thick fur varies from dark brown to black, with white-tipped hairs that give it a frosted appearance. It preys primarily on snowshoe hare, squirrels, and raccoons; it also kills porcupines by flipping them over and attacking the unprotected underbelly. Fishers prefer deep forest, and are present in the Cascades, the northern Rocky Mountains, the Adirondacks, parts of New England, and the upper Great Lakes. Nearly extirpated by trapping and logging, they are making a slow comeback thanks to protective measures and reintroduction programs. **See sites 18, 19, 25, 29, 32, 43, 63, 75, 76, 81, 83, 87, 95.**

Gar

The *Lepisosteidae* family is an ancient family of fish that dates back to the Cretaceous period. Four species are native to this continent (alligator, long-nose, spotted, and short-nose). Gars are formidable-looking fish, with massive cylindrical bodies, large scales, and a long snoutlike maw bristling with teeth. Voracious predators, they will feed on fish, turtles, water snakes, ducklings, and muskrats. Alligator gars, the largest species, sometimes reach seven feet six inches in length and 300 pounds. Garfish, as they are commonly called, frequent rivers and large streams, as well as shallow lakes, where they migrate for spring spawning. Garfish range throughout the Mississippi Basin and larger Gulf tributaries. **See sites 74, 80, 92.**

Gila Monster

America's only venomous lizard won't bite unless molested. And although extremely painful, its bite is seldom fatal to humans. The gila monster (*Heloderma suspectum*) is marked with colorful patterns of black and orange, pink, yellow, or salmon. It typically reaches 15 inches in length and has a large head and short muscular legs with long claws. Gila monsters are subterranean, inhabiting abandoned burrows and rock crevices. Their diet includes carrion, small reptiles, rodents, bird eggs, and fledglings. Gila monsters favor vegetated desert, canyon bottomlands, and lower-elevation mountain slopes. They range from southern Nevada through much of Arizona and Sonora, Mexico; local populations are also found in southern California, southwestern Utah, and southwestern New Mexico. **See sites 4, 5, 23.**

Golden Eagle

The golden eagle (*Aquila chrysaetos*) favors wild, rugged country and preys on small mammals. Its body is typically longer than the bald eagle's, reaching three feet six inches. Its wings are shorter and broader, with a maximum span of six feet six inches. The plumage is dark brown, with a paler nape that runs from yellowish to russet to truly golden. Its bill is smaller and darker than that of the bald eagle. Immature birds show white at the base of the tail and have white patches on the underside of their wings. The golden eagle has endured its share of persecution, particularly from sheep ranchers. It appears to be holding its own, however, and is genuinely common in some portions of the mountainous West. **See sites 2, 4, 6, 8, 9, 12, 13, 14, 18, 19, 20, 21, 22, 24, 26, 27, 28, 29, 30, 31, 32, 48, 51, 55, 77, 91, 93.**

Gray Fox

A common resident of woodlands and scrublands throughout the East, Southwest, California, and coastal Oregon, the gray fox (*Urocyon cinereoargenteus*) stands up to 15 inches at the shoulder and averages 36 inches from tip of nose to tip of tail. The pelt runs from salt-and-pepper to gray; the flanks, legs, and feet are rust colored; a black stripe runs the length of its tail. The gray fox is nocturnal and solitary in habit. Omnivorous, it subsists on rodents, reptiles, fledgling birds, and fruit. The gray fox is the only American canid with climbing ability; it readily scampers up trees in a quest for ripe fruit or to escape predators. Their voice is a weak yap. **See sites 9, 11, 33, 34, 36, 43, 57, 58, 62, 63, 72, 73, 80, 81, 83, 85, 87, 91, 92, 93, 94, 95, 100.**

Gray Whale

Once hunted almost to oblivion, the gray whale (*Eschrichtius robustus*) has rebounded to a population of more than 30,000 animals. This medium-size baleen whale reaches a length of 45 feet. It has blotchy grayish skin, numerous bumps on the back, and no dorsal fin. It is a coastal whale, usually keeping within a mile or two of the shore as it feeds. Gray whales follow a strict migration route, birthing their calves in shallow lagoons in Baja California, and returning to Alaskan waters in the summer. Their migrations thrill legions of whale lovers along the way. Although their populations are currently secure, gray whales face new and dire threats from plans for a huge salt-processing works in one of their nativity lagoons. **See sites 10, 28.**

Gray Wolf

Also known as the timber wolf, the gray wolf (*Canis lupus*) is our largest wild canid, standing up to three feet four inches at the shoulder, reaching five feet in length, and weighing up to 100 pounds. The gray wolf displays a variety of color phases, from pure white to black, and all shades of gray in between. They are social animals, mating for life and living in close-knit family units of four to 17 individuals. Gray wolves will eat anything from rodents to carrion to ripe berries, but they prefer large game, and whenever possible, they take "culls"—weak or injured deer, caribou, and moose. The gray wolf is gradually reclaiming its original range through restocking programs, including one in Yellowstone National Park. Increasingly their mournful and haunting songs are heard in the wilder regions of the West and upper Midwest. **See sites 1, 2, 3, 18, 19, 20, 29, 30, 32, 44, 63.**

Great Blue Heron

Our most widespread heron, the great blue heron (*Ardea herodias*) is found in the lower 48 states and southeastern Alaska. It is also our largest heron, often reaching 48 inches in height. These stately birds are grayish blue, with two black neck plumes, black eyebrows, a white crown, a brownish gray neck, and black shoulder patches. A solitary hunter, this wader stands motionless at the water's edge. lashing out suddenly, spearing its prey with a rapier-like bill. Great blues will forage in a wide range of habitats, from remote wilderness rivers to freshwater marshes and saltwater estuaries. They will also stalk mice and other small rodents in meadows and fields. **See sites 9, 11, 20, 21, 24, 25, 27, 35, 37, 40, 41, 42, 53, 57, 60, 61, 62, 63, 64, 66, 67, 68, 69, 70, 71, 72, 73, 74, 77, 78, 79, 80, 81, 82, 83, 84, 85, 86, 88, 90, 91, 92, 94, 96, 97, 98, 99.**

Great Egret

Once hunted nearly to extinction for its long, lacy feathers, the great egret (*Casmerodius albus*) has rebounded significantly, reclaiming much of its original range. They are now found along the Atlantic, Gulf, and Pacific coasts and in the Mississippi Basin and much of the interior West. Standing up to 39 inches tall, these pure white birds have a yellow bill and black legs, and sport long, delicate plumes during the breeding season. Great egrets favor fresh and saltwater wetlands and prey on fish, which they capture by standing motionless in the shallows, then striking suddenly. **See sites 9, 11, 21, 24, 25, 35, 40, 41, 42, 57, 60, 61, 64, 66, 67, 68, 69, 70, 71, 72, 73, 77, 78, 79, 80, 82, 84, 85, 86, 88, 90, 91, 92, 94, 97, 98, 99.**

Great Horned Owl

Reaching 25 inches in length, with a wingspan of almost five feet, the great horned owl (*Bubo virginianus*) is second only to the great gray owl in size among continental owls. Recognized by its prominent ear tufts and huge yellow eyes, it demonstrates wide color variation. Owls near the Arctic in northern Canada and Alaska are almost pure white. More southernly owls range from gray to brown. Our most widely distributed owl, the great horned owl is found throughout all of North America except the deep Arctic. They will inhabit forests, swamps, plains, deserts, farmlands, suburban backyards, and city parks. Great horned owls have powerful talons and are fierce hunters. They will take mice, rabbits, rats, crows, waterfowl, opossums—even the occasional raccoon, skunk, or neighborhood cat. **See sites 5, 6, 8, 9, 11, 12, 19, 20, 23, 24, 25, 26, 30, 31, 32, 33, 35, 36, 37, 38, 40, 41, 43, 45, 47, 48, 52, 54, 59, 62, 63, 65, 68, 71, 72, 75, 76, 77, 78, 80, 81, 83, 84, 88, 91, 92, 93, 94, 95, 96, 97, 98, 99, 100.**

Grizzly Bear

Most taxonomists consider the grizzly (*Ursus arctos*) and the Alaskan brown bear different races of the same species. The grizzly is the bear of the interior United States and is the smaller of the two—it weighs up to 900 pounds, compared to the 2,000 pounds of the coastal Alaskan brown bear. The difference in size is probably due more to food availability than to genetics— pickings are slim in the mountains and tundra compared to the salmon-rich Alaskan coast. Grizzlies are truly omnivorous, and will eat anything from roots and insect larvae to stranded whales. They can be formidable hunters, sometimes killing mature moose. Distinctive in appearance, grizzlies have concave faces and humped backs, making them easy to differentiate from black bears. Grizzlies range from Wyoming and Montana through the Canadian Rockies and throughout Alaska. They are the lords of whatever realm they inhabit and cannot be depended on to yield ground to anything—including human beings. Attacks are rare, but grizzlies are unpredictable and dangerous. **See sites 2, 17, 19, 20, 29, 32.**

Harbor Seal

The most common seal of the continental United States, the harbor seal (*Phoca vitulina*) is found along both the Atlantic and Pacific coasts. These small pinnipeds seldom exceed five feet in length or weights over 300 pounds. They are brown or gray or somewhere between and usually speckled with small spots. Harbor seals have doglike faces and somewhat lugubrious expressions. They are generally diffident but can become testy if cornered or molested. These seals frequent a wide range of habitats— open coast, rocky headlands, bays, and river mouths. They like to haul out on rocks or beaches, where they indulge in long naps. Harbor seals feed on a variety of fish and will also eat squid. **See sites 7, 11, 28, 75, 84, 89.**

Humpback Whale

About 16 feet long at birth, as an adult the humpback whale (*Megaptera novaeangliae*) typically reaches 50 feet in length. Its humped dorsal surface is black; the throat, breast, and undersides are white. Its head is usually colonized by large aggregates of barnacles; its flippers are extremely long and knobbed along the leading edges. Humpbacks hunt cooperatively, forcing small fish together by blowing "bubble nets" around them. When the fish are compressed, the whales dive in, gulping down great numbers. They are among the most musical of the great whales, exhibiting an astonishing vocabulary of haunting chortles, clicks, and squeals. Humpbacks often thrill whale-watchers with their acrobatics, breaching high into the air before crashing back down. Recovering from near-extinction, they are found in small pods along the Atlantic and Pacific coasts. **See sites 10, 28, 75.**

Least Tern

North America's smallest tern and the only one with a yellow bill, the least tern (*Sterna antillarum*) was almost wiped out by the milliner's trade in the late 19th and early 20th centuries. It has since rebounded, but its long-term future is still unsure. These birds are about nine inches long, with a gray back and wings, white forehead and underbelly, black cap and eyeline, black outer primary feathers, yellow feet, and black bill tip. Least terns breed along the California coast, tributaries of the interior Mississippi River, and along the Atlantic coast. They winter along both coasts of Mexico and South America and favor sandy beaches and interior islands. They feed on small fish, diving into the water from a considerable height to make their catch. **See sites 39, 49, 53, 67, 68, 70, 71, 79, 82, 84, 86, 90, 91.**

Least Weasel

This chipmunk-size weasel is the continent's smallest carnivore, seldom exceeding eight inches in length. The least weasel (*Mustela nivalis*) has a brown back, white underbelly, white feet, and a short brown tail. In northern latitudes it turns white in winter, like its cousin, the ermine (also known as short-tailed weasel). Least weasels are found in a belt that runs from Alaska through the Canadian prairie provinces into parts of Quebec, the northern Great Plains, the Great Lakes, and Appalachia. They frequent open woods, grassy meadows—even suburban lawns. Nocturnal hunters, they prey primarily on small rodents, particularly mice. Their chief predators are foxes, cats, and owls. **See sites 38, 43, 52, 63, 100.**

Leopard Frog

The five species of spotted frog, members of the *Ranidae* family, have suffered drastic declines in recent years. Causes are not known, but habitat destruction, acid rain, ozone depletion, and pesticides all may be to blame. All leopard frogs are markedly spotted; background colors are green, buff, or gray, depending on the species and local variation. Length ranges from two to six inches. Leopard frogs are found throughout the continental United States except the Pacific states. They prefer freshwater marshes but will also inhabit some brackish coastal marshes. Active wanderers, leopard frogs may be found in deep, damp grass far from water, particularly in the summer. **See sites 4, 6, 27, 33, 34, 41, 43, 50, 56, 61, 63, 71, 72, 73, 76, 80, 81, 83, 85, 91, 94, 96, 98, 99.**

Loggerhead Sea Turtle

The loggerhead (*Caretta caretta*) is the most common of the Atlantic sea turtles—which is not to say that it is commonplace. Its numbers have been greatly reduced by overexploitation and habitat destruction. Found from brackish streams to the high seas, the loggerhead roams the ocean from the mid-Atlantic to the Bahamas. Females lay their eggs on sandy beaches at night. After an incubation period of one to three months, the hatchlings emerge almost simultaneously. Adults reach 45 inches and weigh up to 350 pounds. The carapace is reddish brown, with five large plates on each side. The head is large, and the front flippers have two claws each. The loggerhead's varied diet includes jellyfish, fish, mollusks, crustaceans, and eelgrass. **See sites 64, 67, 69, 70, 71, 86, 91.**

Long-tailed Weasel

Our most widely distributed weasel species, the long-tailed weasel (*Mustela frenata*) is found in all of the 48 continental United States. The only North American weasel with brown feet and white underparts, it also has a brown head and back and a black-tipped tail and averages 20 inches in length. Generally nocturnal, the least weasel is sometimes seen in the day. It is a ready climber and haunts farmlands, open areas, wetlands, and second-growth woodlands. Long-tailed weasels typically take smaller prey such as mice, rats, chipmunks, and ground-nesting birds, but they will also tackle animals that outweigh them, such as rabbits and chickens. **See sites 11, 13, 19, 21, 29, 30, 31, 32, 36, 38, 43, 45, 51, 60, 63, 80, 81, 83, 85, 87, 91, 92, 93, 95, 97, 98.**

Lynx

Cats of the far north, lynx (*Felis lynx*) are found in Alaska and portions of Idaho, Washington, Oregon, Montana, Wyoming, and New England. They are larger than bobcats, reaching lengths of 40 inches and weights of 40 pounds. Gray or buff in color, the lynx has long legs, long ear tufts, a black tail tip, luxuriant fur, and huge paws that act as snowshoes when hunting prey in deep snow. Lynx are vulnerable to large population swings that have been linked to the cyclical population crashes of snowshoe hare, a favored prey. In the continental United States these beautiful cats are rare over their entire range. **See sites 1, 2, 3, 18, 19, 20, 31, 32, 76.**

Magnificent Frigatebird

The magnificent frigatebird (*Fregata magnificens*) reaches three feet four inches in length and has a wingspan of seven feet six inches. A deeply forked tail and extremely narow wings give this bird a dramatic silhouette in flight. Its feet are so weak that it can barely walk, and it spends much of its time aloft. Females are black with a white breast; males are glossy black with a vivid red throat pouch that they inflate during courtship. Although frigatebirds are usually seen over water, they seldom stray far from land. They adeptly pick fish from the surface of water and often trail schools of tuna to prey on the baitfish driven to the surface. Frigatebirds make their homes from southern Texas to northern Florida's Atlantic coast, and are particularly numerous in southern Florida. **See site 70.**

Manatee

The manatee (*Trichechus manatus*) is the only North American member of the *Sirenia* order. Completely aquatic and almost hairless, they slightly resemble seals, except that manatees have huge blunt heads and broad paddlelike tails. They reach lengths of 15 feet and weights of 1,000 pounds or more. Manatees are completely vegetarian and quite sluggish. When meeting, they often "hug" each other with their flippers and press their lips together in a "kiss." They are found in rivers and estuarine waters from North Carolina to Texas, with the largest concentrations in Florida. Aptly called sea cows, manatees consume up to 100 pounds of aquatic vegetation each day. Greatly threatened by habitat destruction and human encroachment, many are killed each year by motorboat propellers. **See sites 67, 68, 69, 71.**

Marbled Murrelet

About ten inches in length, the marbled murrelet (*Brachyramphus marmoratus*) is brown, mottled with white in summer; in winter, gray to black with a white shoulder patch and a partial white collar. This little seabird is threatened, a victim of the West's timber wars. It nests high in the crowns of old-growth conifers; as the forests of big trees have been logged, the species has declined proportionately. The murrelet flies out to sea at dawn to forage for fish and comes ashore at night to visit its nest. In the far north, it will nest on the ground. This species ranges along the Pacific coast from California to the Aleutian Islands but is extremely scarce in the southern portion of its range. **See sites 1, 7.**

Marten

The marten (*Martes americana*) was much reduced in recent decades but is making a comeback. This little mustelid is now found in Canada, Alaska, the Cascade Range, the Rocky Mountains, the Adirondacks, parts of New England, and the upper Great Lakes. About 25 inches long, the marten has thick yellowish brown fur, a pale orange or buff patch on its throat and chest, and a bushy tail. It is active in early morning and evening and on overcast days. Extremely territorial, marten tend to keep almost exclusively to the trees, which they mark by rubbing their scent glands on the branches. Red squirrels are a favorite prey, but marten will also eat other rodents, birds, bird eggs, honey, berries, and fruit. **See sites 1, 2, 3, 18, 19, 25, 31, 43, 75, 76, 83, 95.**

Mexican Free-tailed Bat

A medium-size bat with a naked tail that extends beyond its anterior membrane (hence its name), the freetail (*Tadarida brasiliensis*) roosts primarily in huge cave colonies in the Southwest. It reaches six inches in length, and has dark brown fur, a snub nose, and a grooved upper lip. Although the freetail has declined due to pesticides and habitat destruction, it is still one of our most common mammals, probably numbering over a hundred million. It ranges from western Texas north to Kansas and west to California. These bats are known for their spectacular evening displays when they leave their caves in a mass exodus. They sometimes fly distances of 100 miles or more in search of their prey of flying insects. **See site 59.**

Mink

Noted for its luxuriant fur, the mink (*Mustela vison*) typically reaches 25 inches in length and is dark brown with a white chin patch. An adept swimmer, the mink lives along rivers, creeks, lakes, ponds, and marshes. Carnivores, mink prey on fish, reptiles, amphibians, crayfish, rodents, and birds. They are nocturnal, typically solitary, and aggressive toward intruders. Like most members of the *Mustelidae* family, mink emit a strong odor, or musk, when cornered or harassed. Vocalizations are varied and include screeches, purrs, and hisses. They are distributed throughout Canada and the United States except the arid Southwest. **See sites 1, 13, 19, 20, 22, 24, 29, 31, 32, 33, 34, 35, 36, 38, 40, 41, 43, 44, 50, 52, 61, 62, 63, 75, 76, 80, 81, 83, 84, 85, 87, 90, 92, 93, 95, 96, 98, 99, 100.**

Mississippi Kite

This graceful bird of prey is usually seen dipping and diving through the air, where it spends most of its time. The Mississippi kite (*Ictinia mississippiensis*) reaches 15 inches in length and has a wingspan of 36 inches. Adults are gray, with a white or whitish head and underparts, black tail, and black outer primary feathers. They are mainly insectivorous, showing a fondness for dragonflies; they will also take small reptiles and amphibians. Their favored habitats are blackwater swamps and other wet, wooded regions. Mississippi kites range from the Gulf Coast states to the Southwest; they winter in the tropics. They have expanded their range recently and are now sometimes seen as far north as New England. **See sites 33, 34, 36, 64, 73, 80, 91.**

Monarch Butterfly

The monarch butterfly (*Danaus plexippus*) is very large, with a wingspan of up to four inches. The wings are bright orange with black veins and a black margin with white dots. This is the only butterfly that undertakes an annual north-south migration of hundreds of miles. Unlike birds, however, no single individual butterfly makes the entire round-trip. In autumn northern butterflies head south for the winter. In spring they head back north, breed along the way, and die, their places taken by offspring that return to the original starting point. Monarchs range throughout nearly all of the United States, absent only from Alaska and the Pacific Northwest; they are year-round residents of southern California and Hawaii. **See sites 65, 82.**

Moose

North America's largest deer, the moose (*Alces alces*) typically reaches seven feet at the shoulder and can weigh 1,500 pounds. Moose are dark brown and have long grayish legs, humped shoulders, an extremely large protuberant snout, and a long bell of skin and hair below the jawline. Males support massive antlers with small prongs. Moose are common in Alaska and most of Canada and are found in portions of New England, Idaho, Montana, and Wyoming. They favor shallow lakes and are often spotted deep in the water, dredging for aquatic plants. They can be testy, and in Alaska it is moose, not bears, that account for the majority of attacks on humans. **See sites 1, 2, 3, 13, 17, 18, 19, 30, 32, 43, 44, 76, 81, 83, 95.**

Mountain Goat

The legendary "beast the color of winter," the mountain goat (*Oreamnos americanus*) inhabits high peak areas from the northern Rockies to Alaska. These powerful white ungulates stand about 42 inches high at the shoulder and weigh 200 pounds or more. They have muscular bodies, short legs, slightly curved, slender black horns, and prominent beards. In summer they shed their thick, shaggy fur for shorter summer coats. Herbivores, mountain goats migrate up and down the slopes with the season in search of fodder; they favor high, craggy areas and alpine meadows near the snow line in summer, retreating to lower elevations in winter. Renowned for their climbing prowess, mountain goat have hooves with a sharp outer rim for gripping and a rubbery sole for traction, allowing them to leap and saunter along rock faces so steep they look almost vertical. More mountain goats are killed by avalanches and rockslides than by predators. **See sites 1, 18, 19, 21, 29.**

Mountain Lion

With the exception of the jaguar (which is virtually extinct in the United States), the mountain lion is North America's largest cat. Also known as puma or cougar, the mountain lion (*Felis concolor*) is a tawny, graceful cat with small rounded ears, big feet, and a long tail. The tail tip and backs of the ears are dark brown, and the belly is whitish. Males can reach nearly eight feet long from tip of nose to tip of tail, and weigh more than 200 pounds; females rarely top

150 pounds. Mountain lions have adapted to a wide range of habitats, including forests, scrublands, and blackwater swamps. More than 5,000 mountain lions are thought to live in California; they are also found in the Southwest and the Rocky Mountain states. A Florida subspecies, the Florida panther, is endangered. **See sites 4, 6, 8, 12, 14, 18, 19, 20, 21, 23, 29, 31, 60, 69.**

Mudpuppy

At up to 17 inches long, the mudpuppy (*Necturus maculosus*) is one of our largest salamanders. It has extravagant red feathery gills, four stubby limbs, and a large keeled tail. This aquatic salamander inhabits a wide variety of habitats, from clear streams to less-than-pristine bayous, showing a tolerance for polluted water rare in amphibians. Ranging throughout the Mississippi Basin and the Great Lakes, the mudpuppy varies in color from olive to gray-brown, and may be lightly speckled. Generally nocturnal, mudpuppies are often active during the day in muddy or weedy waters. They are omnivorous, feeding on insects, fish, small amphibians, crayfish, mollusks, and amphibian spawn. **See sites 36, 83.**

Mule Deer

The mule deer (*Odocoileus hemionus*) is large and stocky, with bucks sometimes exceeding 400 pounds. It has large ears and a short tail that is black above, white at the base. Bucks sport higher antler racks than their eastern cousins, and the antlers have branched tines. Their coats are reddish in summer and brown-gray in winter. Herbivores, "mulies" follow established migration routes, foraging in the mountains in summer and retreating to valleys in winter. Mule deer are more susceptible to habitat destruction, human disturbance, and winterkill than whitetails and have demonstrated worrisome population drops in some areas. They range from Colorado to California and north to Alberta and British Columbia. A subspecies, the black-tailed deer, is common along the Pacific coast. It is much smaller than either the mule deer or white-tailed deer, seldom reaching 200 pounds. **See sites 4, 5, 6, 12, 13, 14, 18, 19, 20, 21, 22, 23, 24, 26, 27, 29, 30, 31, 32, 48, 49, 51, 55, 56.**

Musk-ox

A native of far northern Canada, the musk-ox (*Ovibos moschatus*) is found in the United States only in the far northern reaches of Alaska. With long shaggy hair that hangs down almost to its feet, it is generally dark brown, with pale silvery hair on the lower back and legs. Bulls may reach five feet at the shoulders and exceed 900 pounds. Both sexes have broad, flat horns that conform close to the skull and curve forward at the tips. The cow's horns are more slender and curved than the bull's. The cow also has a paler face than the bull's. Musk-oxen graze in small herds, seeking lowland valleys in the summer. During winter they graze wind-scoured slopes where snowpack is minimal. When threatened, the adults form a circle around the calves, with their horns facing outward. This defense mechanism made them an easy target for hunters, and they were almost wiped out. They are now being introduced across their original range. **See site 2.**

Northern Goshawk

The northern goshawk (*Accipiter gentilis*) is a denizen of coniferous forests and seems to prefer mountainsides. It is a large raptor, reaching a length of 26 inches and attaining a wingspan of 42 inches. This striking bird has a blue-gray back, barred breast, prominent white eyebrow, and (in mature birds) reddish eyes. The wings are short with rounded tips, and the tail is long and narrow, a combination that allows them to maneuver rapidly through the trees in their pursuit of woodland birds. Goshawks are noted for their fierce disposition, and woe betide anyone who attempts to molest one or approach its nest. The goshawk is found from Alaska through the Pacific Northwest and the Rockies, and east to the Great Lakes and the northeastern United States and Canada. Its fortunes vary with the locale. In some regions it is declining—in others it is expanding its range. **See sites 18, 19, 20, 21, 25, 29, 30, 31, 32, 36, 43, 63, 75, 76, 78, 81, 83, 87, 93, 95, 96, 100.**

Ocelot

A tropical cat noted for its lovely patterned pelt, the ocelot (*Felis pardalis*) has undergone a precipitous decline due to trapping, hunting, and habitat loss. Although the sale of live ocelots or their pelts is now illegal, in the United States ocelots are found only rarely in southern Texas and southeastern Arizona. Reaching 52 inches in length and weights of 40 pounds, the ocelot is easily distinguished from the bobcat by its long tail and spots, which are arranged so heavily and symmetrically that they look like stripes. Ocelots inhabit thick scrublands and wooded areas and hunt at night for rodents, birds, reptiles, amphibians, and fish. **See site 60.**

Opossum

Officially called the Virginia opossum (*Didelphis virginiana*), this is the only American marsupial. It reaches 52 inches in length and has short legs and a long prehensile tail. The face and throat are whitish, the ears naked, the body grizzled brown or black. The female has an abdominal pouch where live embryonic young develop. When threatened, it will sometimes roll over, shut its eyes, and feign death— "playing possum." Adapted to brushy woods, swamps, and farmland, this species ranges throughout most of the eastern United States west to Colorado and Texas, and in the Pacific West. **See sites 9, 33, 35, 36, 40, 52, 60, 61, 67, 68, 69, 72, 73, 74, 78, 80, 85, 86, 88, 92, 93, 94, 95, 97, 98, 100.**

Orca

The so-called killer whale, the orca (*Orcinus orca*) is not a whale at all but a dolphin. The sea's biggest and most voracious predators, orcas grow to 30 feet long. They are jet black, with white oval patches behind each eye and white markings on the belly extending to the rear flanks near the tail. Orcas comprise two races that are differentiated more by diet than appearance. Resident orcas live only in certain parts of the Pacific Northwest, hunting fish (particularly salmon)

cooperatively. Transient orcas range the world's oceans, feeding on whales, dolphins, and seals. These extremely sociable animals range along the Atlantic and Pacific coasts. **See sites 10, 28.**

Osprey

This fish hawk is a welcome sight for any birder hiking or boating along the nation's waterways. Once decimated by chlorinated hydrocarbon pesticides, the osprey (*Pandion haliaetus*) is making a slow comeback. These eagle-like birds reach 25 inches in length and have wingspans of up to six feet. The dorsal surface is brown, the belly and head are white, and a dark streak runs along the side of the face. They fly distinctively, hovering above rivers and lakes before diving and expertly snagging fish from the surface of the water. Their nests are easily identifiable, consisting of masses of sticks jammed together atop dead snags, telephone poles, or rocky promontories. Ospreys range along the Atlantic and Pacific coasts, including much of Canada and Alaska, and also frequent much of the interior West. **See sites 7, 14, 17, 19, 24, 25, 26, 28, 29, 30, 32, 34, 37, 41, 42, 44, 53, 57, 60, 62, 63, 64, 66, 67, 68, 69, 70, 71, 72, 75, 76, 77, 78, 79, 80, 81, 82, 83, 84, 85, 86, 87, 88, 89, 91, 96, 97, 98, 99.**

Painted Bunting

North America's most brilliantly colored bird, the male painted bunting (*Passerina ciris*) has a bright blue head, green back, crimson breast and rump, and a red ring around the eye. The female has a bright green body and paler yellow-green breast. These sparrow-size birds (about five inches in length) prefer brushlands, hedgerows, and thickly vegetated swampy areas. They have fared reasonably well, though they are still captured in Mexico for the cage-bird trade. Painted buntings range from southern Missouri to the Gulf Coast and from western Texas to Mississippi. They are also found along the southeastern Atlantic coast from South Carolina through Florida. **See sites 41, 42, 57, 58, 60, 64, 69, 71, 80, 91, 93, 94.**

Pallid Bat

A buff-colored bat with huge ears, the pallid bat (*Antrozous pallidus*) inhabits the western states, particularly the arid portions. They roost in hollow trees and in buildings, and their colonies include members of both sexes. These bats, which grow to about six inches long, emit a sharp odor when irritated. Unlike most other bats, they prefer ground-dwelling prey to flying insects. Pallid bats fly close to the ground, much more slowly than other bats, beating their wings only about ten times per second. They hunt crickets, grasshoppers, and scorpions. The Jerusalem cricket, a large insect with a soft, juicy thorax and formidable jaws, is a favorite target. Pallid bats will often leave a tidy pile of Jerusalem cricket legs at the site of a kill. **See sites 27, 31.**

Parrotfish

The *Scaridae* family of marine fishes contains several genera and almost 80 species. All are large-scaled reef fish with powerful "beaks" comprising fused teeth that allow them to chew vegetation and polyps from coral. The sound of parrotfish crunching coral may be heard underwater from a con-

siderable distance. All are brilliantly colored, ranging from green to aquamarine to blue, often with white, orange, or purplish markings, although they start as drab-colored young. Some parrotfish may exceed six feet in length. They usually are found in small groups and are extremely wary. Some species secrete a mucous envelope around themselves at night, when they enter a torpid state; the mucous is apparently a defensive device or a means of keeping silt and sand from clogging their gills. **See site 15.**

Peregrine Falcon

The peregrine falcon (*Falco peregrinus*) is the poster child of the American conservation movement, having fought its way back from the brink of extinction by means of tougher pesticide laws and reintroduction, or hacking, programs. Peregrine populations have fully recovered in the Arctic, are recovering in the West, and climbing slowly in the East. These large falcons reach 20 inches in length and have wingspans of 42 inches. They have a black hood, black mustache, and huge black eyes. Adults are gray above and whitish below, with the breast symmetrically patterned in spots and bars. Juveniles are brown above, with a streaked pattern to the breast. They breed on cliffs and escarpments, as well as the ledges of high-rise buildings. Peregrines are renowned for their "stoops," high-velocity dives on prey that can hit 180 mph. They favor birds as prey. **See sites 2, 4, 6, 11, 12, 17, 19, 22, 23, 26, 28, 30, 32, 39, 47, 53, 55, 57, 59, 60, 64, 66, 70, 71, 75, 79, 81, 82, 83, 86, 89, 90, 91, 95, 96, 97.**

Piping Plover

A threatened species, the piping plover (*Charadrius melodus*) has lost much of its natural habitat—the beach—to humans. Some nesting areas are now protected, but the long-term fate of these little shorebirds is very much in doubt. The piping plover, which may reach a length of seven inches, has a short black bill, pale gray back, white breast and rump, and orange legs. In summer a black bar across the forehead and another around the neck are present. Piping plover range along the Atlantic coast from Newfoundland to Virginia and winter in the interior in a belt from Manitoba to Texas and along the Atlantic and Gulf coasts from Florida through Texas. **See sites 39, 49, 57, 60, 64, 70, 79, 82, 86, 97.**

Polar Bear

The world's only snow white bear, the polar bear (*Ursus maritimus*) cannot be mistaken for any other. Second only to Alaskan brown bears in size, they can weigh over 1,000 pounds. Polar bears inhabit the pack ice and barren shores of Arctic Canada and Alaska, preying primarily on seals. Their usual mode of hunting consists of patient waiting by a seal's breathing hole in the ice; when the seal comes up for air, the bear pounces. It will also feed on birds, bird eggs, carrion, seaweed, and berries. The polar bear is a strong swimmer and is often seen paddling in open water, traveling from one ice floe to another. They dig winter dens in deep snowbanks; females den all winter long, but males may be out at any time of the year and at any time of the day or night. **See site 2.**

Prairie Falcon

The peregrine's kissing cousin, the prairie falcon (*Falco mexicanus*) is distributed widely throughout the West. They favor rough country—plains and arid mountains most particularly. These falcons reach 18 inches in length and have wingspans of up to 42 inches. They are light brown above and buff below, with a fine pattern of spots and streaks on the breast. The underside of the wings is pale; the wingpits are dark. Prairie falcons lack the peregrine's dark hood but have prominent diagonal facial streaks that run from the eye to the neck. They hunt a wide variety of prey, most particularly birds, which they chase from the air but usually hunt on the ground. **See sites 6, 8, 12, 13, 14, 20, 21, 22, 26, 27, 30, 31, 32, 47, 50, 51, 55.**

Pronghorn

Neither a deer nor a true antelope, the pronghorn (*Antilocapra americana*) is the only member of the family *Antilocapridae*. Sometimes called the American Antelope, pronghorn stand about 42 inches high at the shoulder and weigh up to 150 pounds. They are beautifully marked, tan on the upper body and the outer legs. Bucks have black patches on the face and sides of the neck; females have black masks with the patches almost absent. Both sexes are horned, and the horn sheaths are shed each year. Bucks have horns longer than their ears; does have horns that seldom exceed ear length. Conservation measures have brought this species back from the brink of extinction, and it is now thriving throughout the arid West. The fastest runners in the Western

Hemisphere, pronghorn sprint across the plains at speeds of up to 50 mph. When alarmed, they display "flags" of erect white rump hair. **See sites 5, 8, 13, 14, 17, 21, 24, 30, 48, 49, 51, 55.**

Prothonotary Warbler

An occupant of eastern swamps and bottomlands, the prothonotary warbler (*Protonotaria citrea*) has declined as its favored habitat has been drained and razed. This large warbler attains a length of six inches and has a long bill and big dark eyes. The head and breast are golden yellow, the back is olive; the wings and tail are gray. Males are brighter in color than females. Prothonotary warblers are quite tame and are often seen perching on branches over still or sluggish water. Most common in the Southeast, these warblers range from the Atlantic coast to central Texas and from the Gulf Coast to the Great Lakes. **See sites 24, 34, 35, 36, 40, 62, 64, 72, 77, 78, 80, 85, 91, 92, 94, 98, 99.**

Raccoon

Perhaps the most familiar of America's predators, the raccoon (*Procyon lotor*) is at home in a wide range of habitats, from forested river bottoms to suburban backyards. It is rapidly expanding its range—not just to the suburbs but even to intensively developed urban areas. Raccoons are found throughout the United States, with the exception of Alaska, Hawaii, and some portions of the Rocky Mountains and the Great Basin. The raccoon reaches 40 inches in length and weighs up to 26 pounds. Its cunning little bandit mask, bushy ringed tail, and distinctive gait make it unmistakable. Raccoons will

devour everything from fledgling birds and fruit to dog food. They are particularly fond of frogs, salamanders, fish, and crayfish. **See sites 9, 27, 33, 35, 36, 39, 40, 41, 43, 49, 50, 52, 59, 60, 61, 63, 65, 67, 68, 69, 71, 72, 73, 74, 78, 80, 81, 83, 84, 85, 86, 87, 90, 92, 93, 94, 95, 97, 98, 100.**

Red Bat

The red bat (*Lasiurus borealis*) is one of the few mammals in which the sexes display markedly different colors. Males are a bright red or red-orange; females are brick or dull red; both have white patches on the back and breast. The average length is seven inches. These woodland bats roost in tree branches about four to ten feet above the ground. Although solitary in habit, they often forage in pairs, describing tight, circumscribed courses as they seek night-flying insects. Red bats are quite common, living everywhere in the continental United States, except the Rocky Mountains and parts of the desert Southwest. **See sites 33, 43, 62, 63, 72, 80, 85, 93, 95, 96, 98, 99.**

Red Fox

The sly fox of fables, the red fox (*Vulpes vulpes*) has several distinct color phases—red, black, and reddish brown—and ranges up to 15 inches at the shoulder, and 42 inches in length. It has a bushy white-tipped tail and prominent triangular ears. The red fox is sometimes mistaken for a coyote or collie—remember that neither of those animals has a white-tipped tail. The red fox favors dry uplands and open areas and is even found in suburbia. It does not den in the winter, but simply curls into a ball, wrapping its luxuriant tail around its feet and nose. It is omnivorous, hunting everything from insects to rabbits. The dog (male) voices a short gargling yelp; the vixen (female) has a high-pitched yipping scream. **See sites 20, 26, 29, 33, 34, 36, 37, 38, 40, 41, 42, 43, 44, 45, 49, 50, 52, 56, 58, 62, 63, 72, 73, 74, 75, 76, 81, 83, 84, 86, 87, 88, 90, 91, 92, 93, 94, 95, 98, 99.**

Red-tailed Hawk

Our most common buteo, the red-tailed hawk (*Buteo jamaicensis*) is found in all the U.S. except Hawaii. Almost any wild habitat is to its liking: forest, farmland, desert, plain, and tundra. Redtails will hunt and breed in the suburbs or even large cities, where they subsist on rats and pigeons. They soar on thermals in search of prey, but birders most often see them perching on dead snags, telephone poles, and fence posts. Redtails reach 26 inches in length, and their wingspans can exceed four feet. They are variable in color, particularly in the West. They range from mottled brown to black on the back; the breast is usually paler and mottled. The rusty red tail of these hawks (grayish in some western birds) is easily observed in flight. They prey primarily on rodents and occasionally on ground-dwelling birds. **See sites 5, 7, 8, 9, 11, 12, 13, 14, 18, 19, 21, 22, 23, 24, 25, 26, 28, 30, 31, 32, 33, 34, 35, 36, 37, 38, 41, 42, 45, 47, 48, 49, 50, 52, 54, 57, 62, 63, 64, 65, 66, 67, 68, 73, 77, 78, 79, 82, 84, 85, 86, 88, 90, 91, 92, 93, 98, 99.**

Red Wolf

An inhabitant of the southern states, the red wolf (*Canis rufus*) reaches a height of 15 inches, length of nearly 5 feet, and weight of 75 pounds. It has reddish flanks, muzzle, legs, and ears and a gray back. These shy little canids favor brushy areas and swamps. They prey primarily on rodents and ground-nesting birds, although they also hunt crabs and other crustaceans in intertidal areas. Red wolves once ranged as far north as West Virginia and southern Pennsylvania and as far west as Texas, but they were driven almost to extinction by trapping and shooting. Through a careful breeding program, enough wolves have been raised to allow the beginnings of restocking efforts in North Carolina. In the wild, red wolves often interbreed with coyotes, which is another threat to their survival. **See sites 91, 93.**

Ringtail

The ringtail (*Bassariscus astutus*), a relative of the raccoon and coati, is recognized by its huge eyes, long ringed tail, and sinuous catlike form. Buff or grayish in color, it has a long body (measuring up to 30 inches) and short legs. Formidable hunters of mice, ringtails were placed in mines during the California Gold Rush, earning the nickname "miner's cat." In addition to mice, ringtails hunt insects, birds, and small mammals or reptiles. They can climb trees with their extraordinarily sharp claws. Strictly nocturnal, they are apt to be glimpsed only fleetingly. When threatened, a ringtail will scream and secrete a foul-smelling fluid from its anal glands. Ringtails prefer rugged, wooded country, particularly along streams, and range from Oregon through California, and into Arizona, New Mexico, and parts of Texas. **See site 4.**

River Otter

A graceful member of the weasel family, the river otter (*Lutra canadensis*) was once common throughout North America. Nearly wiped out by trapping and habitat destruction, however, river otters are only now making a comeback in the South, Northeast, and Pacific Northwest. Their fur is a rich dark or chestnut brown above, whitish below. Sizable animals, river otters can reach 30 pounds in weight and four feet in length. They have long muscular tails and webbed feet well suited to their aquatic habitat. River otters feed primarily on fish, crayfish, amphibians, and reptiles but will also eat rodents, including muskrats. Celebrated for their playfulness and sociability, river otters create slides along mudbanks and snowbanks, apparently for the simple joy of zooming down on their bellies. **See sites 3, 9, 17, 18, 19, 23, 24, 25, 27, 29, 30, 32, 33, 34, 35, 37, 40, 41, 43, 44, 52, 61, 62, 63, 65, 68, 69, 72, 73, 74, 75, 76, 77, 78, 80, 81, 83, 85, 87, 91, 92, 93, 94, 95, 96, 97, 98.**

Roseate Spoonbill

Resembling the flamingo in coloration, the roseate spoonbill (*Ajaia ajaja*) reaches 32 inches in length and has pink wings, red shoulders, and a reddish tail. It is characterized by a long spatulate bill that it uses to strain small crustaceans from the water. Roseate spoonbills were once plentiful in southern Atlantic and Gulf coast marshes and estuaries but were hunted almost to extinction. They have recovered somewhat but still face serious threats from wetland destruction. They are found locally in small flocks, and their range now includes southern Florida and the Gulf Coast from western Louisiana to southern Texas. **See sites 40, 41, 42, 57, 69, 72.**

San Joaquin Kit Fox

The smallest of North America's foxes, the San Joaquin kit fox (*Vulpes macrotis mutica*) ranges throughout central California. Agricultural development in the San Joaquin Valley has destroyed most of the dry upland range needed by this house cat-size fox for survival, and it seemed doomed to oblivion until conservation programs protected several hundred thousand acres of prime habitat. In these areas, at least, this big-eared canid is doing extraordinarily well. San Joaquin kit foxes prefer to hunt their favored prey of rodents and insects at dusk and dawn. They are tractable animals and seem unafraid of human beings if a discreet distance is maintained. **See site 8.**

Sea Otter

The sea otter (*Enhydra lutris*) is not quite as manic as its cousin, the river otter, but its behavior is equally endearing. This large marine otter is often spied floating on its back in kelp beds, cracking shellfish open on rocks balanced on its chest. It also sleeps in the kelp beds, wrapping strands of seaweed around its body to hold it in place. Sea otters can be up to four feet long and can weigh 90 pounds. They have large webbed feet that serve as flippers, prominent whiskers, yellowish faces and necks, and heavy, thick tails. They dote on shellfish, particularly crabs, sea urchins, abalone, and mussels, but also eat fish in quantity. Their luxuriant dark brown fur was almost their undoing—trappers drove them nearly to extinction in the 19th century. Today the only colonies exist in Alaska and the central California coast. **See site 7.**

Snapping Turtle

The common snapping turtle (*Chelydra serpentina*) is extremely aggressive and will not hesitate to bite, especially when on land. These big turtles typically reach 18 inches in length and can weigh as much as 45 pounds. The carapace is brown and has three low keels; the head is large, the tail long. Within their range snappers may be found wherever there is water—lakes, ponds, rivers, creeks, or swamps. Truly omnivorous, they will eat fish, reptiles, amphibians, birds, rodents, carrion, and vegetation. Snapping turtles range from the western Great Plains east to the Atlantic Ocean, and from the Gulf Coast north to Manitoba. **See sites 34, 36, 40, 41, 42, 49, 52, 61, 62, 69, 72, 73, 80, 83, 85, 86, 92, 94, 96, 98, 99.**

Snow Goose

Populations of the snow goose (*Chen caerulescens*) have exploded in recent years, and their continental population is counted in the millions. Snow geese are now so numerous that they are overgrazing their nesting grounds in the Arctic, sometimes displacing rarer species. White geese with black wing tips, "snows" reach about 30 inches in length. They travel in large flocks, flying across the sky in distinctive undulating lines of white, honking continuously. Snow geese range throughout the United States and Canada, with the exception of

Florida, Georgia, South Carolina, and parts of the Southwest. An immature color phase, known as the blue goose (it's actually blue-gray), is found in the East. **See sites 2, 9, 24, 35, 39, 40, 42, 43, 50, 55, 60, 73, 77, 86, 90, 97, 98, 99.**

Spotted Owl

A denizen of the deep forest, the rare spotted owl (*Strix occidentalis*) needs old-growth timber to survive. As the coniferous forests of the West and Southwest have fallen, so have the fortunes of spotted owls. They face another threat from barred owls, a similar species that is encroaching on them from the east. Spotted owls are large, reaching 19 inches in length, and have dark brown backs with white spots, and white breasts streaked with brown. They feed almost exclusively on rodents, dropping down on their prey from perches overhead. Spotted owls are extraordinarily tame, often letting observers approach them closely. They currently range from southwestern British Columbia to southern California. A separate population is found in the mountains of Colorado, Arizona, Utah, New Mexico, and western Texas. **See sites 11, 12, 25, 29.**

Spotted Skunk

A small fine-boned skunk that has declined in recent decades, the spotted skunk (*Spilogale putorius*) is known for its playful disposition. It will often hop up on its forefeet when threatening potential molesters with a jet of musk. Spotted skunks typically grow to 25 inches in length and weigh between six and 14 pounds. They have black fur with irregular spots and stripes over their bodies. They frequent wooded areas and are adept climbers. Like striped skunks, they are omnivorous and will consume almost anything that is remotely edible. Like raccoons, they stage nocturnal raids on campground foodstuffs. Spotted skunks range throughout the West, the South, and the eastern Great Plains. **See sites 11, 29, 63, 100.**

Striped Skunk

The striped skunk (*Mephitis mephitis*) may be our most easily identified mammal, both by sight and by odor. This extremely common species is found in all of the continental United States and much of Canada. It grows to 30 inches in length and has a bushy tail, black fur, and a large white V that runs along the top of its back. When disturbed, the striped skunk can accurately discharge its acrid musk at distances exceeding ten feet. It is an omnivorous animal, feeding on everything from fruit to rodents, reptiles to amphibians, eggs to carrion. Skunks are nocturnal and are found in a wide range of habitats, including open woodlands, scrublands, prairies, suburbs—even inner cities. **See sites 11, 13, 21, 22, 26, 27, 36, 40, 45, 49, 50, 52, 56, 60, 63, 73, 74, 75, 78, 80, 81, 83, 85, 88, 93, 94, 95, 97, 100.**

Timber Rattlesnake

The timber rattlesnake (*Crotalus horridus*) is found in wooded areas from the eastern Great Plains to the Deep South and north to New England. It is the only rattlesnake in much of the Northeast. While still common in some areas, it has been completely wiped out in others, and its long-term future is very much in doubt. In northern latitudes, timber rattlesnakes congregate in large numbers to den for the winter, often with copperheads. Den sites are usually near ledges with southern exposures, where the snakes may sun during spring and fall. Timber rattlers reach five feet in length and may be gray, yellow, tan, or brown; all show distinctive dark crossbands. They prey primarily on rodents. **See sites 33, 35, 36, 72, 83, 85, 86, 93, 96, 98.**

Western Tanager

The male of this species (*Piranga ludoviciana*) has a bright yellow and jet black body, black wings, and a brilliant scarlet head. The female is duller but still handsome, with a yellow-green body, yellow breast, and greenish wings. Both sexes have white wing bars and may exceed seven inches in length. Western tanagers prefer open coniferous forests and are also sometimes found along riparian woodlands. They feed on insects in the spring and summer, often launching themselves from perches and snagging the insects in midair like flycatchers. Later in the season they eat fruit and berries. These western songbirds range from the Mexican border to southern Alaska and from the Rockies to the Pacific. **See sites 9, 11, 14, 19, 20, 24, 25, 27, 29, 30, 31, 32.**

White Ibis

A fairly common resident of the southern Atlantic and Gulf coasts, the white ibis (*Eudocimus albus*) has experienced declines in recent years as a result of habitat loss from wetlands destruction. This striking bird has a white body, black wing tips, and a red bill and legs. Immatures are mottled with brown and white. The white ibis typically reaches 25 inches in length. A wading bird, it forages in both salt-water and freshwater marshes, using its long curved bill to probe the mud for crustaceans and mollusks. White ibises are often seen feeding in groups. Two related species, the white-faced ibis and the glossy ibis, share its range. **See sites 40, 42, 69, 72, 85, 86, 92.**

White Pelican

The white pelican (*Pelecanus erythrorhynchos*) has declined sharply in recent decades because of habitat destruction and pesticides. Huge birds, white pelicans can reach nearly six feet in length and have wingspans approaching eight feet. They are snow white with black wing tips and large yellow bills. During the breeding season they display yellow crests and breast patches. White pelicans are gregarious, breeding in large groups and traveling and foraging in flocks. Unlike brown pelicans, they favor freshwater habitats and they don't dive for their food. Groups of birds will surround fish in shallow water, then scoop them into their pouches. They breed in the upper Great Plains and throughout the Great Basin and winter along the Gulf Coast from Florida to Texas. **See sites 20, 22, 26, 49, 50, 55, 68.**

White-tailed Deer

Unquestionably the most successful large mammal on the continent, the whitetail (*Odocoileus virginianus*) has expanded both its range and numbers, thanks to hunting regulations

and the decline of natural predators. Originally residents of the East, whitetails have pushed inexorably westward and now range throughout the continental United States, with the exception of the arid Southwest and California. They favor second-growth forests, farmlands, and sub-urbs, wherever there is enough vegetation to sustain them. Whitetails can reach four feet at the shoulder; bucks often weigh more than 300 pounds. Antlers are erect, with the main branch forward and unbranched tines behind. The deer have white underparts, and their upper coat changes with the season—blue-gray in winter, tawny or russet in summer. As the name indicates, their tails are a distinguishing feature—when alarmed, they raise the white underside (the top surface is brown) to alert their fellows, "hightailing" it. A dwarf subspecies, the Key deer, is found only on Big Pine Key in the Florida Keys. **See sites 14, 19, 31, 33, 34, 35, 36, 37, 38, 39, 40, 41, 42, 43, 44, 45, 48, 49, 50, 51, 52, 54, 55, 56, 57, 58, 60, 61, 62, 63, 65, 68, 69, 70, 71, 72, 73, 74, 75, 76, 77, 78, 79, 80, 81, 83, 84, 87, 88, 90, 91, 92, 93, 94, 95, 96, 97, 98, 99, 100.**

Wild Turkey

Their gobbles and "perts" were heard throughout the woodlands of the South and the East before the Pilgrims landed. But by the early 20th century, the wild turkey (*Meleagris gallopavo*) was almost wiped out by overzealous hunting. They have since rebounded, thanks to restocking programs and controlled hunting, and inhabit most of their original range. Both sexes have naked heads and iridescent bronze feathers. Toms can reach four feet in length and have long breast plumes and large wattles that change from blue to red, depending on their emotional state. Although they are ground-walkers, wild turkeys can fly short distances; they roost in groups in trees. **See sites 12, 34, 37, 38, 48, 51, 52, 54, 55, 62, 74, 78, 93, 95, 96, 100.**

Wolverine

The largest member of the *Mustelidae* family, the wolverine (*Gulo gulo*) is justifiably reknowned for its aggressiveness and hunting prowess. Weighing up to 60 pounds and reaching 44 inches in length, the wolverine has a heavy, coarse, dark brown pelt. The temples are yellow, and two broad yellow stripes run from the shoulder to the base of its bushy tail. In the wild, wolverines may be mistaken for small bears. They are unequaled as hunters and will take deer, porcupines, rodents, birds—even injured or ill moose and caribou. They typically mark their kills with musk, which repels other predators and scavengers. Wolverines have been known to drive bears and mountain lions from their kills and are disliked by trappers for their penchant for robbing traplines and despoiling cabins and food caches. Wolverines live in Alaska and northern Canada, and have been reported sporadically in the American Rockies, the North Cascades, and the Sierra. **See sites 2, 3, 18, 19, 29, 32.**

Wood Duck

The drake of this species (*Aix sponsa*) has been called the most beautiful duck in North America. Patterned in shimmering purple, blue, black, green, and gray, it has a long crest and tail, red bill, and distinctive white face stripes. The hen is much drabber, feathered in gray-brown plumage, with a white eye ring. Both sexes typically reach 18 inches in length. They haunt riparian forests, wooded swamps, and forested lakeshores. Wood ducks prefer old cavities in mature trees for their nests, but will also use artificial nest boxes. Wood ducks range east of the Mississippi and along the Pacific coast. Once hunted almost to extinction, this species has rebounded as a result of nesting box programs and tough hunting regulations. **See sites 9, 34, 35, 36, 37, 40, 42, 62, 63, 64, 65, 71, 72, 73, 74, 78, 80, 81, 83, 91, 92, 95, 96, 98, 99, 100.**

Wood Stork

Once the wood stork (*Mycteria americana*) was known to nest in colonies up of up to 10,000 pairs. Today, the species is endangered as a result of land development of its feeding grounds—shallow saltwater and freshwater wetlands. Up to 40 inches tall, the wood stork has a naked gray head and neck, which has earned it the nickname "flint head," and a thick, downcurved, black bill. The body is white and the flight feathers are black. These wading birds fly with neck extended, coasting high in the sky on thermal air currents. They hunt their prey by slowly stalking through marshes. Wood storks are voiceless except for low hisses and much bill clacking. Small flocks are found locally along the Atlantic and Gulf coasts from South Carolina to Texas. **See sites 68, 69, 71, 72, 91, 92.**

INDEX

Page numbers in **boldface** refer to photographs.

ILLUSTRATIONS CREDITS

Author **Glen Martin** is a staff
writer for the *San Francisco
Chronicle,* covering natural
resources, conservation, and
the environment. He has also
written for *Audubon, Sierra,
Outside,* and *Discover.*

Book composition by the
National Geographic Book
Division. Printed and bound
by R.R. Donnelley & Sons,
Willard, Ohio. Color separa-
tions by CMI Color Graphix,
Huntingdon Valley, Pa. Cover
printed by Miken Companies,
Inc., Cheektowaga, N.Y.

**Visit the Society's Web site at
www.nationalgeographic.com**